Economics Explored

Martin Brimble

Stanley Thornes (Publishers) Ltd

To the memory of Winifred Grace
An extraordinary grandparent

First published in 1990 by:
Stanley Thornes (Publishers) Ltd
Old Station Drive
Leckhampton
CHELTENHAM GL53 0DN
England

British Library Cataloguing in Publication Data
Brimble, Martin
 Economics explored.
 1. Economics
 I. Title
 330

 ISBN 0-7487-0228-8

Designed by Alan Hamp
Typeset by 𝔸 Tek Art Ltd
Printed and bound in Great Britain at
the Bath Press, Avon

Contents

Preface

When I first commenced teaching Economics at secondary school level seventeen years ago, courses at CSE level in the subject were extremely rare. Enterprising teachers with wide ability range classes were forced to devise their own Mode 3 CSEs to complement the O Level route, and thus was born a movement that allowed whole classes of mixed ability pupils to study the same subject and be entered for a final exam.

GCSE has marked an exciting step forward for Economics teaching nationally in this respect; through the provision of syllabuses and subject specific criteria, there is for the first time a nationwide commitment to ensuring that all students have access to the principles of Economics. Additionally, allied to other countrywide developments, a movement has sprung up to ensure that Economics awareness becomes a curriculum entitlement for all. Current Government plans for the National Curriculum themes will provide further support for this process.

It is hoped that this book will be of value in the teaching of Economics at GCSE level.

Acknowledgements

I have many to thank for their help and suggestions made over the years.

My special thanks go to the staff at both South East London School, ILEA and Elizabeth Garrett Anderson School, ILEA, for their support and guidance; particularly to Brendon O'Reilly, Roy Newman and Brian Hoy at the former and Jeff Lewis and Rikki Lanigan at the latter.

I am indebted to my present head, Miss B E Loveridge, of Elizabeth Garrett Anderson School, for her support of the subject of Economics as essential in girls' education. Particular thanks are owed to Jack Price of the ILEA LAPP project for securing some time off during 1987-1988 which allowed this book a beginning. I owe an enormous debt to all my friends and colleagues in the London branch of the Economics Association and to the many who contributed to its erstwhile journal *Working Capital*. Stephen Romer supplied an idea, in this context, which forms the basis of one of the exercises in the unit on Elasticity.

At an earlier stage in thinking, South East London School's involvement as a trial school for the Economics Association project also left an indelible influence on my ideas.

I thank all my students, particularly those who urged me on to write this work and who helped by testing the material in the classroom. I name only a few: Danny Morgan, David Moule, Gary Renshaw, the Hamilton brothers, Toper Hassan, Harold Wilson (not the ex-prime minister), Jonathan Thomas, Jeffrey Cheeseman, Carrie Miller, Ruth Harvey, Lorissa Allen, Lynne Ankrah, Denise Malcolm and Nicola Ross; all in 5T, my current Economics classes, and for some reason my Friday Law class 1988-1989!

My final thanks go to my youngest son William (who patiently endured visits to my publishers) and to my eldest son James for trying out many of the exercises. My loving gratitude to Catherine, my wife, for all her encouragement and for bearing with the germ of this project so well.

The author and publishers are grateful to the following for permission to reproduce extracts, figures and other text materials:

British Rail for items on pages 83–4; Central Statistical Office for items from the *Abstract of Statistics 1988* pages 25, 57, 89; from *Economic Progress Report 1986*, page 182; from *Economic Trends 87*, page 225; from *Family Expenditure Survey 1986*, page 171; from *Regional Trends 22*, pages 96, 158; from *Social Trends 17*, pages 25, 130, 131, 148, 166, 174, 191, 204 (all Crown copyright, reproduced with the permission of HMSO.) • The *Daily Express* for items on pages 105–6, 136 • The *Daily Mail* for items on pages 105, 148, 173 • The *Daily Mirror* for items on pages 19, 80, 178, 211–2, 223 • The *Daily Telegraph* for items on pages 111–2, 240, 267 • The Department of Employment for item on page 52 • The *Economist* for items on pages 62, 94, 127, 142, 166, 168–9, 186, 187 • The *Evening Post* for items on pages 140–1 • The *Evening Standard* for items on pages 88, 100, 113 • The *Financial Times* for items on pages 117, 192, 209, 228 • The *Guardian* for items on pages 20, 59, 112, 123, 180, 192–3, 222, 243, 244, 262, 262–3, 266–7, 270 • The *Independent* for items on pages 5–6, 29, 52, 68, 80–1, 84, 95, 99, 131, 205, 215, 216, 221–2, 225, 240, 249, 251, 267, 268, 272, 278, 279 • The *London Daily News* for items on pages 32, 45, 216 • The London and East Anglia Group for item on page 149 • The *London Evening Standard* for items on pages 12, 39 • *New Society* for items on pages 166, 174, 210, 212 • The *Observer* for items on pages 86, 86–7 • The *Sun* for items on pages 19, 26, 184–5 • *The Times* for items on pages 88, 89, 167, 167–8, 192, 220–1, 230, 236, 251, 255, 256–7 • Unilver plc for item on page 106 • The *Yorkshire Post* for item on pages 210–11.

We are also grateful to the following for permission to reproduce photographs: AA
Publishing, page 11 ● Air France, page 103 ● ASDA, page 179 ●
Associated Press, page 32 ● Australian High Commission, page 13 ●
Barnaby's Picture Library, page 11 ● British Home Stores, page 179 ●
Cammell Laird Shipbuilders, page 69 ● Central Electricity Generating Board,
page 24 ● Claire Starkey, pages 51 and 181 ● Thomas Cook, page 179 ●
Heinz, page 37 ● *Farmers Weekly*, page 11 ● S & R Greenhill, page 62 ●
Holt Studios Ltd, page 244 ● Hulton Picture Library, pages 62 and 190 ●
Intervention Board, page 238 ● Network: John Sturrock, page 94 ●
Kent Messenger Group Newspapers, page 259 ● London Transport, page
179 ● The Mansell Collection, page 168 ● Mark Edwards Photo Library,
page 240 ● Terry Mealey, page 131 ● National Motor Museum, page 142 ●
Oxfam, page 51 ● QA Photo Library, page 103 ● Regina Health and Beauty
Products, page 216 ● Royal Bank of Scotland, page 197 ● Sainsbury's pages
37 and 179 ● The Scottish Tourist Board, page 51 ● Sealink, page 103 ●
The Times, pages 255 and 256 ● Will Green, page 100.

Every effort has been made to contact copyright holders and we apologise if any
have been overlooked.

1 What is Economics?

Economics is the study of how people's wants are satisfied. The *economy* is that part of our society involved in:

- making
- distributing
- consuming

goods and services.

Dear Santa Claus For Christmas I want a year off school, a sports car, a walkman, my own pet lion (to sort out the school bully), and let's get this quite right, last Christmas you brought me some smashing presents but where did you leave the bike?

Dear Santa Claus For Christmas I want some food for my child.

Activity

Each person in this picture is involved in the economy.

Make three lists headed: Making, Distributing and Consuming.
Put each of the people in the picture under these headings, saying what they are doing. Some people will appear in more than one list. The lists are started for you here:

Making	Distributing	Consuming
	A Van driver, delivering goods	**A** Van driver smoking a cigarette
F Butcher cutting up meat	**F** Butcher selling meat	

The basic economic problem

Economics exists as a study because people have to solve the basic economic problem that they want more than they have. Everyone in an economy is involved in some way with this problem.

Complete these sentences with the appropriate word, given below.

The government may want more ....

A local firm might like to take on more ....

Teachers want more ....

Pupils want ....

(textbooks, schools, school leavers, pay)

2 Infinite Wants

Everyone has **wants**

Everyone in the economy has a need for goods and services.

Needs and wants

Dave wants to go to the disco tonight. He washes his shirt with soap powder and plans to hang it on the line, but it's raining. He doesn't want to be late, so he puts the shirt in a tumble dryer.

Dave has *consumed* a range of economic goods. He has had to pay for this range of goods in order to get his shirt washed.

Can you list what these goods (and services) might be?

Once our immediate wants are satisfied, others usually arise. Wants are *infinite*; this means they go on for ever.

One reason why wants are infinite is that wants are often inter-connected: one want leads to another want.

Test yourself

1 Explain what economists mean when they say wants are infinite.
2 Using the example of a motor car, explain how wants are inter-connected so that satisfying one want can lead on to another want.
3 Make a list of things you need. Make a list of things you want. Use your lists to discuss the differences between needs and wants.

Activity 1

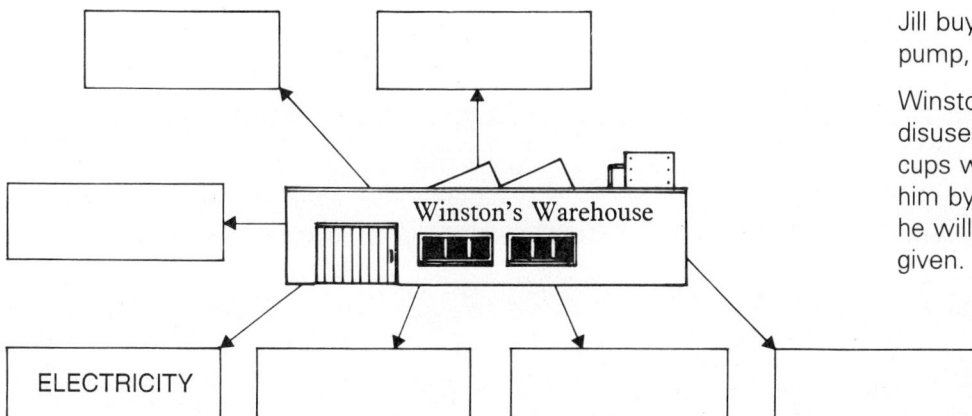

Jill buys a bike, but soon finds she needs a pump, a headlamp, a chain and a padlock.

Winston is starting up in business in a disused warehouse. He will make plastic cups with an old moulding machine left to him by his uncle. Try and think of the wants he will now have. An example of one is given.

Winston's Warehouse

ELECTRICITY

3

Extension 1

People's wants change over time. Make a list of three things Alex and Sharon might want at each of these stages of their lives.

Wants also vary from one situation to another. You can see this with the Williams family. Match each person to the new want that they have.

A
Peter aged 13. Now that he goes to Sandywell Comprehensive he wants to cycle to school.

B
Granny Williams, lives with the rest of the family, but at 80 is finding it difficult to climb the stairs.

C
Mr Williams, deputy head at Sandywell Comprehensive, is to take assembly tomorrow but has a sore throat.

D
Uncle John forgot Peter's birthday and must remember to get him a present this Christmas. He probably needs ....

1
A bungalow or some form of sheltered accommodation.

2
A bike.

3
A new car.

4
A microphone.

E
Mrs Williams recently changed her job. She now works on the new industrial estate outside Sandywell. It's a long journey by bus.

5
A diary for important dates.

Free goods

Usually we must pay to satisfy our wants but sometimes our wants are easy to satisfy because a range of free goods are available.

Mrs Robinson lives on a tropical island. For breakfast she picks fruit from the trees. Her water supply is provided by a nearby stream. The climate is pleasant all the year round, so she hardly needs to heat her home. She catches fish from the stream and can dry any she doesn't use in the sun to cook later. The air is fresh. The air, the sunshine, the wind and the rain are all examples of free goods.

ECONOMIC TERMS
Free goods: items that are so readily available they do not command a price.

Reducing our wants

It is possible at times to reduce the burden our wants can create.

The Keegan family have decided to go abroad for a holiday this year. They will be crossing the Channel by car ferry and spending two weeks shopping and sight-seeing in Paris.

The Barton family, on the other hand, are going to stay with Mr Barton's mother in the Peak District of Derbyshire. They plan to walk across the fells and, being keen artists, will probably spend a lot of time sketching.

Test yourself

1 Who (the Keegans or the Bartons) do you think is more likely to consume economic goods? Who is more likely to consume a range of free goods?

2 Explain which family will be most effective in reducing the cost of their holiday and why.

Some people are more able to satisfy their wants than others. Look at the drawing at the start of this Unit. Decide who will find it easier to satisfy their wants and who might find it more difficult. Why might this be so?

Activity 2

1 Tony and Patricia Kwan left school last year. They have always wanted to own a motorbike. Now they find that although they have satisfied this want their purchase has given rise to other wants. What might some of these wants be? List them for each box **A–G**.

2 Some of these wants are connected with PERSONAL SAFETY, others with LEGAL REQUIREMENTS and others with the OPERATING NEEDS OF THE BIKE.
   Re-group the wants you identified in **1** to classify them under one of these headings.

3 Using this exercise and other examples explain how wants are infinite.

DATA RESPONSE

Mail ship is answer to Saints' prayers

By Nicholas Schoon

THIS MORNING, the Royal Mail Ship St Helena, the 3,150-ton vessel which provides a lifeline for some of the world's most isolated communities, should be rounding Land's End at the start of her long voyage to the South Atlantic.

In six weeks she and her 76 passengers will arrive off Jamestown, capital of the island of St Helena, 47 square miles of extinct volcano rising out of the ocean, 4,500 miles from Britain.

Her arrival invariably causes quite a stir among the island's 6,200 inhabitants, known as Saints. RMS St Helena brings returning residents, a few adventurous tourists, the mail and all the imports the Saints depend on. She's 23 years old and her days are numbered, but a larger replacement is soon to be built.

The island of St Helena, where Napoleon spent his six final, forlorn years does not have an airport or deep-water harbour. The 329-ft ship has to anchor off Jamestown to unload into barges.

The St Helena sails from Avonmouth six times a year, carrying the equivalent of several well-stocked supermarkets, as well as a builders' merchant or two. She calls at Tenerife and Ascension Island twice, and Cape Town once, during each voyage.

Every year she makes an extra trip to Tristan da Cunha, a lonely spot which makes St Helena seem well-connected and cosmopolitan. Some 300 people live there, on an active volcano, and their chief occupation is providing a quarter of the world's crayfish and rare stamps.

The St Helena was badly needed by the Islanders since the Union Castle line had withdrawn its freight, passenger and mail service more than a year earlier, and serious shortages had developed.

"She was greeted as if it was the relief of Mafeking," Andrew Bell, managing director of the tiny but enterprising Cornish shipping line which owns the ship, said.

He put up the idea of running a shipping service subsidised by the Overseas Development Administration, and found a suitable vessel. The service costs about £4m a year, of which the Government provides £1.6m.

The cost of the subsidy has changed little since 1977 but the amount of freight and passenger numbers has risen. By the year's end the Government will order a new ship of twice the tonnage, costing about £20m.

continued on next page

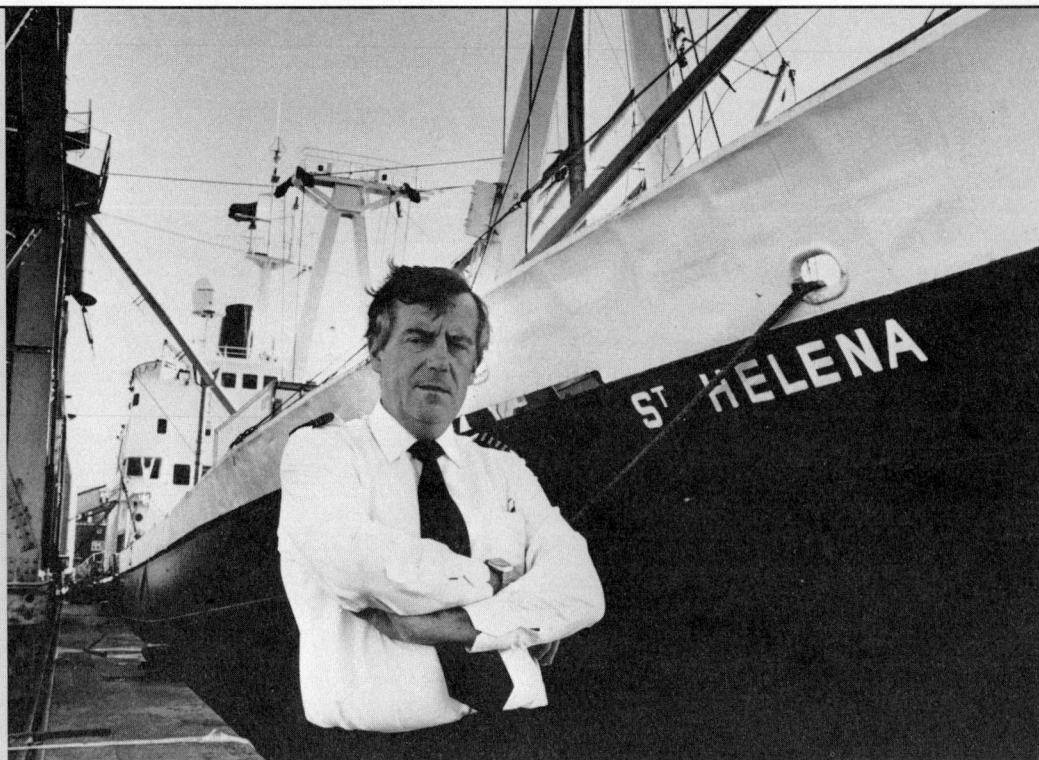

Three yards have been shortlisted for the job – small companies in Aberdeen and Lowestoft, and the large Scott Lithgow yard in Greenock, which needs orders after losing a big Royal Navy contract.

The cheapest return fare from Avonmouth to St Helena is £2,240, the most expensive £3,600, and voyages are booked up months in advance.

Source: The Independent, 12 September 1987

Captain Bob Wyatt and the Royal Mail Ship St Helena at Avonmouth

1 In what way has the Royal Mail Ship St Helena satisfied the wants of the people of St Helena and Tristan da Cunha?

2 Suggest why the 'Saints' find it difficult to satisfy all of their wants.

3 How can the people of Tristan da Cunha pay for the goods they purchase from RMS St Helena?

4 Why do you think Andrew Bell started his service to St Helena? What initially helped to make the service a success?

5 What will be the reward for his company?

6 The service has clearly helped to satisfy the wants of the islanders, but has it helped to satisfy anybody else's wants? If so, whose?

Extension 2

The Sheriff children want a day out. Mr Sheriff suggests a trip to the seaside. He thinks it will be a cheap day out, as access to the beach he has in mind is free and it is a beautiful sunny day. They have swimming costumes and towels and a tank full of petrol in the car.

As soon as the Sheriff family set out in their car they realise that everyone else has had the same idea. The motorway is very busy and they waste time trying to find a parking space near the beach. They end up parking a mile away and walking down to the seaside.

1 Use the following wants and write a short story that illustrates the wants a typical family might have at a seaside.
    ice cream, bucket and spade, cricket set, candy floss, postcard, hot dog, beach ball, wind break, boat trip around the harbour, deck chairs

The Sherrifs end up having an enjoyable but expensive time. "Before we leave," says Mrs Sheriff, "we must send your mother a postcard".
"Remind me not to come again," says Mr Sheriff.

2 In a brief paragraph explain how your story illustrates the fact that our wants are infinite.

3 What sort of costs did the Sheriff family experience during their day out?

4 Was Mr Sheriff correct in his view that the family would be able to have a cheap day out?

Extension 3

1 Ask each of your teachers to identify a want of theirs that would help improve their teaching of your classes; it could be equipment, textbooks, extra staff, more time for preparation, or any other resource.
2 Once you have a range of ideas ask your economics class to decide (from the list you have written) which they think would be the most important improvements that could be made. Construct a bar chart to help you.
3 Take the three most popular ideas and examine the difficulties that might exist in trying to implement them.

Coursework

Aim: To consider who is in the best position to satisfy their wants.

The Butler family live in a semi-detached house in south-west London. They both work in the same advertising agency in the West End, and have two children. Their house will need to be re-roofed in the near future.

The Aktar family live in Calcutta. Mr Aktar is a sales manager. His wife does not work. They have three children and two servants. The house has four bedrooms and two living rooms, as well as a kitchen and bathroom. There is no garage for Mr Aktar's car.

The Khonan family have recently moved to Calcutta from a part of India hit by drought. Mr Khonan has not yet found work. The family are forced to live on the pavement. They have to beg for food.

Simone lives with Jon, a hospital porter, in a council-owned tower block in north London. They have a six-month-old baby. The flat is very damp. Simone and Jon are hoping that the council will re-house them.

1 All these families have one want in common. What is it?
2 Which families are better able to satisfy their wants? Which families are least able to satisfy their wants? Give reasons for your answers.
3 Since Mr and Mrs Butler bought their house, they have discovered that their

purchase has given rise to other wants. Make a list of what some of these wants might be.

4 If Mr Khonan found work and was able to satisfy his family's need of a place to live, what other wants might arise for them?

5 If Simone and Jon were re-housed, what wants might then arise for them because of this?

6 The Aktars could decide to convert part of their house into a garage for the family car. What wants might this create for the rest of the household?

7 What are the similarities and differences between the lists you have made of the wants of these four families?

3 Scarce Resources

A resource is anything that we can use in the making and providing of a good or a service.

If resources were always in plentiful supply, people would better be able to satisfy all their wants. However, this is not usually the case. Instead we find that most resources are scarce and command a price – so we have to pay for them. By *scarce* we mean that there is only a finite or *limited* amount of items compared with people's wants. We always seem to want more than we have.

This is a potato.
He is just a potato.
If you peel him and cut him up, and fry him in oil, you've got a potato crisp.
Call the potato and the oil your raw materials.
Call the effort you've taken your labour.
Call the peeler and the frying pan and the oven your capital equipment.
Call all these things your factors of production.
Call the crisp your product.
If anyone wants a crisp, will you let them have a packet for nothing?

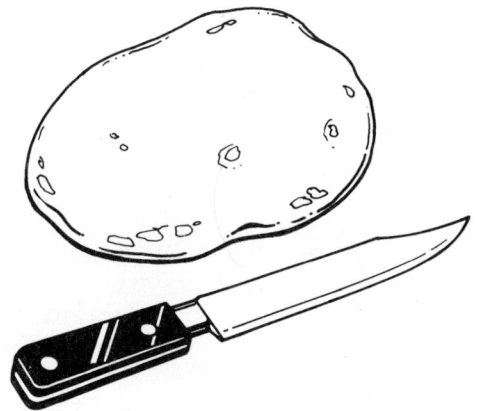

ECONOMIC TERMS

Resources: items used in providing goods and services.
Factors of production: those resources which when combined together produce economic goods and services.
Finite: limited in supply.
Scarcity: a situation that exists when a resource is not plentiful in supply.

Making an apple pie

In the Keegan family only Mike can make the perfect apple pie.

Only the supermarket in town has all the raw materials he will want to use.

When Mike goes to catch the bus to the supermarket, he finds he has to wait. There's only one bus an hour.

When the bus comes he has to stand. He has to wait on the way home, too, and stand again.

As he walks home from the bus stop he passes several houses on his estate that are boarded up awaiting repair. The local council does not have enough workers and materials to repair them all.

Mike stops at Nella's house to borrow an economics textbook for his homework. In their class of 26 the teacher could only afford to issue 13 books.

Outside the paper shop the evening paper headline reads, *Local hospital ward closed: nursing shortage*. When he gets home his mum is in the kitchen.

"I'll be some time," she says. It'll be too late now for Mike to make the apple pie tonight. Even time is scarce.

Mike switches on the TV instead. Tonight's stories are about famine in Africa, drought in India, and serious flooding in Canada. People seem to be in need everywhere. "It's all very depressing," thinks Mike. So he tells his mum he's off to bed.

"Oh, I forgot," she says. "Your Auntie Joan's coming to stay. You'll have to sleep on the sofa tonight."

"If only we could expand our resources to infinity," sighs Mike, "then we could solve all our problems!"

- Make a quick list of examples of scarcity that Mike met on the day he decided to make the perfect apple pie.
- Compare your list with those made by the rest of the class.

Four factors of production

Economists say that there are four types of resources that are brought together in an attempt to provide us with all the goods and services we want. These four types of resources, called *factors of production*, are:

- land;
- capital;
- labour;
- enterprise.

These can be combined in various proportions to produce the goods we require.

Land

As far as the economist is concerned *land* covers all the natural, as opposed to human, resources of our planet.

The land provides us with many of the raw materials we require to make goods. The apples for Mike's pie were probably grown on orchard land, the flour came from a farmer's wheat fields, the sugar from a sugar beet farm.

Capital

Any wealth that is used to make further wealth is called *capital*.

Mike's capital in making his apple pie would include the money he used to buy his bus ticket, the goods he bought in the supermarket, and the raw materials once he had purchased them. It would also include the equipment he used, like bowls and spoons and the oven to bake the pie.

Sometimes capital is used to make *consumer goods* like Mike's apple pie. At other times it is used to make the *capital goods* (for example, a blast furnace) that are needed to make the consumer goods.

Labour

The human beings, who work to provide the economic goods and services that we want, are called *labour* by economists.

Enterprise

The people who run a business in the hope of making a profit take a risk that they will lose their resources if the business runs at a loss. Their service in taking this risk is called *enterprise* by economists. A person who takes such risks is called an *entrepreneur*.

Mike's apple pies

Mike decides to set up in business selling his apple pies. He employs his sister Jackie to help him. Now he is an entrepreneur surrounded by the other three factors of production.

1 What is a resource?
2 List the resources you use in an economics lesson.
3 **a** List the factors of production Mike uses in setting up his 'Sweet as a Pie' business.
  b Describe how he would make use of each of them.
4 Which factors of production are each of the following:
  a a farmer;
  b a fruit picker;
  c a canning factory;
  d apple trees;
  e an orchard;
  f money in a bank account?

The proportion of each factor of production used in an enterprise can be altered. In the past most enterprises were labour intensive; today many in the developed world are capital intensive.

Activity

1 List the resources that are shown in both photographs.

2 Draw up two columns. Label one MODERN FARMING and the other TRADITIONAL FARMING.

   a Count and list the number of workers in each photograph. Estimate the total wages they might earn in a year. Write this figure in the appropriate column.

   b Try to put a value on the equipment used in each photograph. Record this in the appropriate columns.

   c Roughly compare the ratio (proportion) of labour costs to equipment (capital) costs in each photograph. What difference do you notice?

Traditional farming

Modern farming

Chaos blamed on middle-aged

Menace choking London's streets

By NICK FARRELL

MIDDLE-AGED, middle-class men driving expensive company cars are largely to blame for traffic chaos in London.

This is one conclusion of a study published today by environmental pressure group Friends of the Earth.

The 66-page report, called Capital Schemes?, claims the Government is contributing to the havoc by an obsession with new roads as a solution.

More roads, far from easing traffic flow, actually increase it by encouraging more cars and lorries, the study claims.

Public transport users, cyclists and pedestrians are being neglected despite most Londoners wanting better public transport and fewer large road schemes, says FoE.

It wants better use of existing roads and more money spent on public transport.

FoE says there is clear evidence that many motorists could be persuaded to switch to public transport.

In just two years, while the now defunct Greater London Council operated its Fair's Fare policy, bus use increased by 13 per cent and Tube use by 44 per cent while car commuting went down by more than 20 per cent.

"Most people coming into London in the mornings are middle-aged men on their own in company cars taking up a lot of road space," said an FoE spokesman.

"Very little of this through traffic is essential."

London was the only European capital where public transport had taken a back seat to the car, added the spokesman.

"Here we give tax relief to those going to work in company cars."

Source: *London Evening Standard*
9 April 1987

Having read this report carefully, answer these questions.

1 Why in your opinion do many people want to travel to work by car?

2 What resources are provided by the government to help the motorist?

3 If more resources were spent by government to satisfy the wants of motorists, who might suffer?

4 Explain how the report illustrates an economic problem.

5 Would giving more resources to the motorist be a wise solution? Give reasons for your answer.

Extension 1

STOP THE HORROR SLAUGHTER OF KANGAROOS

Adapted from a report in the Sunday Mirror by Steve Bailey and Richard Brecker, 3 August 1986.

"Outraged animal lovers are mounting an international campaign to end the savage, senseless killing of millions of kangaroos.

Officially, over 2½ million kangaroos will be killed this year in Australia's outback. Farmers demand that numbers be controlled to protect crops."

1 Copy the table below and sort out the statements on the next page into the categories given.

Statements supporting the use of kangaroos as a resource	Statements critical of the use of kangaroos as a resource	Statements worried about the effect of kangaroos on other resources

It's not culling, it's killing.

Kangaroos were responsible on one farm for wiping out the entire grazing for the cattle there.

Top sports stars are in the firing line for wearing flash footwear made from kangaroo skins.

Repair bills to fencing came to £50,000 on one ranch.

Five species have already become extinct.

Kangaroo skins can be sold for leather.

Kangaroo meat is good as pet food, claims pet food manufacturer.

2 Write a short summary of the arguments that can be presented for and against the economic exploitation of the kangaroo as a resource.

Extension 2

1 Your parents are contemplating buying a house in Acacia Avenue. They have a choice of three, each with a different heating system:

No 39: Gas fired central heating; average quarterly bill £110.
No 77: Solid fuel (coal) central heating; average quarterly bill £100.
No 68: Oil fired central heating; average quarterly bill £130.

Which would they have to choose if your parents could only afford about £105 a quarter for central heating?

2 Complete the table. (Some words have been given as clues to help you.)

Solid Fuel Heating		Oil Fired Heating		Gas Fired Heating	
Good points	Bad points	Good points	Bad points	Good points	Bad points

CLEAN FUEL   INSTANT HEAT AT THE TURN OF A SWITCH

CHEAP BILLS   MIDDLE EAST DEMANDS HIGHER OIL PRICES

DISPOSING OF WASTE PRODUCTS e.g. ash   LIGHTING THE FIRE

3 Look at these ways of heating a home. Consider the effects on the economy of each method. Present a short report in support of a particular method of generating power.

> **Coal**: A cheap form of heating, particularly if the coal is imported. Possibly contributing like oil, as a fossil fuel, to the overheating of the planet's atmosphere (the so-called greenhouse effect). Creates jobs in areas of otherwise high unemployment.

> **Wind, solar and tidal power**: So far only small amounts of power have been generated by these methods. Development of the necessary capital equipment will be expensive. Offers a cheap, limitless and clean form of power.

> **Atomic power/nuclear energy**: Currently problem of disposal and danger of accidents damaging the environment. Less effect on the environment when compared to fossil fuels. Could be a cheap method of power generation and a long lasting one, if spent fuel is re-used.

Coursework

Aim: To consider the use and abuse of resources.

1 Over a period of time (for example a month) collect newspaper stories about resources. Label and number each item in your collection.

2 Decide which articles are:
  a about how people are wasting resources;
  b examples of how people are finding new resources;
  c describing how people are conserving (looking after) existing resources.

3 Write a short summary setting out what you found under each section.

4 You have recently moved to a beautiful village in the countryside. Write a letter to the Prime Minister complaining about the effects on the environment of a plan to open a coal mine in your area.

5 You are the area manager of British Coal and are worried about people's fears about the new mine. Prepare a leaflet detailing the advantages a new coal mine will bring to the area.

4 Choices

We have seen that wants are infinite and resources are finite. We cannot have everything we want so we have to make *choices*.

Decide for yourself
- What choices would you make if you were Tim or Shaheen?
- Remember that you could choose not to spend but to save your money.

Kay and Rick's night out
Kay and Rick are planning to go to the disco tonight. Here are the economic facts that face them.

Kay and Rick's money	Admission £2 each.
	The disco starts at 9 pm and finishes at 1 am.
	The bus service stops at midnight. A shared taxi is £4.
	Bus fare to the disco is £1 each.
	First drink is £1 each.
	All other drinks are £2 each.
	Take-away food costs £5.
	A girl was recently assaulted in the area at about 12.30.
RESOURCES	WANTS

Kay and Rick's wants are greater than their resources so they will have to make choices.

Discuss how they can make the best use of their resources.

Everyone, rich and poor alike, is limited in terms of their purchasing power to some extent. They are forced to choose between competing wants and to allocate (or direct) their spending towards a certain end or goal.

Decide for yourself
- How would you allocate Kay and Rick's resources?

A diagram about resources
An entrepreneur, such as a farmer, has to decide, within the boundaries of the resources he or she has, how best to use them.

Tim and Shaheen can only spend ten pounds

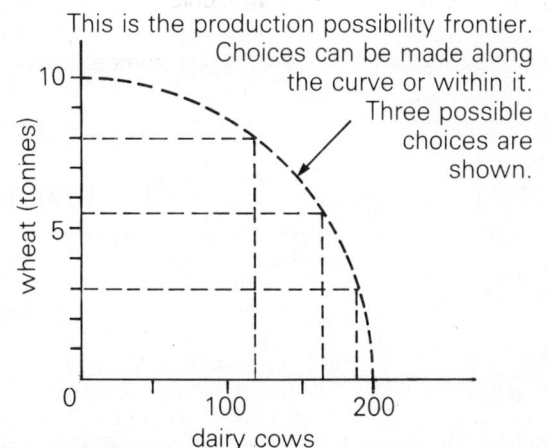

This is the production possibility frontier. Choices can be made along the curve or within it. Three possible choices are shown.

Production possibility curve

Farmer Carter could have a herd of 200 dairy cows or could grow 10 tonnes of wheat on the same land. Alternatively, he could settle for (or choose) a combination of cows and wheat.

We can show the choices we can make with the resources we have on a *production possibility curve*.

If Farmer Carter chose to grow 3 tonnes of wheat, he could also have 190 dairy cows.

Extension 1

How many dairy cows could Farmer Carter have if he grew 7 tonnes of wheat?

How many tonnes of wheat could he grow if he decided to keep 50 dairy cows?

Utility

We choose to spend our money, whether we are consumers, or producers, or government departments, on what we think will give us the greatest satisfaction. Economists call the satisfaction we obtain *utility*.

Jackie's choices

Jackie likes chocolate bars, but she also likes toffee bars. She will buy chocolate bars if they give her more utility (or satisfaction).

There may be a point where she no longer wants to choose chocolate bars and prefers toffee bars.

Decide from this graph when Jackie makes this decision.

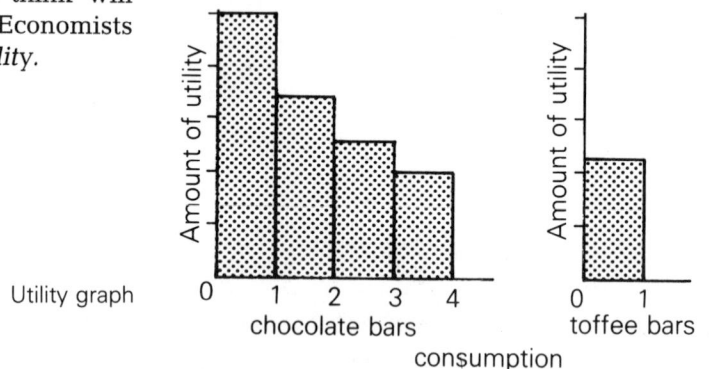

Utility graph

Activity

The Melchester Mirror
The County Paper
Exclusive: Bridge planned over the Shallow!

By our special correspondent
Plans are afoot to considerably shorten the journey time to London for local commuters. The bottleneck at Shallowford will be removed by providing a bridge across the Shallow.

A consortium set up by the County Council and local businesses believe that a toll bridge would quickly pay for itself. The government may grant £3 million to help this new enterprise.

The Shallowford Star

At last the government has recognised the need to reduce the severe congestion on River Road and Ferry Street. The offer of £3 million from the government, dependent on the County Council raising a similar sum, will help, but £8 million will be needed to build the new bridge.

Some people are already worried that the new bridge, whilst solving traffic problems in the town, will lead to a loss of trade.

"Shallowford will become a sleepy backwater," complained one resident. "I'd prefer to use the £6 million central and local government would spend in improving the ferry service. A toll bridge would be a heavy burden on local people too."

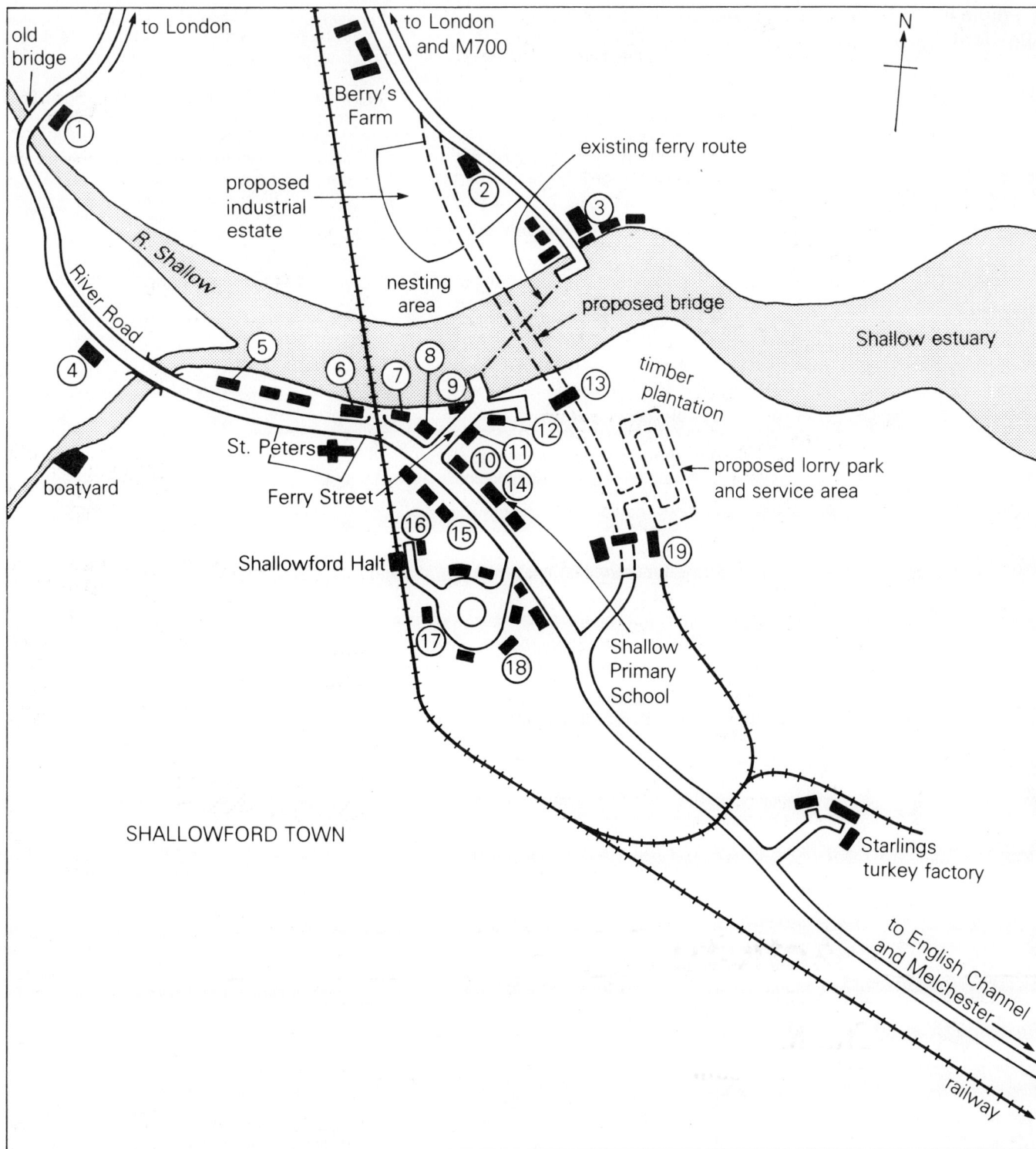

A Bridge Too Many?

ACTIVITY POINTS:

See the further information on page 18.

1 Decide who will be for the new bridge and why.

2 Who do you think will be against the new bridge? Why?

3 Consider some of the ways the town will benefit if they choose a bridge.

4 What risks for Shallowford might exist if they make this choice?

The people of Shallowford

1 Tom Copley owns the Old Bridge pub. As there is no competition in the area he has done very well from the increased traffic on River Road.

2 Heather Owen lectures in economics in London. She is well aware that her land will become very valuable if a bridge is built, but how does she persuade Shallowford that it is a good idea?

3 Jack Upcar runs the northern side of the Shallowford Ferry business.

4 Joan Williams, since the loss of her daughter in an accident on River Road, has thrown all her energies into The Sleepy Joe café. She needs all the passing trade she can get, as she's recently expanded the café, borrowing heavily from the local bank.

5 Helen Crane is the local representative of the Royal Society for the Protection of Birds. She is very concerned that a bridge would disturb the nesting site of the local swan population.

6 Mr and Mrs Mone's house is so close to the railway line and River Road that any plan to move traffic away from the west side of Shallowford would receive their unanimous support.

7 Harry Dickens runs the southern end of Shallowford ferries, with his partner and brother-in-law, Jack Upcar.

8 Mrs Green owns the grocery shop in the centre of Shallowford. Business is thriving. She is worried about rumours that Star Foods, one of the consortium of local businesses involved in financing the bridge project, may ask for planning permission to build a supermarket at the proposed service area.

9 John Danilor, local librarian, complains that the ferry is so noisy that the once quiet life he had has been totally ruined.

10 Josie Brown owns the Cow and Duck pub at the centre of Shallowford. Business is roaring. She benefits enormously from passing trade, but last year had literally to cower and duck when a juggernaut ploughed into the saloon bar.

11 Steve Shepherd is currently unemployed. He was recently made redundant from the position of Motel manager near Aberdeen, and has returned to Shallowford to care for his aged parents. He has been approached to run the Motel the consortium are planning to build at the service area.

12 Mrs Patel retired to Shallowford and purchased Rose Cottage five years ago. The increased ferry business is spoiling her peaceful retirement.

13 Commander Braithwaite, R.N. retired, lives in the Smugglers Rest. After a career at sea defending the nation he now finds he has to defend his own home. His house will be demolished if the bridge is built. He has vowed to lie down in front of the bulldozers. Mrs Braithwaite will join him!

14 Mr and Mrs Boyd teach at the school. They are much respected in the town for their dedication and hard work on behalf of the students. Two years ago Julie Williams, one of their most promising pupils, was killed crossing River Road on her way to school. Since then they have campaigned for a footbridge over River Road. Playing fields would be lost if a new bridge over the Shallow was built, but road accidents in the town would probably decline. The couple are split over the proposals.

15 Rose Evans, the local lollipop lady, sees the children across River Road. She likes doing the job, but agrees that River Road is very dangerous.

16 Bob Thomas is area manager, British Rail. Thanks to his hard work Starlings now send their turkeys to London via rail and Chrissie Crackers, the jokes and novelty firm, are thinking of doing so as well.

17 Ruth Fields lives on the new estate on the edge of Shallowford, close to Shallowford Halt railway station. She works long hours as a merchant banker, and would prefer a quicker journey to and from London, and the chance of trying out her new sports car on the M700. Her husband runs a haulage firm. Both want a bridge.

18 Mr Sage works at Starlings and is fed up with the low wages he gets stuffing turkeys. The new bridge would give him the chance to run the poultry unit at Berry's farm.

19 Mrs McDonald owns Chrissie Crackers. The new approach road for the bridge runs through her factory. She has been promised compensation which will enable her to rebuild those parts of the factory that will have to be demolished. She would then have two alternative ways to send her products to their market. She believes road transport would be more convenient and cost effective.

Shallowford Public Meeting

This is an activity for 22 players. Each player becomes a local person (remember to allocate two 6s, 13s, and 14s). Make sure that the class is fairly evenly divided between those for the bridge and those against it.

The class then divides into pro-bridge and anti-bridge groups and researches their arguments. Each group chooses a spokesperson. The teacher chairs the meeting and calls the two groups together to argue their case. Each person should be given a chance to put their point of view.

Then decide as a class which choice – to have a new bridge or to use the money for another purpose – would be of the most utility for Shallowford.

DATA RESPONSE 1

He earns £73 a second on stage

THE BOSS CLEANS UP

Rich Pickings

STRAWBERRY growers are predicting a record 25,000-ton crop this summer, despite the poor weather.

Source: *Daily Mirror*, 13 June 1985

★ BRUCE Springsteen may insist he is just a regular guy – but he is stuffing close on a million pounds into the back pocket of his tatty old jeans for every night he spends in Britain.

The Boss's six shows have already grossed £5½ million in advance ticket sales, which ensures he should earn about £73 for each SECOND he spends on stage while he is here.

Of course Bruce will have to pay VAT, promoters' fees and security costs out of that.

Then there is the massive cost of keeping his show on the road.

"But he'll still personally be left with at least one and a half million pounds personal profit," a tour insider estimates.

Perhaps now he'll be able to afford to buy himself a new tee-shirt!

Source: *Daily Mirror*, 13 June 1985

Bradford: 'No cash to clear blaze litter'

CLEARING the litter that fuelled last month's tragic blaze at Bradford City ground had not been a priority, club chairman Stafford Heginbotham said yesterday.

"We had so much on," Mr Heginbotham told the public inquiry into the fire which killed 55 fans.

"I inspected the stand many times and had no complaints about the litter.

"I was aware litter would have collected under the stand but it would have been a major task to clear it all."

The inquiry has heard that the club was warned twice that rubbish gathered under the stand was a potential fire risk.

In a hushed voice, Mr Heginbotham said: "I have thought a thousand times what more could have been done in order that such a tragedy had not occurred."

Source: *Daily Mirror*, 13 June 1985

BRITAIN OFF TO MOW MEADOW!

BRITISH gardeners will spend £120 million on lawn mowers this year... more than anywhere else in the world.

Fourteen million machines were bought in 1985, mower manufacturers Qualcast reported yesterday – and this year, sales should be even higher.

Qualcast say that most people go for electric machines – they accounted for 80 per cent of the mower market in 1985. Petrol mowers grabbed a 15 per cent share, and push machines 5 per cent.

Source: *Sun*, 3 February 1986

1 Which extract deals with consumers making choices?

2 How did they tend to choose and why?

3 Which extract is about a worker facing a choice?

4 Which extracts show how entrepreneurs can be successful if they make the right choices?

5 Which extract highlights the dangers involved in making the wrong choices?

6 What do the extracts have in common?

Traffic noise drowns bridge critics

One year after the opening of the £90 million Humber crossing, traffic figures start to justify optimism. Malcolm Pithers reports

THE Humber Bridge, one of the most dramatic and controversial pieces of engineering in Britain for years, is slowly beginning to justify its existence and silence its critics.

It is the longest single span suspension bridge in the world.

Opponents said it was a bridge from nowhere leading nowhere, a costly white elephant that would hardly be used.

The more optimistic said that the area desperately needed the bridge, despite its vast expense. Its very existence would generate traffic, help local industry, and, might even bring new industries to the north and south banks of the Humber at a time the recession was biting home.

Mr Roger Evans, a civil engineer, who is deputy bridge master, believes that the bridge has already proved its value. "Some people said we would never have more than 4,000 vehicles a day, crossing the bridge, and we have already doubled that figure."

But interest on the outstanding debt runs at around £20 million a year and critics say that the returns will never keep pace. Viewed strictly financially, they are probably correct.

Councillor Michael Wheaton, as leader of Humberside County Council, uses other colossal projects to put matters in perspective.

He pointed out that when the bridge opened it cost less than half the Tyne and Wear metro system, less than a quarter of the Thames surge barrier, an eighth of the Drax L power station, and less than one-tenth of the Sizewell nuclear power station.

What social and industrial changes have been wrought by the bridge are not yet known, but a detailed analysis of figures and movements which has been carried out this year should show how it has changed the area.

Revenue from all this traffic totalled £4,228,542. That is not enough to permit talking in terms of real profits, but it is a steady, healthy income and far exceeding the hopes of some people.

The actual running costs of the bridge are around £1 million a year, leaving a return of £3.2 million, and proving sufficiently healthy to persuade the operators to provide refreshment facilities and even consider a larger car parking area.

Source: *Guardian*, 9 August 1982

---

1 a How much did it cost to build the Humber bridge?

 b Why is it unique?

2 Why was the decision to build the bridge criticised?

3 What did those in favour of a bridge point out?

4 Although the bridge makes a profit in terms of its revenue and running costs, why is it possibly a financial disaster?

5 How could the Humber area have spent £90 million if they had decided not to build a bridge?

Extension 2

All our fuchsias?

1 Rose Gardiner runs a garden centre. She can choose to grow either 100 pots of geraniums or 150 fuchsias, or she could grow a combination of these two plants.

   a Can you construct a graph to show this? (See page 15.)

   b If Rose Gardiner decides to grow 60 pots of geraniums, how many fuchsias can she grow as well?

2 You too have to choose what to produce. You have 10 hours for homework this week. You have only two lots of homework set (Economics and English).

   a On a graph show how you would share out your time equally between the two subjects.

   b Now allocate more time to Economics. Show (by labelling) how much time Economics now has.

3 Governments have to choose as well. Let us say that the government has £200 million spare this year. It costs £40 million to build a new hospital and £25 million to build a new school.

   a How many hospitals or schools could they have?

   b Make a choice yourself of a combination of hospitals and schools. Show this on a graph.

   c Write a short letter to your Member of Parliament giving the reasons for your choice.

Coursework

Aim: To investigate possible choices of transport.

Select, either in your own neighbourhood or among teachers and other workers at your school, a range of people who commute to work either by car or public transport.

1 Ask them to estimate the weekly cost of their journey to work. In the case of car drivers devise a way of allowing for those costs that appear less frequently (insurance, service charges, motor tax, capital repayments etc.).

2 Find out the distance they commute in a week and work out the average cost of a mile of travel.

3 Ask them to list some of the benefits of their chosen method of commuting.

4 Ask each group to list some of the costs involved in their chosen method of commuting.

5 Compare the cost of commuting for each group. What differences do you find? Do these costs or the other costs and benefits that you have identified help to explain why they choose to commute in the way they do?

5 Costs and Benefits of Choosing

NOW OPEN WIDE. THIS MIGHT PROVE COSTLY BUT THINK OF THE BENEFITS.

Whenever an individual makes a decision they have to consider the benefits they will receive and the costs that they will have to bear. We call the costs an individual has to carry their *private costs*.

As well as the costs of a decision, we also obtain benefits. If these benefits are gained by individuals, we call them *private benefits*.

The costs society receives from an economic decision are called *external costs* and the benefits society receives are called *external benefits*.

Activity

PRIVATE COSTS

If I buy a Choffee, I'll have to walk home

20 p.

I really must lose weight – I'm 15 stone.

Oh, no! Not another filling!

Sorry I'm late for lessons but I had to queue in the sweet shop for my Choffee bar.

If I buy a Choffee bar then I can't afford an evening paper.

PRIVATE BENEFITS

Yummy yummy! It fills your tummy!

Choffee gives me get up and go.

After eating a Choffee bar I feel really satisfied.

It's only 20p. Other bars that size are at least 30p.

EXTERNAL COSTS

Dentists report that the state of children's teeth is a national scandal.

ADVERT: Chewing gum scraper operator required to clean station concourse.

DOCTORS SUGGEST THAT 30% OF THE POPULATION ARE OVERWEIGHT.

Litter's not much fun when you're only five foot one.

MILK CHOCOLATE TOFFEE BAR 20p
Choffee
The Bar with the chewy centre

EXTERNAL BENEFITS

Wages bill for Choffee £300 000 a year.

Choffee cover printing contract brings jobs to Shallowford.

Jobs for doctors, dental technicians.

VAT on sweets helps pay for new hospitals and schools.

Ghana's cocoa exporters record increased sales.

ACTIVITY POINTS:
1 What are the costs of eating sweets for the sweet eater?
2 What are the benefits for the sweet eater?
3 What are the costs to others in society if you eat a lot of sweets?
4 What are the benefits to others in society if you eat a lot of sweets?
5 Consider the costs and benefits from smoking cigarettes.

22

Jane's watch

Jane is trying to choose a watch. Some look very smart, but their faces are not too clear. On some the straps are too narrow. Eventually she finds what she wants: a reliable watch with a clear face and a wide strap.

Jane has acted rationally in making her choice. We assume in economics that all people who make economic choices act in a similar way to Jane: they choose in order to maximise (make the most of) the benefits of a decision. These benefits could include a saving in money and time, or an increase in utility.

Opportunity cost

Making decisions, however, also involves us in costs. If Jane buys her watch she can't afford a new dress. The real cost of choosing the watch is not the money cost, but the benefit Jane has given up by not consuming the next most desirable alternative. Economists call this the *opportunity cost*.

Decide for yourself

- What would be the opportunity cost of each of the following decisions?
- Match each situation with the best suggested answer.
1 Jill buys a water pistol.
2 Mrs Cohen borrows money to expand her flower shop.
3 Developers build the Channel Tunnel.
A She cannot replace the van she uses to make deliveries.
B They abandon plans to build a bridge.
C She has to go without a kite.

ECONOMIC TERMS

Opportunity cost: the benefit given up when choosing an item, measured in terms of what you lose from not consuming the next best alternative.
Private costs and benefits: the advantages and disadvantages experienced by individuals who make economic decisions.
External costs and benefits: the advantages and disadvantages of an economic decision as experienced by the wider society.
Social costs and social benefits: the total or net costs and/or benefits arising from producing a good or service. They are calculated by adding the private benefits and external benefits together and subtracting the private and external costs.

John's accident

John buys a motor scooter with his savings, but he cannot also afford to have driving lessons. He decides he will be able to teach himself from a book.

John tries to turn into a No Entry street and is knocked down by a van.

Let's look at some of the costs of John's decision:

- The police and ambulance are called and John is taken to hospital. His leg has been fractured.
- John spends a fortnight in hospital during which time he cannot work or pay his taxes.
- He has to attend physiotherapy for the next year. The government has been planning to cut the budget for physiotherapy and put extra resources into medical research. With people like John around, they decide to change their plans.

John's accident has resulted in a number of external costs. Make a list of as many of these costs as you can and compare your list with those of other students.

Switch on the light

When you've switched on an electric light, have you ever thought of the costs and benefits involved? When we add the total private costs and benefits of an economic decision and the total external costs and benefits together, we arrive at the *net cost* or *net benefit* of an economic decision. This is called the *social cost* or *social benefit*.

Think of some of the personal costs of switching on an electric light. One is that someone has to pay the bill. The personal benefits, however, are enormous. Can you think of some of them?

The external benefits are high too. For example, many power stations are situated in rural areas where they bring employment which would not otherwise be available. Can you think of others?

The external costs also have to be considered. Some of these power stations generate electricity from nuclear sources. The ecological pressure group Friends of the Earth claims that between 1977 and 1986 there were 121 radiation leak incidents at one power station. Some of these affected workers, and others the surrounding community. The opportunity cost of further expanding nuclear energy might be what we lose by not researching into a 'cleaner' and, perhaps, cheaper form of energy.

Berkeley Power Station

1 You wish to buy a watch. You have the choice of two that offer you identical quality. One is 5% cheaper. Why do you choose it?

2 What is meant by the term opportunity cost?

3 You have 50 pence and could spend it on sweets or the bus fare home. You decide to buy the sweets. What is the opportunity cost of your decision?

4 What private benefits would you receive from buying and using a minty gel toothpaste?

5 Describe how social cost/benefit is calculated.

6 Describe the costs and benefits of one of the following:

a smoking; b motorways; c nuclear power generation.

DATA RESPONSE 1

Look at this information carefully before you answer the questions. It may help if you glance through all the questions first to see what you are looking for.

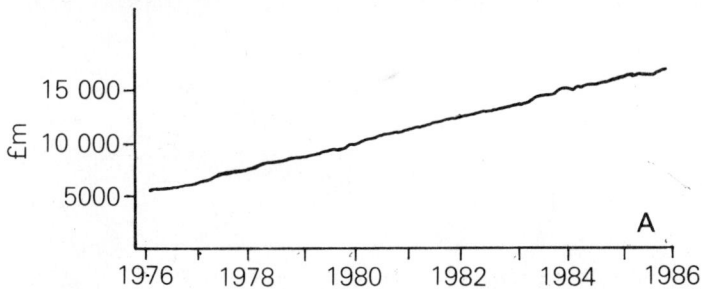

CSO *Abstract of Statistics, 1988*

Consumers' alcohol expenditure at current prices

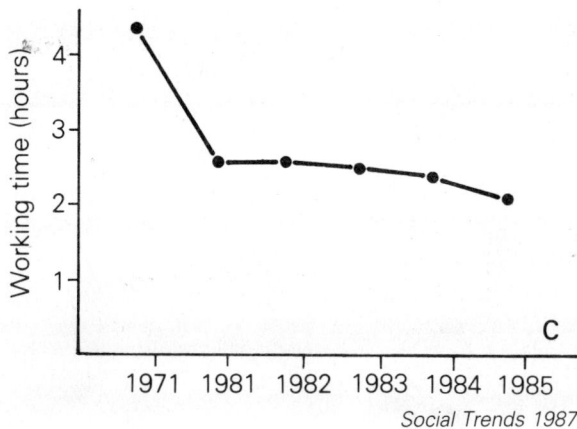

A Great and Growing Evil 1987 Royal College of Physicians

Consumption of alcohol

Social Trends 1987

Length of time needed to earn enough to buy one bottle of whisky

Hospital admissions re. alcohol		Convictions for drink-driving	
1952	1982	1968	1980
512	13 916	23 900	78 000

Problem Drinking Heather and Robertson

D

A Great and Growing Evil 1987 RCP

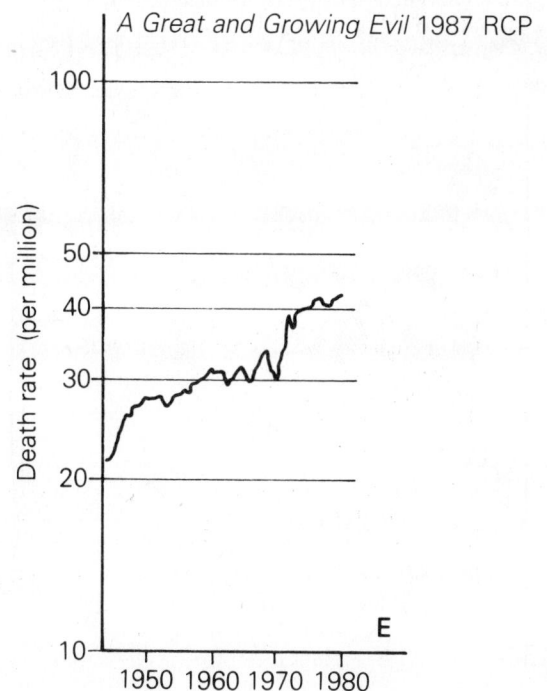

Death rate from alcoholism and related diseases

1 Using **A** and **B**, explain what changes have occurred in the pattern of expenditure on, and consumption of, alcohol.

2 Explain how the information in **C** can be used partly to account for the changes you observed in your answer to **1**.

3 Using **D** and **E**, explain what consequences there could be for society if consumers choose to drink more (increase their consumption of) alcohol.

4 What increases in resources will society have to provide to cope with the problems created by an increase in alcohol consumption?

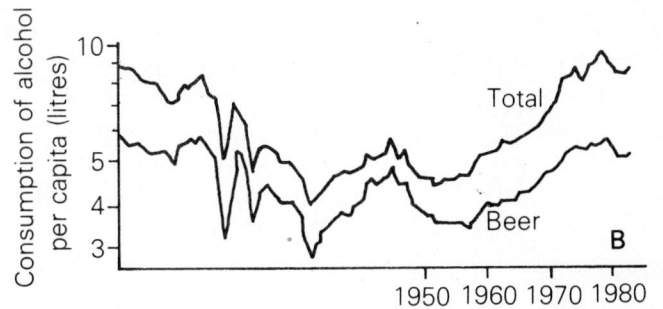

Extension

There would seem to be nothing more natural than having a well-cooked British breakfast of bacon and eggs to start the day. Farmers and shopkeepers benefit from it. Tourists seek it out. But others are not so happy. Animal welfare groups worry about 'factory' farming methods. Doctors and dieticians, worried about Britain's high rate of heart disease, have urged people to think again about the way they start their day.

1 What might be the various costs and benefits of having a great British breakfast? Draw up a chart like the one here, filling in as many costs and benefits as you can think of in each section.
2 What might be some of the consequences for farmers if consumers changed their breakfast eating habits?

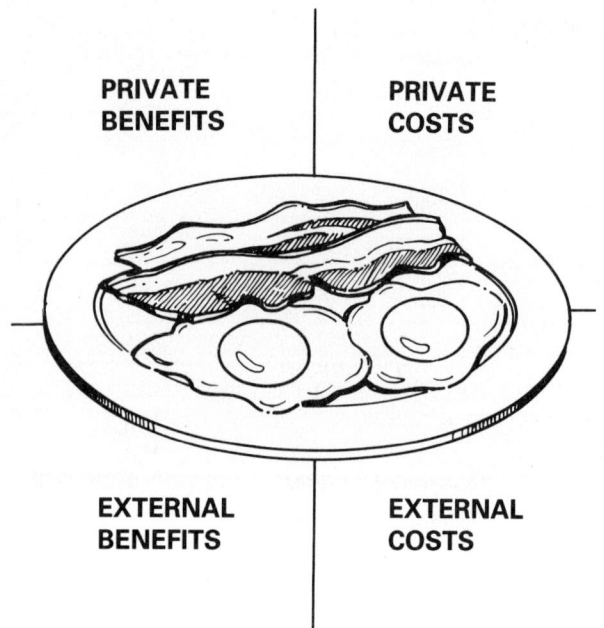

PRIVATE BENEFITS   PRIVATE COSTS

EXTERNAL BENEFITS   EXTERNAL COSTS

DATA RESPONSE 2

IT'S THE killer that comes with ice and lemon. Or in pint jars.

Many people spend their happiest hours with a glass in their hand – cheerfully sentencing themselves to an early, painful death.

Drink is now Britain's third biggest killer behind heart disease and cancer.

It causes more deaths than smoking.

• PREGNANT WOMEN. They are particularly at risk, and so are their unborn babies. They give birth to low-weight, premature babies.
• YOUNG PEOPLE. They haven't developed the same tolerance to alcohol as older people, and are therefore more likely to be involved in accidents.

* One in five road accidents involves a driver over the legal limit – a threat to his own life, his passengers, and all other road users.

Costs?

* Two out of three accidents causing serious head injuries involve drink.

This year, more than 3,000 people in Britain will die from cirrhosis of the liver – and that figure is up 63% in the last ten years.

* More than half of all murders involve drink.
* Two out of every three suicides and attempted suicides involve alcohol.

The cost to the health service is staggering – one in every five patients admitted to general hospitals have alcohol-related illness or disability. And many more people are admitted to psychiatric hospitals each year.

The cost to industry is equally phenomenal, with between eight and 14 million days a year lost at work because of heavy drinking. Industry loses £1.6 billion a year through absenteeism and premature death caused by drink.

Adapted from the *Sun*, 3 February 1986

1 Describe the costs of drinking for the individual.

2 What are the effects of drinking on young people?

3 What are the consequences, in the form of external costs, of drunken driving for other road users?

4 What are the external costs and benefits of drinking for those employed in
a industry;
b the health service?

Coursework

Aim: To examine whether young people are more aware than the elderly of the costs of smoking, and to consider the effects on the economy of a programme to make them more aware.

1 a Consider what the costs of smoking might be: money costs, opportunity costs, private costs, social costs.
b Consider what the private and social benefits might be.

2 Interview people of different age groups to gather data. What costs were highlighted by them?

3 a What benefits did they offer to explain their smoking habit?
b Were the young people more aware of the costs of smoking?

4 What reasons would you advance to explain why young people started to smoke and why old people continue to smoke?

5 Consider the ways in which the tobacco industry benefits the economy.

6 Consider the ways in which smoking is a cost for the wider community, e.g. passive smoking, cancer and related illnesses, costs for industry in lost production, and for the community in the use of hospital services.

7 a Would a programme of health education be successful in reducing the tobacco habit?
b How might such a programme
i damage
ii improve
the economy?

6 Choice and Economies

Just like individuals, countries have to make economic choices. They have to decide what to produce and who to produce for. They must decide how to allocate goods and services. Should they provide for all their people or only for those who can afford to pay?

How shall we run our economy?

Countries can run their economy in one of three basic ways:
- They can operate a *free market* (capitalist) economy. In a free market economy all resources are given a price and people purchase the goods and services that they want, if they can afford them.
- A country can be run as a *command economy*. This is sometimes known as a centrally planned or collectivist economy. In a command economy the government decides what will be produced and how resources will be distributed.

- A country can choose to combine these two economic systems by operating a *mixed economy*. Such a country would have both a private sector and a public sector. Some goods are left to individuals to produce and consume freely (within a private sector), others are provided by the government (within a public sector).

For some people in the world a fourth type of economy exists. For the people of places like Tristan da Cunha (see page 6) it is difficult to do more than just manage to exist. Such economies have few opportunities to trade. The people find it difficult to concentrate on providing one good or one service (to specialise). They tend to live in small groups and try to be self-sufficient (provide for their own needs). In such countries economic decisions are organised in a traditional way that has remained unchanged for many years. People are said to live at a *subsistence level*. Their choice is simply about how to survive.

Activity

The Great Storm

PUBLIC NOTICE

Because of the very high level of storm damage throughout the Borough, the Council will not be able to move the obstruction to the road known as The Beeches, caused by a fallen tree, for at least two weeks.

The Council regrets the inconvenience caused and assures residents it will do everything in its power to restore all services as soon as possible.

Mrs Smith lives at 2 The Beeches. She is a pensioner and is not well. At the best of times she finds it difficult to walk to the shops. She can't afford a taxi. She does not know how she will manage over the next two weeks.

Mr Hickling of 3 The Beeches works in the Midlands and commutes from Beechester by train. The fallen trees means he has a long detour to get to the station. He sympathises with the Hensley's desire to move the tree, but wants the council to be in control of the disposal of timber and repair of the street. He is a keen supporter of his local council's desire to provide services for the community.

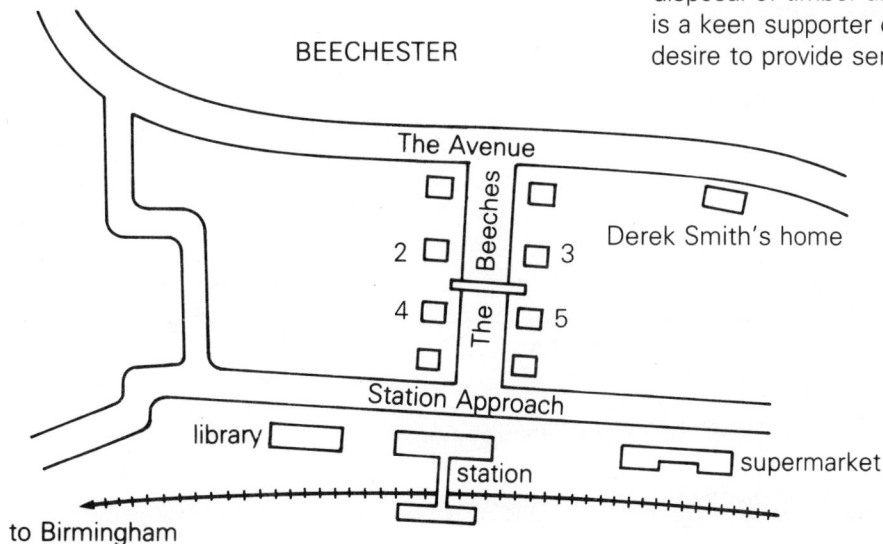

BEECHESTER

The Avenue

The Beeches

2

3

Derek Smith's home

4

The

5

Station Approach

library

station

supermarket

to Birmingham

The Mehmet family live at 4 The Beeches. They own the supermarket in Station Approach. They would be very concerned if local rates went up. They think the government should find the money to clear up after the storm.

The Hensleys of 5 The Beeches own a thriving timber business. They would be quite happy to clear the obstruction so long as they could keep the beech tree.

Government to meet storm bill

By Colin Brown
Political Correspondent

THE GOVERNMENT is to pay emergency aid to local authorities faced with multi-million pound bills after the storms which have brought havoc to England and Wales in the last four days.

But ministers could still face protests from Conservative council leaders that the help is not enough. Tony Hart, the Tory leader of Kent county council, which is one of the worst hit authorities, said he was disappointed because the Government is refusing to pay the entire cost of the emergency.

Kent county council could present the Government with a bill for £13.5m, although Paul Sabin, the council's chief executive, estimated last night that the total bill in the country would be £20m. Under the rules for emergency aid, the Government will pay 75 per cent of the cost, but councils must first meet the product of a penny rate – £2m in Kent.

Kent ratepayers will also be liable for a further £4.5m, the remaining 25 per cent of the emergency bill.

Furniture makers queue for rare timber

WOOD from the exotic trees blown down when Friday's hurricane tore through Kew Gardens and Chelsea Physic Garden in London could be turned into some of the finest furniture made in Britain this century, *Nick Cohen* writes.

Furniture makers and timber merchants were in contact with both botanical gardens yesterday, hoping to buy woods which are rarely seen on the open market.

Source: *The Independent*, 20 October 1987

1 Why are Mrs Smith and Mr Hickling at a greater disadvantage than the Mehmet and Hensley families?

2 What are the arguments for allowing the Hensleys to clear the obstruction?

3 What are the arguments for not allowing them to clear it?

4 Which of these people favours some form of local or central government intervention, and why?

5 Who is the least able to make a decision and why?

6 Mrs Smith's son Derek chops several branches off the tree with a chain saw he hired and gives some of them to his mother for firewood. The rest he sells locally. He keeps all the money he earns and does not declare any income for tax purposes.

Derek Smith's daughter is a student in your class. Your mother is the local magistrate. The police arrest Derek. Advise your mother on the handling of his case. Bear in mind the economic as well as the legal points that could be raised in Derek's defence and prosecution.

ECONOMIC TERMS

Free market economy: resources are priced. Individuals with purchasing power are free to choose the goods and services they want.
Command economy: a few individuals in government decide what is produced and how it is distributed.
A mixed economy: combines some parts of a free market economy with some parts of a command economy. It has a well developed private and public sector.
Informal (or Black) economy: illegal economic activity in any of the above economies.

Choices and attitudes

Mrs Spring is separated from her husband. She lives with her two children, Jason and Julie. She is an example of someone who, in our society, is very poor.

One day to her astonishment, she receives this letter.

Dear Mrs Spring,

You will probably have noticed that we have removed the street light and paving stones from the public highway outside your house.

When you have paid the arrears in rates that you owe the Council, we will be delighted to return the above items.

Yours sincerely

Your friendly neighbourhood Council

Mrs Spring reads the letter out to Jason and Julie. "Why should I be held responsible for the pavement and street light outside my home? I know I get a lot of benefit from them, but so does everyone else who uses the street."

"You're right, Mum," says Jason. "They are examples of public goods. The council shouldn't remove them."

"What's a public good?" asks Julie.

"A public good," says Jason, who is studying Economics at school, "is one used by lots of people. You shouldn't be the only person who pays for it if other members of the community use it. All the community should share the cost as all benefit from its provision. That's one of the reasons it's difficult to have a totally free economy."

Julie left college a couple of years ago and has started her own hairdressing business. She is very keen that everyone should live in a free market economy. "Consumers should be allowed to buy what they want if they can afford it," she says. Employers, she believes, should be allowed to hire workers or any other factor of production. "That way," she says, "you cut out shortages and surpluses of goods because people only provide what others want to buy." If someone hits on the right idea then they can get very rich selling it. "People, if they work hard," says Julie, "are entitled to a reward."

Julie saved very hard and then spent a lot of money to set up her business. She's behind with the rent she pays her mother.

Decide for yourself
- Were the council right to remove the street lamp and paving stones?
- How would you solve this problem?

Free and command economies

Jason doesn't always agree with Julie. Since Dad left home his mother has had to work very hard as a nurse to support the family. He reckons not everyone can afford to choose and that when people need help (when they're sick or out of work or need help to go to college), someone else has got to intervene, or get involved.

Jason believes that the government should provide for such basic needs as health and education and caring for people who cannot care for themselves.

He is critical, too, of the waste he sees. He accepts that competition in a free economy can reduce costs and provide a better service. "But," he points out to Julie, "look how wasteful advertising is. And look what happens if one firm dominates the market. The consumers end up with no choice and the government has to intervene to stop workers and consumers being exploited. And," he goes on, "governments have to stop organisations polluting the environment because they are only interested in making a profit."

"Perhaps you'd like to live in Russia," says Julie. "There the government provides most of the goods and services. You wouldn't have half the choice you have here. You can't tell the government you don't like the goods they sell, so the quality is terrible. Everyone has to queue for goods all the time and there are often shortages."

One answer to Julie's and Jason's arguments is to combine aspects of both free and command economies.

Mixed economy

In the United Kingdom we have a mixed economy which seeks to do just that. One part is called the *private sector* and provides private goods and services. The other part is called the *public sector* and provides state financed goods and services. There are three types of these: *merit goods, public goods* and *uneconomic goods.* Merit goods are goods provided below the market price, by a government, because they are considered important to the welfare of the community. Train services in rural areas are often a merit good. Public goods are goods provided by the government because it is largely impossible to prevent people who do not pay for the item from benefiting from the provision of the good or service in question. Street lighting is an example of a public good. Uneconomic goods may be provided by a government for political reasons. For example, to keep a factory open in an area of high unemployment the government might subsidise the output produced.

Three types of economy

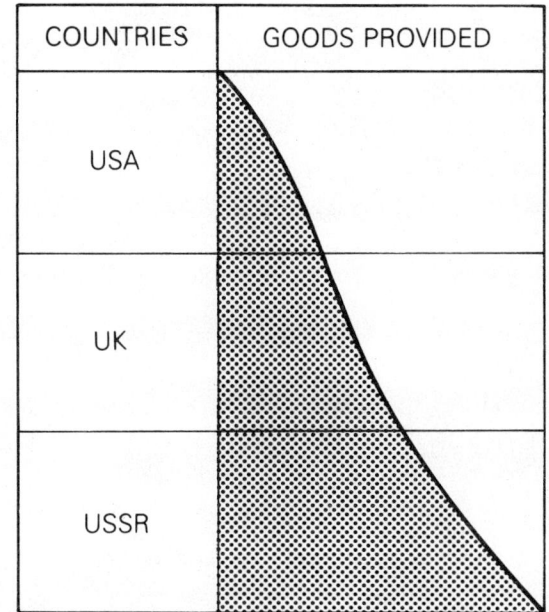

COUNTRIES	GOODS PROVIDED
USA	
UK	
USSR	

▨ Public sector   ☐ Private sector

Test yourself

1 List four ways in which economies are organised.
2 Look at what Jason and Julie say and explain the advantages of a free market economy.
3 What disadvantages in free markets does Jason point out?
4 What is a subsistence economy?
5 What is a mixed economy?
6 What part does the public sector play in such an economy?
7 Working in pairs, decide that one of you is to be dictator for a week. The other asks him or her what economic choices he or she would make for the country. What problems does your interview reveal?
8 Assume that you have no alternative but to attend the nearest school. What are the benefits of this (for example, a cheaper use of resources) and what are the costs (for example, there may be poor quality of service)?

DATA RESPONSE

Disaster in the desert

DUSA MAREB: The rain which has begun to fall on the arid plains of central Somalia has come too late to help three million nomadic herdsmen. In a cruel but largely forgotten drought they have lost much of their livestock. Six hundred people have died, and many more are close to death.

Undernourished children with swollen bellies and matchstick legs are everywhere in this dusty town of thatched huts. The air is filled with the stench of dead cows and camels, whose rotting carcasses litter the roadside.

Now, with the onset of the long rainy season, three weeks late, water-borne diseases pose a new threat, say United Nations officials.

But the biggest tragedy is that most of Somalia's nomadic herdsmen, who account for 60 per cent of the five million population, have lost the camels, cattle, goats and sheep which provide their only livelihood.

The officials said 80 per cent of the livestock in 12 of Somalia's 18 regions perished during the drought.

Local officials are angry that foreign donors have been slow to come to the aid of the drought victims. But the government in Mogadishu did not launch an international appeal for aid until recently and the drought, which affects a remote and inaccessible region, has gone largely unreported.

Source: *London Daily News*, 13 May 1987

1 Using the photograph and report what evidence exists to show that the families of Dusa Mareb are living at a subsistence level?

2 What reasons could be given to explain why they are living at this level?

3 What immediate difficulties will the people face once the disaster is over?

4 The Government ask you to mount a relief operation to bring aid to the nomadic people of Dusa Mareb. What difficulties might you meet in trying to do so?

Extension 1

Check the meaning of each type of economy given here in the ECONOMIC TERMS boxes.

From Svetlana in Leningrad, USSR. Svetlana lives in a *centrally planned economy*.

> Dear Jocelyn
>   Thank you for your letter and school photographs. I did not realise you went to a private school. Do you think this is fair on others? In our country, hospitals and many other services are provided free by the state government.
>   Please can you send me some more copies of the pop magazine you enclosed last time. We do not have this kind of thing here. I thought the dress you wore in the school photograph was very fashionable; I am envious of you.
>   Your friend,
>   Svetlana.

From Bob, in Detroit, USA. Bob lives in a *free market economy*.

> Dear Jocelyn
>   I've included our new address overleaf. We had to move to a smaller house as my dad was very ill last year and the medical fees were astronomical. I've also moved to the local state school. It's O.K. but some of the kids just think they are there for a good time.
>   Dad's back at work now, which is really great. He's promised us a holiday in Bermuda this year, even if we have to sell our second car.
>   Your pal,
>   Bob.
> P.S. Air fares to the States are cheap. Why not come over for a vacation.

From Philip in Dusa Mareb, Somalia He lives in a part of Somalia where *subsistence* agriculture is the means of obtaining a living.

> Dear Jocelyn
>   Thank you for sending me the parcel of food and clothes. We are very grateful. We are suffering terribly because of the drought. We may have to leave this district to search for water for our animals.
>   This will be hard on us, as we will be leaving the area our ancestors have always lived in, but we have no choice.
>   Yours sincerely,
>   Philip.

Jocelyn hears from her pen pals all over the world

1 Which of Jocelyn's three pen pals is best able to make a lot of choices, and why?
2 Who is least able to choose and why?
3 Who has a lot of choices made for them? What advantages are there in this?
4 What are the disadvantages of having choices made for you?
5 What sorts of problems has Bob's family had because of the type of economy they live in?
6 Imagine that you are Jocelyn. Write a letter to one of your pen pals describing the good and bad aspects of living in the British economic system.

Extension 2

The USSR is often given as an example of a command economy.

Here is an account of what Mikhail Gorbachev, one of the current Soviet leaders, has said in describing and criticising this system (adapted from the *Daily Mail*, 1 November 1987):

- research showed that the practice of providing the same things for everyone was unjust;
- too much effort was directed into production plans rather than caring about the real needs of the consumer;
- in spite of increases in output the market suffered from a lack of goods;
- we produce more metal, tractors, and combine harvesters than any country in the world;
- we lose out because they are of low quality;
- we are the world's leading grain producer;
- we have to import millions of tons of fodder grain;
- we have the greatest number of physicians and hospital beds per head of the population of any country;
- the quality of medical assistance is inadequate;
- our spacecraft went to Venus;
- many of our domestic appliances are inadequate;
- there is no unemployment, health care is free, so is education;
- people are protected from the hardships of life;
- some use this, they know only their rights and not their duties.

1 Describe the advantages for a consumer living in the USSR.

2 Describe the disadvantages for a consumer living in the USSR.

3 In the USSR a Central Committee used to decide what would be produced, the people then had production targets that they had to work to in order to produce the goods. What sorts of problems do you think this system produced?

Coursework

Aim: To investigate services provided by the state.

1 Talk to a person employed in the provision of a state service, for example, a nurse, teacher, doctor or police officer. Ask them to explain to you how the service is paid for. Once you have interviewed them, rewrite their explanation in your own words.

2 What are the benefits of the system according to the person?

3 Investigate a range of other sources (e.g. newspapers, textbooks) to determine other possible benefits to be gained from the provision of this service by the state.

4 What problems have consumers experienced with the provision of this service? Identify and talk to consumers who have had problems like:
   a consumer waiting a year for a hip replacement;
   b parent unhappy with discipline/ homework standards in the local school;
   c a person who has recently been burgled and is unhappy with the local crime detection rates.

5 Now assume people had to pay the full costs of the service they receive. Find ways of estimating what this would be. What problems would be created for some people?

   On balance consider whether the service should continue to be provided by the state or left to individuals as part of a free market.

7 Production

In economics *production* is the term used for the creation of goods and services to satisfy those wants that consumers are prepared to pay for. Business organisations or firms are the individuals or groups called *producers* that seek to provide such goods or services. For goods or services to be produced, producers have to make use of resources which are called *factors of production*. These factors include land, labour, capital and entrepreneurial skill. A place involved, in some way, with production is called a *production unit*. A firm can own one or more such production units.

Activity

Let them eat cheesecake

Ingredients for a Mandarin Cheesecake
125 g butter
225 g digestive biscuits
1 tsp gelatine
1 can of Mandarin oranges
900 g curd cheese
150 ml double cream
2 eggs
125 g caster sugar
peel and juice of one lemon

1 There are three stages involved in the making and selling of cheesecake. The first stage is called *primary production* and is the *extractive stage*. In this stage raw materials are obtained from the earth. Which photograph opposite illustrates this stage?

2 The second stage is called *secondary production*. In this stage raw materials are converted into manufactured items. Which two photographs illustrate this stage?

3 The third stage is called *tertiary production* and is the stage that provides services and retails or sells a product. Which photograph represents this stage?

4 Draw a flow chart showing how each of these stages is related to form a *chain of production*. Start with raw materials and end with the shops that sell cheesecake.

5 Using the recipe, construct a more complex chain of production that includes all the ingredients in a cheesecake.

6 What are the benefits to the following from the production and supply of cheesecakes?
   a Consumers of cheesecakes
   b Producers of cheesecakes
   c The government

7 What social costs might be associated with the production, distribution and consumption of cheesecake?

A

B

C

D

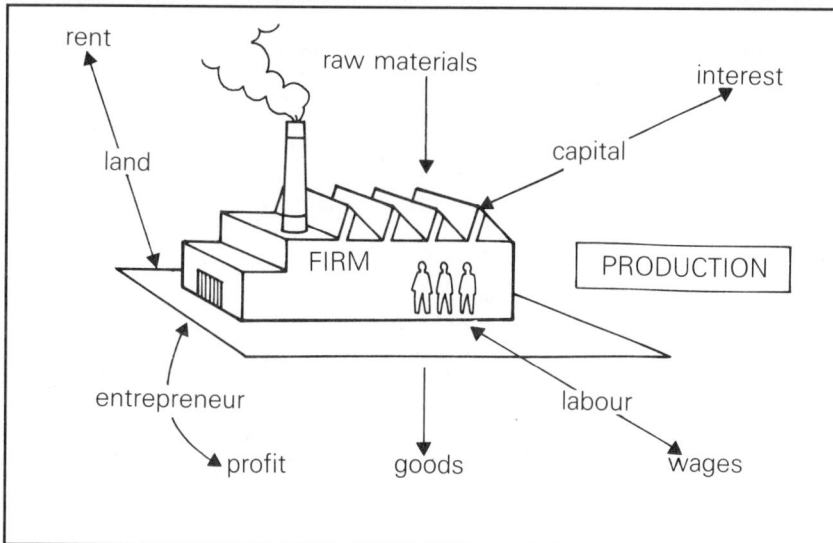

Paying for your cheesecake

When you buy a cheesecake, or anything else you want, you have to pay for all the factors of production that went into that item:

- each ingredient in the cheesecake;
- the people who produced the ingredients;
- the people who made the cheesecake;
- the people who package the cheesecake;
- the people who sell the cheesecake to you;
- the people who provide the money to finance the business.

In fact, as economists say, all factors of production have to be rewarded.

The milk shake chain

The Mackenzie family are out shopping and Alex, the youngest Mackenzie, wants a milkshake. "That shouldn't cost much," he says. "They just make it out of milk and that comes out of bottles." The rest of the family know that the production of even an apparently simple product can be quite complicated. They try to explain to young Alex.

"There's more to milkshakes than just milk, Alex," says his sister, Liz. "There are other ingredients too."

"I didn't expect you to know that there's a chain of production which stretches from obtaining raw materials through to turning the materials into goods or services and then on to selling them," said Mr Mackenzie. "But I would have thought you'd know that milk doesn't just come out of bottles."

"No," said Liz. "It comes out of cows. And think of the problems and costs of looking after the cows and getting the milk to the dairy."

"And then," said Mrs Mackenzie, "the animals need feeding in winter and tractors need fuel. The list is almost endless, isn't it?"

"When the milk comes to our house," said brother Rick, "someone has to be paid to bring it."

"The workers at the dairy," said Mr Mackenzie, "the people who bottle the milk, have to be paid. So does the tanker driver who brings the milk from the farm to the dairy."

"Oh well," said young Alex. "I'll just have a glass of water please. That's free, isn't it?"

"Well no, not really . . ." Mr Mackenzie begins to say.

The three stages of production

If you were drawing up a chain of production to show how milk got to young Alex's doorstep, an economist would be able to help you by pointing out that production is organised in three stages:

Primary production: raw materials are extracted from the land (for example, coal, fish, wheat, cotton, poultry, diamonds).

Secondary production: raw materials are turned into finished goods in places like factories, mills, breweries, and workshops, as well as in canning plants and refineries.

Tertiary production: goods are distributed and sold and services to all stages of production are provided. For example, hairdressers, the delivery of goods, or quantity surveying.

Decide for yourself

- At what stage of production is the milk sold?
- At what stage is milk turned into butter and cheese?
- At what stage is the milk when it is being taken from the cows?
- At what stage is the milk when it arrives on your doorstep?

Other ways of classifying production:
- much production takes place in the private sector but production also takes place in the public sector;
- much production takes place for consumers and involves making consumer goods but production also involves making capital goods so that in future we can make more consumer goods.

Decide for yourself

- Which of the following are most likely to be provided by the private sector?
- Which are most likely to be provided by the public sector?

    gloves   railway journeys   medicines
    fertilisers   radios   eye operations
- Which of the following are consumer goods and which are capital goods?

    a bicycle   sandals   a petrol pump
    a railway carriage   a ticket machine
    a teddy bear   an icecream

Under-production

The Mackenzie family were lucky to get the last cheesecake in the supermarket. The cashier explained to them, "Last month we found we weren't selling our range of cheesecake. But this month there's been an advertising campaign. They've gone like hot cakes. The manager will have to order more or we'll have a lot of angry consumers."

Over-production

"I wish people would buy boats like they buy cheesecake," said Mr Mackenzie. He builds boats in the local shipyard. "Even with financial help from the government in the form of subsidies, it's hard to find a lot more people who want our product."

Decide for yourself

When there is under-production of an item, shortages develop. However, when there is over-production of an item then stockpiles build up. Workers may have to be made redundant in such circumstances.

- Should firms be allowed to solve the problems created for them by over-production through advertising? What if this involves supplying consumers with goods that the consumers don't really want?
- Should governments provide finance for industries that over-produce? Or should they encourage such industries to close and new ones to develop?
- Is production simply to keep workers employed the most efficient use of resources? Is such production providing consumers with what they want?

ECONOMIC TERMS

Production: the creation of goods and services to satisfy consumer wants.

Primary production: the first stage in the process of production, known also as the extractive stage.

Secondary production: the second stage in the process of production, known also as the manufacturing stage.

Tertiary production: the third stage in the process of production in which goods are distributed and services provided.

Test yourself

1 What are the factors of production?
2 Explain how each factor of production is needed in the production of a good – use any of the following examples:
 a cars;
 b pens;
 c typewriters.
3 Draw a simple flow chart which shows how a newspaper is produced. Start with the raw materials and end with the paper boy or girl delivering the newspaper to your house.
4 What problems are caused by the under-production of a product?

DATA RESPONSE

Sport for all comes under a Mars bar

by Valentine Low

A MARS a day helps you work and rest – but left-wing councillors have decided it will not help you play in a London borough.

Haringey Council has turned down plans for a Sports For All leisure promotion because it is organised by Mars.

The councillors reckon the damage done by Mars to children's teeth and health is more important than any benefits they get from sport.

The promotion was supported by the Sports Council and had been recommended by Haringey council officers. They said it would be a good use of the council's leisure facilities, at no cost to ratepayers.

Ron Blanchard, leisure committee chairman, said: "We turned this down because we are genuinely concerned about what people are eating."

Opposition Tory councillors accused the ruling Labour group of opposing private sponsorship in the borough.

Under the promotion, Mars wrappers can be collected and exchanged for vouchers which can be spent at sports centres.

"This is no loony Labour council nonsense. We feel too many are eating sweets, fat-containing foods and too much meat.

Disappointed

And a Mars spokesman said: "We are disappointed that Haringey Council are denying children and others this chance to try out different sports at very little cost.

"We would certainly have no problem in assuring Haringey that our Mars bar should cause them no concern."

Source: *The London Evening Standard*, 25 March 1987

1 Why did the council decide not to let the Sports For All promotion go ahead?

2 What products does the council think people consume too much of?

3 How did the sweet company plan to finance sports centres?

4 Imagine that you are a spokesperson for a sweets manufacturer. Write a letter explaining why the production of sweets is good for the United Kingdom's economy. Use these terms to help you: utility, taxation, exports, employment, freedom of choice.

5 You are a keen sports fan. You want more facilities locally, but at the same time you recognise the need for a healthier population. Write a letter to the council supporting or opposing their position.

Extension 1

Butcher, baker, and candlestick maker!

Butcher	Cashier	Hairdresser
Baker	Police constable	Civil servant
Candlestick maker	Solicitor	Word processor operator
Miller	Pop star	Pilot
Farmer	Sewing machinist	Social worker
Plantation worker	Footballer	Bus driver
Teacher	Actor/Actress	Builder
Optician	Coal miner	Publican
Potter	Assembly line worker	Nurse
Quarry worker	Doctor	Lumberjack
Fisherman	Brewer	Watchmaker

1 Sort out these occupations (jobs) into three groups under the following three headings;
   a Extractive workers;
   b Manufacturing and construction workers;
   c Workers providing a service.
2 What makes a worker in any one group different from workers in other groups but similar to other workers in their own group? Explain this with reference to each of your headings.
3 Select one worker from each group. Explain how each worker chosen could be of benefit to the other workers you have chosen.

Extension 2

1 Copy these terms exactly as they are here. Connect, by drawing straight lines, all the terms that describe in some way the same type of production.

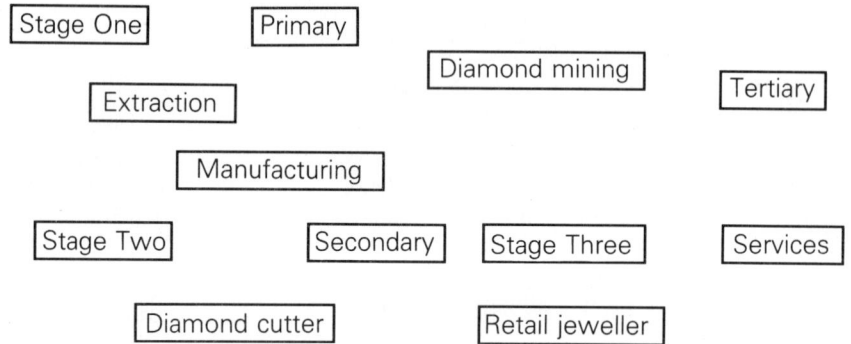

Stage One   Primary   Diamond mining   Tertiary   Extraction   Manufacturing   Stage Two   Secondary   Stage Three   Services   Diamond cutter   Retail jeweller

2 Construct a simple chain of production for the petrol industry. It should have three stages. Name each stage and briefly describe the industrial plant/building used in each stage. For example, if this was for brewing beer you would include farms, breweries, public houses/off licences.

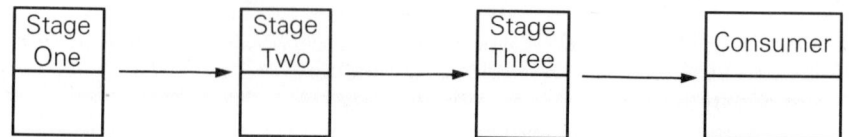

Stage One → Stage Two → Stage Three → Consumer

3 Now try and describe the chain of production for each industry given below.

	Coal	Timber	Demerara sugar
Primary			
Secondary			
Tertiary			

Coursework

Aim: To investigate a local business.

1 a Select for study a particular business in your local area.

b Record the name and address of the organisation.

2 Identify and record at what stage(s) of production the business operates.

3 What organisations does the business rely on for its components and raw materials? Use a chart to record this information.

Products	Name of organisation	Stage of production

4 Describe briefly how the work within the business is organised. Look at one production unit only.

5 a Identify who the major customers are for the business's services/products.

b How do they benefit?

6 Consider how:

a the local economy

b the government

benefits from the existence of the business you are investigating.

7 Consider to what extent there are external costs arising from the firm's actions.

8 The firm wishes to expand production in your area. Compare the points you have discovered in **6** and **7**. Imagine you are the chairperson of the local council's planning committee and have to give the casting vote on a planning application made by the firm. Explain what points you would make for and against the firm's planned expansion.

8 Capital and Enterprise

Production cannot take place unless someone organises the factors of production to satisfy wants.

The person who tries to bring together these factors (land, labour and capital) in the most profitable combination is said to show *enterprise* and is called an *entrepreneur*. Entrepreneurs set up businesses in the hope of making a profit. But entrepreneurs also take the risk that the business will make a loss and end up in bankruptcy.

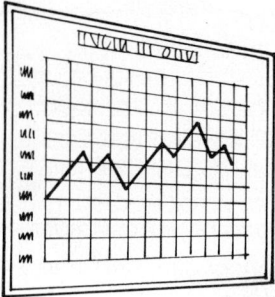

Activity

Dee Walker is 17. She left school with three GCSEs. She works for Mrs Johnson who owns Mode Hairstyles. Dee earns £80 a week, plus tips. Dee plans to set up her own hairdressing business when she has learnt as much as she can from Mrs Johnson.

Mrs Johnson likes Dee and thinks she has a lot of potential ability. She is thinking of taking her on as a partner one day, but she hasn't said anything about this yet.

This is how Dee describes her job:

"I really like working as a hair stylist. At times, though, I get the boring jobs to do. Mrs Johnson doesn't trust me yet with some of the more difficult styles. I feel I'm not being stretched. Sometimes if I do something wrong she tells me off in front of customers. But the pay's good. I'm saving up so I can start my own business. You don't need a lot of money to get started, I reckon."

Ariana Georgiades is 19. When she left school she had one year's youth training in catering. Now she runs a business offering meals to the housebound and elderly and catering for larger functions. In a good week she can make £120. She has a driving licence and a small car so she can travel to her clients.

This is how Ariana describes her job.

"I like being my own boss. At first the business was based at home. I had to stop when we had a small fire from an appliance overheating and the council found out. Now I travel from customer to customer. This works well, but I can lose a lot of business if my car breaks down."

1 Dee is an employee. Compared to Ariana, what advantages does she have?
2 Why doesn't Dee like working for someone else?
3 What problems does Ariana have in running her business that Dee does not have?
4 Ariana likes being her own boss. Describe some of the good points that she or someone else might find in being self-employed.

What do entrepreneurs have to do?

Entrepreneurs have to:

- choose the best work force (labour) they can and pay them a wage/salary;
- site the firm in the best location, where necessary paying a rent (for the land used);
- consider how best to finance and run production, for example by borrowing money and purchasing machines (capital). They have to pay interest on any money borrowed.

Many people in Britain own shares in a company and receive a share of the profits (in the form of a *dividend*). But they are not entrepreneurs in the strict sense of making day-to-day decisions about the running of the company. This is left to the firm's board of directors and team of managers.

What is capital?

The *capital* of a firm is the wealth used by that firm to provide future wealth, or the wealth used in making goods and providing services. The goods made can be either capital goods or consumer goods. The *industrial capital* of a firm includes:

- factory buildings and offices;
- machines, lorries and other vehicles;
- raw materials;
- money in the bank used to finance the business;
- the stocks of finished goods waiting to be sold.

Mr and Mrs Bedley in a jam

The Bedleys have a small business making marmalade and jam. What industrial capital might they employ?

At present they have a particular problem. Their labelling machine keeps breaking down. A piece of capital equipment wears out a little each year and this is known as *depreciation* (or loss of value). Each year we can overcome this problem by adding new equipment to the capital stock of the country. This process is called *investment*.

The Bedleys had hoped to expand production next year by buying a larger vat to cook the jam in. Now, nearly every day, Robin, their engineer, has to repair the labelling machine. Because of this he's beginning to fall behind in his regular maintenance work.

The Bedleys decide to buy a new labelling machine and leave the expansion of production to next year. They have scarce resources and have to make a choice.

<table>
<tr><td>ECONOMIC TERMS</td></tr>
<tr><td>Entrepreneur: the person who organises the other factors of production in order to make a profit.
Capital: wealth used to create more wealth.
Depreciation: the wearing out of capital equipment.
Investment: the addition of new capital.
Capital goods: equipment which enables the production of other goods and services, such as consumer goods.
Consumer goods: products on sale to the consumer.</td></tr>
</table>

The Bedleys, by deciding to buy a capital good (the new labelling machine), have had to accept that the flow of consumer goods (jam and marmalade) cannot be increased in the short term. This is the opportunity cost involved.

Consuming or investing?

Economies produce consumer goods and services because of the utility these goods and services give to consumers *now*.

Economies produce capital goods because of the wealth in the form of consumer goods that can be produced by this capital at some point in the *future*. This diagram shows how choices have to be made between consuming now or investing so that consumer goods are available in the future.

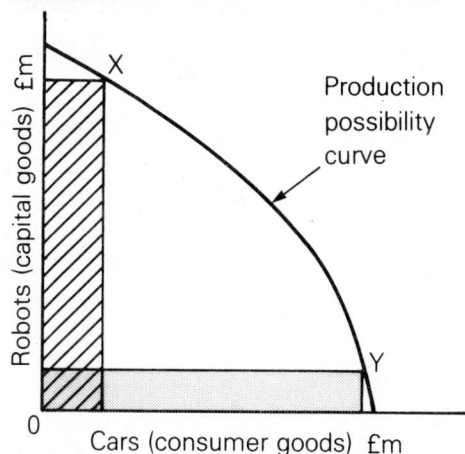

KEY   £m: Value of goods produced

Choice X: this economy chooses robots
Choice Y: this economy chooses cars

The Bedleys are not the only producers who have to make choices. All industries have to make investment and production decisions. In the car industry manufacturers (the producers) might have to decide whether to manufacture a new model sports car or make labour savings by increasing the number of robots they use when making such cars.

The Success Motors story

Success Motors have £2 million available to invest. Let us look at their choices. They can increase their current stock of *working* or *circulating capital.* (That is the capital of a firm that is used and changes shape during the making of goods.) The managing director of Success can take money out of the firm's bank account and purchase steel and rubber to make the bodywork and tyres of their latest sports car. In doing so, capital (money) in the bank is turned into capital in the form of raw materials. It still remains working capital.

In the Success Motors parking lot there are further examples of working capital in the form of the cars ready for sale. Once the cars have been sold, money from the sales can be used to replenish capital in the bank.

Alternatively Success Motors could choose to expand their stock of fixed capital. (That is the machines and buildings used by the firm to make the goods.) These items of fixed capital have a longer life than working capital, but in the long run they will also need replacing.

Success Motors could, for example, finance their plan to reduce their work force by switching over to cars built by robots. What savings will they make in the future if they do decide to switch production to robots?

Test yourself _____

1 Who is an entrepreneur?
2 What is capital?

3 If an entrepreneur purchases a new machine, what might have to be sacrificed? What economic principle does this represent?
4 Which of the following are not capital goods?
 a your watch;
 b the teacher's pen;
 c a railway line;
 d the local hospital;
 e the local factory's machines;
 f the local factory manager's private car.
5 What is the difference between consumer and capital goods?
6 What is the difference between investment and depreciation?
7 What is working capital?
8 What is fixed capital?

Infrastructure

Not all the capital in an economy is owned by industry. Capital that we use to provide us with goods and services that we do not pay for directly is called *social capital.* For example, roads, schools, hospitals and houses are social capital. Most social capital is owned and provided by the state.

The social capital of an economy that is used to aid the production and physical distribution of goods is called *infrastructure.* For example, roads, drains, telephone cables, railways and power lines are all parts of the infrastructure of a country.

Decide for yourself

● Think of the infrastructure that exists in the street where you live. List it and then compare your list with other students'.

ECONOMIC TERMS
Forms of capital: Fixed capital, working capital and social capital. **Infrastructure**: All human-made systems that aid the production and distribution of goods and services: for example, drains, telephone, roads, airports.

DATA RESPONSE

☐ GOLDEN boy Andrew Lloyd Webber can't put a foot wrong.

The diminutive genius behind riotously successful musicals on both sides of the Atlantic – from Cats to Starlight Express – made another £1 million yesterday when shares in his Really Useful Company jumped on the back of good figures.

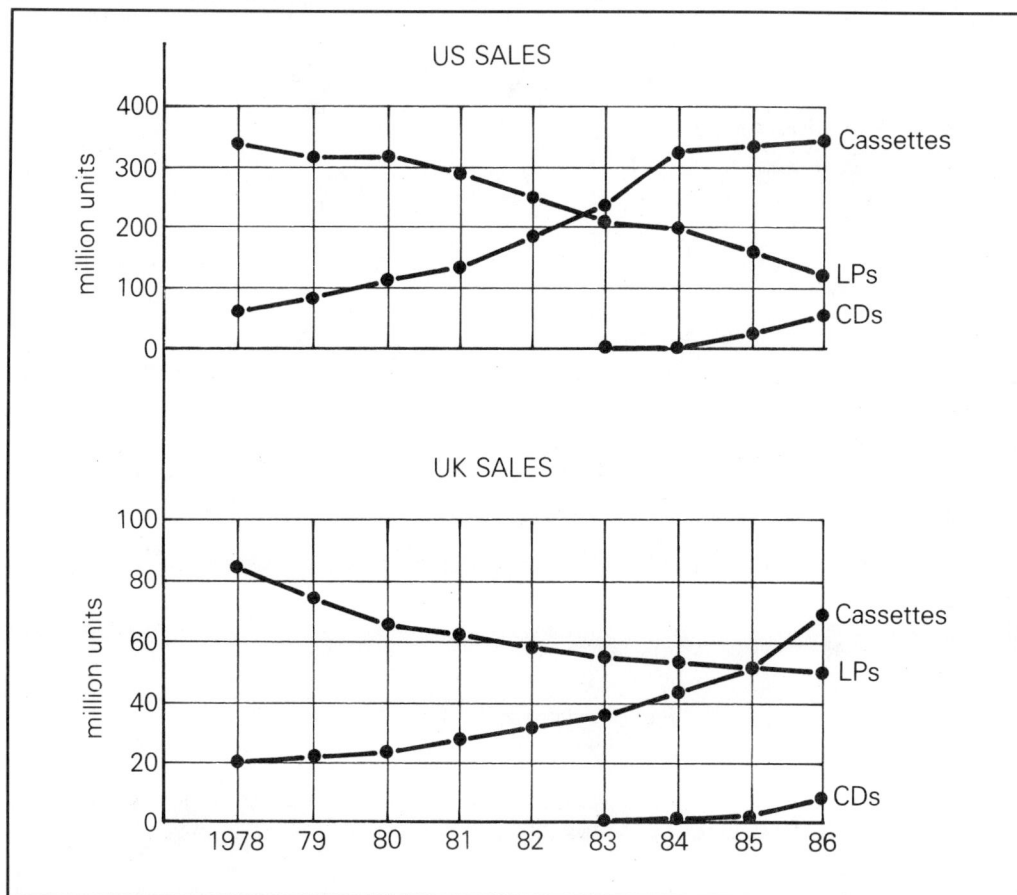

US SALES / UK SALES graphs showing million units for Cassettes, LPs and CDs from 1978 to 86.

Andrew's Really Useful £500,000 increase

by SARAH BARCLAY

ANDREW Lloyd Webber's Really Useful Group continues to be a box office smash. Half-year profits are up £500,000 at £2.5 million to the end of January, its first anniversary on the stock market.

With Cats and Les Miserables keeping the tills ringing and the audiences rolling in, turnover for the group increased from £7.5 million to £9.3 million. There is the prospect of selling the film rights in the long term.

Profits from Phantom of the Opera are not expected until next year but when they do it will be a question of megabucks. The show opens on Broadway in the autumn.

Royalties for the group jumped from £4.6 million to £5.3 million with income from theatre productions raised from £2.1 million to £2.5 million.

The record and video production division dropped into the red with a £74,000 loss while music publishing brought in income of £89,000, up £10,000.

The interim dividend is raised from 3.75p to 4.1p a share and the stock market applauded with an extra 3p on the shares at 481p.

Source: *London Daily News,*
28 March 1987

Having looked at this information carefully, can you answer these questions?

1 Why is Andrew Lloyd Webber's company successful?

2 What evidence is given that it is worth buying shares in the Really Useful Group?

3 Which areas of the company seem to be:
a doing well?
b making a loss?

4 From the information on the graph, describe the sales trend for:
a cassettes
b CDs
c LPs

5 Explain why these trends exist.

6 You are considering investing in the pop music business. Using the information given here, describe the type of investment you would consider making.

Extension 1

a

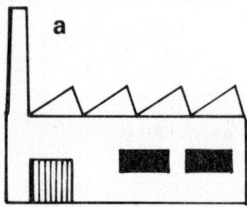

Factory building

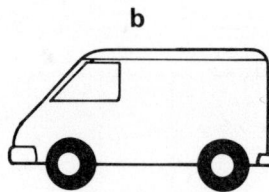

b

Delivery van

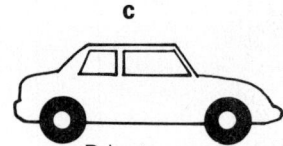

c

Private car

d

Office cleaning machine

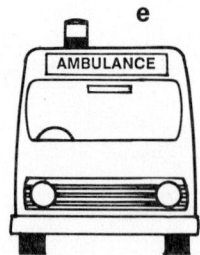

e

AMBULANCE

Ambulance (NHS)

f

BEANS

Beans ready to be baked and canned in a baked beans factory

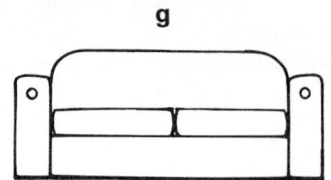

g

Sofa, sold to Mrs Brown in the January sales

h

Domestic washing machine owned by Mrs Keegan

i

Washing machine in the launderette

j

Sunnyvale Private Nursing Home

k

PORRIDGE OATS

Porridge Oats in the Sherrifs' larder

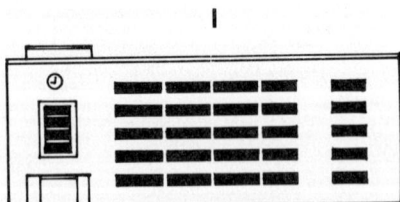

l

Sunnyvale Comprehensive School

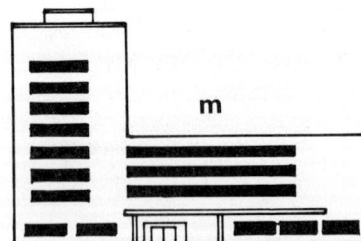

m

NHS District hospital

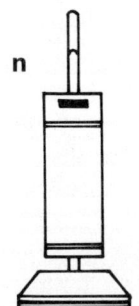

n

Vacuum cleaner

1 Sort out the above examples into three groups:
   a Consumer goods;
   b Capital goods (industrial);
   c Social capital examples.
2 Explain why you should put example **b** and **c** into separate categories.

3 Explain why **j** and **m** should be in separate categories.
4 Explain why **h** and **i** are in separate categories.
5 List another three examples of social capital.

Extension 2

Spot the circulating or working capital

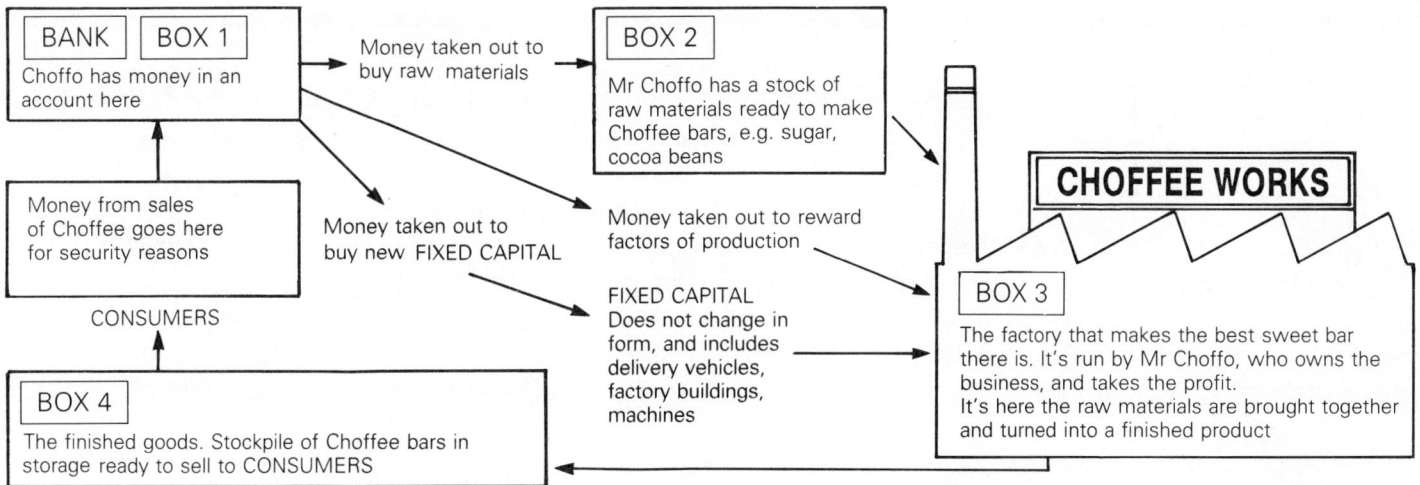

BANK | **BOX 1**
Choffo has money in an account here

Money taken out to buy raw materials →

BOX 2
Mr Choffo has a stock of raw materials ready to make Choffee bars, e.g. sugar, cocoa beans

Money from sales of Choffee goes here for security reasons

CONSUMERS

Money taken out to buy new FIXED CAPITAL

Money taken out to reward factors of production

FIXED CAPITAL
Does not change in form, and includes delivery vehicles, factory buildings, machines

CHOFFEE WORKS

BOX 3
The factory that makes the best sweet bar there is. It's run by Mr Choffo, who owns the business, and takes the profit.
It's here the raw materials are brought together and turned into a finished product

BOX 4
The finished goods. Stockpile of Choffee bars in storage ready to sell to CONSUMERS

1 Who is the entrepreneur in the above example?

2 What reward does he receive?

3 Mr Choffo takes money from the bank and purchases a sugar beet crop. Which box has his capital moved from and in which box is it now to be found?

4 Mr Choffo sells off his stockpile of finished goods and banks the money. Where has his capital moved from and to on the diagram? (Name the boxes.)

5 Mr Choffo takes on a new order, runs down his stock of ingredients and expands production of Choffee bars. Which two boxes are now involved?

6 List as many examples of circulating capital as you can find mentioned in the diagram.

7 List as many kinds of fixed capital as you can find in the diagram.

8 a Explain to a non-economist the difference between fixed and circulating capital.

   b Why are they both forms of capital?

Coursework

Aim: To investigate the use of capital.

1 Select two different types of firms in terms of the goods or services they produce or provide (for example, a dentist and a baker, a butcher and a newsagent, a washing machine maker and a garage). Ask them if they will help you with your research.

2 Identify the most expensive piece of capital equipment (excluding buildings) that they possess.

3 How much did this capital equipment cost when new? How much is it valued at now?

4 Why do you think there is a difference between these two values as revealed in question **3**?

5 How much would the item of capital equipment cost to replace at current prices?

6 Display your answers to **3** and **5** on a bar chart. Construct one bar chart for each of your two firms.

7 Interview the owners of the business to discover:

   a What sacrifices had to be made when originally purchasing the equipment (that is, what was the opportunity cost?).

   b The benefits they have gained from being able to use the equipment.

   c Assuming that they have to replace the equipment, investigate some of the ways they would finance its replacement.

8 If you were able to provide them with more capital, what item of capital equipment do you consider would be of greatest value to the firm? Give reasons.

9 In what way might the introduction of new capital affect workers in each firm?

9 Population Growth

Economists study changes in the population because people are:
- the workers or producers paid to make goods and perform services;
- the consumers of these goods and services;
- the citizens who, as taxpayers and voters, are involved in the decisions a government makes about the economy.

The population explosion

The Owens have a population problem. Mrs Owen is expecting triplets; Auntie Glenys, who lives in Germany, is coming to stay for a while to help.

"Well," says Mr Owen, "it's not too bad. We can use Mum's old room." (Mrs Owen senior died last year.) Their son, Rob, is not so sure. "I hate screaming babies. I think I'll emigrate to Australia."

The population of a country increases and decreases in the same sort of way as the Owen household is changing. There are four factors involved:
- **births** (measured as the Birth Rate) ADDS to the population;
- **immigration** (people coming into a country) ADDS to the population;
- **deaths** (measured by the Death Rate) REDUCES the size of the population;
- **emigration** (people leaving the country) REDUCES the population.

Immigration less emigration gives the **net migration rate.** If more people are entering a country than are leaving it, the flow is *positive.* If more people are leaving than entering, the flow is *negative.*

When the birth rate is higher than the death rate there is a *natural increase* in population.

A natural increase in the population and positive net migration results in the total population growing.

Decide for yourself
- What would happen to the population if there was a natural decrease in the population and negative net migration?
- What would happen to the total population if there was a natural increase in the population and this was matched by a negative net migration flow?

ECONOMIC TERMS

Birth rate: the number of live births for every 1000 of the population for each year.

Death rate: the number of deaths for every 1000 of the population for each year.

Net migration rate: the amount of immigration less the amount of emigration. Net migration is positive if, on balance, more people are entering a country than leaving it. It is negative if, on balance, more people are leaving a country than entering.

Natural increase in population: when the birth rate is higher than the death rate.

Total population growth: result of a natural increase and/or positive net migration.

Activity

Population growth

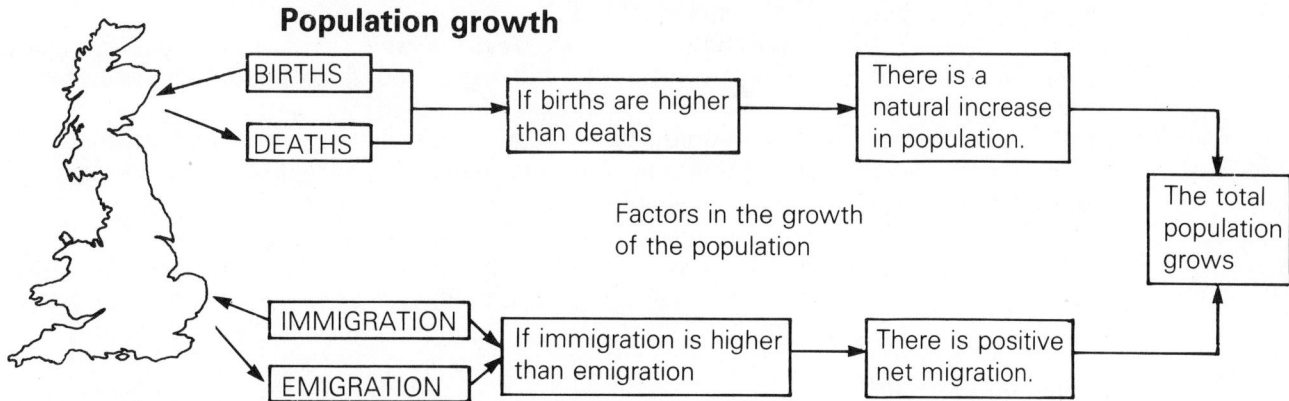

BIRTHS

DEATHS

If births are higher than deaths → There is a natural increase in population.

Factors in the growth of the population

IMMIGRATION

EMIGRATION

If immigration is higher than emigration → There is positive net migration.

The total population grows

1 Which two factors, other than births and immigration, help determine the size of a population?

2 If the birth rate is lower than the death rate will there be a natural decrease or a natural increase in the population?

3 ECONOMIA'S POPULATION IN A GIVEN YEAR

Total population on 1 January	50 000
Birth rate during the year	16
Death rate during the year	15
Net migration during the year	+20

Was there a natural increase or decrease in the population of Economia during the year? What was the size of the change?

4 What was the total population growth during the year in question?

5 During this century both the birth rate and death rate in the UK have fallen. But, with the birth rate falling faster than the death rate, population growth has slowed to a halt.

Sort out the following into two lists headed:

Reasons for a falling birth rate	Reasons for a falling death rate

Improved diet and food supplies
Use of contraception
Equal opportunities for women
Development of the NHS
Better medicine
Better sanitation
Introduction of state pensions so people do not need children to support them in old age

What is the ideal population size?

The Owen family have to consider whether they have enough resources to cope with their population explosion. Some countries have this problem too. Other countries have lots of natural resources and not enough people to exploit them. The ideal population (or what economists call the *optimum population*) occurs when the output of each person is at its highest possible level. At this level, the best use is being made of the country's resources.

If a country is under-populated, it has less population than the optimum. It can increase its income by expanding its population or by encouraging immigration.

Australia and Canada are examples of such countries.

If a country is over-populated, it has more people than the optimum. Bangladesh is such a country. Population growth outstrips resources – a fact first noted by Malthus in 1798. Today a number of developing countries find themselves in this position.

Providing for dependents

With triplets on the way Mr and Mrs Owen will need to earn as much as they can. Having three extra mouths to feed will be quite a burden. This need to provide for dependents is a problem in the wider economy too.

The population of an economy can be divided into two groups:

The working population

Those people of working age (16–60/65) who work, and those who want to and are available to work (considered as economically active).

The non-working population

Young people up to 16; people who have retired; those of working age who are not available to work (the ill, disabled, those bringing up children, students).

Decide for yourself

- Young people need health care, schools, hospitals. Can you think of other things they need?
- Old people need day-care facilities, meals-on-wheels, health care, hospitals. Can you think of other services they need?
- Many of these services are provided by the government, but who really pays for them?

The dependency ratio

You can work out the number of workers available to support the dependents in a country by what is called the dependency ratio:

> The number of dependents per 1000 of people of working age, for example 750:1000

So, in this example, for each dependent there are 1.3 workers to provide for them.

In the cartoon the ratio is 3 dependents to each worker. If the number of dependents is 45, what is the number of workers?

Test yourself

1 Which four factors decide the size of the population?
2 100 people left a country as emigrants; 50 immigrants arrived. Was the net migration rate positive or negative?
3 The birth rate in a country was 20 per 1000 in a given year; the death rate was 30 per 1000. Was there a natural increase or a natural decrease in the population?
4 You are a toymaker. The newspapers are carrying stories about 'a baby boom' and 'the birth rate rising'. Why would you be smiling?
5 What does an economist mean by the optimum population of a country?
6 In an imaginary economy ten years ago there were 3 workers for every 4 dependents. Now there are 3 workers for every 5 dependents. What has happened to the burden of dependence?

Extension

The Scottish Highlands

A bazaar in Bangladesh

A British street

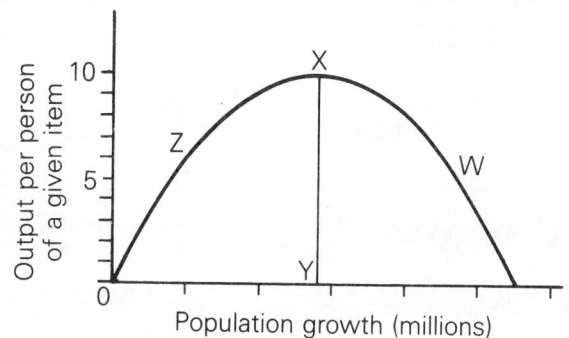

Output per person of a given item / Population growth (millions)

1 What is the output per person (per capita) at points X, Z and W (see graph)? What does this tell us about how well off people are at each of these points?
2 Z shows an under-populated country; X shows a country with an optimum population; W shows a country with over-population; which of the points (Z, X, or W) shows an ideal level of population?
3 Look at the photographs and decide which of the countries best shows:
   a under-population;
   b optimum population;
   c over-population.
4 Which country best fits the ideal and why?
5 Consider the factors of population growth and describe how an over-populated country can become over-populated.
6 What can an under-populated country do so that its population has higher living standards?

DATA RESPONSE

Economic Status of the British Population of Working Age: 1984–1986

Economically active %		Males					Females				
		White	W. Indian or Guyanese	Indian Sub-con.	Other	All males	White	W. Indian or Guyanese	Indian Sub-con.	Other	All females
in employment Employees	—full-time	64	53	47	47	63	31	41	22	27	31
	—part-time	2				2	24	14	7	14	24
	—all	66	55	49	49	65	56	56	29	41	55
Self-employed		11		15	10	11	4		4		4
On government scheme		2				1	1				1
All in employment		79	63	64	60	78	60	58	34	45	59
Out of employment		10	21	17	12	10	7	13	9	10	7
All economically active		88	84	81	72	88	67	71	43	55	66
Economically inactive %											
Long-term sick or disabled		4		4		4	3				
Looking after home		0				0	22	14	41	24	22
Full-time student		4	7	10	25	4	4	9	7	12	4
Retired		2				2	1				1
Other inactive		2		3		2	5		4		5
All economically inactive		12	16	19	28	12	34	29	57	45	34
Total of working age (thousands)		16,312	179	410	213	17,361	14,807	199	351	176	15,764

Source: Labour Force Survey, combined data for 1984 to 1986 inclusive.
Department of Employment

Growth of workforce due to women

By David Felton
Labour Editor

A 1.8 MILLION increase in the workforce over the last 15 years is entirely due to the growth in the number of women working.

More women took jobs, particularly part-time employment, because of a rise in the average age at which they have their first child and the comparatively lower birth rates in the 1970s compared with the 1960s.

The trend of steady growth in the overall size of the civilian workforce since 1971 stalled between 1981 and 1983 when numbers fell by more than 300,000. The trend picked up again and the workforce in 1986 was 26.7 million.

The study reveals that in addition to the growth in part-time and women workers, the other key employment change has been a large growth in the number of people working for themselves.

In 1979 fewer people were self-employed than in 1971, but since then rapid growth meant that by 1986 the number in self-employment had risen from 1.9 million to 2.6 million.

The number in work fell by two million in the four years after 1979 but then rose by 500,000 over the next three years. The unemployment rate, excluding school leavers, rose from 4.3 per cent in 1979 to 11.5 per cent seven years later.

In 1971 an average 750,000 people were claiming unemployment benefit, compared with an average 3,187,000 in 1986.

Source: The Independent, 14 January 1988

1 From your reading of the text explain why there has been an increase in the size of the workforce.

2 Identify and describe two other changes in the working population mentioned in the article.

3 List some of the reasons why some of the population of working age are economically inactive.

4 From the chart identify the single biggest reason why some females were economically active.

5 What reasons could be given to explain why unemployment is higher amongst ethnic minority members of the community than whites?

6 What factors can you think of that would lead to an increase in the working population?

Coursework

Aim: To Investigate why the birth rate has fallen.

1 a Find data and information about the overall decline in the birth rate in the UK during this century.
  b Display and analyse your research findings using bar charts or line graphs.

2 Using textbooks (secondary sources of data), identify the reasons advanced for why the birth rate has fallen. You could use a frequency chart to show the most popular reasons given.

3 Undertake a survey of teachers who have children. Divide them into two groups, those with two or fewer children, and those with more than two.

4 Ask each group why they think the birth rate has fallen. Let them choose from a list of possible reasons extracted from the textbooks you have used.

5 How does the primary data you gather compare with the secondary data?

6 Would you get the same set of reasons from people in another occupation?

7 What other problems did you encounter in undertaking such a survey?

10 Population and its Distribution

| The population of an economy is structured or distributed in a number of ways.

To discover how the population is structured
sort out the following:

Type of distribution	Example
By sex	**a** Some people are under school-leaving age; others are of working age; still others are above retirement age.
By occupation	**b** More males are born, but more women survive into old age.
By age	**c** Some people work on farms; more people make goods in factories; most people work in offices and shops or provide services.
Geographically	**d** People who work support those who because of age or circumstances are unable to work.
Between workers and dependents	**e** 3% of the population live in Wales; 12% live in south east England.

Activity

THE DEPENDENT POPULATION
We can see that some rely on others
for their means of support
e.g. pensioners, children, students.

GENDER AND ETHNIC DISTRIBUTION
The population is divided
into males and females
AND there are people of many different
races or ethnic backgrounds.

AGE DISTRIBUTION
We can divide the population
into age groups, e.g. the
young, middle aged and the elderly.

GEOGRAPHICAL DISTRIBUTION
We can look at
where the population lives.
Some areas are more
densely populated than others.

THE WORKING POPULATION
Those who work or who want to
work – the dependent population
relies on this group.

OCCUPATIONAL DISTRIBUTION
We can examine how people are
distributed across a range of
occupations, for example as
farmers, car workers, teachers.

The Owen family include:

- Mr Owen, an insurance clerk in London.
- Mrs Owen, tester and packer in a local factory.
- Grandpa Williams, Mrs Owen's father, currently staying with the Owens on holiday. He is a retired miner and normally lives in Swansea.
- Auntie Glenys, Mr Owen's sister, helps the family with the triplets. Formerly she worked for a German firm exporting lager to the UK; now unemployed but not seeking work.
- Polly Owen, pupil at the local comprehensive.
- Rob Owen, a student of economics in Exeter.

1 What is a dependent? Who in the Owen family is a dependent?

2 What is the working population? Who in the Owen family are members of the working population?

3 Divide the Owen family into three age groups: the young, the middle aged and the elderly, placing each member of the family into one of the three groups.

4 Explain how and why the Owen family are geographically distributed.

5 Where in the country is the densest concentration of this family?

6 Undertake a survey of the occupational distribution of the parents of members of your class.

Population distribution and the Owen family

The Owen family know only too well that the distribution of the population, in all its forms, affects them. Here are some of the reasons why it does:

- The Owens looked after Grandma Owen when she retired and she lived to be 95. ("The older she got, the more she seemed to need things," said Mr Owen.) Mrs Owen used to live in Swansea but she moved to London to find work.
- The Owens have five children to support now the triplets have arrived. ("The government should give more help to families," says Mr Owen "After all, children are the country's future.")
- Mr Owen is an insurance clerk. He knows that he is in a job where demand for his services has grown. ("Prospects for his promotion are good too," says Mrs Owen proudly.)

Decide for yourself
- How does the topic of population distribution affect the Owens?

Producers and population

Producers are also interested in the population. People provide the workforce for employers in return for a wage or salary. As consumers, people consume the goods and services produced.

Can you see why geographical distribution of the population is of interest to producers?

- If a firm is located near to where the people who buy their goods live, then transporting the goods to market will be cheaper.
- If a firm is located near to a supply of labour, then they will find it easier to hire workers.

55

Why is the age distribution of interest to producers?

At present the numbers leaving the workforce or reaching retiring age are higher than those entering the workforce. Given this development, producers have to think of the change in spending patterns for their goods and services that might result. For example, if you were making a well-known brand of baby powder, you might have to consider advertising it in such a way that 'older' babies are attracted to buy it. As the workforce ages they might not be so willing to learn new ideas or to move to a new area if you choose to relocate your firm.

If it is not easy to recruit labour you, as a producer, will consider buying labour-saving machinery such as computers, automated lines, robots, etc. You might also consider it made good economic sense to introduce crêche facilities in order to attract mothers back to work, or to introduce more part-time jobs.

Decide for yourself

Young school leavers will be in heavy demand. Why?

Changing patterns of employment:

- increasingly employers are moving into high technology industries and into providing services;
- there has been a decline in the UK in the numbers of workers employed in primary industry (e.g. mining and agriculture;

- there has been a decline in the staple manufacturing (secondary) industries connected with Britain's first industrial revolution (e.g. textiles and shipbuilding).

One reason for the change in the pattern of occupational employment has been competition from industries in other countries. But the move into the tertiary industry is also associated with the fact that Britain is wealthier today and demands more services. Our ageing population also needs more welfare support (e.g. home helps, doctors, social workers) than our younger population once did.

Test yourself

1 Every ten years the government counts the population in a census. How might the information gathered eventually help the Owen family?
2 Describe two ways in which the population is distributed, giving an example for each.
3 You want to make and sell refrigerators. Give two reasons why you might want to base your firm in London.
4 Assume the population in your area is an ageing one. Give three examples of goods or services the elderly might demand.
5 What economic problems might employers have to face with an ageing population?
6 Describe how and why the occupational distribution of the population of Britain is changing.

DATA RESPONSE 1

1 Using the chart about the working population, complete the table. Fill in the totals of workers in each of the following stages: primary, secondary and tertiary.

	1982	1987
PRIMARY		
SECONDARY		
TERTIARY		

2 How many fewer people worked in primary industry in 1987 than 1982?

3 Give an example of one trade or profession to be found in:
   a the construction industry;
   b the financial services industry;
   c the distributive trades.

4 Which of the sectors listed in your table has grown the fastest?

5 Give some reasons to explain this growth.

The distribution of the working population: a comparison between 1982 and 1987

NUMBER OF WORKERS IN '000s		1982	1987
Agriculture, forestry & fishing	PRIMARY INDUSTRY	358	302
Energy & water supply		680	488
Other mineral and ore extraction		885	757
Metal manufacture & non-metallic mineral products	SECONDARY INDUSTRY (MANUFACTURING)	473	387
Chemical industry		355	335
Metal goods, engineering and vehicles		2730	2231
Mechanical engineering		852	705
Office machinery		79	94
Electrical and electronic engineering		633	546
Motor vehicles and parts		318	239
Other transport equipment		350	251
Instrument engineering		111	102
Other manufacturing		2247	2056
Food, drink and tobacco		658	543
Textiles		268	222
Footwear and clothing		311	291
Timber & furniture		203	206
Paper, printing & publishing		501	484
Rubber and plastics		196	207
Construction		1067	984
Retail distribution	TERTIARY INDUSTRY	2026	2074
Hotels & catering		973	1095
Repair of consumer goods/vehicles		208	245
Transport		1380	1326
Postal services & telecommunications		437	438
Banking, finance & insurance		1798	2299
Other services		6130	6496
Public administration & defence		1594	1587
Sanitary services		287	388
Education		1598	1646
Research		112	107
Medical & health		1304	1266
Personal services		178	191
Recreational		445	517

Source: CSO, *Annual Abstract of Statistics*

Extension

IN INDUSTRIES LIKE TEXTILES AND VEHICLE CONSTRUCTION THEY NOW USE ROBOTS.

THERE HAS BEEN A WORLD WIDE DEPRESSION. A LOT OF MANUFACTURERS HAVE MADE WORKERS REDUNDANT.

MANY OF OUR OLDER INDUSTRIES CANNOT COMPETE WITH THEIR RIVALS ABROAD SO THERE HAVE BEEN PARTICULARLY BIG LOSSES IN TEXTILES, SHIPPING, STEEL.

WHICH WOULD YOU BUY? A TRANSISTOR RADIO FROM JAPAN FOR £40 OR A UK MODEL AT £55? (ASSUME THE QUALITY IS THE SAME.)

FARMERS ARE USING MORE MACHINES AND FEWER WORKERS.

WE NEED MORE WORKERS IN OUR NEWER INDUSTRIES LIKE PLASTICS AND LIGHT ENGINEERING, BUT NOT AS MANY AS IN THE OLD DAYS. NEW INDUSTRIES TEND TO BE CAPITAL INTENSIVE NOT LABOUR INTENSIVE.

A MACHINE CAN NOW CUT COAL CHEAPER THAN MEN CAN DIG IT OUT.

WE HAVE MORE OLD PEOPLE SO WE NEED MORE NURSES AND DOCTORS AND HOME HELPS AND SOCIAL WORKERS . . .

WE NEED A MORE HIGHLY TRAINED WORKFORCE SO LET'S ORDER MORE TEACHERS/LECTURERS.

THE UK NEEDS MORE FINANCIAL SERVICES TO TRADE IN A MODERN WORLD. WE MUST HAVE MORE STOCKBROKERS, TYPISTS, SECRETARIES, BANKERS.

IF WE ARE TO SELL OUR GOODS WE NEED TO ADVERTISE THEM SO WE NEED MORE ARTISTS, DESIGNERS, PUBLICITY MANAGERS.

WE HAVE SEEN THE GROWTH OF A WHOLE NEW INDUSTRY – TELEVISION – IN OUR LIFETIME.

CHANGES AFFECTING
SECONDARY INDUSTRY

CHANGES AFFECTING
TERTIARY INDUSTRY

1 Look carefully at these reasons for changes in the occupational distribution of the population.
Sort the reasons for these changes into three groups.

CHANGES AFFECTING
PRIMARY INDUSTRY

2 In your own words explain what you have discovered to account for the decline in primary industry in this country.
3 What reasons could be given for the contraction of manufacturing industry?
4 Consider the effects on the economy of the changes that have taken place in the distribution of workers between the three sectors of industry.

THE YEAR OF THE CHILD, MARK 2
by Malcolm Stuart

Britain's toy manufacturers, teachers worried about redundancy and the entire babywear industry can afford to be cautiously optimistic about statistics emerging from maternity hospitals – 1980 looks like being a boom year for babies.

Births throughout the country suggest that the birth rate could be 15 per thousand head of population this year – the highest figure since 1972.

'People have all sorts of ideas about the reason but I think one of the main factors is concern about the safety of various forms of contraception,' said Miss M.M. Turner, the senior nursing officer at the Aberdeen Maternity Hospital.

The ever-rising mortgage interest rate is considered to be another contributory factor. 'A surprising number of newly-pregnant women have told me they had planned to put off families until they could afford their own homes, but now the repayments are so far beyond their capabilities they have decided they had better have their babies anyway.' Additionally, a considerable number of women now expecting first babies are in their late 20s or early 30s, products of career-oriented and home-buying 1970s.

This has led some demographers to feel that the baby slump – a one-third drop in births from 1966 to 1976 – was in fact misleading. Many women, they now believe, were merely delaying families.

Source: *Guardian* 26 February 1980

Well, Bagley, if the birth rate gets any lower the school will be empty. You must help to put a stop to the baby slump.

1 Why would toy manufacturers be happy if they read the article *The year of the child*?

2 Look at the cartoon. Who else has been worried about the fall in the birth rate?

3 What was the birth rate expected to be in 1980?

4 What was the main reason given for the sudden rise in the birth rate? Why would this concern increase the birth rate?

5 What other reasons given might account for the rise in the birth rate?

6 What effects might changes in the birth rate have on an economy? Think of the following areas when preparing your answer: consumers, producers, government, trade with other countries.

Coursework

Aim: To investigate population distribution.

1 Find out the changes that have occurred over the last ten years to the migration pattern for your area. (Government reports like *Economic Trends* and *Social Trends* provide such information.)

2 Has there been an increase in migration into your area from other parts of the UK, or a decline?

3 Consider possible reasons for this using economic textbooks, local library information, council data for migration.

4 Try and determine what will be the most important economic consequences of the migration patterns you have discovered.

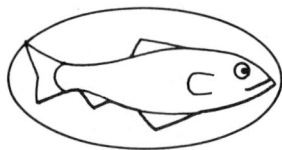

11 The Division of Labour

In most organisations each worker specialises in a particular task. Economists call this the division of labour.

The surplus output produced can be exchanged for the goods and services others produce.

Did you know?

The manufacture of the Model T Ford was divided into 7882 different jobs. According to Henry Ford, 670 jobs could be done by legless men, 715 could be done by one-armed men, and 10 could be done by blind men.

Activity

The division of labour

The "You can have a fishy in a little dishy" experiment.
For this activity you need to work in two groups.

TEAM ONE: Three people, *The Collaborators.*
Person One: Makes a copy of the fish on a piece of card and traces out as many copies as can be fitted on sheets of paper.
Person Two: Cuts out the outlines.
Person Three: Draws on the mouth and eyes.

TEAM TWO: Three people, *The Isolates.*
Each person makes the fish from beginning to end, following the instructions given for each of the three people in team one.

Resources you will need

Both teams are to be given the following:
- a pair of scissors
- a sheet of tracing paper
- a pencil
- a sheet of stiff card
- sheets of paper, *as and when required.*

These are the only resources you may use.

You will also need

One or two people to act as quality controllers.
They must be unbiased and should check the output of each team and reject poorly produced fishes.

How to carry out the experiment

a Each team should start and finish at the same time, and should have approximately 20 minutes to make as many fishes as possible.

b The fish outline should be copied on tracing paper and then a template made on stiff card. The template should be used to draw outlines of the fish on the paper provided. Finally the paper fishes should be cut out and eyes and mouth should be added as shown.

c The quality controller is responsible for announcing the output (total of fishes) produced by each team.

1 Briefly describe the experiment and how it was carried out.
2 What was the result: which team had the greatest output?
3 Explain why you think the team that won did so?
4 Make up a table comparing each team in terms of **a** quantity of output; **b** quality of product; **c** effective use of equipment; **d** job satisfaction. Simply tick the team that you think was the best on each of these points.
5 From analysing the chart describe what you have discovered.
6 Write up your results, using the relevant economic terms.

Dividing the work

Mr Boyd designs boats, but he has to rely on lots of other people to help before he can sell a boat and get paid for his efforts.

Match the workers to the job they do in the boatyard:

Mechanic	**a** Constructs the hull of the boat.
Rigger/ sailmaker	**b** Assembles the engine and places it on board.
Electrician	**c** Types up and sends off orders for new materials
Shipwright	**d** Installs all lighting and power.
Secretary	**e** Erects the mast and sails.

Over the years Mr Boyd has observed these good points about this division of labour:
- if a person does just one job, they can become quicker at that job and produce more units of work;
- if they do just one job they are more practised and skilled at that particular job and produce a better finished article;
- there are savings in terms of time and the use of equipment if people don't have to move from one job to another. For example, in the boatyard only the mechanic needs a set of monkey wrenches;
- because of these savings more units can be produced at a lower cost per unit;
- the workers find that working separately and pooling their efforts can result in their making a complicated boat which one person would find very difficult, if not impossible, to make on their own.

Dividing the work at home

The Boyd family have problems getting to work on time in the morning. So Mr Boyd decides to divide the labour between them.

Jack cleans everyone's shoes.
June makes the beds, and because she's the last to leave, checks all the doors are locked.
Mr Boyd cooks the breakfast.
Mrs Boyd washes and dries the dishes.
Young Robert sets the table and clears it after breakfast.

After a few weeks Mr Boyd said, "Surely you agree that life has been easier at home now we've divided up the jobs we have to do." Here are some of the replies he received:

"Yes, but I'm bored making beds."
"I didn't have time to clean the shoes yesterday because Robert hadn't set the table and I had to do it for him."

Discuss these replies. How do they show that the system of specialising has broken down?

At work too Mr Boyd had observed some bad points about the division of labour:
- some of the workers become very bored doing the same monotonous job every day. The amount they produce and the quality of each article declines. Bored workers are likely to be absent more often;
- sometimes a skill is no longer in demand and the worker involved then becomes unemployed;
- not everyone wants to buy a mass produced article. They would like to have something a little bit different from other people.
- when an organisation divides its labour, each unit is increasingly dependent on each other unit.

"When the electricians went on strike last year", says Mr Boyd, "eventually we all had to stop working."

Why would this happen?

"After a while," Mr Boyd went on, "we had to cancel our orders to other firms and they had to lay off their workers too. They relied on us for their livelihood."

ECONOMIC TERMS

Division of labour: where workers concentrate on one task, in other words, specialise and exchange the surplus of what they produce.
Specialisation: the process of concentrating on one task.
Interdependence: where a person or firm has to rely on others, who in turn have to rely on them.

Factory automation

Living with smart machines

Is the half-century-long replacement of workers by machines going to slow down? Consider the case of the car industry

The first generation of robots was brought into car factories about a decade ago to replace workers and cut costs. These automatons repeated one or two tasks – welding, say, or nut-tightening – on a single car on one long production line, endlessly and flawlessly. Ten years later the most advanced robots are capable of lots of tasks; they operate in parallel, switching from one model to another as different cars flow down the production line.

These machines have increased skills all round: all workers have to know how their robots work. This, in turn, has meant up-grading the jobs of workers and a blurring of the distinction between unskilled and skilled.

The pain of new ideas can be great. When Ford's British factories went on strike in February this year, the conflict was not primarily about wages but about the new skills which threatened to upset established hierarchies. In many companies the main reason for introducing new robots in the first place was to get past such difficulties. Robots at Britain's Rover Group and Italy's Fiat have cleared away union-set demarcation lines.

The second feature of the new machines, however, is that they are not so labour-saving as the old ones. As the chart shows, in Fiat's factories the first generation of automation cut manning levels by half; in the second generation – the move from semi-automated factories to complete automation – the manning level fell by only 20%. If this is a good guide to the future of manufacturing work, then the often-expressed worries – that robots will take over factories, leaving a few computer scientists in charge and the rest of the workforce unemployed – are too pessimistic. As automated factories become more complex and more reliant on computers, the quality of the staff, rather than cuts in their numbers, emerges as the vital issue.

Source: *The Economist*, 21 May 1988

Which is the robot?

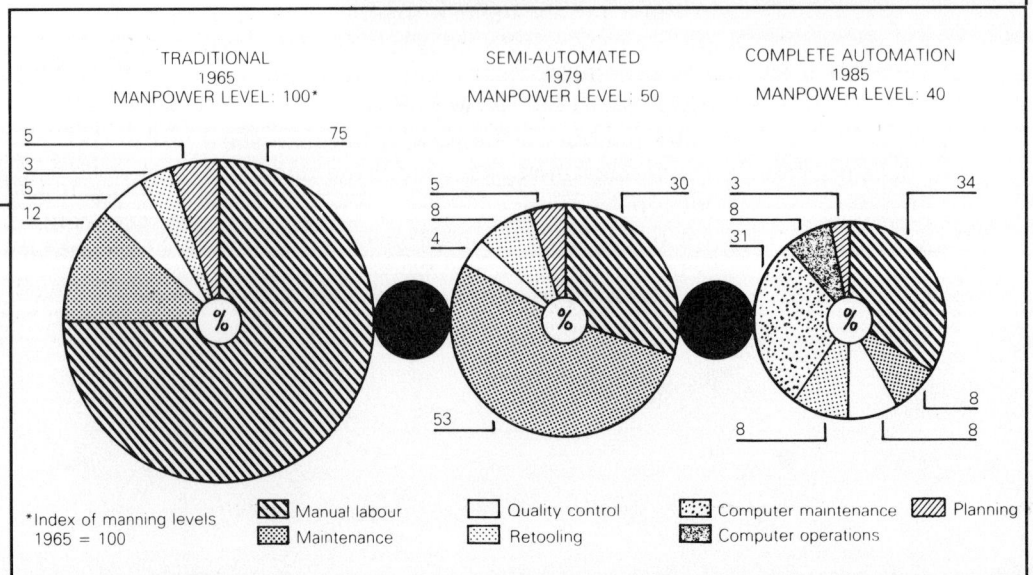

Changes in work practices at FIAT

TRADITIONAL 1965 MANPOWER LEVEL: 100*	SEMI-AUTOMATED 1979 MANPOWER LEVEL: 50	COMPLETE AUTOMATION 1985 MANPOWER LEVEL: 40

*Index of manning levels 1965 = 100

Legend: Manual labour · Quality control · Computer maintenance · Planning · Maintenance · Retooling · Computer operations

1 Describe how the photographs illustrate the division of labour.

2 Why have robots been introduced to replace human beings in performing routine tasks?

3 What effect has the introduction of robots had on the manning levels (levels of employment) in Fiat's factories?

4 What evidence is there that the introduction of robots has
a increased
b reduced
the importance of the division of labour?

Extension 1

The day the world went on strike!
One morning you wake up to find most of the world is on a one-day strike. You have to get to school because you know your Economics teacher will be in, and your coursework assignment is overdue.

1 Write a short account describing
a the problems you find in getting ready to leave for school;
b the problems people face on the way to school and work;
c the difficulties you face during the day. Share the accounts with others in the group.

2 Make a list of some of the people who you have written about in your account, briefly describing how each person helps you in a normal day.

3 "The more we specialise the more we have to depend upon others." Explain why this is so.

Extension 2

Mrs Inman
Packer and tester
in a factory.

Waiting for an eye operation.

Her firm supplies
pumps for fish tanks.

Dr Kwan
Eye surgeon.
His hobby is
tropical fish.

John Williams
Owns a pet shop
chain in South London.

Michael Beckford of
Beckford Enterprises,
Kingston, Jamaica.

Has built up a thriving
business employing six
people in exporting tropical
fish to his cousin
John Williams in the UK.

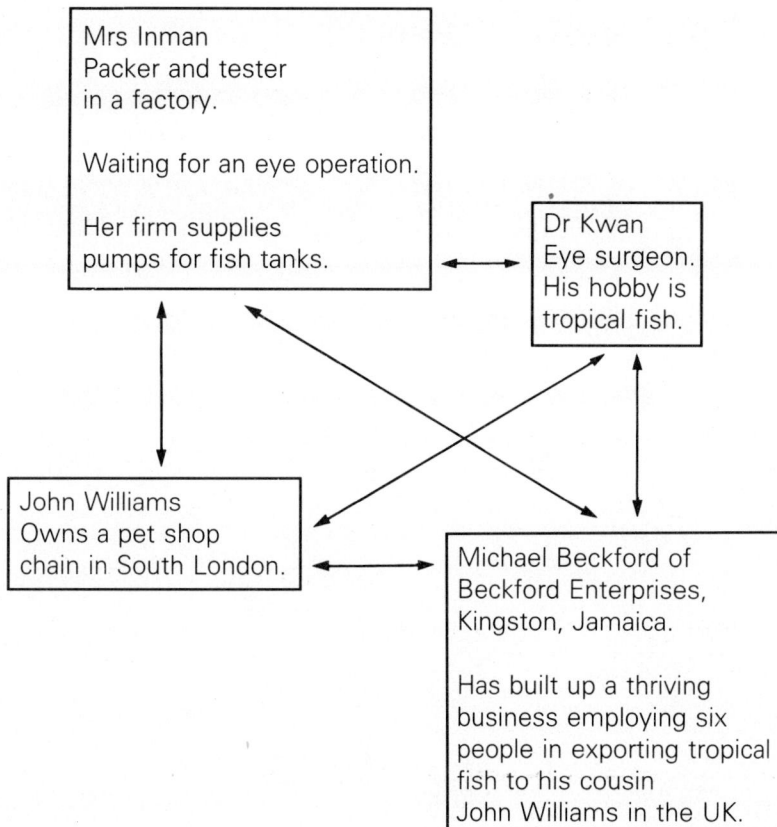

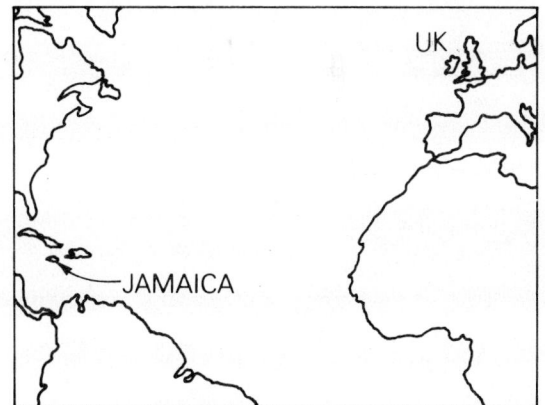

1 List the occupations of these four people.
2 Describe how Mrs Inman relies on
a Dr Kwan;
b John Williams.
3 Describe how Mrs Inman also depends upon Michael Beckford.
4 Explain how Michael Beckford relies on John Williams, Mrs Inman and Dr Kwan.
5 There is a strike in Mrs Inman's factory. Assume the factory is the only supplier of pumps for fish tanks. How will the strike affect each of these people.
6 If John Williams was made bankrupt, how would each of the others be affected?

Coursework

Aim: To investigate the division of labour at home.

1 Devise a simple questionnaire to collect evidence about the division of labour based on activities within the home.
An example follows.

Q. Could you tell me who does the following jobs in the home, a male or female?
(Copy the table and put M or F in the appropriate box depending on whether the man or woman does the job; put p (person) if either does the job. Interview an equal number of men and women.)

	P1	P2	P3	P4	P5	P6	P7	P8	P9	P10
Cleans the house										
Shops										
Makes beds										
Does MOST cooking										
Does the ironing										
Decorates										
Gardens										
Locks up at night										
Puts out the dustbin										

2 Analyse the division of labour in your school (or in a factory or office if you go on work experience).
3 What advantages did you discover existed from dividing one's labour in the situations you investigated?
4 What disadvantages did you note from the way the division of labour operates?
5 It has been argued that the advantages of the division of labour are economic (e.g. increased production) but the disadvantages are the social effects (e.g. increased boredom, the uneven distribution of "unpleasant" jobs). Use the data you have collected to comment on this.

12 Factor Mobility

Labour, as a factor of production, can be mobile (or willing to move) in three ways:

- **Geographically**: when there is movement from one place to another. For example, when a teacher moves from Cardiff to Leeds.
- **Occupationally**: when there is movement to a different job within the same industry or in another industry. For example, when a car worker becomes a shopkeeper.
- **Industrially**: when there is movement to another organisation but in the same job. For example, a secretary who moves from an estate agent to work in the town hall.

I'd like to apply for the job of gamekeeper.

Mobile or not?

People in a modern economy tend to be specialists. This means that they concentrate on the provision of one particular task or job. They exchange (or swap) what they produce as specialists for the goods and services produced by other people.

This specialisation has its problems. There may come a time when the goods or services one person provides are no longer demanded by others This is because new goods and services are always being developed to replace older ones and because people's wants change.

When goods or services are no longer wanted, the producers and the resources they use can become unemployed. Unemployment can hit individuals, firms, a particular region or even a whole nation. Unemployment can, however, be reduced if a person (or for that matter any other factor of production) is mobile and willing to move from one form of employment to another.

Labour is supposedly the most mobile of the factors of production. In theory it should be quite possible for an unemployed shipbuilder to become a nuclear scientist. In practice there are lots of reasons for immobility (the fact that a factor of production cannot move). This is an example of occupational immobility brought about by differences in qualifications.

Geographical mobility, however, is often taken for granted yet in practice because of commitments to family, property and monetary differences between one location and another, it is not easy for some individual workers to move.

ECONOMIC TERMS

Mobility: the movement of a factor of production between jobs. Examples of mobility include:

Geographical mobility: movement to a different place.

Industrial mobility: movement from one organisation to another.

Occupational mobility: movement to a different industry or to another job within the same industry.

Immobility: when a factor of production finds it difficult to move from one form of employment to another.

Activity

A moving experience

The four families in this Activity live in the terraced houses by Choffee's.

Headlines:
"Choffee site earmarked for new sports centre says local council".

"Japanese firm offer £10m to develop Choffee site as a commercial vehicle assembly plant. Would demolish nearby cottages."

Mrs Wilkins,
Choffee's Sales manager.
Age: 30
Family details:
Divorced, one son and one daughter.
She is loyal to the firm, and a move would give her the chance to make a fresh start in her personal life.

Supply of unskilled jobs will decline if robots employed in new factory.

Mr and Mrs Smith,
unskilled workers at Choffee.
Aged 60 and 58.
Looking forward to retirement. The firm have offered generous redundancy terms.
They love their terraced cottage and have no plans to move.

James Martin,
stores clerk at Choffee.
Age: 55
Stores were computerised 5 years ago under his direction.
Family details: Married, two sons, both left home.
House is paid for.
Other factors: Lots of friends in the area. Both he and his wife would like to live in the countryside when they retire.

Ranjit Singh,
driver for Choffee, delivering to local wholesalers and sweet shops.
Age: 45
Family details: Married, one son and two daughters.
Other factors: Children are at local schools; their house is rented from the council.
It is quite easy to find work driving for local firms. He's not certain this will be the case elsewhere.
Would be rehoused by council in the same area if the site was re-developed.

CHOFFEE
FOR SALE
CLOSING DOWN AND MOVING TO A GREEN SITE

The Choffee Chocolate firm is moving to a new site in the countryside.

1 Land cannot move, but suggest two different uses for the Choffee site in the future.

2 What would be the opportunity cost if the Japanese firm developed the site?

3 Why might James Martin be happy to move with the firm when it moves to a site in the countryside?

4 Look at each family. Decide which of the families is least likely to move from their home and why.

5 Why are the Singh family geographically immobile?

Why are some people *occupationally immobile*?

- **Training**: a lot of jobs require long periods of training or special educational qualifications. (Would you let an optician repair your leaking tap?)
- **Finance**: people who might want to start their own business might not have enough money, and might find it difficult to borrow the necessary capital.
- **Restrictions**: many professions and trade unions try to prevent too many workers entering their occupation by, for example, demarcation practices or operating a closed shop. The laws of the country also restrict people from setting up business in certain occupations (for example, pharmacy and the law). Can you think why?
- **Ability**: not everyone has the necessary skill, talent or ability to do well in a particular job. (A singer might not make a good nurse.)

  What skills do the following jobs require? Would you be any good at them?

  a footballer

  b actor

  c artist

  d police constable
- **Discrimination**: quite often a person finds it difficult to get a job because of their sex, age, class, race, size or another social feature.
- **Ignorance**: in a large economy ignorance of job opportunities can be another reason why people do not move from one job to another.

Decide for yourself:
- Why are there so few female engineers?
- What height do you have to be to become a police constable?
- What percentage of teachers in your school are members of an ethnic minority group?
- Two people of equal ability apply for re-training under a government scheme. One is 55; the other is 26. Who would you choose?

People can also be geographically immobile
- The costs of moving: if you own your own house, you may have to sell it at a loss or need a larger mortgage in the new area. People moving from the North to the South of Britain, or moving from Northern Ireland, often find it almost impossible to find a new home at a similar price and size to their existing one.
- **Lack of accommodation**: with restrictions on council house building, it is increasingly difficult to transfer to similar housing in another area.
- **Personal reasons**: not everyone is willing to leave family and friends, particularly if they are older people. Parents do not want to move if it upsets their children's education.

Moving other factors of production
Capital
An alternative to people having to leave a depressed area to find work is for new forms of capital to move to these areas to replace the derelict factories. But capital is not always mobile.

Decide for yourself
A bulldozer can be sent from a motorway site in the south of England to a gravel pit in North Wales.
- How has the bulldozer been geographically mobile?
- How has it been occupationally mobile?

Other forms of capital are harder to move. Your school could be converted into offices, but it would be almost impossible to move it even five miles up the road. A nuclear power station, on the other hand, would be *both* geographically and occupationally immobile. Can you think why? The clue is, does it have an alternative use?

Land
Of all the factors of production, land is probably the most immobile. Geographically speaking land cannot change its position. A shortage of land in one area cannot be made up by moving land to another area. In densely populated areas one solution has been to increase the number of multi-storey buildings for a variety of uses: e.g. shops, car parking, housing and offices.

Land can, however, over a period of time, change in its occupational use.

Decide for yourself
- Discuss how the following could be changed from one occupational use to another:

  a a gravel pit   **c** a supermarket

  b a factory   **d** a rubbish tip.

Another restriction on the occupational mobility of land is the planning regulations of central and local government. For example, the Green Belts around major cities, and commercial and residential zoning, place severe limits on how land is used.

- Why do you think these regulations are made?

Test yourself

1 Who is more mobile? An unskilled labourer with no savings or a dentist who owns her own house?
2 A surgeon in Swansea moves to Ipswich. Is he geographically or occupationally mobile?
3 Why might you find it difficult to become an electrician?
4 You live in Newcastle with an elderly grandparent. You have £500 savings. Why might you be geographically immobile?
5 Why might a firm choose to expand an existing factory in the south east of England rather than move to a new one in Scotland?
6 The local cinema is closing. Explain why this might be happening and suggest alternative uses for the site.

DATA RESPONSE

Ridley rules out curb on M4 housing boom

By Richard North
Environment Correspondent

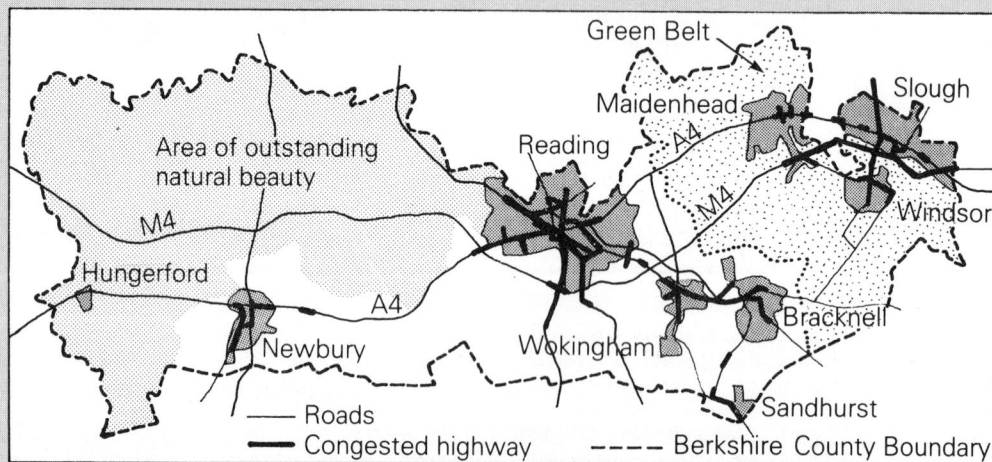

Green Belt
Slough
Maidenhead
Reading
Area of outstanding natural beauty
M4
Windsor
Hungerford
A4
Bracknell
Newbury
Wokingham
Sandhurst
—— Roads
▬▬ Congested highway
- - - - Berkshire County Boundary

BERKSHIRE County Council's hopes that it might dramatically slow the growth of private housing in its 700 square miles of territory along the booming M4 corridor have been dashed by Nicholas Ridley, Secretary of State for the Environment.

Mr Ridley's decision has been given in his proposed revisions of a replacement structure plan the county sent him for consideration two years ago. He wants Berkshire to find land for 43,500 houses by 1996, rather than the 36,530 the county wanted.

Though Mr Ridley's plan would represent a slowing of present growth rates, Berkshire believes it has already gone as far as reasonably possible, given its concern that its roads and services are strained after phenomenal growth in housing.

The county's population has trebled this century. Its housing stock has grown by more than 10 per cent this decade, a rate of growth surpassed only by Buckinghamshire, where Milton Keynes accounts for much new housing.

Sixty per cent of Berkshire is designated as green belt or area of outstanding beauty.

The county council believes that many of its difficulties flow from being told to allow new houses, while being forbidden by the Government to raise the kind of money that would allow services and infrastructure to catch up.

Source: *The Independent*,
30 January 1988

John Smith lives in a bed-sit in Reading during the week. He travels home to Newcastle each weekend to be with his wife and children. During the week he works in Bracknell as a skilled engineer. Job prospects in Berkshire are very promising. John has not been able to find work in Newcastle.

The Smith family own a house in Newcastle which could be sold for £25,000. The cheapest house they could find in Reading is for sale at £50,000. John spends £20 each weekend travelling home to Newcastle. It's a price he's prepared to pay to be with his family. Skilled workers can earn about £10,000 in Newcastle but nearer £16,000 in Berkshire.

1 Why does it make economic sense for John and his family to move to Reading?

2 Look at the map and read the attached article. What two restrictions are limiting the release of land for building purposes?

3 If the council did release land would this help the Smiths?

4 Explain why the council is reluctant to release further supplies of land for building purposes.

5 What would be the private costs and benefits for the Smith family if they could afford to find somewhere to live in Berkshire?

6 Consider the social costs and benefits of Mr Ridley's ruling that land must be found for 43,500 houses in the area by 1996.

Extension 1

It's just capital!

a Typewriter
b New lathe for woodworking firm
c Computer
d Power station
e Docks
f Photocopier

1 Which four of these items of capital are most mobile geographically?

2 Which three items would be most mobile in an occupational sense?

3 Explain why a power station site might remain disused for a period of time once the economic decision to shut the enterprise down has been made.

4 a Which of the items would be purchased by an engineering firm interested in expanding its production of precision equipment and why?

b Explain why this purchase would be an example of the industrial mobility of capital.

Extension 2

Meanwhile back in the boat yard

DAILY GRIM NEWS
Work in boat yard at a standstill.

Skilled workers walk out.
Union back the dispute. Mr Boyd, the firm's brilliant designer, faces the sack . . .

COMPANY NOTICE TO WORKERS
Orders for new boats have slumped recently. Overtime will be reduced accordingly.

BEHIND THE NEWS
The facts seem to be as follows. A welder was ill so Mr Boyd decided to have a go at welding so that production could be speeded up. Mr Boyd made a mess of the welding and sparks from the welding torch flew into an apprentice's face.

Profile of Mr Boyd
Aged 55½
BSc in marine design.
The family live locally.
Mr Boyd prefers watching TV to playing sport, as he's not very athletic.
His favourite pastime is singing in the bath. His family say he sounds like next door's cat.

69

1 Why would it be difficult for someone like Mr Boyd to enter a new occupation, retrain, or change jobs?
2 Why do you think the boat yard directors are considering dismissing Mr Boyd?
3 Who else in the boat yard objected to Mr Boyd's action and why?

4 Mr Boyd has been offered a job in a boat yard in Glasgow. Why might he not take it? Use the ideas below.

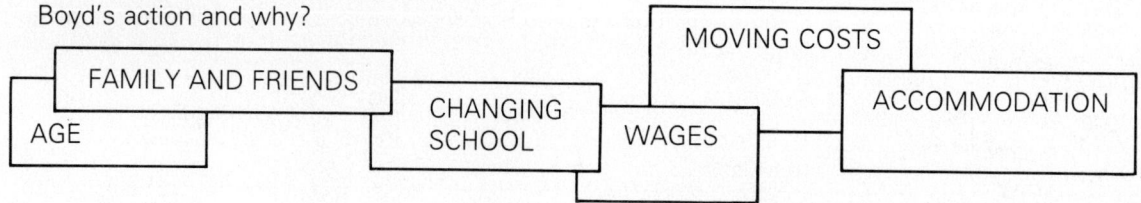

```
                                    MOVING COSTS
   FAMILY AND FRIENDS
                     CHANGING              ACCOMMODATION
 AGE                  SCHOOL      WAGES
```

Coursework

Aim: To investigate movement of the population.

Consider the reasons for geographical mobility either by exploring the movement of workers from one region of the UK to another or from a country abroad (e.g. Bangladesh) to the UK.

1 Explain what is meant by geographical mobility.
2 Consider the factors that push a family from one region to another, and the factors that pull a family from one region to another.

3 a Choose a family that has recently moved to your area. (You could start with your class by asking where each pupil was born.)
  b See if you can identify the costs and benefits for this family of moving to your area and of staying in their former area.
  c Consider why the family might have been geographically immobile and what the causes of geographical immobility are.
4 Interview the family to see if any of these factors presented difficulties to the family when they decided to move.
5 Describe what you have discovered.

13 Private Enterprise 1

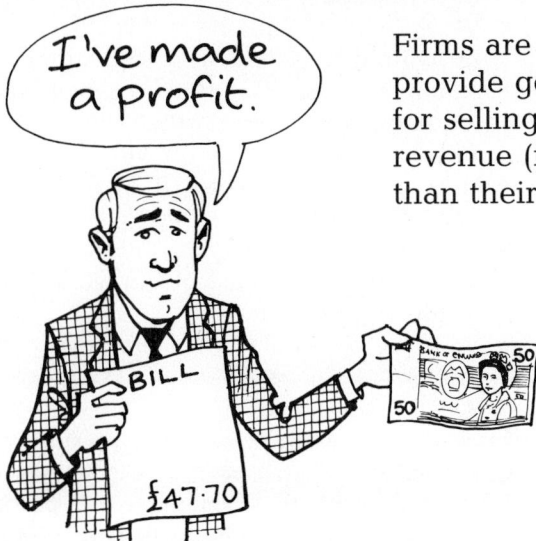

I've made a profit.

Firms are organisations involved in running a business. Businesses provide goods and services for households and other firms. In return for selling their goods and services at a given price, firms receive revenue (money coming in). As long as a firm's costs are smaller than their revenue, the firm makes a profit.

BILL
£47.70

In my firm I want to make the maximum profit possible

I try and make a reasonable profit but I have lots of other interests

WHOSE AIMS?

I enjoy selling as much as I can

We provide a public service at the lowest possible price

We try and provide a public service at a reasonable price

What a firm seeks to do when running its business depends upon the aims of those who own and control the organisation.

Decide for yourself
- Look at the diagram, right:
  Which aims would you select when running a business? You can choose more than one.

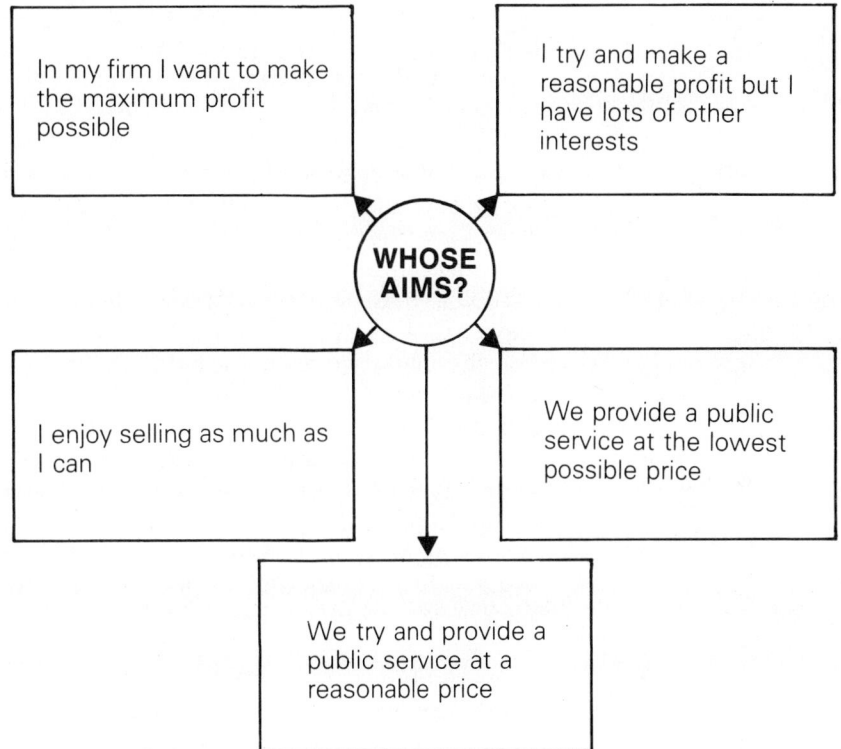

The private sector
In the private sector of an economy individuals and groups of people are free to set up firms in different ways. (Public sector firms are set up in other ways. See Unit 15.)

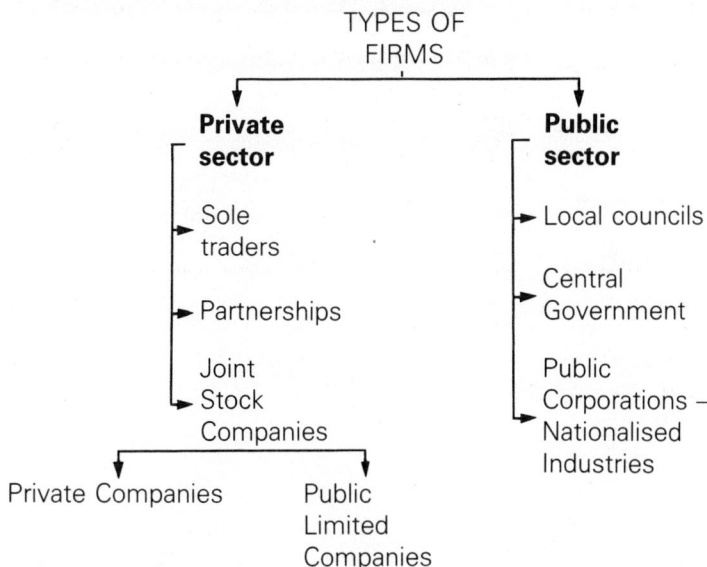

TYPES OF FIRMS

Private sector
- Sole traders
- Partnerships
- Joint Stock Companies
  - Private Companies
  - Public Limited Companies

Public sector
- Local councils
- Central Government
- Public Corporations – Nationalised Industries

Sole proprietor (or sole trader)
This type of organisation of a producer is the oldest and simplest type of firm. The sole proprietor or trader is the only person who owns the business. Such people often work for themselves, but sometimes they also employ other people.

The owner makes all the decisions about how the business is run. He or she receives all the profits from the enterprise. However, in law, sole traders have *unlimited liability* for their losses. If they make substantial losses and are declared bankrupt, they could be forced to sell all their assets to meet their liabilities (debts). Their assets include not only their business, but any personal belongings and possessions. For example, a car, house, furniture and jewellery are all assets.

71

Karl Phillips, sole proprietor

This is how Karl Phillips, painter and decorator, describes how he set up his firm.

"I'd always liked working with people, but now my children were older I decided to set up my own business."

"By taking a second mortgage on my house, I had enough money to purchase all the equipment I needed, the van to travel to the customers' premises and set up an office in the High Street.

"It was really nice at first being my own boss. I could decide when to work and how to organise my day. I enjoyed being able to plan and make decisions without having to ask someone else's permission. What I really liked was being able to keep the money I earned.

"I soon found I had more customers than I could manage, so I employed Ann and Steve to help. They like working for me. They say they know who to come to if they've got problems.

"Once they started working for me, it wasn't so easy and I had to work very hard. For the first two years I didn't have any holidays. I had no one I could really trust to run the business and I didn't want to close in case I lost business to bigger firms. To keep my customers, I kept my prices low and tried to offer a personal service.

"It was quite worrying sometimes. I had to pay all my costs and I'd used up all my savings to set up my business."

Partnerships

A partnership is an *unlimited liability* business. An ordinary partnership is easy to set up. Each partner signs a deed of partnership. This sets out the important details of their future business relationship, for example:
- the salary of each partner;
- the share of the profits of each partner;
- the name of the firm.

There can be between 2 and 20 partners in most firms. In some professions (like accountancy) more partners are allowed.

Taking on a partner gives you someone to share in the problems of running the business. It can lead to the new partner injecting much needed new capital and new ideas and skills. With several partners in a business, it becomes possible to introduce specialisation to the firm.

Decide for yourself

There are problems with partnerships as well as advantages. Ask yourself:
- What would you do if you and your partner began to disagree about how to run the business?
- What would you do if your partner turned out to be unreliable? (Imagine, for example, that you run a sweet shop together, and your partner buys 50 000 surplus Easter eggs on 1st May.)
- How would you cope if your partner became ill or died?
- Your partner could turn out to be lazy and not do their share of the work. What would you do then?
- Your partner could bring less money into the firm than you needed. What would you do about that?

One solution to such problems is to take on a *limited partner*. This type of partner shares in the profits of the firm in proportion to the amount of capital they put into it. However, in all other ways they are a 'sleeping' partner, in that they make no decisions about the running of the partnership and the firm. In return their liability for debts is limited to the amount of money they originally invest in the business. In all limited partnerships, one partner must remain with unlimited liability.

ECONOMIC TERMS

Private sector: that part of the economy made up of firms run by groups and individuals aiming to make a profit.

Sole proprietor (also known as **sole trader**): a person who owns and controls their own business.

Partnership: a business owned and, in some cases, run by at least two individuals.

Unlimited liability: when the owner, or owners, of a firm have to be prepared to sell even their personal possessions to pay off the firm's debts.

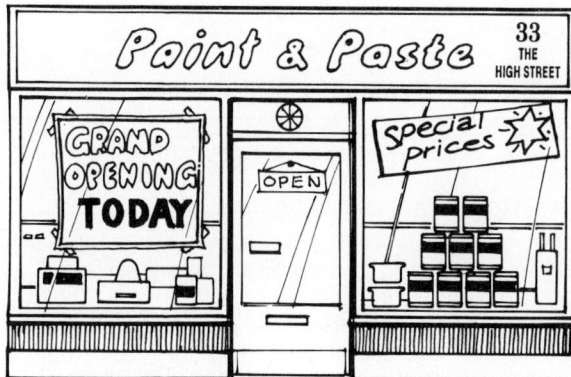

Paint & Paste — 33 THE HIGH STREET

The 'Paint & Paste' partnership seems to be going places. Yet another branch of this successful organisation has opened up. Ann Reilly's imaginative decorating ideas and Karl Phillip's Customer Care Campaign seem to appeal to all age ranges.

Bank report:
Revenue from the existing business is rising steadily.

The partners have requested a loan of £20 000 in order to open a third branch.
The proposed branch is close to the Fourways shopping centre which since opening last year has proved very popular.

Ann's assets
Cash in bank   £3000
Personal jewellery   £200
Furniture   £500
Other assets   £2000
Ann lives with her mother and pays her a rent.

Activity

Dear Jon
   At last I've decided to take things a little bit easier. My new partner has proved to be wonderful. Although she takes 40% of the profits, I can't complain as we've doubled the profits to £40,000. Ann is so reliable and she has had some good business ideas too.
   Yours,
   Karl.

P.S. I enclose a photo of my new car!

1 Why has Karl taken on Ann as a partner?

2 Why might the bank be willing to loan the new business money?

3 If the new business failed Ann and Karl would be responsible for all the debts. What risks would this involve for Ann? In what ways would the risks be greater for Karl?

4 Describe why Karl Phillips is better off, now that Ann has 40% of the profits.

5 Imagine you are Jon. Write a letter to Karl agreeing and disagreeing with his decision to take on Ann as a partner.

Test yourself

1 What is a sole proprietor?
2 What is unlimited liability? Why is it a threat to the small business person?
3 When Karl Phillips set up his business, what were the advantages and disadvantages he found?
4 What is the difference between an ordinary and a limited partnership? What sort of partnership do Karl Phillips and Ann Reilly have?
5 What are **a** the advantages and **b** the disadvantages of taking on a partner?
6 What is a sleeping partner?

7 What is limited liability?

8 You run a power station. The smoke emissions have caused 'acid rain' damage of £20 million to nearby forests and lakes. It costs you £1 million to dispose of waste as you do now. Alterations to the power station to reduce waste emissions would cost £5 million. Disposal costs would also rise to £1.5 million.

a What should you do to make the most profit?
b What should you do to provide a public service to the community?

Open all hours by Jane Roberts

"SINCE we opened, we've had no holiday and no days off," said Mr Mahmood Ahmad.

"We can't afford holidays," added his wife Zubedah, and laughed.

Until three years ago Mr Ahmad was a photographer, doing advertising and commercial work. Then he decided to open a grocers on Lupus Street, Pimlico, on a modern parade of shops already well served with three grocery stores. Since then another has opened, on the opposite side of the road.

The shop, called MSR Foodstore, is open seven days a week, from 9 am to 9.30 pm Monday to Saturday, and from 9 am to 9 pm on Sundays.

"We decided to work hard because there's some competition around here and to compete with it we had to stay open a bit later," said Mr Ahmad.

"When we first took over these premises, we used to stay open until 10.30, but unfortunately we were robbed once at about that time of night, and since then I decided we should not take any more chances. I got some bruises around my face," he said, rubbing the side of his nose. There was no bitterness in his voice.

Although the shop is small, there is a good variety of stock on the shelves. I noticed at least six different types of real coffee, six different mayonnaises, and more than 20 kinds of cheese biscuit. There are tights, fuse wires, tin openers and Turkish Delight.

"It's best to have a small quantity of everything," explained Mr Ahmad. "If someone wants something we haven't got, we will order it specially, if possible. We tell them it will be here on a certain day, and if it is available it is here then. I think customers and their wishes are more important than anything else.

"Occasionally we get some awkward customers, and you really want to serve them, and you can't satisfy them. Some people complain about our prices. What we do is price the things according to our suppliers' recommended selling price. There's not much difference in our prices from the prices in other small shops. But there's no way we could challenge the big supermarkets on prices."

"We get up between half past six and seven. My wife prepares our lunch, which we bring over here with us and heat it up at lunch time. She cooks dinner when we get home at 10.30, sometimes at 11 o'clock," he said, smiling at his wife.

"Sometimes half past eleven," she said, laughing again.

In what free time they have, they watch a bit of television, or read. "Every day and every night I am tired," said Mrs Ahmad. "At night time I am very tired."

She leant her head against the door, beside her cash desk. She looked worn out. A lady came up to pay for some cornflakes, bread and a tub of cottage cheese. She dropped the cheese, and Mr Ahmad rushed to pick it up for her as it rolled across the floor.

Why did he think service was so important?

"Because, in my opinion, if you respect others, they will respect you. And if you give them good service then they will come back again.

"Sometimes people try to come in after we've locked the shop. We let them in, we don't want to disappoint them. They have usually run out of butter or tea or cigarettes.

Polite

"I have been told by customers, at least eight times to my face, that this is the best place where service is concerned. We do try to be polite to people, even to young children.

"Although it is self-service, we are on hand if anyone needs any help."

Right on cue, a small ginger-haired boy came into the shop, and asked for a packet of rice, and Mr Ahmad led him towards the right shelf.

Source: adapted from
The New Standard,
20 May 1981

1 Briefly describe how the Ahmads earn their living.

2 Why do you think the Ahmads have been successful in building a prosperous business?

3 What sorts of costs will have been involved in establishing and developing their business?

4 What can the Ahmads offer their customers that a larger business might not provide?

5 Why do you think Mr Ahmad said, "But there's no way we could challenge the big supermarkets on prices"?

Extension 1

MacLeod Fruit and Vegetable Merchant

Donne and Ellis owners of "Superfruit"

Look at the statements below which relate to these two firms.

A
The business could do better with taking on someone with a few new ideas.

B
Together we have plenty of capital.

C
I make all the decisions. I enjoy that.

D
The jobs involved in running the business can be shared.

E
One problem is that I have to share the profits.

F
Sometimes there is no agreement on how to run the business.

G
My employees know I'm the boss, so they come straight to me if they have a problem.

H
My business is efficient and flexible because I can respond rapidly as I don't have to consult anyone else.

I
If I'm ill the business still continues.

1 Sort the statements into those that might be said by MacLeod and those that Donne and Ellis might make.
2 Using the comments made by MacLeod, write a short account of the problems and benefits of running your own business.
3 What disadvantages do Donne and Ellis have in running their partnership?
4 Explain why Donne and Ellis have a greater chance of being effective in business than MacLeod.

Extension 2

This is the tale of Jack and Jill.
Jack and Jill each have their own businesses making and selling skateboards. Jill's business is very successful, but Jack's business is threatened with bankruptcy.
Jack and Jill live next door to each other and often chat about their business plans. They both own their own homes. Jack has a car and Jill a van. Jack has £1000 in savings in a deposit account at the local bank. Jill has £15 000 in a local building society account.

Jack's business is in his own name.
Jack rents his TV.
He and his wife have a cottage in Wales – in his wife's name.
His wife has jewellery worth £3000, again in her own name.
Jack has recently inherited a valuable stamp collection worth £1000.

Jill has recently been on holiday to the Caribbean and is planning to go skiing in Austria this winter. She is planning to buy a sports car.

1 Jack's business is not doing very well and he is threatened with bankruptcy because he owes £50 000. Using the idea of *unlimited liability* explain why Jack stands to lose more than just his business.

2 Look at what he and his wife own and make a list of the property that is at risk.

3 What evidence is there that Jill is doing well in her business?

4 a Why can't a creditor (a person Jack owes money to) seize Jack's TV?
 b Why can't a creditor seize the cottage?

5 What advantages would there be if Jack and Jill went into business together for
 a Jack;
 b Jill?

6 What would be the advantage to Jill if Jack went bankrupt?

Coursework

Aim: To investigate ownership of firms.

Undertake a survey in your area to find out how various firms are owned.
Here is a sample questionnaire for you to use:

> Name of firm: ....
>
> Does it sell a product? ....
>   supply a service? ....
> Is it owned by:
>   one person? ....
>   partners? ....
>   some other form of financial
>   organisation? ....
>
> Is the firm small/medium/large? (Refer to the number of branches and the total number of employees in deciding.)

1 What advantages do the people you interview see in the way their business is organised financially?

2 What disadvantages do they feel exist?

You could use bar charts or pie diagrams to display your results.

3 Looking at the data you have collected, what differences did you find existed between firms owned in different ways? How would you account for these differences?

14 Private Enterprise 2

A company differs in a very important way from a partnership or sole trading firm:

- All shareholders in companies are protected by *limited liability*. A shareholder is someone who invests money in a company, or buys and holds a 'share' in it. The company can be sued for any money it owes (debts), but the shareholders are protected. Their liability for the debts of the company are limited. They only stand to lose the money they spent purchasing shares in the company.
- Companies are *joint stock enterprises*. This means that a company is jointly owned by its shareholders. There must be at least two shareholders in a company.

The Bedley Business

The Bedleys are a family business operating as a private limited company manufacturing jams and marmalade. Each member of the Bedley family owns a share or portion of the company, which is called Bedley Jams Ltd. (A private limited company must have Limited (Ltd) in its title.) Mr Bedley has 40% of the company as his share. Mrs Bedley also has 40% of the firm. Their son Jack owns 8% and their daughter Kay owns the rest of the shares.

Decide for yourself

- What percentage of the shares does Kay own?
- How many owners of the business are there?

What does a company have to do?

All companies have to register their existence. Two documents are required:

- **The Memorandum of Association:** this states the company's registered address, its title, the form of business engaged in, and the amount of the authorised capital.
- **The Articles of Association:** these describe how the internal organisation of the firm is to work.

A company must hold an Annual General Meeting (AGM). At this meeting a Board of Directors and a Chairperson are elected by the shareholders. All shareholders have a right to vote at the AGM, having a vote for each share they hold. They also have a right to a *dividend* or share of the profits, in proportion to the number of shares they hold. (These rights depend on the kind of shares they own as we shall see later when we look at the Stock Exchange.)

Public limited companies

Bedley Jams Ltd is a private limited company. There are also *public limited companies*. These must have the letters PLC or plc after their names (as in J. Sainsbury plc).

Shares in a public limited company can be resold on the *Stock Exchange*. Firms with PLC status are 'quoted' or 'listed' on this market. Shares in a private limited company cannot be offered to the general public although some small companies are allowed access to the Exchange's Unlisted Securities market, or to the Third Market.

The Bedleys 'go public'

Mr Bedley wants the family company to 'go public' or apply for public limited company status.

"If shares in the company are sold to the public," he says, "we'll attract more capital to re-equip our factory. We can expand and produce more varieties of jams and jellies or more jars of those we make already. We could afford to lower our prices and capture a larger share of the market. Just think," Mr Bedley dreamed on, "that could mean increased profits for all of us. The increase could more than make up for the profits we lose by selling a share of the company to the public."

77

Kay is not so certain everyone will want to buy shares in Bedley Jams plc. "It's a risk buying shares," she says.

"That's not a problem," says Mr Bedley. "When members of the public buy shares in a plc they know they have two advantages. Firstly, their liability is limited to the shares they have bought. Secondly, they can always resell their shares to other members of the public by offering them on the market for secondhand shares: the Stock Exchange."

Mr Bedley is right. These two advantages have helped joint stock companies become very effective in raising the money they need to develop and expand their businesses.

Mrs Bedley, like Kay, is not so certain about going public. "If we go public, we'll have to issue our accounts to the public. To get people to buy shares we'll have to publish a prospectus setting out all the details about our company."

Then Kay adds, "If we issue too many shares, we could lose control of the company. Then someone else would be making the decisions."

"We'll have to keep 51% of the shares," says Mr Bedley. "If we do so, we'll keep control in the family."

Jack had been silent. "Well, I'll be honest," he says now. "If we go public, I won't need permission to sell my shares. If I do sell them, you could lose control. There might be a takeover bid."

Test yourself

1 What percentage of shares must the Bedleys retain if they want to keep control of the firm?
2 How does a company differ from other types of firms?
3 What protection and rights exist for:
   a shareholders;
   b anyone else who might have to deal with a company?
4 What advantages does a person buying shares in a plc have?
5 What are the benefits for a firm of 'going public'?
6 Why do some firms remain private ventures?

Activity

The great Easter egg race

Daily Leak

CHOFFEE MAY BE GOING PUBLIC ACCORDING TO OUR SOURCES . . .

FUTURE PROSPECTS
Expansion of the domestic chocolate bar sector will continue. The quality end of the confectionery market is likely to be penetrated by foreign firms, particularly Swiss and American.

PROPOSED EXPANSION PROGRAMME

Choffee is planning to enter the Easter egg market and also wants to increase its share of chocolate bars. In order to achieve this Choffee needs
2 more factories
1 warehouse
7 additional lorries.

CHOFFEE THE CHEWY
CHOCOLATE BARS.
THEY'RE MUCH MORE FUN THAN . . .
Sshh . . . you know what . . .

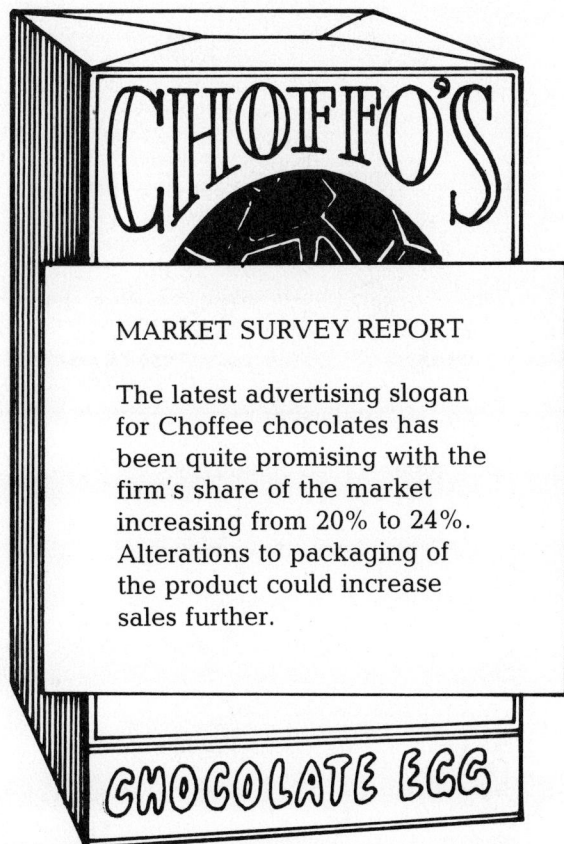

FINANCIAL SITUATION
Current valuation of firm: £50 million.
Profits in last year: £1.5 million.
Expected profits if expansion undertaken
£5 million.
Cost of expansion programme: £20 million.
Finance to be raised by selling 40% of
firm to the public.
Liquid assets and deposit account savings
£6 million.

CHOFFO'S

MARKET SURVEY REPORT

The latest advertising slogan
for Choffee chocolates has
been quite promising with the
firm's share of the market
increasing from 20% to 24%.
Alterations to packaging of
the product could increase
sales further.

CHOCOLATE EGG

1 Describe the Choffee firm's expansion
 programme.

2 Why does the firm want to expand?

3 Explain how the recent advertising
 campaign has benefited the firm.

4 "Choffee" is owned by Mr Choffo, who is
 the sole proprietor. What costs will there
 be to Mr Choffo and his family if he sells
 40% of the firm to the public?

5 What will be the social costs and benefits
 to the community if Mr Choffo is allowed
 to expand his enterprise?

6 Describe the alternative ways Mr Choffo
 could find to get the capital to finance his
 expansion programme.

DATA RESPONSE 1

A

	1982				1984			
	Businesses	Outlets	Persons engaged	Retail turnover (inclusive of VAT)	Businesses	Outlets	Persons engaged	Retail turnover (inclusive of VAT)
	Number	Number	Thousand	£ million	Number	Number	Thousand	£ million
Total retail trade	232 948	349 659	2 264	69 784	230 789	343 153	2 326	82 342
Single outlet retailers	203 157	203 157	828	21 093	201 633	201 633	813	24 268
Small multiple retailers	28 657	76 346	355	9 609	28 207	73 670	349	10 604
Large multiple retailers *of which*	1 135	70 153	1 081	39 082	949	67 850	1 164	47 469
Co-operative societies accounted for	*148*	*6 945*	*116*	*4 061*	*114*	*5 813*	*108*	*4 349*

Source: CSO, *Annual Abstract of Statistics*: 1988

FACT BASE: Co-operatives are yet another kind of business organisation.

Co-operatives (co-ops) are private sector firms aiming not to make a profit so much as to run an organisation where shareholders can benefit or help each other.

Producer co-ops are owned by workers making goods.

Consumer co-ops (first set up in Rochdale in 1844) run shops and are owned by those shoppers who are members. Members elect a committee. A share in a co-op entitles you to a "divi" (dividend) – but only one vote.

WHY CO-OPS ARE OF VALUE

- They are run by the people who own them.
- They are concerned with social issues, e.g. education.
- They provide local retail outlets in rural areas and jobs in urban areas.

WHY CO-OPS HAVE PROBLEMS . . .

- Workers lack management experience.
- Unlimited liability applies.
- Committees are not an efficient way of running a business.
- It is difficult to raise enough finance.
- Lack of interest in profit.

SHARE OF THE ACTION

JUDITH Shaw and Louise Crosby have their own answer to unemployment.

They launched their painting and decorating workers' co-operative after leaving college seven months ago.

Theirs is just one of the thousand co-ops around the country – covering everything from bicycle repair to publishing.

But starting a co-op requires cash and, even more important, know-how.

Mancoda, a Manchester city funded agency, provides people with both. They offer training courses, free advice and help in applying for loans and grants.

Twenty seven co-ops have been set up in Manchester – 11 by Mancoda – and they provide jobs for 156 people.

It took Judith and Louise three months to get their co-op organised.

"We got a £1,000 grant through Mancoda and an overdraft at the bank for another £1,000."

They are now working on two sites in the city, and have taken on three part-timers to help out.

Source: *Daily Mirror*, 13 June 1985

---

1 What are the two types of co-operatives that exist?

2 How are co-ops different from joint stock companies?

3 How did Judith and Louise solve the problem of unemployment?

4 Where did they get finance and advice?

5 Look at Table **A**. Describe the percentage change that has occurred in the co-operatives' share of retail trade.

6 What does this suggest about the organisational advantages of other types of multiple retailers (many of which are joint stock companies)?

DATA RESPONSE 2

Caped crusader helps TV-am to £13m result

By Neil Thapar
City Reporter

BATMAN and Robin may be a trifle long in the tooth but their role was no bit part in helping TV-am to beat market estimates with a £13.1m pre-tax profit for the year to 31 January, despite an industrial dispute.

The dynamic duo were used to good effect by the breakfast channel's managers to keep audience ratings up after Bruce Gyngell, managing director, locked-out and then finally sacked 232 striking technicians.

The company said the latter part of the year was significantly influenced by the ACTT dispute, but reduced manpower will make it much more cost effective this year.

Reduced overheads are also thought to have had some beneficial impact on the year just ended. But the bulk of the profits growth came from rising advertising revenue through increased air time and higher advertising rates. The channel share of the independent television revenue market increased by 15.8 per cent.

Its average number of viewers was up by a million to 15.7 million and a record viewing figure of 16.5 million in Christmas week.

"We are considerably enhancing our news and current affairs output. Our regional studios are being substantially enlarged with the installation of remote cameras and opening of international bureaux," the company says.

Source: *The Independent*, 25 March 1988

1 What profit did TV-am make in the year to 31 January?

2 How did Batman and Robin help TV-am?

3 How had the company reduced their costs during the year?

4 Where had the bulk of the company's profits come from?

5 Describe how and why the company was able to increase its revenue. Why might this be good news for its shareholders?

Extension

Type of firm	Ownership	Control	Capital	Profit
Sole trader	Only 1	Held by the sole owner	Little capital required to start up. Lack of capital can affect growth.	Profits are kept by the sole owner. Unlimited liability for all losses.
Partnership	2 to 20	Shared by partners	Capital is provided by each partner; amounts may not be enough.	Profits are shared by partners according to partnership agreement.
Private limited company (e.g. Brown Ltd.)	2 or more	Run by directors appointed by shareholders. Takeovers are not possible.	Capital is provided by shareholders; more capital may be required.	Profits are shared by shareholders. Limited liability provides protection from losses.
Public limited company (e.g. Brown PLC)	2 or more	Run by directors appointed by shareholders. Takeovers are possible.	Larger amounts of capital can be raised. Must have at least £50 000 capital when formed.	Profits are shared by shareholders and opportunity to make profits are greater. Limited liability provides protection from losses.

1 Which of these types of firm might run the following businesses:
 a a large firm manufacturing cars;
 b a firm of dentists;
 c a small publishing business owned by a family.

2 Which of the above firms have the disadvantage of unlimited liability?

3 In terms of profit what is the difference between a sole trader and a joint stock company?

4 Use the chart to write a short account of the benefits of a joint stock company compared to either the sole trader or partnership as a type of business organisation.

Coursework

Aim: To investigate the performance of a variety of joint stock companies.

Collect information from newspapers on the performance of joint stock companies.

1 **a** Collect a range of newspaper reports (as in Data Response 2) from the financial pages of your daily newspaper.

  b Using bar charts, display the profits and losses achieved by each of the companies you have examined.

2 From the reports, identify those factors which have contributed to these profits or losses.

Alternatively collect information about one firm in particular. (It would be quite acceptable to choose a local firm that is not a joint stock company but might be interested in the publicity and ideas your work generated.)

1 Organise your information in such a way as to show prospective investors:

  a how the firm is organised;

  b how the commodity (whether a good or a service) is produced;

  c how the commodity is marketed/sold.

2 Prepare the material you have gathered in the form of a brochure encouraging people to become shareholders in the company. Include photographs of the products, bar charts (or pie charts) to show costs and revenue, biographies of key personnel. Write a short conclusion setting out the key advantages of investing in the firm.

15 Public Enterprise

Public enterprises are business organisations operating within the public sector of the economy. Public enterprises provide goods and services:
- free at the point of need; or
- at a reduced price (for example, as in merit goods which we will look at later); or
- through the price system in a similar way to firms in the private sector.

Some public enterprises are:
- owned by a local authority (and sometimes referred to as *municipal enterprises*), for example swimming pools, libraries, children's homes;
- others are run by central government departments – for example, the armed forces are answerable to the Ministry of Defence;
- others are owned by central government on behalf of the nation, but run as *public corporations* like private firms. Examples include British Coal and British Rail.

The idea of public corporations has recently been the subject of much public debate. As a result of the policy of successive Conservative governments public enterprises, like British Telecom and British Gas, have been increasingly sold to the private sector as part of a programme called 'privatisation'.

Public corporations are sometimes referred to as *nationalised industries*. They aim to serve the public interest rather than just make a profit. They are usually large organisations that raise their capital by issuing *stock* (a fixed interest long-term loan). Any profits they make are kept by the government. Any losses are paid for by the government.

Public corporations are financed from retained profits, borrowing from banks and other financial institutions in the UK and abroad, by government loans and by injections of new capital by government. The government keeps any profit saved.

Public corporations are set up by Act of Parliament. They are run by boards of directors appointed by the body that owns them, that is by government. The board is free to organise the business, but a minister of the government is answerable to Parliament for the actions of the corporation.

The government also has shares in a number of private firms, the so-called *mixed enterprises*. Examples of these are British Petroleum and Rolls Royce.

Activity

Public enterprises

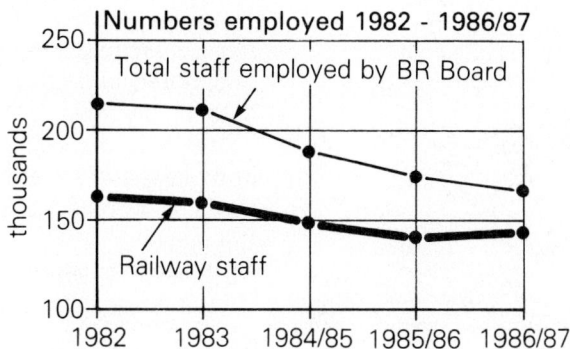

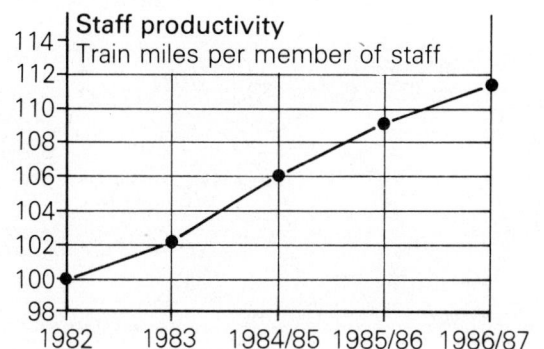

A

Numbers employed 1982 - 1986/87
Total staff employed by BR Board
Railway staff
thousands
250 200 150 100
1982 1983 1984/85 1985/86 1986/87

Staff productivity
Train miles per member of staff
114 112 110 108 106 104 102 100 98
1982 1983 1984/85 1985/86 1986/87

	Year to 31 March 1985		Year to 31 March 1986	
	British Rail	Average of 8 European Railways	British Rail	Average of 8 European Railways
Train kilometres (loaded and empty) per member of staff employed	2,752	2,060	2,903	2,130
Average train loading (passenger kms, divided by passenger train kms loaded and empty)	90	124	94	132
Average train loading (freight tonne kms, divided by freight trains loaded and empty)	197	295	230	307
Support from public funds as proportion of Gross Domestic Product (%)	0·30	0·76	0·26	0·75

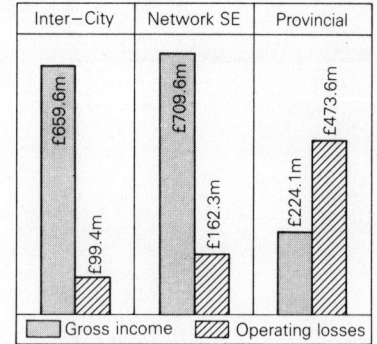

Inter–City £659.6m / £99.4m; Network SE £709.6m / £162.3m; Provincial £224.1m / £473.6m

Gross income / Operating losses

C

Changing Face of the Railway

	December 1962	December 1963	December 1968	March 1987
Number of employees	502,703	464,286	317,478	166,989
Passenger route miles	12,915	12,631	9,471	8,912
Passenger miles travelled	19,728m	19,575m	17,835m	19,150m

E

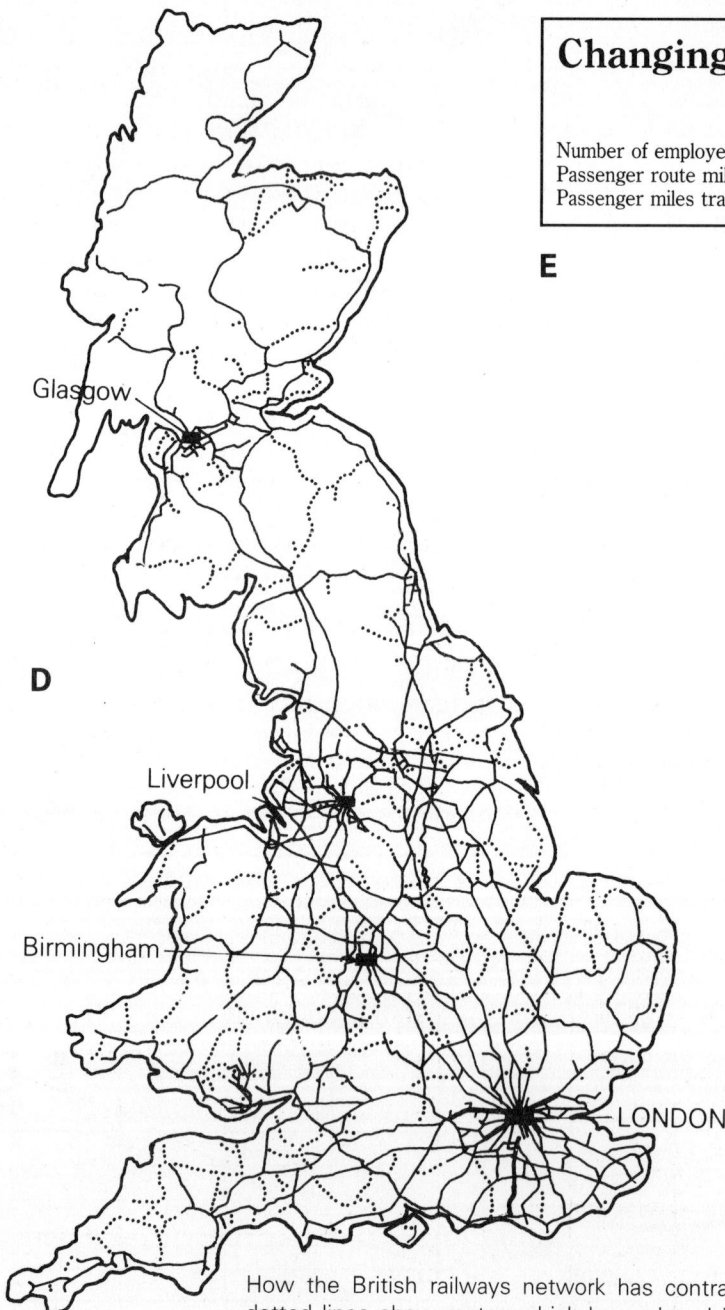

D

How the British railways network has contracted: dotted lines show routes which have closed in the 25 years since the Beeching Report.

Profit and service conflict

F Passenger watchdog councils and railway unions argue that BR should run the railways as a public service, but instead BR is cutting back on services to increase profits regardless of social and environmental costs. For example, unmanned stations, closed waiting rooms, and fewer coaches on trains are more common and the quality of service has declined. Overcrowding is the most frequent complaint.

The arrival of a Gravy Train

G 150 stations have opened since Dr Beeching resigned as BR chairman in 1965. There is more money in the economy and trains have been marketed more effectively. The Channel Tunnel is expected to transform the economics of travel by rail.

The new Sprinters on provincial lines will be faster and quieter and will save on maintenance and repair costs. There will be telephones and privatised hot and cold catering services on trains.

The figures show that, where the service improves, it often attracts extra passengers to trains. Motorists leave their cars at home or at the station.

BR emphasises that it is not a monopoly: it competes with cars, coaches and airlines.

(Adapted from *The Independent*, 21 March 1988)

1 Using **C**, describe the income and losses of British Rail.

2 Using the information in **A**, **B**, **D** and **E**, describe how British Rail has improved its business performance.

3 Read **F** and suggest how consumers have been affected by the drive to be profitable.

4 Using **B** and **G**, compare British Rail's performance with that of other European railways and describe its future prospects.

5 Consider the costs and benefits for a commuter travelling by British Rail.

Two sides to the debate
Arguments for nationalised industries

The arguments for nationalising industries or keeping them in public ownership include:

- If the government owns a firm it can be run on behalf of the people and not just the lucky few who can afford to purchase shares.
- Nationalisation has helped many private sector firms that had declined as a result of changes in economic circumstances (for example, the railways) or lack of investment (for example, coal).
- Helping these industries has prevented even higher levels of unemployment.
- Firms that are important to the nation's survival and defence are protected.
- Economists have argued that nationalisation allows the government to control the economy more effectively. The government is able to achieve national targets because of its control of this part of the economy. (Such targets might include action on relocation of offices, unemployment, sex equality, investment or inflation.)
- Because many nationalised industries operate across the country (like British Rail or, formerly, British Gas), they benefit from economies of scale (see Unit 20). Smaller private sector firms cannot enjoy these benefits.
- Such industries are often *natural monopolies*. This means that it would be wasteful to have more than one firm operating in the market place. This is particularly the case for *public utilities*. For example, competition in the supply of water could lead to different companies supplying water through different pipes to houses in the same street!

- If a private individual or firm controls a natural monopoly, there is a danger that consumers would, through lack of choice, be forced to pay high prices or suffer from a poor level of service, or both.
- To keep an eye on public corporations, because of their monopoly position, the government set up consumer councils for each corporation, like the Central Transport Consumer Council with its Regional Transport Users' Consumer Councils.
- Because nationalised industries are not concerned primarily with profits, they can take account of the external costs of their activities. For example, the pollution from power stations can be regulated and controlled. The supporters of nationalised industries, therefore, would argue that they can provide cheap services for people at the point of need, rather than for profit. They can provide services in areas that other firms might consider uneconomic (for example, railways to remote parts of Wales or post to isolated farms in the Lake District).

It was a combination of these arguments that led the post-war Labour governments to nationalise many firms.

Arguments for privatisation

There are many reasons for favouring a policy of privatisation.

- Nationalised firms making heavy losses can be a drain on government funds because they can only survive if funding is provided (in the form of subsidies – these allow the goods or services being produced to be sold at below the cost of production). Some people benefit: the workers in the industry and the consumers of the product. The rest of the community has to share in subsidising them.
- A firm returned to the private sector and controlled by shareholders and forced to compete with other firms is better able to respond to the needs of consumers.
- Many nationalised firms, it is argued, have not been effectively managed, or have been subject to political control rather than economic decision-making.
- Privatisation can encourage greater choice, less inefficiency, and the production of better quality goods and services.
- Allowing firms to make a profit would act as an incentive to more efficient management.

Privatisation

During the 1980s the Conservative governments have privatised a large number of public corporations: British Airways, British Gas, British Telecom, among others. There are four aspects to their programme of privatisation:

- the sale of government shares in public limited companies such as BP (British Petroleum);
- a vigorous policy of encouraging local authorities to put services out to tender to private firms (this has happened in the case of cleaning in schools and hospitals and of refuse collection);
- the return of public corporations to the private sector by the sale of shares in such enterprises to the general public, or to institutions, with the aim of creating a 'people's capitalism' (in effect, denationalisation);
- selling council houses to their occupants or others.

Following privatisation consumer watchdog bodies have been retained or created, although often in a limited form, in an attempt to prevent consumer exploitation. For example, Oftel has a role in regulating British Telecom's activities.

ECONOMIC TERMS

Nationalisation: the purchase or takeover by the state of a private sector firm.

Public corporation: an industry owned by the government and answerable to Parliament.

Natural monopoly: a situation where, either for reasons of efficiency, or to prevent wasteful duplication, only one firm exists (for example, electricity, water and gas supplies to homes).

Privatisation: the transfer of public sector firms to the private sector.

Test yourself

1 Name three types of public sector enterprise and give an example of each.
2 Why might a government consider nationalising an ailing shipbuilding firm making frigates in a town where the firm provided 20% of all employment?
3 What do you understand by the term privatisation?
4 What are the arguments in favour of privatisation?
5 Why were many firms nationalised in the UK after the Second World War?

DATA RESPONSE 1

Shareholders in privatisation stocks

| | SUCCESSFUL APPLICANTS | | | | |
Company	First Issue	Second Issue	Third Issue	Current number of shareholders	Date
AMERSHAM INTERNATIONAL	65,000	n/a	n/a	6,940	30.9.87
ASSOCIATED BRITISH PORTS	45,500	8,000	n/a	9,006	30.9.87
BAA	2,187,500	n/a	n/a	1,500,000	12.10.87
BRITISH AEROSPACE	155,000	260,000	n/a	102,768	6.10.87
BRITISH AIRWAYS	1,100,000	n/a	n/a	404,000	6.10.87
BRITISH GAS	4,407,079	n/a	n/a	3,000,000	30.9.87
BRITISH TELECOM	2,300,000	n/a	n/a	1,417,905	31.8.87
BRITOIL	35,000	450,000	n/a	178,000	31.7.87
CABLE & WIRELESS	26,000	35,137	218,588	174,758	8.10.87
ENTERPRISE OIL	13,695	n/a	n/a	11,100	30.6.87
JAGUAR	125,000	n/a	n/a	24,918	30.8.87
ROLLS-ROYCE	2,000,000	n/a	n/a	1,250,000*	19.10.87
TSB	3,000,000	n/a	n/a	1,970,000	2.10.87

■ *Rolls-Royce register currently being compiled. After 2nd call overseas holdings 21 per cent against ceiling of 15 per cent. Arrangements being made for last overseas investors to register to divest holdings. *Appointments.*

Britain's shareholder profile

TOTAL SHARE OWNERSHIP

	%	Approximate number
1983 (pre-BT)	5	2 m
1984 (post-BT)	8	3.2m
1986 (post-TSB)	17	7 m
1987 (post-Gas)	23	9.4m

SHARE OWNERSHIP BY AGE

	1983 %	1987 %	% Change
Under 25	5	10	+ 5
25–44	28	44	+16
45–64	40	30	−10
65+	27	16	−11

SOCIO-ECONOMIC GROUPING

Class	1983 %	1987 %	% Change
AB	56	29	−27
C1	26	34	+ 8
C2	12	26	+14
DE	6	11	+ 5

Source: *The Observer* October/November 1987

NUMBER OF COMPANIES INVESTED IN

	%	Approx no of investors
One	56	5.4m
Two	22	2.1m
Three	9	0.8m
Four-nine	8	0.8m
10-plus	3	0.3m

1 What increase in the number of people owning shares took place between 1983 and 1987?

2 List two firms that were privatised in 1987.

3 What has happened to share ownership by age and social class since 1983?

4 How many companies have the majority of shareholders invested in?

5 Use the data to assess whether privatisation has been successful in extending capitalism to the people.

DATA RESPONSE 2

In 1984 British Telecom was privatised. Look at the data and answer the questions.

1 a When British Telecom was privatised, was it making a profit or loss?

b What light does your answer throw on the case for privatising this state asset?

2 What evidence can you find that privatising British Telecom was not in itself effective in increasing the firm's efficiency?

Profits in major nationalised companies (pre-tax 1983–84)

	Profit
The Electricity Council	£1,842m
British Gas	£1,017m
British Telecom	£ 990m
British Airways	£ 185m
The Post Office	£ 131m
British Rail	£ 80m
Bank of England	£ 65m
British Airports	£ 61m
British Leyland	£ 4.1m
National Oil Corporation	£ 2.6m
Civil Aviation Authority	£ 2.3m
Crown Agents	£ 1m
British Shipbuilding	−£ 161m (loss)
British Steel	−£ 207m (loss)
National Coal Board	−£ 410m (loss)
BALANCE	+£3,137 million

Source: *The Observer*, 5 August 1984

BT rings in good news on callboxes

by Tony Maguire

NINE out of ten British Telecom phone boxes are finally working normally, the company claimed today.

Less than six months after being savaged by telephone watchdogs for the deplorable state of phone kiosks, BT chiefs believe they have achieved their target of getting more than 90 per cent of boxes in working order.

The company's internal figures show that in some parts of the country up to 95 per cent are now working, although in run-down inner-city areas the success rate is around 85 per cent.

In central London broken down phone boxes are now fixed within three hours, according to BT, although the company is reliant on the public to report faulty phone kiosks.

"We can only fix them quickly if faults are reported. Payphones are checked regularly, but we rely on our customers to report any difficulties," said a spokesman.

Millions of pounds have been spent by BT in an attempt to rebuild the image shattered by highly critical surveys from the Office of Telecommunications and other phone watchdogs.

Target

The investment appears to have paid off. Engineers have been switched to payphone maintenance, more cashless phonecard kiosks have been installed and the company has tried to cut down vandalism by introducing new, open, payphone housings in the most vulnerable sites.

BT chairman Iain Vallance pledged before Christmas that 90 per cent would be working by the end of March and the company's figures indicate that the target has been achieved.

The company's main rival, Mercury, is pressing ahead with plans to introduce its own payphones after being given the go-ahead by Oftel. And other organisations, such as hotels, can now apply for licences to run payphones.

One of the most frustrating problems for coin box users, the "999 calls only" sign displayed on faulty kiosks, is being resolved.

Source: *Evening Standard*, 7 April 1988

BT overcharging customers by millions of pounds

By Tony Dawe

British Telecom is overcharging its customers by millions of pounds a year because of faulty telephone lines and metering equipment.

Telephone engineers and organizations representing both individual and business users have told *The Times* independently that they estimate the faults are bringing BT an extra 10 per cent on call charges.

That would amount to £500 million a year, a quarter of BT's current profits of £2 billion.

Last night BT dismissed *The Times*'s findings and said: "With a company with 22 million exchange line connections, there will be times, albeit very rarely, when things go wrong. When that happens, they tend to err in favour of the customer."

But overcharging has become such a common complaint among commerce and industry as well as individual subscribers that a handful of companies are now specializing in "telephone bill troubleshooting". For a consultancy fee and half the savings they achieve, they study a company's bill to see if it has paid too much.

In the past year both the Telecommunications Users' Association, an independent body, and the Office of Telecommunications (OFTEL), the formal BT watchdog, have reported sizeable rises in the number of complaints.

Proving the complaints has, however, always been difficult because of lack of independent access to telephone equipment and because BT, unlike its one rival, Mercury, and some overseas telephone companies, does not provide itemised bills.

But the association has now obtained firm evidence of meter faults after one of its members, Mr Danny Dee, a London businessman, installed his own "call logging" equipment to check his phone.

He discovered that he was being charged peak rates over two bank holidays, when calls should be at the cheap rate, and during weekday afternoons when they should have been at the standard rate.

In a separate case, BT has admitted that it overcharged subscribers in two North London exchanges, 340 and 341, for nearly three months earlier this year because the meter timing local calls was faulty. The company claimed that the "average customer would have been overcharged by about £2" but tomorrow all 14,000 subscribers on the exchanges will be offered a £4 rebate.

Source: *The Times*, 8 September 1987

3 What is OFTEL? To what extent has OFTEL been able to achieve improvements in the provision of a payphone/call box service?

4 What has BT done to improve the call box service? Why do you think it has responded in the way it has?

5 In what areas do consumers remain critical of the service BT provides?

A privatization too many
John Humphries urges total opposition to the water sell-off

"It droppeth as the gentle rain from heaven
Upon the place beneath: It is twice blessed:
It blesseth him that gives and him that takes"

In 1974 the local authorities "gave", without compensation, their water service assets in trust to the water authorities. In return Mr Heath's government promised that local authority representatives would thenceforth be in a majority on water authority boards. If the local authorities felt blessed in 1974, they certainly did not in 1983 when the present administration reneged on that promise and handed over control of the authorities to "businessmen".

On the other hand the Government, which now proposes to sell off the water authorities – for which it has not yet paid a penny piece to anyone – must feel happy indeed. Blessed has been he who has taken!

But is privatization the answer to the future of this essential public service? For water is the truest monopoly of all. There will be no Mercury to offer a rival service. No one is going to build competing reservoirs or sewage works or lay new pipes. And there can be little growth in the basic service since 99 per cent of our homes already receive public

water supplies and 96 per cent are connected to main sewers. Privatization will simply farm out a right to raise a tax, something that takes us straight back to the Middle Ages.

The new shareholders, though, could be in for a rough time. For a start, will they be buying assets or liabilities? Even at Thames, which inherited the best assets from its predecessors, all is far from well. In that region alone 13,000 homes are still regularly flooded with raw sewage. In the bitterly cold February of last year the major reservoirs ran dry as pipes burst all over London. After the wettest summer since 1939, Hertfordshire rivers such as the Ver and Misborne and the Cotswold aquifers are running dry through over-abstraction.

Pollution levels of the Thames itself have, according to government research, risen steadily over the past three years. Less fortunate areas with similar problems, and with largely Victorian systems, will have to spend vast sums to put things right. In addition, a whole host of organizations will be watching over the privatized bodies. There will be the National River Authority (the new government quango) and environmental groups whose successful campaign brought about the breakup of the

authorities in the present proposed legislation. There will be the EEC with its strict new regulations, the director general of water and the pollution inspectorate.

Against this background it is not surprising that some MPs are saying that the Control of Pollution Act will have to be set aside to get the flotation off the ground. The Government will have to break its own laws in order to sell something it does not own. This will be an issue in which Sid will *not* be encouraged to participate.

And what of the consumers? At the end of the day they will pick up the bulk of the bill, as we are constantly being warned by Nicholas Ridley, the Environment Secretary. In addition to having to fund all the future replacement and maintenance of the failing systems, they will have the dubious privilege of providing dividends for the presently non-existent shareholders (on an increasing basis). They will also have to pay VAT on their bills once water becomes a product and is no longer a public service. And since the privatized water authorities will also be paying tax to the Treasury on their "profits", that too will have to come out of the customers' pockets.

So what should we do as the 300-page Water Bill lands in Parliament shortly and

starts to churn its way laboriously through both Houses? My advice to every householder in the country is: write to your MP and create hell. There was never a more immoral, improper or unwanted piece of legislation.

Already two thirds of the population has instinctively objected. It is puerile for the Government to say it has a mandate merely because water privatization was included with a whole host of other proposals in the last Conservative manifesto. Because you like one item in the shop window, it does not mean you have to buy the lot.

If the British public do not awake smartly to what is being perpetrated upon them in this most basic and essential monopoly public service – and one, moreover, bearing directly for good or ill on the state of the nation's health – then every man, woman and child in this country will assuredly be soaked.

© Times Newspapers, 1988

The author, formerly chairman of the Water Space Amenity Commission, is deputy chairman of the Council for Environmental Conservation.

Source: *The Times,*
7 November 1988

1 Who previously owned the Water Authorities?
2 Why in this article is water described as the 'truest monopoly of all'?
3 What evidence is there that potential shareholders will not obtain a good return on any money they invest in the new water authorities?

4 What organisations will oversee the performance of the privatised water authorities? How will this possibly affect future profits?
5 What burdens will possibly fall on the consumers when the water authorities are privatised?
6 What benefits do you think will come from privatisation of this service?

Coursework

Aim: To investigate the hypothesis that privatisation increases the efficiency of a business enterprise.

1 What is privatisation?
2 Consider why the government has introduced privatisation.
3 Take one of the reasons advanced (e.g. privatisation increases efficiency) and test this as your hypothesis.
4 Examine a firm recently privatised (e.g. British Telecom) and collect evidence about the firm's recent business performance.
5 Is your hypothesis proved or disproved?
6 Would further competition, e.g. from Mercury in the case of British Telecom, contribute to further efficiency?

16 Locating Production

One of the most important decisions made when setting up a production unit is the decision regarding where to locate the enterprise. This decision is usually based on profit.

"I think it's time we relocated our enterprise; the customers are objecting to scrambled eggs!"

A firm is often first attracted to an area because of a range of **natural advantages.** These include:

- **Geographical factors**: the area might have the right climate, soil type or other physical features, like a deep water harbour or an estuary. For example, Port Talbot in South Wales is able to import iron ore in bulk for steel-making because of its siting on the Severn Estuary.
- **Nearness to raw materials**: when the raw materials used to make a product are bulky they cost a lot to transport. Firms will therefore set up near to the sources of the raw material. This is particularly the case where a lot of waste is involved in making the finished article. Bulk-losing industries, like steel-makers, fall into this class.

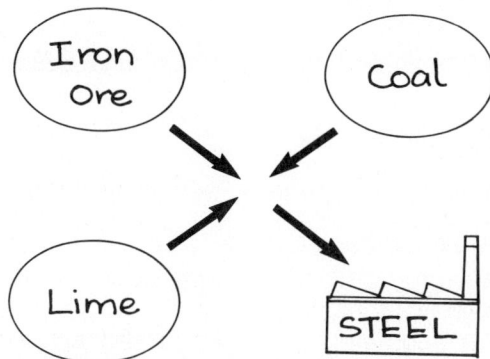

- **Transport facilities**: access to road, rail, sea or air transport is important, both for bringing in raw materials to the firm and for distributing the finished product. Many electronics and computer firms have located in towns along the M4 motorway, where they have good access to a number of different forms of transport (that is, there is a well-developed infrastructure).
- **Nearness to the market**: for many products being near the market is important. In particular, industries whose product is bulk-increasing in its manufacture (like refrigerator assembly, for example) are located near to where potential consumers live.

  Food manufacturers, brewers and bakers are often based close to large centres of population, too, as their product can deteriorate if it has to travel long distances.

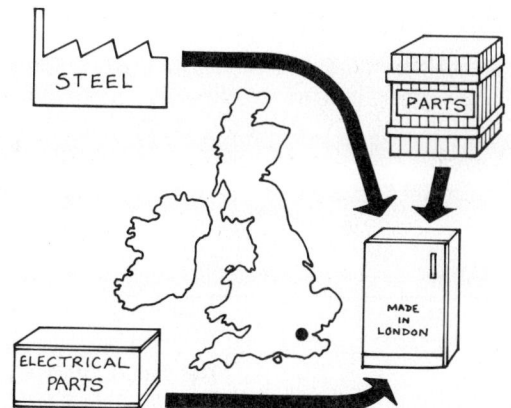

- **Labour supply**: firms needing a cheap supply of unskilled labour are often attracted to areas of high unemployment. Why do you think this is so?

  Firms needing skilled labour will often gather around an area where there is a concentration of higher education opportunities. Why do you think they do this?

91

Activity

Where to locate?

1 The following factors are essential for the location of an enterprise. Find an example for each factor: a market; raw materials; source of power; land; source of labour; transport facilities. Using the map find and match the letters **A–F** to each of the above factors.

2 Using the following information, work out whether steel works **G** or steel works **H** produces the cheapest tonne of steel by the time the steel has reached its market.

To make a tonne of steel you need to transport:

a 15 tonnes of coal from the Ivor coal mine; and

b 11 tonnes of iron ore from either Old Faithful or Bonanza mines to your steel works.

You must then transport the tonne of steel to its market in Steeltown where it is used by a range of industries.

You can only use existing forms of transport (the railway, canals, sea lanes, motorways).

Your transport charges are:

- £2 per tonne by railway for each square passed through or entered;
- £1 per tonne by ship for each square passed through or entered;
- £1 per tonne by motorway for each square passed through or entered.

3 Now calculate how much it would cost to manufacture a tonne of steel at steel works **J** and transport it to Steeltown.

4 Use your result to explain why, if materials reduce during the making of a product, it is sensible to locate your factory near a source of supply of these raw materials rather than near the market.

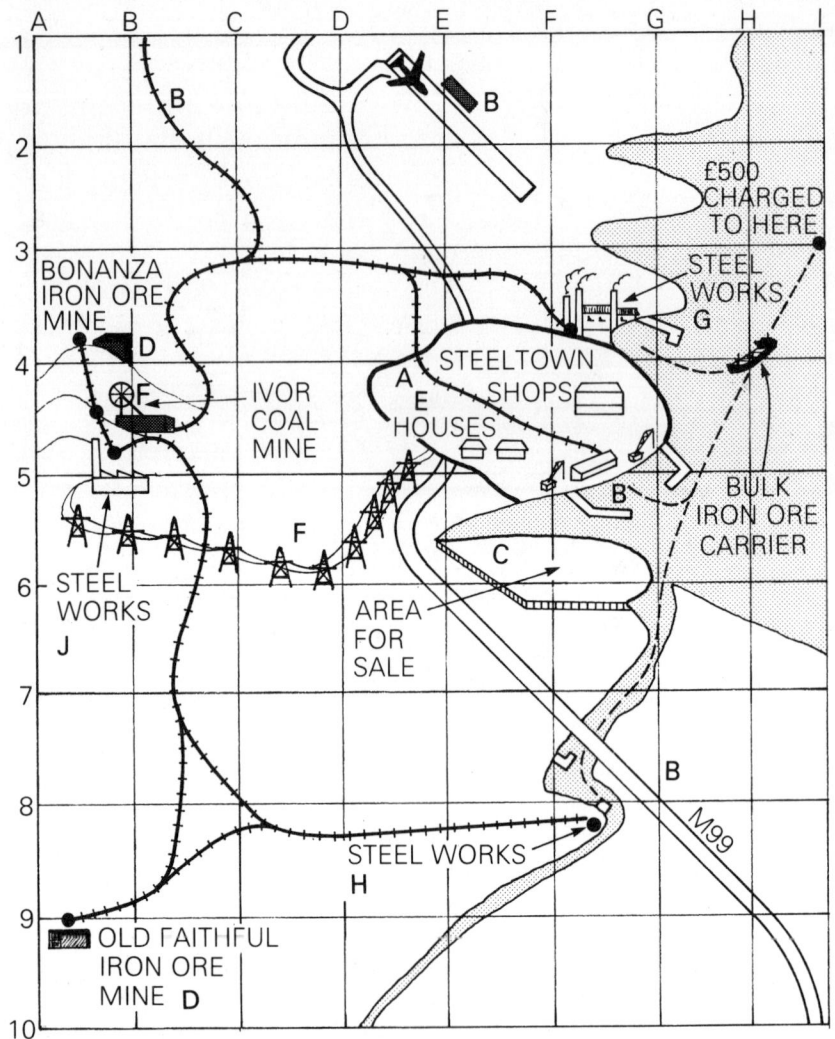

5 Explain why steel works **G** would be in a better position than steel works **H** or **J** if the iron ore mines were exhausted and iron ore had to be imported.

The Shallowford Boatyard

The owners of the boatyard where Mr Boyd works are considering moving to a new site. The founder of the firm chose Shallowford to locate his enterprise because the town had a supply of skilled workers and the Shallow Estuary provided an ideal place for launching and fitting out boats. However, another important factor was that the founder of the boatyard lived in Shallowford.

Many firms are located in a particular place because of the original entrepreneur's decisions. For example, the Pilkington family continue to make glass in St Helens where the firm was founded.

Acquired advantages

Once a firm has come to an area, other firms in the same line of business are often attracted to the area, too. These firms benefit from what we call *acquired advantages*. These are also referred to as *external economies of scale*. Can you think why? These acquired advantages include:

- **Education**: local colleges run courses that are suited to the manpower needs of local firms.
- **Disintegration**: this is a process that occurs within an industry once it is located in an area. Firms within the industry come to specialise in one particular part of the process. In the car industry, one firm will make the body and fit the engine; another will make the lights; yet another will supply the wheels. Each firm benefits from the specialisation that results.
- **Skilled labour**: firms can reduce their training costs if they are in an area where there has been a tradition of working with the skills they require. For example, pottery firms are gathered around Stoke-on-Trent.
- **Sharing information**: if similar firms are gathered together they can share information about common problems. They gain from the reputation the area acquires because of the concentration of an industry in that area. For example, Sheffield is thought of as a 'steel town'.

Footloose industries

For some firms it is not necessary to be located in any one place. The costs (particularly those of transport) are not greatly different wherever the firm is based.

These industries are called 'footloose industries' because small changes in the locational factors of an area could influence a firm's decision to move. Other firms continue to be based on a site even when the original reasons for being there have disappeared. For such firms the costs of moving and the loss of acquired advantages keep the firm on its original site even though there may be considerable cost in remaining. In London, for example, the problems of finding enough trained staff and the difficulties and expense of transport are examples of such costs. We say that 'industrial inertia' stops such firms from moving.

External diseconomies of scale

Industrial concentration in any one area can bring costs as well as benefits for a region. Pollution of the area is one such cost. In many mining areas, for example, the landscape has been ruined by the industrial waste left behind by the mining process.

ECONOMIC TERMS
Natural advantages: benefits that an area has that explain why firms are originally attracted to that region. **Acquired advantages**: these exist when an area has developed benefits from firms in a particular industry being concentrated there. **Localisation**: the increasing concentration of industry in one area.

A major problem occurs if the industry that has made an area famous then declines. This results in very high levels of unemployment in the area or region where the industry has come to be localised. When an area suffers costs on this scale as a result of industrial concentration it is experiencing external diseconomies of scale.

Government policies to aid depressed regions

Governments have tried to alleviate the problems that can result from an uneven distribution of industrial enterprises:

- In areas of high employment encouragement has been given to firms to relocate elsewhere.
- In some regions of high unemployment special areas called *assisted areas* have been established. Specific help is given to firms that move to these areas in order to reduce the high levels of unemployment. (See Extension 2.)

In the late 1980s the government reduced the level of such regional support and targetted the help they provide towards small firms. In specific areas where large firms have closed, special areas called *Enterprise Zones* have been set up and given a range of special privileges. (See Extension 2.)

Test yourself _____

1 The boatyard where Mr Boyd works wants to make much larger boats. Use this fact to explain why they wish to relocate the firm.
2 You are a car-making firm. The windscreen wipers are made in Dover. Explain why you choose to be based at Oxford instead.
3 Oil refineries are often located near estuaries. Why do you think this is so?
4 Explain why you would aim to have a steel plant located next to an iron ore mine.
5 What is industrial inertia?
6 Explain how *and* why a government can help an economically depressed region.

Up in the real world

TEESIDE'S last shipbuilding yard has become an offshore technology base. Hartlepool's south docks are to be a marina. The flattened site of what was Middlesbrough's Britannia steelworks is earmarked for a cinema, shops and business park. Stockton's derelict racecourse will be an £80m edge-of-town shopping and leisure centre. In short, Teeside Urban Development Corporation (UDC) is replacing the old world with the new.

Teeside, birthplace of the railway age, and flourishing into the early 1970s, has lost well over 25,000 jobs in its mainstays, chemicals and steel, since then. The area still has slimmed-down ICI plants on both sides of the river Tees, and British Steel at Redcar

and Lackenby south of it. But overall unemployment even now is around 18%, and in pockets of the huge council estates 30–60% of the men are jobless.

Quite simply, the area's traditional skills fell into a black hole.

Where are the new jobs to come from? Shipbuilding skills have been converted to building offshore oil modules; successfully, at present, but that is an up-and-down industry. The docks on the Tees and at Hartlepool make money – Teesport's container and ro-ro facilities serve the new Nissan plant – but employ only about 1,000. In a free-market world, Redcar's steel might have profited at the expense of Ravenscraig; but the Scots have more clout than Cleveland does.

Whitehall came to their help, designating enterprise zones at Hartlepool and Middlesbrough in 1981 and 1983. Rather than challenge Silicon Glen and the M4, local leaders aimed to build on existing skills; the heart of Middlesbrough's thriving enterprise zone is a CADCAM centre aiming to bring small metalworking firms into the computer age.

Yet a UDC arguably was still what the area needed; a single-minded, business-oriented body to pull things together. Chaired by the former boss of a Hartlepool building firm, it has the goodwill of local politicians.

They want development, money and jobs in the area now.

Source: *The Economist*, 6 February 1988

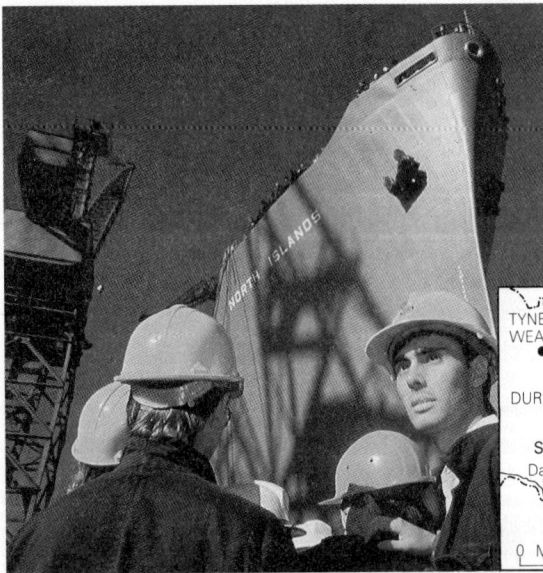

The last new ship leaves Teeside

1 Describe the sort of industries that used to exist in the Teeside area.

2 These industries have now declined. How has this decline affected the level of unemployment in the area?

3 What new jobs have been created in the area?

4 What help has come from local and central government?

5 Why do you think Scotland is more able to get help for its steel industry than Cleveland?

6 Why are the docks in the area able to make money but only employ a few people?

Extension 1

SURE FIRE HAIRDRYERS

You have developed a cordless hairdryer. It could be, according to your research, a market leader if production costs are kept *low*.

The question is: where should you site your production plant in order to keep costs low?

You have two final sites, London and Newcastle. Score each site for each factor on the table below. You can score from 1–6. The higher the number you give indicates the greater the profit you think will be gained from that factor for that site. You can add on bonus points as indicated.

LABOUR:
London:
Staff are available, but often move to other jobs. You could bring in workers from other areas, but would have to house them.

Newcastle:
Plenty of staff, as there are high levels of unemployment.

MARKET
London:
There are 10 million people as a market. If this is important you can award five bonus marks to this point.

Newcastle:
High unemployment. People don't have a lot of money to spend.

SITE:
You can only find a site on the edge of **London**. Take off 3 points from London's market prospects as your transport costs to the market will now rise.

Newcastle:
Plenty of sites for a factory.

GRANTS:
Government will give you £1 million if you go to **Newcastle**.

COMPONENTS/RAW MATERIALS
All the parts you need are made in the South East of England. (**London** gets 3 bonus points here.)

OTHER FACTORS:
Your elderly grandma lives in **London**.

FACTORS	LONDON	NEWCASTLE
Site		
Labour		
Transport of raw materials and components		
Transport to market and size of market		
Grants		
Other factors		

Total:

1 Which site did you choose (i.e. which site has the highest score)?
ANSWER: ....

2 Explain the advantages of the site you have chosen compared to the other site.

═══════════ **Extension 2** ═══════════

1 Using this map and an atlas to help, list the areas of the UK that have development area status.
2 Consider what economic problems these areas might have in common.
3 What kind of assistance is given by the government to such areas?

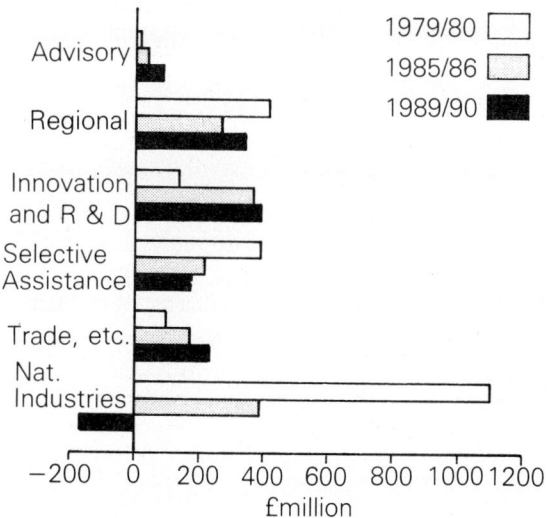

Changes in DTI's spending pattern between 1979/80 and 1989/90

Advisory
Regional
Innovation and R & D
Selective Assistance
Trade, etc.
Nat. Industries

1979/80 ☐
1985/86 ▨
1989/90 ■

−200 0 200 400 600 800 1000 1200
£million

The New Regional Aid Map   Source: *The Independent*, 13 January 1988

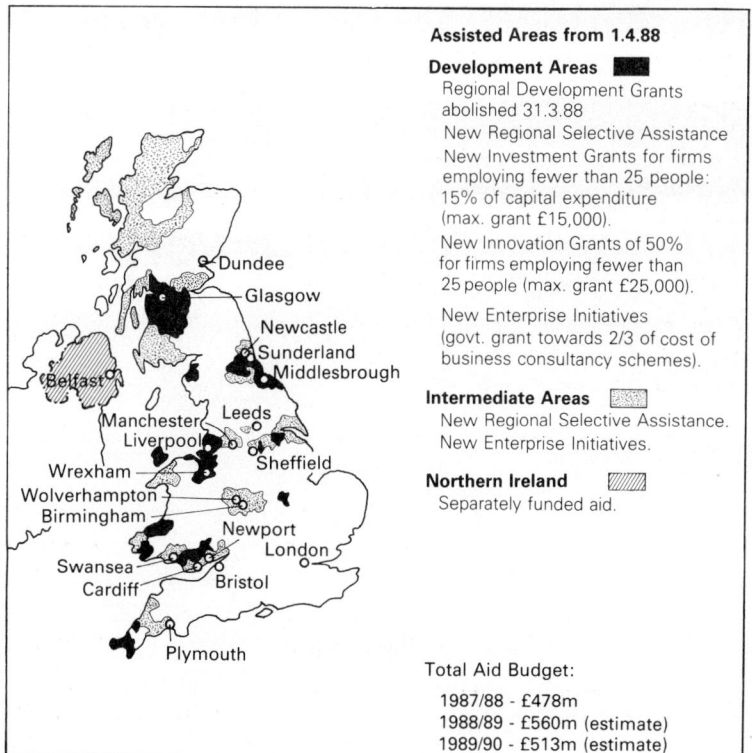

Assisted Areas from 1.4.88
Development Areas ■
Regional Development Grants abolished 31.3.88
New Regional Selective Assistance
New Investment Grants for firms employing fewer than 25 people: 15% of capital expenditure (max. grant £15,000).
New Innovation Grants of 50% for firms employing fewer than 25 people (max. grant £25,000).
New Enterprise Initiatives (govt. grant towards 2/3 of cost of business consultancy schemes).

Intermediate Areas ▨
New Regional Selective Assistance.
New Enterprise Initiatives.

Northern Ireland ▨
Separately funded aid.

Total Aid Budget:
1987/88 - £478m
1988/89 - £560m (estimate)
1989/90 - £513m (estimate)

Enterprise Zones

	Year designated	Percentage increase in employees from designation to December 1985	Rates revenue foregone 1984/85 (£ 000)	Public sector investment from designation to March 1985 (£ 000)		Investment in building from September 1984 to October 1985 (£ 000)
				Land acquisition	Infra-structure investment	
Great Britain		70[1]	19,950	25,417[1]	87,189[1]	143,796
North						
Hartlepool	1981/82	602	314	42	1,189	2,357
Middlesborough	1983/84	-48[2]	241	299	447	10,457
Tyneside	1981/82	-10	3,260	..	4,047[1]	1,821
Workington (Allerdale)	1983/84	253	127	106	2,353[1]	1,215
Yorkshire & Humberside						
Glanford	1983/84	1,851[3]	66	1,470	160	79
Scunthorpe	1983/84		261	418	1,000	17,771
Rotherham	1983/84	107	252	83	389	10,147
Wakefield	1981/82	42	532	369	726	6,515
East Midlands						
Corby	1981/82	..	1,688	–	5,910	..[3]
Wellingborough	1983/84	3,338	74	1,300	2,205	..[3]
South East						
Isle of Dogs	1981/82	321	2,430	14,400	22,680	7,214
NW Kent	1983/84	286	886	–	742[6]	..[3]
West Midlands						
Dudley	1981/82	24	1,545	225	1,134	4,976
Telford	1983/84		225	–	1,496	..[3]
North West						
NE Lancashire	1983/84	157	260	..	549	4,979
Salford/Trafford	1981/82	86	2,097	2,522	3,172	16,593
Speke	1981/82	24	1,484	–	1,693	..[3]
Wales						
Delyn	1983/84	39	367	1,958	2,336	2,579
Milford Haven Waterway	1983/84	..	259	627	725	365
Swansea	1981/82	64	1,239	1,175	5,950	3,293
Scotland						
Clydebank	1981/82	105	2,149	200	9,728	4,500[7]
Invergordon	1983/84	94	25	223	4,094	866[7]
Tayside	1983/84	83	171	–	14,464	10,328[7]
Northern Ireland						
Belfast	1981/82	-4[4]	936	851[5]	3,667[5]	8,000[8]
Londonderry	1983/84	12[4]	534	–	227[5]	424[8]

1 Incomplete data.
2 Employment at designation included a large temporary work force.
3 Data not shown separately for confidentiality reasons.
4 From designation to September 1985.
5 From designation to March 1986.
6 From designation to November 1985.
7 From September 1984 to September 1985.
8 From September 1985 to October 1986.

Source: *Regional Trends 22* (1987)

4 What other types of areas within the UK have been given help by government?

5 Select an Enterprise Zone (preferably one near where you live), and, using the information in the table, describe the forms of help and the sums of money given to businesses within the zone.

Coursework

Aim: To investigate why firms with clear disadvantages in their industrial location do not resite their operations.

Use the idea of industrial inertia in your work (see page 93).

1 Select a firm which might have problems, given its location, and describe the business it engages in.

2 Identify the natural advantages of location the firm might have originally enjoyed.

3 Consider the acquired advantages that have arisen for the firm.

4 Consider the natural advantages that might remain.

5 Examine the costs and benefits of moving for the firm.

6 Using all the information you have collected, explain why the firm continues to remain in its location.

17 Costs of Production

Every firm has two sets of costs. There are *fixed costs* (like rent, salaries and insurance charges) that have to be paid even if there is a temporary halt in production. These costs are sometimes called *overheads.* Then there are *variable costs* that vary or change (like buying raw materials or paying for electricity used). The total costs of production are a combination of a firm's fixed costs and variable costs.

The office cat. You have to feed it, so it's a fixed cost. But if there aren't any mice around you'll have to feed it more. So it's also a variable cost!

Activity

NUMBER OF PAINT & PASTE'S
CUSTOMERS EACH MONTH

April	200
May	300
June	0

COSTS OF POWER USED
PER CUSTOMER £1

MELCHESTER
BOROUGH BUSINESS RATE
DEMAND

April	£40
May	£40
June	£40

RENT BILL

April	£60
May	£60
June	£60

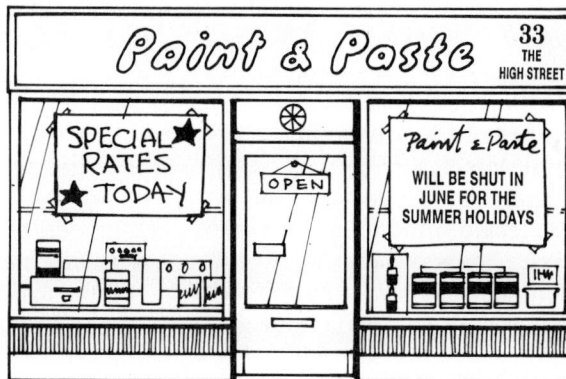

Paint & Paste
33 THE HIGH STREET

SPECIAL RATES TODAY

OPEN

Paint & Paste WILL BE SHUT IN JUNE FOR THE SUMMER HOLIDAYS

SALARIES
The two directors
of Paint & Paste
each receive £400
every month.

Costs of paint, wallpaper, paste
(and other raw materials)
£50 per customer.

INSURANCE
£20 every month.

£ — Total cost — Variable costs — Fixed costs

0   Output (number of clients)   **A**

1 **a** List the variable costs involved in running the Paint & Paste business.
 b Calculate the total variable costs for the month of May.
2 **a** List the fixed costs involved in operating.
 b Calculate the total fixed costs for the month of May.
3 What were Paint & Paste's total costs for the month of May?
4 Explain why Paint & Paste will still have bills to pay for the month of June, even though everyone in the firm is away.

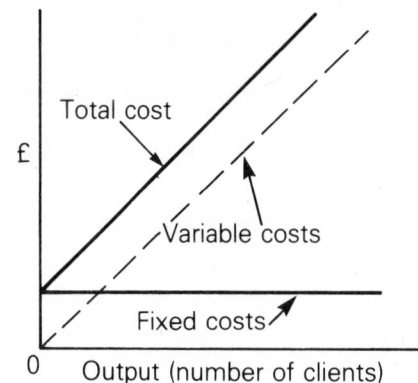

5 On a graph (like diagram **A**) show the fixed costs of the business for April.
6 Calculate the variable costs to be added if Paint & Paste have:
 a 20 customers;
 b 75 customers;
 c 100 customers during April.
Add this information to your graph.

Total costs

When we add the total fixed costs of a business to its total variable costs, we have the total costs of production. We can show this on a graph like this:

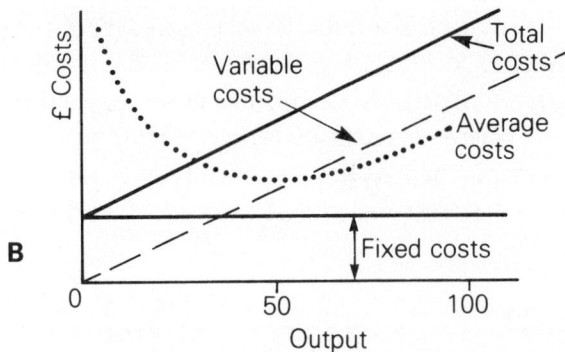

B

Average costs of production

When we divide the total costs of production by the total units produced, we get the average costs, that is the cost per unit of production. This can be shown on the graph, too.

Decide for yourself

Look closely at diagram **B**. As production increases, the average cost, to start with, will fall but in the long run it will begin to rise. Why do you think this is so?

If you can't think why, consider the fact that very large scale production involves the hiring of extra units of labour, the purchase of raw materials that others might want, and can result in an increase in inefficiency and problems resulting from managing a large enterprise.

Marginal costs

Economists call the cost of adding one more unit of output to the total number of units produced the *marginal cost*.

When marginal costs are less than average costs, then the average cost curve will fall and each unit of output will be produced at a lower cost. But if marginal costs are greater than the average cost, then the

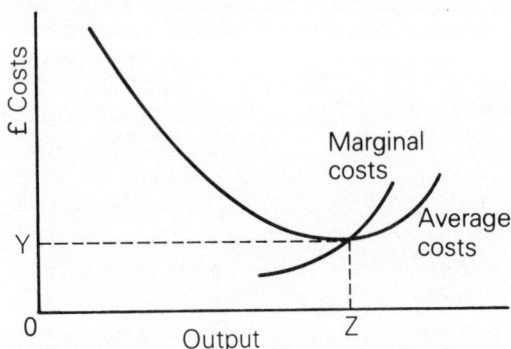

average cost curve will begin to rise. What does this show about the firm's economic position?

ECONOMIC TERMS

Fixed costs: costs that do not change when output changes.
Variable costs: costs that change when output changes.
Total costs: the cost of producing the output in question calculated by adding total fixed costs to total variable costs.
Average costs: this can be calculated by dividing total costs by the total number of units of output.
Marginal costs: the cost of producing an additional unit of output.

Test yourself

1 If you take fixed costs from total costs what are the costs that remain?
2 Give three examples of:
   a a variable cost;
   b a fixed cost.
3 List these items (costs involved in running a paper mill) under the headings Fixed Costs and Variable Costs:
   wages; wood pulp supplies; paper dye; salaries; rental of a paper cutting machine; power; rent paid for use of the site.
4 A firm making watches produces 1000 at a total cost of £10 000. The marginal cost of making a further watch is £9.
   a What is the total cost of making 1001 watches?
   b What is the average cost of making 1001 watches?
   c Explain why the firm should produce more than 1000 watches.

98

DATA RESPONSE

Compact disc puts vinyl in the shade

WHEN Philips and Sony launched the hi-fi compact disc in March 1983 they were taking a considerable gamble.

The digital and laser technology involved had taken many years and millions of pounds to develop.

To recoup the investment the new format had to make a strong challenge against the long playing vinyl record, which had reigned supreme for more than 30 years as the leading hi-fi medium.

The gamble seems to be paying off; the record companies agree that the days of the LP are numbered. Vinyl records could struggle on for five more years or 15 before becoming museum pieces.

This year the value of compact disc sales in Britain is likely to be higher than LP sales for the first time; in 1989 the number of discs sold will overtake the number of LPs.

Philips and Sony get a 2 per cent royalty for every player sold by rival manufacturers licensed to make CD equipment; most goes to the Dutch multinational.

While player costs have fallen sharply, the price of the discs has remained stubbornly high.

Record factories charge about 40p to press an LP, while the exworks price of a CD is roughly £1. A simple analysis suggests that in the shops the discs should cost about £2 more than a full price £6.99 LP; in fact they cost about £5 more.

Peter Scaping, business information manager at the record industry pressure group, British Phonographic Industry Ltd, says member firms have more generous profit margins for CDs than for LPs.

But he and most of the industry expect prices to fall in 1988 – perhaps to under £10 – because of a world-wide overcapacity of compact disc factories and a more competitive attitude.

There are already six CD factories in Britain which can make 60 million discs a year.

At first CDs were the preserve of classical music enthusiasts, who tended to be more well-off than rock and pop music listeners and more concerned with sound quality.

But high fidelity is no longer their strongest selling point. Convenience, the resistance to wear and tear and the desire to own the latest electronic status symbol are now as important.

Source: *The Independent*, 5 April 1988

HOW THE COST OF A FULL PRICE, £11.99 COMPACT DISC BREAKS DOWN

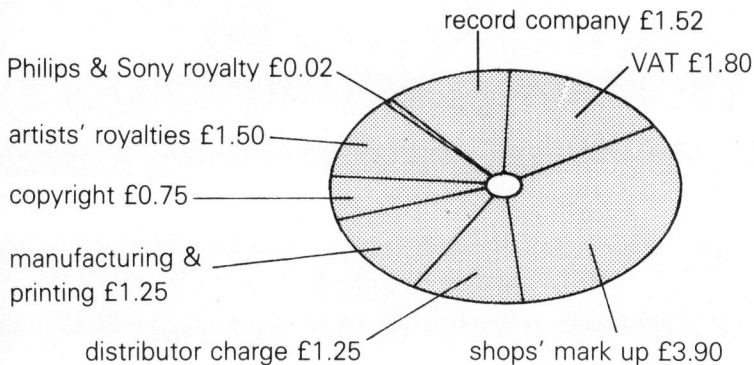

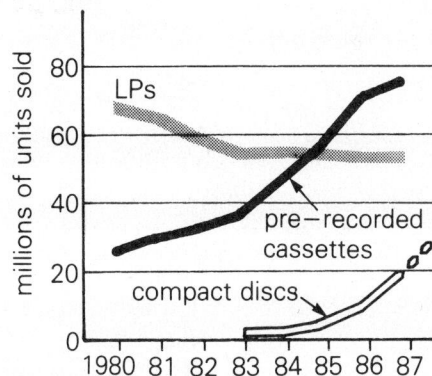

record company £1.52
VAT £1.80
Philips & Sony royalty £0.02
artists' royalties £1.50
copyright £0.75
manufacturing & printing £1.25
distributor charge £1.25
shops' mark up £3.90

millions of units sold
LPs
pre-recorded cassettes
compact discs
1980 81 82 83 84 85 86 87

1 What is the price of a compact disc in this example?

2 How much does it cost to:
a make the disc?
b market the disc?

3 Explain why the eventual price of compact discs in shops is higher than the cost of making the disc. Refer to some of the additional costs involved.

4 Why was the launch of the compact disc a 'gamble'?

5 Why, despite the high price involved, are people prepared to buy compact discs?

6 Explain why a consumer's interest in the product is of benefit to those involved in manufacturing compact discs.

Highway robbery of drivers' £630 a year

TRAFFIC jams cost every car owner in the capital at least £630 a year. A new report today is the first of its kind to put a figure on the waste of time and money caused by the hold-ups.

The British Road Federation report, called The Cost of Congestion, says traffic delays now cost Londoners £1.4 billion a year.

And the 2.3 million cars and 400,000 lorries registered in London, together waste an estimated 310 million hours stuck in stationary or slow-moving traffic.

The report found that congestion in Britain's main cities was now costing £3 billion a year in wasted petrol, vehicle wear and tear and loss of work time. And it warns that worse is to come.

Predictions

"The chronic traffic congestion now experienced on a daily basis on some of the major national roads, such as the M1, M6 and M25,

will become more widespread and last for longer periods unless the rate of investment is increased to meet traffic needs," it says.

Pressure

Traffic on major roads was growing three times faster than Government predictions while road construction was only two-thirds of what it should be, according to the last White Paper.

Analysing the figures, the roads pressure group Movement for London, to which the British Road Federation belongs, said the average vehicle in the capital spent 111 hours every year sitting in jams – or 18 minutes a day.

Movement for London chairman Ralph Cropper said: "The only realistic way to end chronic traffic delays in the capital is to plan and build a network of good-quality roads."

Source: *Evening Standard*, 20 June 1988

RAPID REMOVALS
Delivery in 24 hours or your money back

1 Imagine you own and operate a fleet of lorries engaged in the house removal business.
   a What stage of production is your business operating at?
   b List some of the major costs you will have in trying to keep your fleet of lorries on the road.
2 The report, 'The Cost of Congestion', argues that traffic delays cost a vehicle owner at least £630 a year.
   Explain why this is so, referring to the costs highlighted in the report.
3 Describe how these costs could affect your house removal business.
4 Your local council is prepared to solve the delays being caused to commuters by constructing a six lane motorway. In the process 150 houses will have to be destroyed.
   Form two groups, one as business leaders, the second as politicians in the local community representing unhappy home owners. Organise a debate on the proposal to build the motorway.
   The following points may help you and should be borne in mind if the motorway is built.

Assume there is a shortage of private houses for sale.

Business profits will increase.

Rates will have to rise.

Workers will be on time for work and not held up in traffic jams.

Traffic is growing faster than the road building programme.

Extension 2

RATES BILL

SALARIES
Paid monthly

VARIABLE COSTS
These are those costs that change as production/output changes

FIXED COSTS = THE ENTREPRENEUR'S CONTINUAL WORRY. THESE HAVE TO BE MET EVEN WHEN PRODUCTION HAS TEMPORARILY STOPPED

Maggie's Marge Factory

POWER COSTS

DEPRECIATION
A regular sum of money put aside because the entrepreneur's capital wears out

WAGES BILL
Paid each week

RAW MATERIALS

POLY WHAT'S ITS NAME

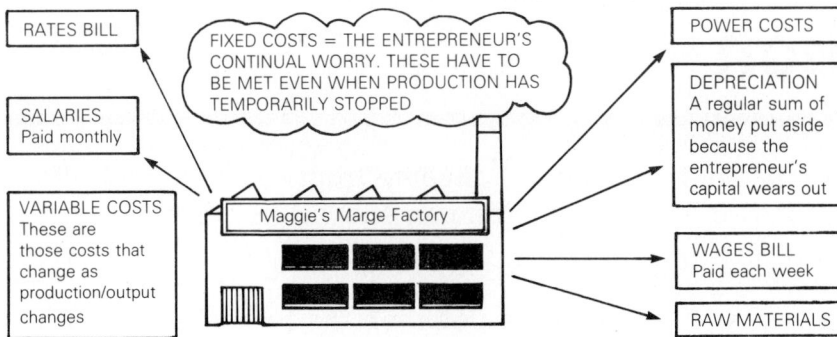

Ingredients:
Animal oils, vegetable oils, water, whey, salt, sugar, E471, E322, E160, Vitamins A and D.

1 Make a list of the fixed costs and a list of the variable costs involved in running Maggie's Marge Factory.

2 You own the margarine factory in question. Your workers strike for a fortnight. Explain what will happen to your variable costs during the month in question. What will happen to your fixed costs?

3 There is a surplus of vegetable oils, cement, and sugar available on the world market. How might these surpluses affect your variable costs?

4 You decide to increase the overtime rate you pay to your workers. What will happen to your variable costs if you then increase the number of hours worked over a weekend by them?

5 Fixed costs are sometimes called overheads. Can you think of a reason why?

6 At the beginning of the month no margarine has been produced for the month, yet total costs are £2000. When output for the month starts 1000 tubs an hour are produced during a 10 hour daily shift, for 5 days a week. Total costs at the end of the first week have increased to £5,000. Calculate the average cost of producing tubs of margarine during this first week.

7 In the following week production increases to a total weekly output of 60,000 tubs. Total costs for the fortnight stand at £7,600 by the end of the second week. What are the average costs now of producing a tub of margarine?

8 Explain what has happened to average cost as one moves from Week 1 to Week 2.

Coursework

Aim: To test the hypothesis that fixed costs are likely to be a higher proportion of total costs in a small business compared to a large scale enterprise.

Select two firms in the same line of business: one that you consider to be a large scale enterprise (e.g. in terms of output or number of production units); the other one that you consider to be a small scale enterprise. Examples might include comparing a supermarket and a corner grocery store, or a hairdresser in the nearest large high street to you with a hairdresser in your neighbourhood.

1 Devise a simple questionnaire in order to collect information from each business:
- name of firm; _____
- address; _____
- number of customers on average per week; _____
- examples of prices charged; _____
- fixed costs: salaries; rent/mortgage; others; _____
- variable costs: raw materials; power; wages. _____

2 Explain why you expect to find that the variable costs involved would be a smaller proportion of total costs in the smaller firm and why fixed costs might be a higher proportion.

3 After carrying out your survey, display your findings. Do they prove your hypothesis?

4 Collect more information for a range of small firms and for a range of large scale enterprises. (You could do this by comparing your findings with those of other students in your class.) Calculate the average fixed and average variable costs for each group.

What differences/similarities exist when comparing this information with your first survey?

5 Explain why results from a range of enterprises are likely to be a better test of the point you are trying to prove than results from a smaller number of firms.

18 Revenue, Profits and Competition

The total revenue from a firm is the income from the sale of all the goods and services they provide. You can show it like this:

Price of the product × the quantity sold

Profit is measured as the difference between the total revenue of a firm and its total costs.

Burglar Alarm Bells

Mick and Anita Bell run a business installing domestic burglar alarms. They charge each customer £200 for the installation of a complete system.

Decide for yourself

- How much would their total revenue be in a week if they installed 7 burglar alarm systems?

The Bells' average revenue is the revenue received for each unit sold. (It is really the same as the average price.)

Last week they had 15 customers; this week they had 8 customers. Next week they will have 20 systems to install. The average revenue per customer is the total revenue divided by the number of units sold.

Decide for yourself

- What will be the average revenue for this three week period?

Mick and Anita were particularly pleased with last month's trading figures. Their total costs came to £15,000. They fitted 100 burglar alarms.

- How much profit did they make?

What happens to profits?

To stay in such a healthy trading position Mick and Anita have to compete with other firms that install burglar alarms. For this reason they are constantly putting some of the company's profits back into their company. In this way they are able to re-equip their business. They can buy a new van, develop better alarm systems, and increase their advertising, for example. This money is called the *retained profit* of the firm.

Some of their profit is paid as a dividend to those who own shares in their company. A *dividend* is the income shareholders receive in return for owning shares in the business and, therefore, risking the possible loss of their wealth.

The government also receives part of the Bells' profits in the form of taxes.

Competition

Firms compete in many ways. The Bells work long hours. They make use of advertising and offer free gifts and other inducements in order to win contracts.

For large contracts firms often have to put in tenders. To win the contract they will sometimes offer to do the work at a special discount price or within a special time limit.

Firms compete with each other in particular through *product differentiation*. This simply means making a product unique in the customer's eyes. This can be done by:

- **Branding**: that is giving the product a name. Sometimes the branding becomes so successful that people confuse the product and the brand name. Do you say Hoover or vacuum cleaner? Do you say Biro or ballpoint pen? Can you think of other examples of successful branding?
- **Sales promotion**: this can be attractive packaging and display of the product, or it can be offering a special service, like delivering the goods to the customer's home.
- **Advertising**: the product can be advertised on television, in newspapers, on posters or by delivering handbills in a locality.
- **Inducements**: these can be free gifts, competitions and special offers like a price discount during a certain month.

- **Price cutting**: firms often offer certain of their products as *loss leaders* (goods sold at a reduced price) in order to attract customers to their business and therefore increase their revenue.

They may arrange frequent sales or discounts from the price of their goods. These are all techniques designed to keep the consumer interested in their product. Sometimes firms get involved in price wars in order to defeat their rivals.

Activity

1 You are planning to go on holiday and will be travelling from Liverpool to Paris to visit old friends.

You can travel by car or train using a cross-channel ferry, by car or train using the Channel Tunnel or by plane. Select one way of travelling and give reasons for your choice.

You can travel to Paris by plane, ferry, car or train.

2 Consider:
 a the opportunity cost of your decision;
 b the effects your decision will have on the profits of the different firms that could transport you across the Channel.

3 Imagine you own a ferry company. Explain how the following events could effect your profits by either increasing your costs or reducing your revenue:
 a delays to crossing caused by an increased amount of shipping in the Channel;
 b a dispute with your workers about a new productivity deal leading to a strike/work to rule;
 c an increase in holiday prices in most Mediterranean countries;
 d an increase in the price of oil;
 e a closure of the newly opened Channel Tunnel because of emergency engineering works.

4 Each picture shows a different way of crossing from Britain to France. Using these different possibilities, explain why it would be difficult for you as a ferry operator to increase your profits by raising the prices you charge. Present your answer in the form of a speech to your shareholders.

5 Explain how the opening of the Channel Tunnel affected your business. How did you combat this threat to your business?

Perfect Competition

In a perfect situation:
- there are lots of firms;

- they each produce an identical (homogeneous) product;

- all the firms have perfect knowledge of the market;

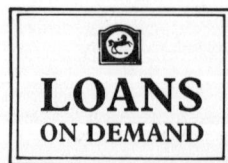

- new firms can enter the market place with ease.

Decide for yourself
- Why do you think there is seldom a situation in which perfect competition exists?

Competition and the consumer

When firms are competing with each other, the consumer can benefit in various ways:
- less efficient firms go out of business because no one wants their over-priced or poor quality goods;
- efficient firms can increase their share of the market and are able to expand the future production of items at prices consumers can afford. They gain economies of scale and these savings may lead to further reduced prices for customers.

If a business becomes very profitable, new firms are attracted into the industry. This serves to keep prices low and profits at a reasonable level.

ECONOMIC TERMS

Total revenue: the income received from the sale of all goods and services.

Profits: what you have left if you take total costs from total revenue.

Losses: what you owe people when your total costs are greater than your total revenue.

Average revenue: the average price received from the sale of each unit of a good or service.

Competition: when you are battling with another firm (or firms) to gain or retain the customer's loyalty.

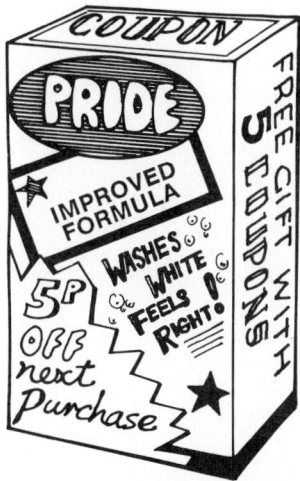

Test yourself _____

1 Bob sells Carol five bottles of wine priced at £7, £9, £13, £5 and £6 respectively.
   a What is the average revenue per bottle that Bob receives?
   b What is the total revenue received by Bob?
2 a If the total cost involved for Bob was £20, how much profit has he made?
   b What loss would he have made if the total cost was £60?
3 Suggest two different things firms can do with their profits.

4 You sell bread in your small supermarket, but so does the bakery along the street.
   a What does competition mean?
   b Are you in competition with them?
   c How can you compete with the bakery?
5 How might buyers of loaves benefit from your competition?
6 What forms of product differentiation are being used on the packet of washing powder?

DATA RESPONSE 1

Bar Wars erupt over Rowntree

By JOHN HAMSHIRE and RICHARD CASEBY

CHOCOLATE makers were preparing last night to do battle for control of Rowntree. At stake is domination of the vast European sweets market.

The British firm rejected a £2.1 billion bid from Nestlé of Switzerland. But three other companies were thought to be ready to launch their own assault on the makers of Britain's best-loved bar, the KitKat.

Bar Wars, as City pundits are calling the battle, will be resolved before the ending of EEC trade restrictions in 1992 blows the European confectionery market wide open.

Sweet firms are the latest to ditch the 'small is beautiful' concept in favour of 'biggest is best' – if only because market muscle increases their chances of survival.

An estimated 40 KitKats are eaten in Britain every second and the snack itself is sold in 100 countries.

THE BIG PRIZE IS EUROPE, CHOCK-FULL OF PROFITS

Yet despite this and other famous products, like Fruit Gums, Black Magic chocolates, Polo mints and Yorkie bars, Rowntree commands just 8 per cent of the European market.

The York-based company's chairman Kenneth Dixon promptly denounced yesterday's bid from Nestlé as 'unwelcome.'

He claimed it did not reflect the value of Rowntree's 'unique collection of brands' and said his board believed the business could best be developed as an independent group.

But within minutes of Nestlé unwrapping its 890p a share offer, speculators began pouring their cash into Rowntree in anticipation of a takeover battle. Shares rose 176p from 752p to close at 928p.

Safeguard

The other companies tipped to enter the fray are Nestlé's Swiss rivals Jacobs Suchard and U.S. giants Hershey and RJR-Nabisco.

Suchard already owns nearly 15 per cent of Rowntree. Hershey could be drawn in in an attempt to safeguard its worldwide markets against an enlarged competitor.

Ironically, it was Rowntree which began European hostilities 20 years ago when it started manufacturing KitKat in Hamburg, After Eight mints in Dijon and Lion bars in Paris.

Rowntree expanded abroad during the inter-war years, at the same time launching Aero, Smarties and all-conquering KitKat bars.

In 1969 Rowntree turned down a takeover bid by the American giant General Foods, then merged later that year with the British company Mackintosh.

Last year the group made a trading profit of £130 million on a turnover of £1,427 million.

Source: *Daily Mail*, 27 April 1988

'Last year we spent over £3,000m on confectionery'

The battle of the chocolate bars has broken out in Britain and it would appear that only Trade Secretary Lord Young has the power to stop Kit Kat, Smarties and Black Magic falling into foreign hands.

Two Swiss chocolate giants – Nestlé and Jacobs Suchard – are slugging it out for control of Britain's number two confectionery group, Rowntree.

They are greedy for Rowntree's hugely successful portfolio of brand names, including the world's favourite snack bar, Kit Kat.

Nestlé is ready to pay more than £2,100 million to get its hands on the York-based sweets company. And Rowntree has very little armour to defend itself.

Awareness

Yet the company, under the stewardship of Ken Dixon, should be sitting pretty. Britain has the sweetest tooth in Europe.

continued on next page

Last year we spent almost £3,100 million on chocolate and sweets and Rowntree lays claim to roughly one-quarter of that.

And confectionery sales are rising again, despite our growing health awareness, after a two-year trough. Last year Britons ate 741,000 tonnes of sweets – almost nine ounces a week each.

Lord Young and Nestle have their eyes fixed on 1992, when many of the barriers to free trade within Europe will be removed. Companies will have much greater freedom to expand, sell products and take over other firms in Continental countries.

Before that date, many big groups are trying to swallow their competitors in other countries to position themselves for the Common Market's "big bang" in trade.

Cadbury would cost well over £3,000 million, but the giant confectionery and food companies around the world seem ready to spend almost any sums to net top quality brand names.

They are particularly keen on Britain's companies, which spend enormous sums each year on promotion and development to build up their products.

Some, like Wispa, are considered to have such potential that Cadbury spent £6 million on its launch.

Last year sales of Rowntree's Black Magic and Yorkie bars grew by 3½ per cent, whereas the overall chocolate market grew only 2 per cent.

The hard-nosed men in the City did not understand what Rowntree has always known – that children weaned on Kit-Kat and Rolo will continue to eat them well into their dotage.

That is why UK chocolate companies spend a phenomenal £100 million a year on advertising.

Source: *Daily Express*, 28 April 1988

1 Which Swiss companies were competing to gain control of Rowntree?

2 What famous brand names were the Swiss firms seeking to gain control of?

3 Describe how Rowntree's business has grown and developed. What share did Rowntree have of the British and European chocolate and sweets market in 1987?

4 Why might a Swiss firm want to gain control of a British company before 1992? (If you have problems answering this question see the maps in the activity in Unit 40.)

5 What other advantages are there for a company in buying a share of the British chocolate market?

DATA RESPONSE 2

THE UNILEVER GROUP

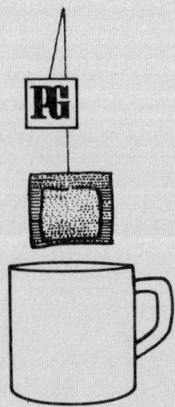

Year ended 31st December	1984	1985
Results		
	£ million	
Turnover	16 172	16 693
Operating profit	930	949
Profit on ordinary activities before taxation	925	953
Profit on ordinary activities after taxation	537	556
Profit on ordinary activities attributable to shareholders	503	516
Extraordinary items	(26)	–
Ordinary dividends	(165)	(179)
Profit of the year retained	308	333

Our European tea businesses continued to make excellent progress both in terms of market share and profits. The *Lipton* brand was strongly marketed, and flavoured teas and herbal infusions contributed to the gain in share. In the United Kingdom Brooke Bond has also improved its position and the successful test launch of *PG Tags* was the most significant recent development in the United Kingdom tea market. Lipton Export had another successful year and Fralib in France also did well. In the United States Lipton gained market share and again improved dollar profits despite the lower growth of the tea market. In other territories performance was generally good and in some countries our tea interests were strengthened by the incorporation of the local Brooke Bond business.

Our *Cup-a-Soup* instant soup continued to grow and was market leader in most countries where it is sold.

The Unilever Group is an example of a multinational firm. Multinationals are companies that usually have their head office in a developed country but operate in several other countries as well. Unilever is a joint British and Netherlands company.

1 List two other countries that Unilever operates in.

2 The turnover of a business is its total revenue during a given period of time. What was Unilever's total revenue in 1984?

3 By what percentage did Unilever's total revenue increase between 1984 and 1985?

4 Give some possible reasons for the changes in revenue that took place between these dates.

5 Profit is the difference between total costs and total revenue (turnover). Calculate the total costs of Unilever's business for 1985 if the level of profit was £949 million.

6 Profit is the return or income entrepreneurs receive for risking their money or capital in a business enterprise. Give reasons why only a portion of profits were distributed to the shareholders.

Extension

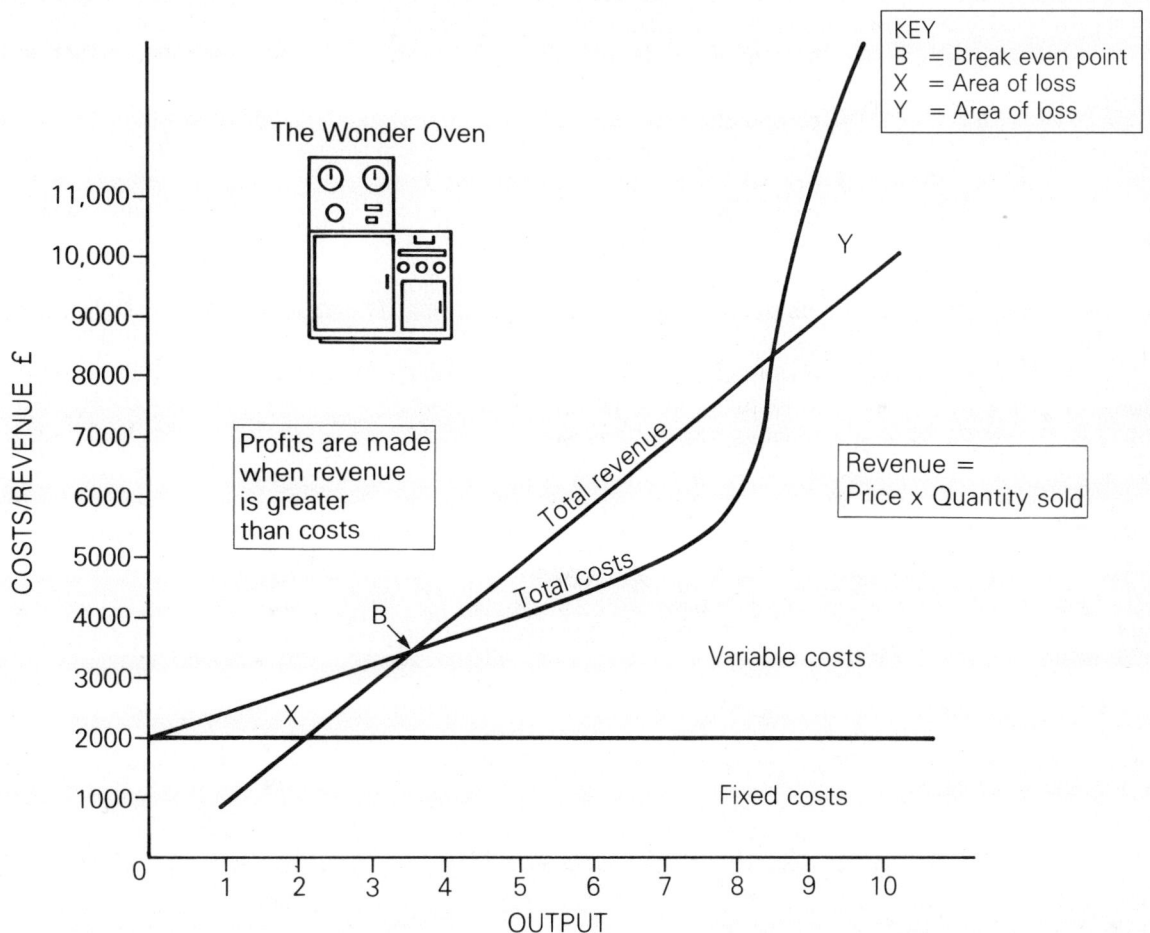

The Wonder Oven

KEY
B = Break even point
X = Area of loss
Y = Area of loss

Profits are made when revenue is greater than costs

Total revenue

Total costs

Revenue = Price x Quantity sold

Variable costs

Fixed costs

COSTS/REVENUE £

OUTPUT

1 What is the price at which the Wonder Oven is being placed on the market?
2 What is the total revenue the firm receives if it sells 7 ovens a week?
3 What is the fixed cost of making a Wonder Oven? Explain whether or not these fixed costs change if:
a 3 ovens are produced;

b 8 ovens are produced; giving a reason for your answer.
4 What type of cost has to be added to fixed costs in order to obtain the total costs of producing a Wonder Oven? If 5 ovens are produced how much of this cost would be involved?

107

5 Look closely at the diagram. Explain what happens to costs and revenue at Break even point, **B**.

6 Identify a level of output where if the firm produced goods it would:
   a make a loss;
   b make a profit.

Coursework

Select one or other of these subjects.

Aim: To investigate competition.

1 Choose a local supermarket. Interview a member of the management, asking them to identify the firms they consider to be their major competitors in the local area.

2 Examine a selection of these competitors and seek to identify the factors that might account for their ability to compete. These factors might include:
   a price of goods retailed;
   b size of business/number of branches;
   c reputation for service;
   d location of the business.

3 Consider the extent to which the firm/supermarket you originally selected has responded to meet this competition from its rivals. For example, what has it done about: opening times; prices; free gifts and other inducements?

4 Is your chosen firm likely to be successful in warding off its competitors? Give reasons for your answer.

Aim: To investigate profits.

1 Collect reports from the financial sections of newspapers which give details of the performance of a range of companies.

2 Classify your information into two groups:
   a information about firms making losses;
   b information about firms making profits.

3 Analyse the reasons given for the loss-makers (strikes, bad weather, poor management, high interest rates, competition from rivals, perhaps). Present your information in the form of a table or bar chart.

4 Now undertake a similar analysis, but this time concentrate on the profit-making firms and the reasons given for their success (good management, excellent labour relations, good export performance, a high level of consumer demand, etc.).

5 Select a loss-making firm. Write an imaginary letter to the directors of the firm suggesting how their revenue could be increased and their costs reduced to bring the firm back into a profit-making situation.

19 Integration

One way a firm can grow is by *amalgamating* (or joining up with another firm). This process is called *integration*. If both firms agree to join together we call it a *merger*. For example, Cadbury-Schweppes is a famous company formed as the result of a merger. If one company buys up at least 50% of another company's shares, then this integration is called a *takeover*. Sometimes the target firm may resist the takeover bid.

Decide for yourself
- Try to collect evidence of recent takeover bids.
- How do the target firms try to resist being taken over?

The direction of integration

Firms can integrate with other firms in various ways. We call this the *direction of integration.* The direction frequently gives a firm particular advantages.

If the integration is with another firm producing a similar range of goods and services (that is, it takes place at the same stage of production) then the process is described as *horizontal.* For example, if two farmers merge their farms, this is horizontal integration.

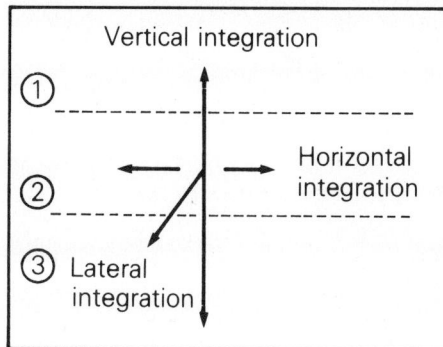

Forms of integration

If the integration is with a firm at an earlier stage in the same production process, or at a later stage in this chain of production, then the process is described as *vertical integration.* For example, a brewery buying either a hop farm or a chain of pubs would be vertical integration. There are two types of vertical integration:
- *Backwards vertical integration*: amalgamation with a firm that you buy products from.
- *Forwards vertical integration*: amalgamation with a firm you are supplying your products to.

How should Choffee integrate?
The Choffee Company's expansion programme has produced a strong and powerful firm. The company now plan to expand further because they want to become the largest company in the chocolate market, and increase the firm's amount of profits.

Choffee are planning to merge with a firm that makes toffees and chocolates. Mr Choffo, the managing director, argues that this is a good plan:

"We'll be a bigger firm with a larger share of the market and more control over our future. We'll be able to gain internal economies of scale. We can cut down on the numbers of office staff and slim down the sales and delivery services. We could reduce our prices and, if we did that, we might get an even larger market share."

Mr Choffo warmed to his argument:

"We can sell off some of the spare warehousing we'd be left with. We'd be able to rationalise our production. That should reduce our costs too. We'll become very competitive, particularly against foreign firms trying to enter our home market. Once our competitors have disappeared, we'll be abe to make even more profits."

Sarah Choffo, the youngest director, has different ideas:

"If we're going to integrate," she says, "I think it should be with a sugar company. We'll have a guaranteed supply of raw materials. Alternatively I'd like to see us integrate forwards vertically. I want to set up a chain of Choffee Chocolate Shops, one in every high street. Then we'll be able to sell our products direct to the consumer. That way we'd eliminate many of our sales and marketing costs."

Activity

INTEGRATION:

A

(RAW MATERIALS)

VERTICAL – BACKWARDS

HORIZONTAL

HORIZONTAL

(LATERAL MOVING INTO ANOTHER INDUSTRY)

J TYPE CAR WORKS

ABC CAR FACTORY

POP CORN MAKER

VERTICAL – FORWARDS

LATERAL DIVERSIFICATION (MOVING INTO ANOTHER INDUSTRY)

CAR SHOWROOMS (RETAIL OUTLET)

RESTAURANT CHAIN

FLYING SCHOOL

LATERAL (INTO ANOTHER INDUSTRY)

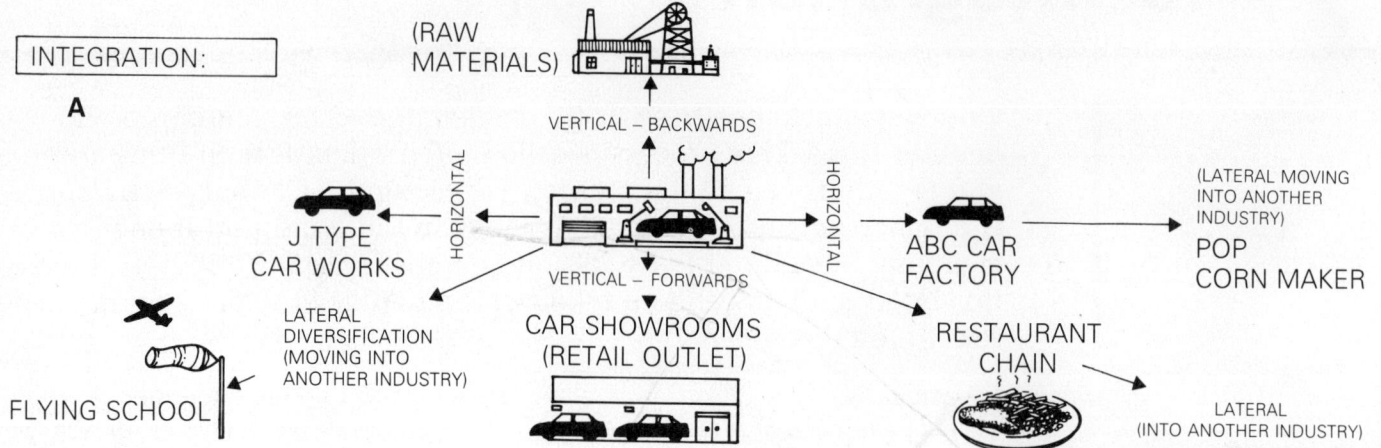

STAGES OF PRODUCTION	BREAD		CARS			SCHOOLS		OIL
PRIMARY (Extraction) 1	Kent Farms Ltd	Sugar Plantations Company	ABC Coal Mines	Iron ore mine				BP oil wells
SECONDARY (Manufac-turing.) 2	Islington Flour Mills PLC		Austin	Morris	Leyland			BP refineries
TERTIARY (Services and selling) 3	June's Cakes	Tasty Pastry	London car sales			Eton	Harrow	BP petrol stations

Table 1   A range of firms in a variety of industries

KEY: Arrow shows direction of integration

1 Look at diagram **A** and then examine table 1, and using the table answer the following questions. Find:
   a three examples of horizontal integration;
   b one example of forward vertical integration;
   c a firm completely integrated in the vertical direction;
   d a firm diversifying;
   e and two examples of backward vertical integration.

2 Sort out the examples below into appropriate columns in table 2.
   a a brewery takes over a chain of pubs.
   b A shoe maker merges with another shoe maker.
   c A weighing machine maker buys out a moulding maker.

Diversified firms	Backward vertically integrated firms	Forward vertically integrated firms	Horizontally integrated firms

Table 2

   d A chemist buys a newspaper shop.
   e A football club buys a ticket agency.
   f Tesco purchases Safeway food shops.
   g An oil firm buys up a crisps firm (oil here meaning petrol).

June Choffo, joint managing director, has yet another scheme. She favours what is called *lateral integration*. This would involve expanding the firm into an unrelated industry. She thinks Choffee should buy up a word processing firm:

"After all it's a growing area of business. We can't rely on selling chocolates for ever. We need to diversify (spread our risks). Then we won't have all our eggs in one basket. If the demand for chocolate declines, we have another source of income to rely on."

Decide for yourself
● Given that Choffee could afford any of these alternatives, what do you think Choffee should do?

Test yourself
1 A market garden buys a chain of greengrocers. What sort of integration is involved?
2 A sweet shop is taken over by another sweet shop. What form of integration is involved?
3 Explain what advantages there are to a firm that has diversified by integrating laterally.
4 What benefits does a firm gain from integrating:
   a horizontally
   b vertically?
5 What is the difference between a merger and a takeover? In what ways are they similar?

ECONOMIC TERMS

Integration or amalgamation: the joining together of two firms.
Merger: a merger occurs when two or more firms agree to join together.
Takeover: an amalgamation that takes place when one firm buys a controlling interest in another firm.
Horizontal integration: the amalgamation of firms producing similar goods or services and operating at the same stage of production.
Vertical integration: the amalgamation of firms operating in the same line of business but at different stages of the business. Integration can be either *backwards* (towards the raw material) or *forwards* (towards the market).
Lateral or conglomerate integration: the joining together of firms in unrelated areas of production.
Diversification: the process of trying to reduce risks by operating in several rather than one area of the economy.

DATA RESPONSE 1

180 mph car plan after Ford buys Aston Martin

By John Langley, Motoring Correspondent

FORD HAS BOUGHT Aston Martin Lagonda, the British sports car maker known world-wide as the producer of the James Bond car. The deal was announced last night at the Frankfurt Motor Show but the price was not disclosed.

Aston Martin Lagonda, based at Newport Pagnell, will now go ahead with production of a new 180 mph supercar next autumn. A smaller, cheaper model costing around £45,000 will follow within five years.

Ford is planning to turn Aston Martin into a British Ferrari, to compete with the Italian firm owned by Fiat, its European arch rival.

In the motor industry, the deal is also seen as a tit-for-tat move against General Motors, which surprised Ford 18 months ago by buying the British Lotus sports car group for £22.7 million.

All the major Western car makers are also aware of the growing threat from Japanese manufacturers, who are planning to move into the more luxurious car sector.

Mr Kenneth Whipple, Ford of Europe chairman, said the deal would enable Aston Martin to expand its production and pursue its own product programme. It would also give Ford an opportunity to enter a market where Aston Martin had earned an outstanding reputation.

"They are long on automotive know-how and engineering expertise. We will certainly gain from their experience and they will gain from our support," he added. Mr Victor Gauntlett will remain Aston's chief executive.

Aston Martin produces five cars, including one Lagonda, a week, ranging in price from the basic V8 saloon at £65,000 to the £145,000 volante Zagato-bodied open model.

The price Ford paid is likely to have been considerably more than the £833,500 paid by Automotive Investments, the American firm which bought it

continued on next page

111

from the British company C.H. Industrials three years ago.

Aston's forthcoming smaller car "will be aimed at the top end of the Porsche market," Mr Mike Haysey, marketing director, said last night. The company had been profitable for the past three years – "probably for the first time in 60 years."

Aston Martin has had a variety of owners in a financially chequered existence. It was rescued from bankruptcy in 1974.

Source: *Daily Telegraph*, 8 September 1987

1 What motor company did Ford buy?

2 What form of integration was involved?

3 What plans does Ford have for the company?

4 Why will the merger improve the Ford company's chances of competing?

5 What advantages does the deal offer the companies involved?

Extension 1

Imagine that you are in charge of the new company described in the above Data Response exercise. Describe what new firms you would seek to acquire, to make certain your plans for a new sports car were successful. Give your reasons.

DATA RESPONSE 2

A

RHM will resist £1.7 bn bid from Australia

Rosemary Collins

The Australians launched their bid for a big slice of the European food industry yesterday with a long-awaited offer for Ranks Hovis McDougall, makers of Mother's Pride, Mr Kipling cakes, Bisto gravy mix and Paxo stuffing.

The ... bid from Goodman Fielder Wattie values RHM at £1.7 billion or 465p a share and it will be fiercely contested by the UK group ...

"This bid is resistible and will be resisted," said Stanley Metcalfe, RHM managing director.

Mr Goodman wants to buy RHM because he has a vision of global food brands manufactured and marketed by the global food company he hopes GFW will become.

He does not regard Mother's Pride or Bisto or any other RHM products as potential world brands. "We are looking for process economies and a manufacturing base in Europe," said GFW managing director, Mr Duncan McDonald.

At RHM's Windsor headquarters they said Mr Kipling cakes were popular in France, and 5 per cent of last year's £1.5 billion turnover came from European sales.

Ranks' shares rose 9p to 477p after the announcement. Goodman already has a 29.4 per cent stake, built up over two years, and no other shareholder owns more than 2 per cent of the equity. RHM believes it has many small, private shareholders to whom it intends to appeal on the grounds of loyalty and gratitude for at least two years of generous dividends.

Goodman Fielder Wattie is Australia's biggest food group, the creation of Pat Goodman, a New Zealander and fifth-generation baker who, with his brother, inherited a rundown family bakery and now controls a group whose output includes flour, cooking oil, cakes and branded groceries, gelatine and meat – a range similar to that of his takeover target, RHM.

None of GFW's principal brands are marketed in Britain. In Australia best-sellers include Meadow Lea margarine, the White Wings range of flour, cake mixes and snacks, and Steggles' chickens.

Source: *Guardian*, 21 July 1988

P&O takes a berth at Woodrow

by Michael Foster

TAYLOR Woodrow shares leapt 43p to 481p today, following news that Sir Jeffrey Sterling's P&O shipping conglomerate has bought a 6% share stake.

Anyone hoping for a hostile bid will be severely disappointed. Both Sir Jeffrey and Woodrow chairman Sir Frank Gibb made it clear today that relations are friendly and joint ventures with a focus on Europe and the US are being explored.

Hostile bids just aren't Sir Jeffrey's style. But his negotiating skills mean that a long-term agreed merger between the two companies cannot be ruled out. Both sides are strong in construction and property, even though P&O's shipping interests tend to hit the headlines.

Confidence

Sir Jeffrey said today: "We have an excellent relationship with Sir Frank Gibb and with Taylor Woodrow." To the sound of mutual backslapping Sir Frank said: "We see this as an expression of confidence in Taylor Woodrow and its growth potential."

Source: *Evening Standard*, 20 July 1988

1 Using Sources **A**, **B** and **C** answer the following.
  a Which of the sources describes a merger? What evidence in the extract supports your choice?
  b Which of the sources describes a takeover bid? What evidence in the extract supports your choice?

2 What type of integration would take place in each of these cases?

3 Explain why Mr Goodman wants to buy RHM.

4 Why might the integration of P&O and Taylor Woodrow be of value to both companies?

5 What further percentage of RHM would Goodman's firm have needed to seize if it was to gain control of RHM?

Extension 2

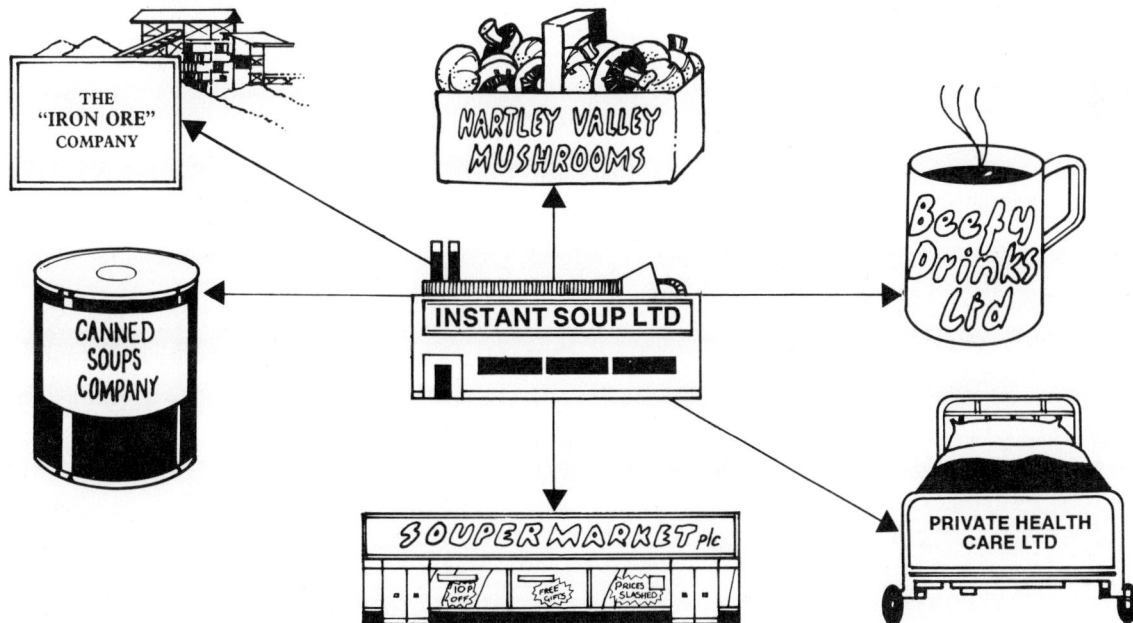

1 If Instant Soups merges with Beefy Drinks or Canned Soups, what form of integration will be involved?

2 What type of integration would take place if Instant Soup:
  a merged with Private Health Care Ltd?
  b merged with Soupermarkets plc?

3 What example of backward vertical integration is given in the diagram? What advantages would such integration bring to Instant Soups?

4 In your view would a merger between the Iron Ore Company and Instant Soups be of great economic value to the companies involved? Give reasons for your answer.

5 Explain how the economic value of the merger of Iron Ore Company and Instant Soups would change if Instant Soups acquired Canned Soups.

6 You have been appointed managing director of Instant Soups Ltd. You have £1 million to invest. You can either develop a new line of packet soups or acquire one of the firms listed above (each is priced at £1 million).

  a What is the opportunity cost if you decide to purchase Beefy Drinks Ltd?

  b Select a firm to purchase, giving reasons for your choice.

Coursework

Aim: To investigate two mergers.

Select two examples from newspaper accounts of proposed mergers. Gather further information about the firms involved.

1 Compare the mergers and describe the direction of integration involved in each.

2 Consider the advantages and disadvantages to each of the proposed mergers.

3 Which would you support? Give detailed reasons for your answer.

20 Economies of Scale

Large firms are often in a better position to compete with other firms because of the *internal economies of scale* that they enjoy. Economies of scale are the benefits to be had when the size of a business's operation is increased. Economies of scale are internal if the expanded production is brought about by changes within the firm. *External economies of scale*, on the other hand, are the benefits to be gained from an increase in the number of related firms that come to be located in the immediate area.

If you had a bigger car, Mum, you wouldn't need to take three trips to get us all to school.

Activity

Curls

Perms only £7 Style by Loriessar

So I says to Bert, it's only £7 – I deserve a treat.

I only came here for peace and quiet.

Kate Mann and Marc Edwards own Curls hairdressing salon. They are open for business six days a week. The current price they charge for a perm is £7. They have an average of 90 customers a day.

The variable costs per customer are as follows:

Power (use of electricity)	£1
Raw materials (hair lotion, shampoo for example)	£2
Wages	£1.50

Each day they also have to find the following amount to cover fixed costs

(insurance/salaries for directors/rates/rent) £40

1 **a** What is the total daily cost of the Curls business?
  b How much on average does it cost to provide a perm?
  c What price is charged for a perm?

2 **a** How much revenue does Curls earn in a day?
  b How much of this is profit?

3 If Kate and Marc had only 20 customers in a day what would be their:
  a total daily cost
  b the average cost per customer?

4 Assuming Curls still charge a price of £7, what would be the amount of profit made each day?

5 Kate secures an exclusive deal with a world famous supplier of hair lotions. If she can increase business to 100 customers a day Hair International will supply her with raw materials at a special discount of £1 per customer.
  a What would the average cost then be?
  b What would the new daily profit be?

6 Kate and Marc are considering taking on the next door shop and expanding their business to cater for 110 customers a day. To do this they need to take a loan from the bank. This will increase their daily fixed costs by £20. They would also need a manageress, at a wage of £60 a week. Their rates bill would rise by £24 a month and their insurance bill by £4 a day. Should Marc and Kate expand their business?

Internal economies of scale

This diagram shows some of the most important internal economies of scale.

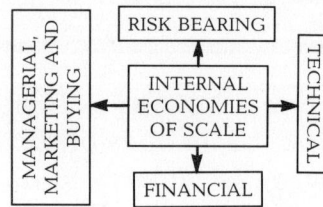

Managerial, marketing and buying economies

When a firm needs raw materials and is able to buy them in large quantities (bulk buying) it is often able to obtain a discount. Again when a firm comes to sell its finished product it will be able to gain substantial savings in selling costs. Think about why the costs of delivery, in particular, could be lowered.

Advertising costs can be kept to a minimum. It costs the same to advertise 1000 articles as it does to advertise 100.

In a large firm there can be several managers and each manager can specialise in a specific area. This can lead to huge savings for a firm.

Technical economies

When firms expand they can afford to subdivide their labour throughout each stage of production. They can thus get savings in the process of production.

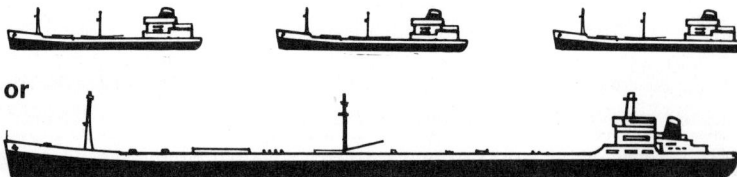

or

Which method can transport oil more cheaply?

By using larger machines, a firm can gain from the economies of increased dimensions. A large canning plant, for example, can afford to purchase a large potato peeling machine, but in a smaller firm the potatoes might have to be peeled by hand by the workers.

Better use, too, can be made of machines at different stages in the production process. This can be done by expanding pro-

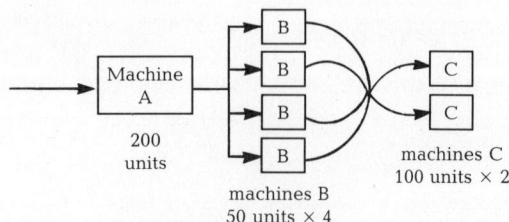

Chain of production

duction to a point where there is an even flow of output through the machines provided for each stage in the chain of production. (This idea is sometimes called the principle of multiples.)

Risk bearing economies

Economies can be gained if production is spread into a range of markets and not just expanded. The firm will then benefit because the chance of anything going wrong, like a particular market declining, will have been lessened because the risk will have been spread. This is a benefit that is said to be had from "the law of averages". The old saying "Don't keep all your eggs in one basket" is another way of describing risk spreading.

Financial economies

A large firm with large-scale production can often borrow money at a lower rate of interest than a small firm. The large-scale enterprise is also in a better position to raise the finance necessary for future expansion.

Decide for yourself
- Why do you think this might be so?

Diseconomies of scale

However, now consider what can happen if you get too big.
- You often have to *standardise*, that is make the same product in order to supply a mass market. Some customers would, instead, prefer an individualised product. For example, Marks and Spencer can provide good, cheap suits, but they cannot provide custom-made suits made personally for each customer.
- It can become very much harder to control the firm. As the boss it is more difficult to be certain that your orders are being carried out. With many people to consult, decision-making becomes slower. Waste can creep in with a firm finding that it is employing too many workers. (We call this *over-manning*.)
- Because it is harder to keep in touch with all that is going on in a very large enterprise, there is always the danger of misunderstandings. This can lead to labour unrest. The personal touch is lost.
- There is an increased tendency to follow rules for their own sake rather than to benefit the firm. We say there is too much "red tape" or bureaucracy.

1 Which factory, A or B, is experiencing economies of scale?

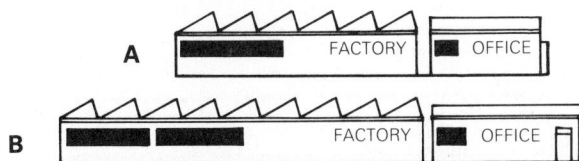

2 Give one example of a technical economy.

3 What benefit do you gain by buying in bulk?

4 What does the expression "Don't keep all your eggs in one basket" mean?

5 What problems can occur if a firm grows too much?

6 Explain what is meant by economies of increased dimensions.

DATA RESPONSE 1

How the future of ice cream is being reshaped by Wall's

BY DINA MEDLAND

THE MAKING of ice cream has come a long way since the fourth century BC, when Alexander the Great is credited with dreaming up the first ice-lolly, during his campaign in Asia Minor, by asking his slaves to fetch snow from the mountains to freeze a mixture of honey and fruit juice.

At Wall's new ice cream factory in Gloucester in the UK, the world's largest computer-driven mix plant is capable of producing 32,000 litres of ice cream per hour. Lollies have their place here as well.

Discussions with the trade early in the season (and before too much money has been spent) provide important feedback regarding consumer tastes and market segmentation for different products, while the marketing division is responsible for testing the products and selling them at a later stage.

Without innovative technology there would be few new ice cream products along the lines of Viennetta for example – a frozen ice cream dessert aimed at the take-home market and launched in 1982 with considerable success.

In 1980 a small team began work on the ideas behind Viennetta, and patented a recognisable new concept the following year. By 1982 extrusion nozzle technology had been added to the existing manufacturing process for ice cream "logs", moulding them into ornate and diverse designs.

The Viennetta manufacturing process is a flexible one, involving the undoing of a coupling connection and recoupling it to different extrusion units in order to change the product flavour or design.

This is a job that can take just half an hour, although cleaning the lines is a time-consuming process – the company spends 20 hours a day manufacturing ice cream, with four hours set aside for cleaning the manufacturing equipment. Vats mixing ice cream are cleaned steadily through the 24 hour period.

By the time potential buyers for new products are approached, Wall's is able to manufacture products that look like the original concept, but there is not necessarily a commitment to large-scale manufacture at this stage.

Rotating extrusion nozzle technology is used in the manufacture of the Twister, a strawberry and vanilla ice cream in a twisted spiral shape with a chocolate centre. In this process, separate pipes come out of the freezer – one for each flavour – and extrude, or force through under pressure, the ice cream in its spiral shape.

The same technology is used to manufacture the chocolate Romero, marketed as "the snack bar with a twist."

The development division also scrutinises competition outside the ice cream industry in its search for new ideas, and confectionery is a prime target. In an attempt to lure chocolate and toffee lovers, Wall's has developed a range of products such as choc bars, which use the same basic technology in their manufacture, but differ in flavour or presentation.

There are limits on how far Wall's can delve into new flavours for the same product, however, and this places more emphasis on the need for the development of entirely new designs.

Source: *The Financial Times*, 6 October 1987

1 What evidence in the extract supports the view that Wall's is a firm engaged in the large-scale production of ice cream?

2 Given this large-scale production, how do Wall's make sure that they produce a product that will be in demand?

3 a What new form of technology was introduced by Wall's when it produced the Vienetta?

b Explain why Wall's might find it easier to develop a new product than might a smaller ice cream firm.

4 What limits exist for Wall's in the making of ice cream?

5 Describe one of the new products Wall's has developed.

Extension 1

Wide World: Flights to six continents. Hundreds daily connecting all the world's major airports.

Westair: A daily flight from Cornwall to the Scilly Isles.

Technical economies: These allow more efficient use of resources. Increased dimensions and specialisation are possible.

Marketing economies: Materials required can be purchased in bulk and selling costs, for example advertising, per unit sold will be lower on average.

Risk bearing economies: A small firm might find itself in trouble through operating in only one market or area, but a larger firm can spread its risks.

Financial and managerial economies: A small firm may have to pay higher interest rates to borrow capital. A larger firm can make more effective use of management.

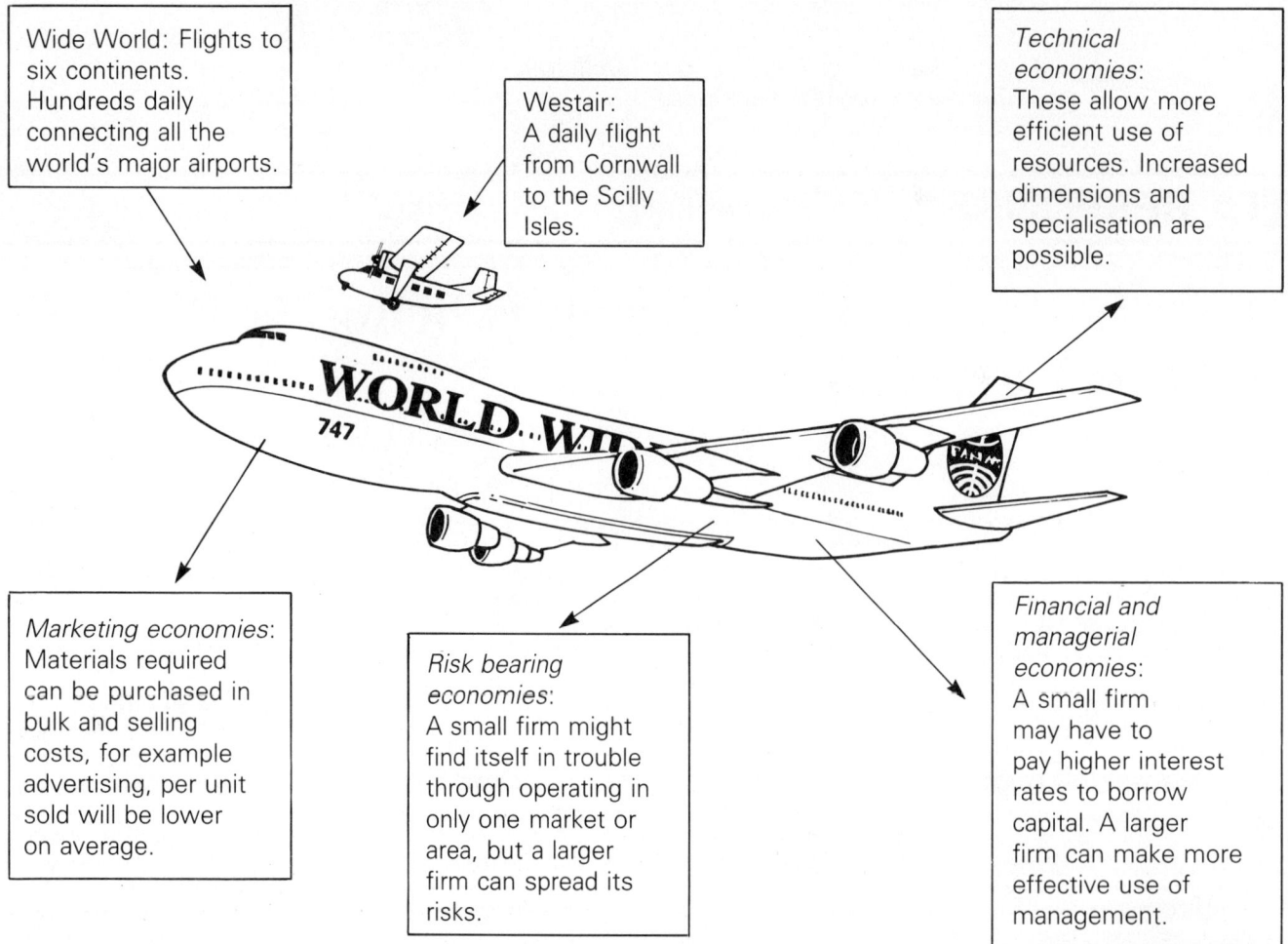

Look at examples **1–7** and decide which type of economy of scale is either missing or present.

1 Wide World can fly 600 passengers and their baggage across the Atlantic in only one flight.

2 "I don't think we are in a position to let you have more credit." (Bank manager to Chairman of Westair Ltd.)

3 We can service and refuel our planes very quickly because of our excellent ground crew. This cuts down the time our planes are on the runway (Wide World pilot).

4 We buy in the in-flight meals that we offer. We are such an important customer that our supplier gives us a special discount price (Wide World spokesperson).

5 Last month the weather was so bad in the Cornwall area we had to suspend all flights for five days (Westair).

6 We've been able to launch a special management training programme and this has greatly improved our performance (Wide World chairman).

7 Our special sales campaign was cheap at the price and increased our sales of airline tickets by 15% in Europe alone (Wide World sales staff member).

Extension 2

A. 'The advertising costs for 1000 boxes of chocolates are the same as the costs for a 100 boxes of chocolates.'

B. 'Now that we're bigger we should really take on a production manager. That'll get things moving. No one seems to know what's happening and who's in charge.'

C. 'The workers have a complaint. When we were a smaller operation we could all sit down and sort the problems out. Now we could be heading for a strike.'

D. 'The bigger we get the more workers we can hire, and then we'll make better use of the division of labour.'

E. 'We can buy our sugar supplies in bulk now at a special discount.'

F. 'The site's too big now, we've begun to lose equipment and materials. We'll need to take on a security guard. But that'll push our costs up.'

G. 'Of course we're quite happy to lend you the money you require.' (Bank manager to the Choffee board.)

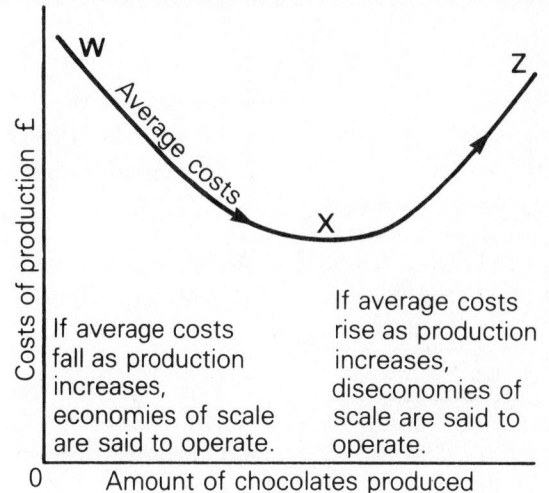

If average costs fall as production increases, economies of scale are said to operate.

If average costs rise as production increases, diseconomies of scale are said to operate.

1 Look at the graph. What is happening to average costs between points **W** and **X**?
2 Which of the comments describe the economies of scale that can be gained as average costs decline?
3 Look again at the graph. What is happening to average costs between points **X** and **Z**?
4 Which of the comments describe the diseconomies of scale that operate as average costs increase?
5 **X** is described as the optimum point of production. Can you explain why?

Coursework

Aim: To investigate evidence of economies of scale in two schools: a primary school and a secondary school.

1 Consider what economies of scale the primary school shows evidence of.
2 To what extent does the secondary school you attend show more effective examples of economies of scale: specialist staff, better provision for subjects like music, art, science?

3 What diseconomies of scale are present in your secondary school? (boredom/absenteeism are possible symptoms of problems). To what extent do you think these outweigh the benefits to be had from life in a secondary school?
4 Which school is operating at an appropriate scale of operation? Give reasons for your answer.

21 Monopoly

A *monopoly* exists when one producer or seller controls the supply of goods or services to a market. A monopoly comes about when a firm erects barriers that prevent other firms from entering the market and competing with them.

> The beer here is awful, but it's a two mile walk to the next pub.

> I'm not going to Joe's cafe for chips again. I'll go to the Happy Frier in the High Street.

> Look at this bill! £30 for an oil change. If only there was another garage in this village.

Decide for yourself
- Can you identify examples of a monopoly?

The barriers to entry
The various barriers to entry are:
- **Concentration of raw materials**: if the raw materials for a process are only to be found in one place, a firm can, by obtaining this source, eliminate competitors.
- **Technical barriers**: an existing firm engaged in large-scale production and probably enjoying economies of scale would have low costs of production. A new firm's initial output would probably be smaller and its average costs higher. It would not be able to obtain the same level of profits. The new firm would also find the cost of developing and marketing their new product very high.
- **Price wars**: the firm holding the existing monopoly could reduce the new firm's chances of survival by cutting their own prices. These price wars occur from time to time in a number of industries, for example newspapers, petrol and computers.
- **Legal barriers**: these are probably the most effective barriers a firm can erect. If a firm has a *patent* on a product that it has invented or developed, then other firms are not allowed to make identical products. A patent gives the sole right to make or sell an invention for a period of time.

  Firms can register their brand names and copyright (protect the right to reproduce) original work too. For example, this book is copyright and other people cannot copy material from it to sell.
- **Marketing barriers**: firms with well known brand names are often faced by attempts from market intruders to 'counterfeit' their work. ('Rolex' watches and 'Gucci' handbags may be sold for a few pounds in a street market, for example.) But branding is an effective way of preventing new firms from entering the market. They would need to launch their product with an expensive advertising campaign if they were to have any success in persuading consumers to switch brand loyalties.

Activity

Jane has recently opened a brand new branch of her Janesburys supermarket chain, opposite Bert's general store.

1 How has Jane made her supermarket more attractive for customers than Bert's general store?

2 How is Jane keeping potential competitors from entering the retail business?

3 What other factors has Jane used, or could use, to build her business?

4 Explain why Bert is unhappy about the opening of a new Janesburys supermarket.

JANESBURYS STORE –
Reasons for success

PRACTISING PRODUCT DIFFERENTIATION (see Activity Q.1)	Tick here
Branding 'J' food	
Janesbury ® – registered trade mark	
Advertising, e.g. newspaper, plane, shop display, carrier bag	
Packaging and display of goods	
Inducements – free gifts (Jane's Jam), June competition vouchers, trolleys	
Price cutting – various goods as *loss leaders* – sale now on	
BARRIERS TO ENTRY (see Activity Q.2)	
Owns foods factory – supply of its 'raw' materials	

Legal barriers – ® mark; pat pending; suing counterfeiters	
Evidence of price war	
Technical barriers – management expertise/ economies of scale	
'Captive' market – local people now wouldn't go anywhere else – largely through advertising	
BACKGROUND FACTORS (see Activity Q.3)	
GCSE Economics course – knowledge	
PLC – therefore access to capital	
Could issue more shares e.g. to pay for extension or fund new branch	
JB's Foods – evidence of backward vertical integration	
Chain – evidence of horizontal integration	
Economies of scale – bulk buying, delivery lorry	
Evidence of division of labour in advertisement for staff	

Monopoly power: a cost to economy?

Monopolies are often accused of misusing their economic power. Critics of monopolies argue as follows:

- monopolies put up their prices to consumers (this may be as a result of a cartel agreement between a group of firms in which they agree to act together in order to dominate a market);
- monopolies make abnormal (or super) profits;
- the consumer is left without the choice of an alternative source of supply;
- with no competitors, the monopolist can often become lazy and inefficient.

Other people, however, argue that monopolies can benefit the economy:

- with a monopoly there is no need to spend a great deal of the firm's money on advertising to try to persuade consumers to buy your product;
- prices can be offered on a stable basis. There are no price wars and no need for sudden fluctuations in price;
- economies of scale are possible with more being produced at a lower average price. Both consumers and the monopolist benefit from this.

Price of goods supplied by a monopoly enjoying economies of scale:	£28 each
Average price of goods with nine firms competing and sharing the market	£35 each

In this case, even if the monopolist is making an abnormal profit, say £10, it is clear that the consumer is better off by £7 every time they buy a good.

- The profits a monopolist enjoys are the rewards for successfully developing a product the market has come to prefer. If a firm takes the risk of investing its money, then it should also, some people say, reap the benefits of such enterprise.
- Monopolies are in a better position to compete with overseas firms because they enjoy economies of scale in the home market. They therefore contribute to economic growth and prosperity.
- The success of a monopolist acts as an incentive to other firms. This might eventually lead to their entering the market with a better and/or cheaper product. They would be attracted by the chance of making abnormal profits.

Natural monopoly

For a variety of reasons there are situations where only one firm is really needed in a market. Any other situation would lead to higher costs to the consumer. In these circumstances, a *natural monopoly* is said to exist (as discussed in Unit 15).

Decide for yourself

- Should such situations be brought into public or private ownership?
- Why do you think this?

Watching over monopolies

The government has powers to protect the public if monopolies misuse their power. It does this through its Office of Fair Trading. The Director General of this body can arrange for either the Monopolies and Mergers Commission or the Restrictive Practices Court to investigate cases of unfair trading. Any firm that has at least a 25% share of a market is, in law, considered to be a monopoly and can be investigated by these two bodies. This includes government monopolies, like British Rail.

Decide for yourself

- Why do you think that a merger of two companies, each with less than 25% of the market, may also be referred to these bodies?

ECONOMIC TERMS
Monopoly: where there is one supplier of goods and services in a market.
Barriers to entry: situations that prevent new firms from entering the market.
Super-normal profit: profit made above the level needed to keep an entrepreneur in a particular line of business.
Cartel: a secret understanding between firms to fix the price or control the quantity at which they will sell to the market. (OPEC is a cartel of oil-producing countries. Their action resulted in a sharp increase in oil prices in the 1970s.)

1 What is a monopoly?
2 Give one example of a technical barrier to entry that a monopolist can use to keep competitors out of a market.
3 Give one example of a legal barrier that a monopolist can use.
4 Explain how brand loyalty can reinforce a monopoly situation.

5 What sort of barriers to entry could a monopolist erect in industries which produce:
a cars;   c glassware;
b lawn mowers;   d breakfast cereals?
6 What government bodies have been set up to watch over monopolies? Name some examples of monopolies that they could investigate.

DATA RESPONSE

MPs urge monopolies inquiry into petrol sales

Patrick Wintour

Evidence of price fixing by petrol companies should be investigated by the Monopolies and Mergers Commission, an all-party committee of MPs recommended yesterday.

Lack of consumer power meant that oil companies had little need to engage in price competition. The Office of Fair Trading was too impotent and, in the case of petrol retailing, too dependent on the oil companies for information to monitor effectively the evidence of price collusion.

The Tory-controlled committee found that the leading petrol wholesalers are also the leading retailers and supply most of the independents.

Independents enjoy little autonomy in fixing prices because companies such as BP and Shell either run price-support mechanisms through subsidies or impose maximum sales prices and profit margins. Shell admitted to the committee that it would not sell to hypermarkets because they might undercut its own sites.

The number of petrol retailers had fallen from 30,383 in 1976 to less than 20,197, and the proportion of the leading oil companies' sales through independent retailers from 50.9 to 44.7 per cent. In towns and cities the big companies now owned 71.3 per cent of sites. The committee found that the oil companies had highly sophisticated information gathering techniques to monitor competitors' prices, but admitted it had uncovered no conclusive evidence of a cartel. Nevertheless, the committee said, "we are not convinced that market forces operate unchecked".

The committee says that to increase the level of competition and diversity the display of prices should be made compulsory, the Office of Fair Trading should investigate the true costs of supply to rural areas to ensure against overcharging, the powers of the Office of Fair Trading should be strengthened and unleaded petrol should be made more attractive to car owners.

Source: *Guardian*, 27 July 1988

1 Which two government bodies mentioned in the report have power to investigate cases of unfair competition?

2 Which two large petrol companies are mentioned?

3 Describe some of the ways by which the big petrol companies have been able to control the market for selling petrol.

4 What evidence is given that the leading petrol companies dominate the market for the sale and purchase of petrol?

5 What did the committee of MPs recommend to improve the situation?

6 The article refers to:
a price fixing;
b cartels.
Explain what each of these terms means.

Extension 1

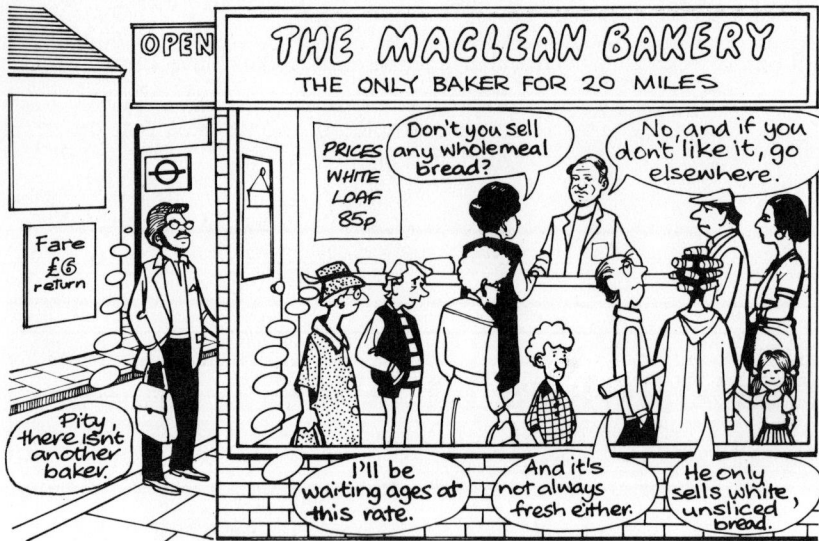

1 Why is the MacLean bakery in a monopoly position?
2 What advantages does this position give the MacLeans?
3 Why might you not like being a customer at the MacLean bakery?
4 Examine how easy it would be for someone to set up in business selling bread in the village.
5 In what ways would the arrival of a second shop benefit the villagers?

Extension 2

1 What legal barriers is the Blunt Calculator Company employing to prevent other firms from entering the electronic calculator market?
2 What technical barriers does the firm enjoy?
3 Explain how the price Blunt is able to sell their calculator for acts as a barrier to other firms entering the market.
4 You are given £1 million to develop a new product. As a group, examine the arguments for using the money to produce electronic calculators or a new range of cosmetics for men.
5 Explain why it might be easier to enter the timber business than the electronic calculator business.

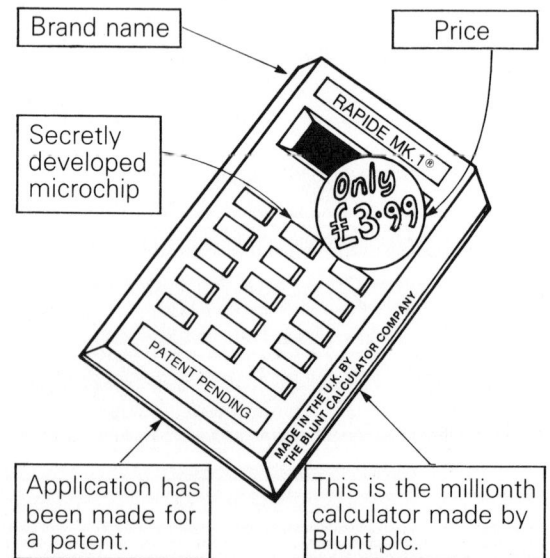

Coursework

Aim: To investigate brand loyalty.

Select a product sold in a local supermarket. Identify the number of brands of this product sold.

Devise a way of identifying the market leader. Observation at random periods linked to a frequency chart would be one way.

Construct a questionnaire to establish why brand loyalty exists. Could it be price, taste/use, packaging, advertising, inducements?

22 Demand 1

Demand is the amount consumers are willing to purchase at any given price. If prices rise then the quantity demanded will fall. If, on the other hand, prices fall, then the quantity demanded increases. People who can now afford the item will purchase it, and those who could already afford it may be encouraged by the lower price to increase their purchases.

Activity

1 Assume everyone in your class each receives £60 pocket money every week. Make a list of four items you would prefer to spend this money on, in the order of their importance to you. Include cassettes in your list.

1 _____

2 _____

3 _____

4 _____

2 Now imagine the price of each cassette is £4. How many would you buy? Put your answer against person 1 in the table below. Fill out the rest of the grid by asking others in your class the same question.

	Number of cassettes purchased
Person 1	
Person 2	
Person 3	
Person 4	
Person 5	
Total:	

3 Repeat the exercise. Each person still has £60 but the price of cassettes has risen to £10. How many cassettes would now be bought by each person?

Person 1	
Person 2	
Person 3	
Person 4	
Person 5	
Total:	

4 Repeat the exercise for a final time. Each person still has £60, but a cassette now costs £16.

Person 1	
Person 2	
Person 3	
Person 4	
Person 5	
Total:	

5 Transfer your information to a graph. On the vertical axis show each price. On the horizontal axis record the quantity of cassettes your group has bought at each of these prices.

6 Describe the kind of curve that appears on your graph.

Jack Boyd and the power boat

Jack Boyd wants to own a power boat. So do many other people. Jack's father designs boats, so he knows that although many people would like to buy his product, few ever do.

"It's not enough to want a product, Jack," Mr Boyd points out. "You have to be able to pay for it."

Economists call this combination of willingness and ability to pay *effective demand*. Effective demand has to exist before a product can be purchased.

"I've saved £500," says Jack. "If only your boats cost less, I'd buy one and so would lots of my friends."

Jack has discovered one of the laws of demand: the lower the price of a good, the more of it will be demanded. A second law states: the higher the price, the less will be demanded of a good.

We can see the relationship between price and the quantity demanded on a *demand schedule*. This is simply a table that lists the quantity of a product that will be demanded at a given price.

Demand schedule: Speedboats	
Quantity	*Price*
20	£20 000
300	15 000
4 000	10 000
50 000	5 000

Usually this information is displayed on a graph. The relationship between the price and quantity appears as a line known as the *demand curve*.

If we assume that other factors that influence demand can be kept the same, then, when prices change, we can observe the effect of the price change on demand:

● If prices rise, then the quantity demanded will fall, or contract, and move back along the demand curve. People are unable to afford the same level of purchases that they made before. Some may be priced out of the market altogether.

● If prices fall, then the quantity demanded will increase. There is said to be an extension of demand along the curve. People can now afford the item and will purchase it. Those who could already afford it may be encouraged by the lower price to increase the quantity they purchase.

ECONOMIC TERMS

Demand: the amount consumers are willing to purchase at any given price.
Effective demand: willingness to pay for an item backed by purchasing power.
Demand schedule: a table listing the quantity of a product that will be demanded at given prices.
Demand curve: a line on a graph that shows the relationship between price and quantity demanded.
Movements along the demand curve:
Extensions = forward movements (increases in quantity demanded).
Contractions = backward movements (decreases in quantity demanded).

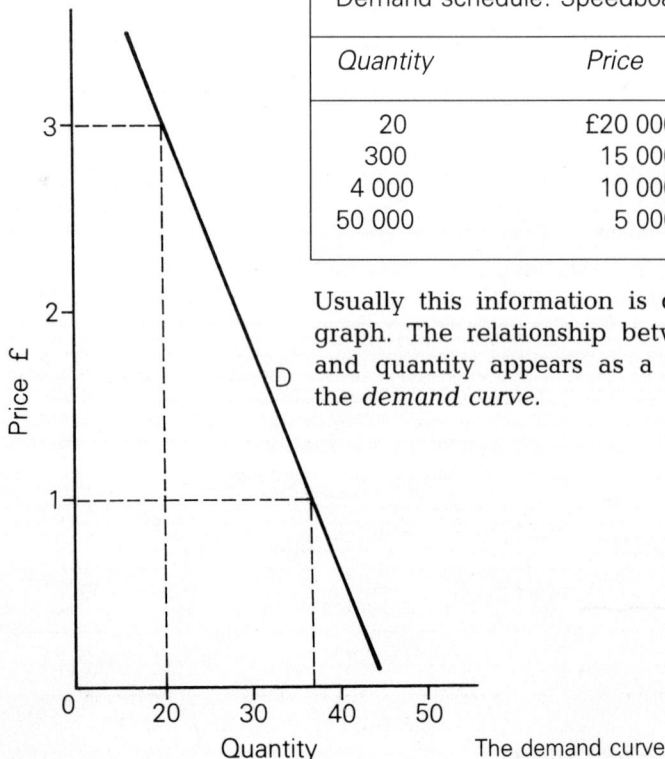

The demand curve

1 What is meant by the phrase 'effective demand'? Illustrate your answer by referring to the purchase of a Rolls-Royce motor-car.

2 **a** If the price rises, what happens to the quantity demanded?

   b Why can some people be upset by a price rise?

3 What is meant by the phrases:

   a an extension of demand;

   b a contraction of demand?

4 The Smith family love tomatoes, but cannot afford them in winter months. Explain why. Illustrate your answer with a demand graph.

DATA RESPONSE

Eyes down

A YOUNG woman, smartly dressed, stands on a large podium at the front of a London cinema, reading out strings of numbers which have been randomly generated by a computer in Feltham, 15 miles away. Below her, in a kind of orchestra pit, some 40 staff are checking numbers, counting tickets and entering information into the house computer. Beyond, 700 men and women of all ages sit at tables in the stalls and in rows of seats in the cinema's vast balcony, earnestly filling in their cards. This is a Monday night. Bingo has come a long way since the days of ball-popping numbers, old dears in tea-cosy hats, and cries of "Two fat ladies—eighty-eight!".

The Mecca leisure club in Essex Road, north London, does well to attract nearly 1,000 bingo players seven nights a week. Since its peak in the early 1970s bingo-hall business has been hit by the proliferation of new, competing leisure industries and the introduction in the early 1980s of newspaper bingo, which lures punters with huge prizes. Business has fallen 30% in real terms since 1974 (see chart). The clubs know that, to survive, they will have to update bingo's image. As long as it is seen as an outmoded form of small-time gambling, loyal old ladies keep on coming, but young customers stay away. A survey in 1982 showed that 83% of bingo players were women, and 70% were aged over 38.

In widening its market, the bingo industry has had to cope with a straitjacket of regulations, policed by the Gaming Board. One of the biggest problems has been posed by limits on the size of the prizes: a £200 prize at the local bingo hall is unlikely to lure people away from their £1m newspaper bingo cards. Two years ago the government agreed to the setting up of a national game, which links some 800 clubs by computer. That allowed clubs to offer a single game with an "at least one in the audience" chance of winning a £200 house prize, some hope of a £3,000 regional one and a long shot at a £50,000 national prize. Bingo managers say that the husbands, sons and daughters of the regulars have started to come along.

The figures confirm their view that the fall in receipts has been stemmed since 1986.

Now the Home Office has agreed to allow bingo halls to open in the morning, from 10am rather than from noon. The Bingo Association, which pressed for the change, believes that this will allow more housewives to have a flutter while out shopping. Some managers will not play; they say no great surge in business followed the last occasion when opening time was brought forward, from 2pm in 1984. True, old ladies dislike staying out after dark, but in most clubs business is concentrated in the early evening. (The national game starts half an hour after "Eastenders" finishes on television.)

One silly remaining restriction is the ban on bingo-club advertising. Newspapers may advertise their games because they do not charge to play them. Bingo managers believe they could compete well with other leisure industries—if only they were allowed to tell customers where to come and when.

Source: *The Economist*, 9 July 1988

Bingo

Value of stakes, 1988 prices
Years ending March 31st

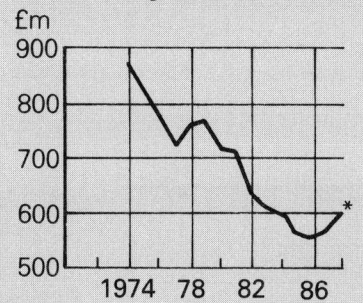

Number of licensed clubs
End year

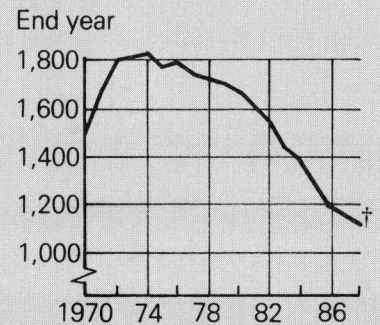

The demand for a product changes over time. Read this article carefully and then answer the questions.

1 Why do you think young customers have kept away from bingo halls?

2 What evidence is given that bingo is only a game for 'loyal old ladies'?

3 How had the decline in demand for bingo affected:

   a the number of clubs;

   b the value of stakes?

4 The article describes a number of ways by which the demand for bingo could be raised. Identify two of these ways.

Extension 1

1 During their first week in operation Video Hire of Melchester offer free rentals of video tapes as an inducement. Explain why only 400 video tapes are demanded. Use the following ideas to help you: time/ distance/lack of knowledge/opportunity cost/number of video players owned or rented in Melchester.

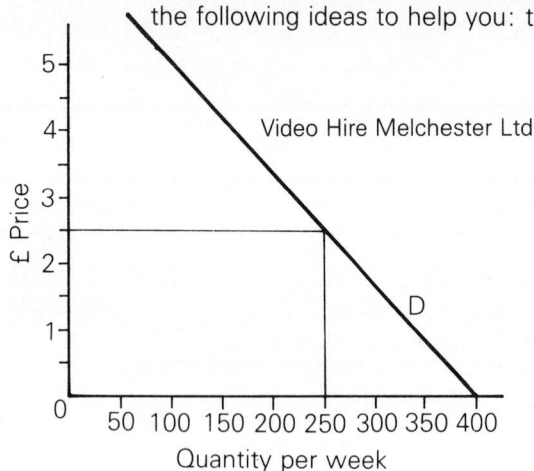

2 At a price of £5 a video tape what would be the quantity demanded?

3 In their second week Video Hire set a price that results in 300 video tapes being hired. What is the price?

4 How many more video tapes would be hired if the price fell from £5 to £1?

5 The government is concerned about the growing number of young people who are hiring and watching horror videos. They decide that a price of £4 should be the minimum price for hiring a video tape. What will be the quantity demanded now? Why might Video Hire be unhappy with this decision?

(Graph: x-axis "Quantity per week" marked 50 100 150 200 250 300 350 400; y-axis "£ Price" marked 1 to 5; downward sloping demand line labelled D; label "Video Hire Melchester Ltd")

Extension 2

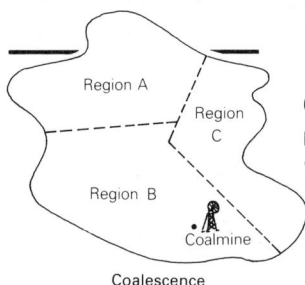

Coalescence is a mythical country with three regions and one coal mine.

(Map of Coalescence showing Region A, Region B, Region C and Coalmine)

Coalescence

1 Look at the demand schedule below for coal in each region.
What is the total demand for coal in Coalescence if the price is £4 per tonne?

Price per tonne	Region A Demand in tonnes	Region B Demand in tonnes	Region C Demand in tonnes
£5	100 000	50 000	10 000
£4	200 000	60 000	20 000
£3	300 000	70 000	30 000
£2	400 000	80 000	40 000
£1	500 000	90 000	50 000

2 Using the information, construct a graph that shows the total demand curve for coal in Coalescence. As a first step you will need to add up the total demand for coal at each price.

3 Explain why when the price becomes lower the total demand for coal increases.

4 The government of Coalescence decide that the minimum price for coal shall be set at £3 per tonne. How many tonnes of coal would be demanded at this price?

5 Explain why many potential customers will be unhappy with the government's decision.

6 If the price of coal was £1 per tonne how many tonnes would be demanded?

Coursework

Aim: To investigate the basis of demand for different products.

1 Compare the demand for:
  a a brand of cornflakes which has many well-known rivals, with
  b the demand for a popular brand of cigarettes.

2 Collect data that allows you to construct demand curves for each product, showing the relationship between price and quantity.

3 What difference do you notice in the positioning of the curve for each product?

4 Interview people to discover their attitudes to the product in question.

5 Display your results on a bar chart.

6 To what extent do your interview results help you to account for differences in the positioning of the demand curve for each product.

23 Demand 2

In order to show the effect of price on demand economists assume that the underlying conditions that determine demand are held constant. Movements along the demand curve can then be isolated and examined. However, the underlying conditions that determine demand in the real world rarely stay constant. These conditions produce changes that shift the total demand curve's position, either to the left or to the right.

For example:

- if total demand for the product expands/increases at all price levels, the demand curve will move bodily to the right;
- if total demand declines or decreases at all price levels, the demand curve will shift bodily to the left.

There are a number of underlying conditions of demand that produce shifts in total demand. These conditions include:

- advertising;
- changes in tastes and habits or preferences;
- changes in population;
- changes in the price of substitutes;
- changes in government policy;
- changes in the price of complementary goods;
- changes in income.

Let us examine this further by looking at the demand for skateboards.

Let us say skateboarding has become a national craze. People have switched from other leisure activities to spend time skateboarding. So the total demand for skateboards has increased. If there were more people in the economy and they had more income, this might also increase the demand for skateboards.

An advertising campaign spelling out the health advantages of skateboarding or its glamorous nature could also increase total demand.

In these circumstances the increase in the total demand for skateboards means that at all levels demand increases and the demand curve will move to the right (see diagram **A**).

However, suppose suddenly the demand conditions change: skateboarding is shown to be dangerous; a government publicity campaign warns people of these dangers; parents encourage their children to consider an alternative, for example, roller disco; and, at the same time, the price of roller boots (a substitute) falls dramatically. The demand for skateboards at all levels will decrease and the demand curve will move to the left.

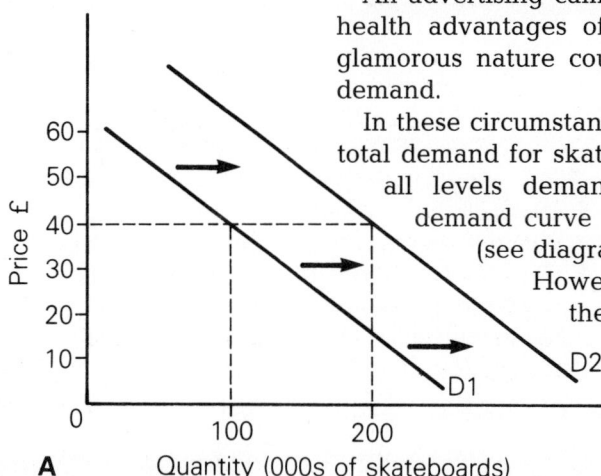

ECONOMIC TERMS

Total demand: the amount demanded in an economy for a good or service.
Conditions (or determinants) of demand: the underlying factors that produce shifts in total demand.

Test yourself

1 If there are changes in the conditions that determine demand, how is the demand curve affected?
2 The government gives every worker in the country a 15% pay rise. What might happen to the demand for computer games?
3 A series of new and exciting computer games are advertised on television. What would happen to the demand for computer games?
4 A report in a national newspaper warns parents that "We are fast creating a nation of computer game junkies." How might demand for these games alter?
5 Show this last change in demand on a price/quantity graph. You will need to record the position of both the original and the new demand curves. Label the original curve **D1** and the new curve **D2**.
6 On the graph show what might happen to demand for computer games at all price levels if home computers became 50% cheaper to buy. Label the curve **D3**.

A Quantity (000s of skateboards)

129

Activity

Escape to the sun

A In 1981, a then-record 382,000 passengers went through British airports to or from the West Indies. A year's worth of recession later, the figure had dropped by 7%. It stayed there in 1983, then grew steadily to 419,000 in 1986, the latest year for which figures are available. British Airways has seen "fantastic" demand for Caribbean flights this winter; some islands, like Antigua, want more laid on.

The rush is not just to the Caribbean. Thomas Cook Ltd has sold 37% more long-haul holidays worldwide this winter than last. Among other people's packages, it sells its own; on February 2nd it said that side of its business would pull out of Mediterranean holidays, to concentrate on long-haul.

Australia's bicentenary is boosting demand for holidays there, and travel agents see future growth in Canada, Egypt and India. Above all, the weak dollar – while helping the Caribbean, whose prices reflect its weakness – has renewed interest in the United States.

In sum, either vastly more people than before can afford a long-haul holiday, or many can afford two a year. Either way, the economy is plainly stuffed with cash for discretionary spending.

Source: *The Economist*, 6–12 February 1988

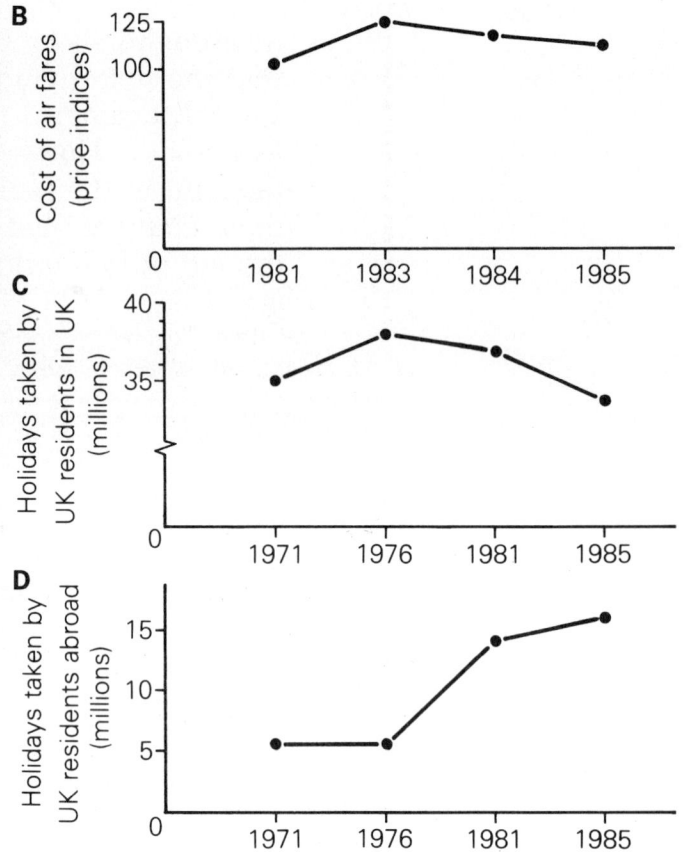

B Cost of air fares (price indices)

C Holidays taken by UK residents in UK (millions)

D Holidays taken by UK residents abroad (millions)

And I'd like some tomato ketchup with my saltfish and yams.

E Household income:

Table shows real disposable income per head (index number)

1980	1981	1982	1983	1984	1985
100	98	99	103	107	111

Source: *Social Trends 17 HMSO*

1 Using **A** and **D** explain what has happened to the demand for holidays abroad since 1981.

2 Using **C** explain what has happened to the demand for holidays at home since 1971.

3 Using all the information, try and explain why demand for holidays abroad is rising.

4 Consider the effects of this change in the pattern of holidaying on seaside holiday resorts in Britain. If possible collect evidence to illustrate your answer.

DATA RESPONSE

Shopkeepers put up the shutters By Phil Reeves

NEARLY three hours before the match, large numbers of police began patrolling the centre of Middlesbrough. Shopkeepers in Linthorpe Road, the main route to Middlesbrough's ground, Ayresome Park, began putting up metal shutters from about 4.40pm onwards. Some closed early in case of trouble.

One shop assistant warned: "If you are not local to Middlesbrough, you are not safe around here from half past four onwards on the day of the match. I should clear off if I were you." The match began at 7.30pm.

Several severely cracked shop front windows bore testimony to previous running battles between Middlesbrough fans and visiting rival supporters.

The general view among shopkeepers appeared to be that violence was likely and, even if none came, it was best to be prepared.

"There's always trouble between us and Chelsea. Always," one Middlesbrough fan told me. "They have got to be the worst fans in the country," he added with some relish. "They've got knives and hammers and all that sort of thing. And we hate each other."

The match, the first leg of a two-match play-off for a place in the First Division, was all-ticket – one of several measures taken to deter hooligans.

Several thousand Chelsea fans who boarded a "football special train" from London's King's Cross to Middlesbrough were allowed to travel only if they held a ticket for the match. Tickets were restricted to club members. A spokesman for Chelsea FC said yesterday that it was not possible to join the club until next season – a further deterrent to trouble makers.

Source: *The Independent,* 26 May 1988

Average attendances at football matches[1]

Football League (England & Wales)				
	Division 1	Division 2	Division 3	Division 4
1961–62	26,106	16,132	9,419	6,060
1966–67	30,829	15,701	8,009	5,407
1971–72	31,352	14,652	8,510	4,981
1976–77	29,540	13,529	7,522	3,863
1980–81	24,660	11,202	6,590	3,082
1981–82	22,556	10,282	5,159	3,621
1982–83	20,120	10,768	5,333	2,812
1983–84	18,856	11,601	4,946	2,822
1984–85	21,129	8,725	4,832	2,519
1985–86	19,562	7,696	4,522	2,554

1 League matches only.

Source: *Social Trends 17*, HMSO

1 What were the shopkeepers expecting would happen on the day of the match? How could their businesses suffer as a result?

2 Using the table, construct a graph to illustrate how attendance at fooball matches has declined.

3 What possible connection exists between the evidence in your answer to question **1** and the information on your graph for question **2**?

4 What other reasons could be advanced to account for the decline in the demand to attend football matches?

Extension 1

Demand depends upon many factors other than price. These factors are called *determinants of demand*, and can lead to a change in the position of the demand curve. Examples of determinants of demand are shown on the chart.

Changes in taste	Seasonal factors e.g. festive occasions	Population e.g. rise in number of elderly	Existence of substitutes

1 Now copy the chart, then take this list of goods and classify them on the chart under the most appropriate determinant of demand. Use the information about the change in the pattern of demand for each good.

> **a** a rise in the sale of mini-skirts during summer months;
> **b** an increase in the sale of wheelchairs;
> **c** a decline in the sale of turkeys at Christmas time;
> **d** an increase in the sale of prams and pushchairs;
> **e** a decline in demand for ball-point pens following the development of fibre-tip pens;
> **f** an increase in the sale of bedsocks;
> **g** a rise in demand for ice skates;
> **h** a fall in demand for fireworks during November;
> **i** an increase in the demand for anti-freeze during a sudden cold spell;
> **j** an increase in demand for large print books;
> **k** a growth in demand for cigarettes following a successful advertising campaign;
> **l** the decline in demand for clockwork alarm clocks and an increase in demand for digital alarms.

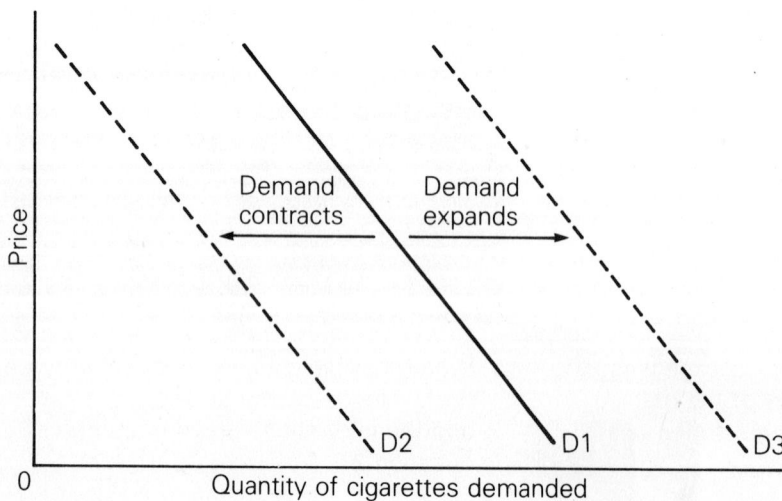

2 A change in the determinants of demand for a product can result in a shift of the demand curve *to the left* if total demand contracts and *to the right* if total demand expands. Decide whether the curve will move to the left or the right in the following situations:
   a the income of the population rises;
   b health warnings about smoking are issued;
   c the death rate falls;
   d a tobacco substitute is marketed;
   e smoking is banned in all public places;
   f office workers are made aware of the dangers of passive smoking;
   g a pro-smoking pressure group is successful in persuading the government to allow television advertisements promoting the sale of cigarettes.

Extension 2

Everything is eventually a substitute for something. Examine the chart carefully.

The Palmer family would like fresh fish for their supper. The chart shows the various alternatives open to them.

a Fresh cod from Macs of Upper Street.
↓
b An alternative might be fresh cod from another shop.
↓
c An alternative might be some other type of fresh fish, e.g. haddock.
↓
d An alternative might be frozen/smoked/canned fish.
↓
e An alternative might be fish fingers.
↓
f An alternative might be fish cakes.
↓
g An alternative might be poultry.
↓
h An alternative might be eggs.

Now answer the following questions.

1 If the Palmers could not afford fish fingers, what might be an acceptable alternative for them?
2 When the Palmers go to Macs they find the shop has been closed. What can they do?
3 Look closely at the items below. Construct a 'Substitution chain' for perfume, using the items in the box. It has been started for you.

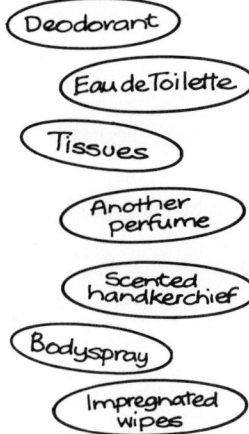

Deodorant   Chanel No 5

Eau de Toilette

Tissues

Another perfume

Scented handkerchief

Bodyspray

Impregnated wipes

Coursework

Aim: To test the hypothesis that the demand for cinema tickets has fallen because people prefer TV/video as a substitute.

1 Find evidence in your local area and from libraries (ask for *Social Trends* published by HMSO) that confirms that demand for cinema tickets has fallen.
2 Explain what economists mean by the conditions that determine demand.
3 Devise questions that will find out:
   a how often people in different age groups go to the cinema;
   b reasons why they go when they do;
   c reasons why they do not go.

4 Display your results using bar charts.
5 Have you proved your hypothesis to be true?
6 What other underlying demand conditions might also provide an answer?
7 What differences did you find between age groups?
8 Using the points in **5**, **6** and **7**, what advice would you give to the manager of your local cinema?

24 Supply

By the term *supply* economists mean the amount producers are willing to offer for sale at any given price.

Activity

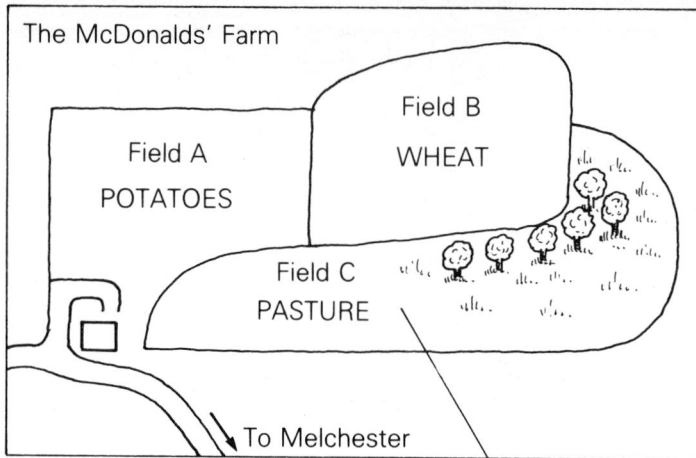

A

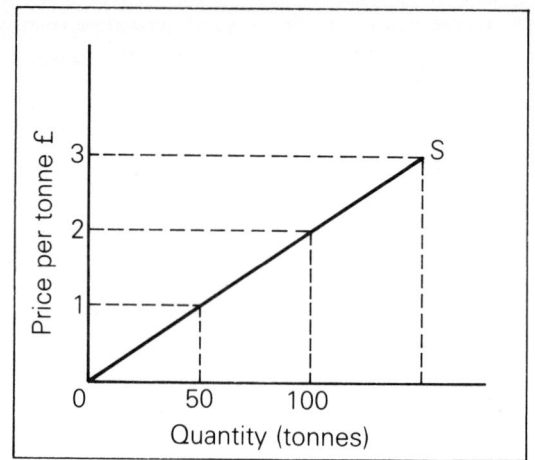

B

Topside £2 a lb

WHEAT PRICES
HIT NEW LOW

The McDonalds own a farm and have been asked to supply potatoes to a local crisp factory in Melchester.

The McDonalds supply the crisp factory from field A with 50 tonnes of potatoes at £1 a tonne.

They have three fields. Each field is capable of producing 50 tonnes of potatoes for the market.

1 Melchester Crisps are delighted with the quality of the potatoes supplied by the McDonalds, and increase their order from 50 tonnes to 100 tonnes. Look at **B**. What price will the McDonalds charge? Explain why they will supply more when the price rises.

2 If the prices for potatoes reaches £3 a tonne the McDonalds would be prepared to plough up all their fields in order to plant potatoes for the market. Why are they prepared to do so at a price of £3 a tonne?

3 At a price of £2 a tonne how many tonnes of potatoes will the McDonalds supply, and which fields will they use?

4 What is the opportunity cost for the McDonalds of allocating all their production to potato growing? What are the advantages and disadvantages of doing so?

5 Construct a graph and record the information in the above activity showing:
 a the quantity of potatoes supplied; and
 b the prices involved.

We want potatoes!

Melchester Crisps Ltd are desperate for supplies of potatoes. The McDonalds can supply them with 40 tonnes which they hold in their cold store now: they can let them have the whole of this year's crop. But that will not be ready for at least two months. In this situation, the supply is fixed and we can show it on a graph like this:

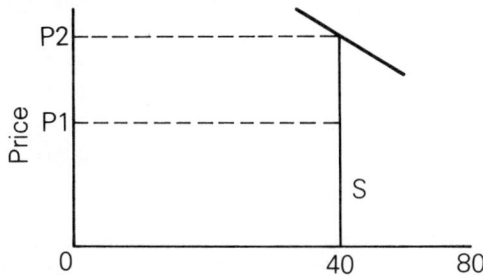

A

However, Melchester Crisps are prepared to increase the price they offer for potatoes. As a result, the McDonalds have decided to grow potatoes in *all* their fields next year. Can you think why this is so? The answer is a simple but very important one in economics. The higher the price offered for an item, the more of that item will be supplied. So, over a period of time, supply can expand.

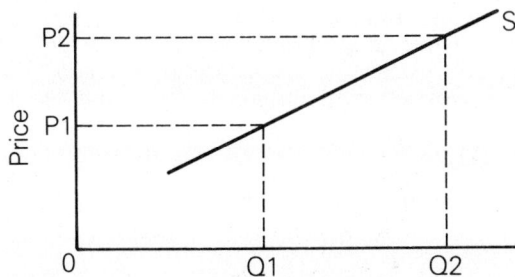

B

If we assume that the conditions of supply have not altered, then we can isolate and examine the effect a price change has on the quantity supplied:

- If prices rise there will be an extension in the quantity supplied (on diagram **B** from $0Q_1$ to $0Q_2$).
- If prices fall, there will be a contraction in the quantity supplied (from $0Q_2$ to $0Q_1$).

Changing conditions of supply

Over time the conditions that underly supply can change. If they do, then the supply curve will shift its position. The conditions underlying supply include:
- costs;
- the price of other products;
- weather;
- government policy.

Economists call such factors the *conditions* or *determinants of supply*.

An increase in total supply will lead to a shift in the supply curve to the right. A decrease in total supply will lead to a shift in the supply curve to the left. (See diagram **C**.)

If, for example:
- there is excellent weather next year;
- the government decides to subsidise potato production;
- the cost of fertilisers falls; and
- a new machine for harvesting potatoes rapidly is developed;
- the supply of potatoes will increase.

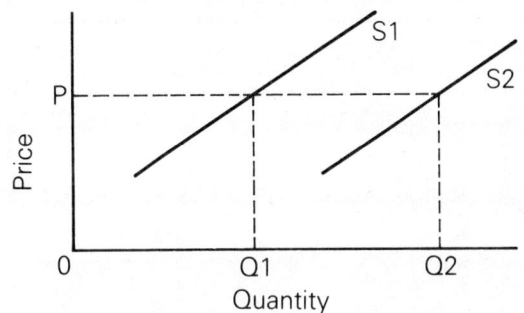

At the same price as last year, the McDonalds would be willing to supply more potatoes.

However, in other circumstances, total supply could fall. For example:
- if the McDonalds thought it would be more profitable for them to plant sugar beet given the rising price of this market;
- the weather over the next year was unsuitable for potatoes;
- the cost of pesticides increased;

then the supply conditions for potatoes would lead to a fall in total supply.

Instead of supplying (at the price $0P_1$, the quantity $0Q_1$, the McDonalds would only be prepared to supply $0Q_2$ (See diagram **D**.) They will only be willing to supply the former quantity at a higher price: point **X**.

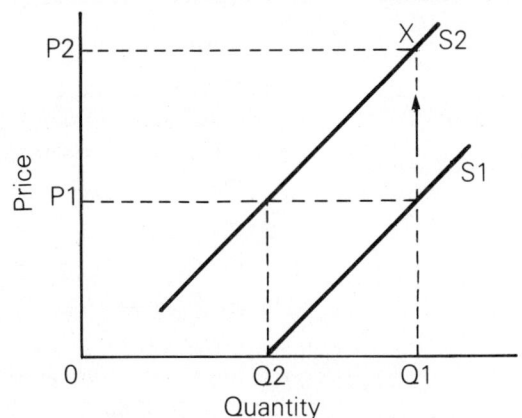

D

135

DATA RESPONSE

Hurricane blows in price rise policy

By Lisa Buckingham

HOUSEHOLD insurance premiums look set to rocket—despite a UK profits boom for major insurance companies. **Commercial Union** and **General Accident** yesterday joined **Royal** and admitted they were looking at their premium charges for buildings cover.

The reason, say the companies, is the hefty loss incurred after last October's hurricane.

But the big storm cost Commercial Union only £15 million. General Accident's bill was £20 million. That compares with £100 million for Royal, which did not have its own re-insurance in place.

And the weathermen say the hurricane—for which claims totalled £1 billion—was a one-off.

Insurers are not so confident. They think weather patterns are changing. And householders look likely to have to pay.

Premiums rates could rise from 18p to 20p for every £100 insured.

But there is some brighter news for motorists. After years of premium increases, ranging from 25 to 30 per cent, relief is on the way.

CU says it will raise premiums on average by just 4 per cent this April, against last year's 11.5 per cent. More rises may come in the autumn.

But both CU and General Accident had much better results from motor business. GA, the country's motor giant, saw losses fall from £44 million to £19 million. That is before investment income earned on the premiums.

Profits

Commercial Union topped most analysts' expectations with a 43 per cent profits rise to £170·1 million. Roman Cizdyn at stockbroker **Sheppards**, expects £270 million this year. The shares put on 3p to 339p.

General Accident was in the middle of expectations with profits £81 million higher at £204 million. **County NatWest** is looking for around £300 million this year. GA shared plunged 14p to 877p.

The big insurers are all looking over their shoulders for predators.

CU, where Aussie John Spalvins has 4·8 per cent and Robert Holmes a 'Court has a stake, decided to increase its dividend 23 per cent to 16p. It also promised to keep giving shareholders increases above inflation.

General Accident gave a 25 per cent lift to 35p. A week back Royal, where Spalvins is also on the books, lifted the dividend 24 per cent.

Source: *Daily Express*, 3 March 1988

1 Why according to the article were some insurance companies increasing the price at which they are prepared to offer household insurance?

2 Why did the Royal suffer more than other insurance companies?

3 At the same time as price increases are occurring in household insurance policies, the price at which motorists are supplied with policies may fall. Why is this so?

4 a Why is it important that insurers keep investors in their business happy?

b How do they intend to do so?

c What effect will this have on the price at which future insurance premiums are supplied?

Extension 1

Supply possible now

Supply possible in the short run

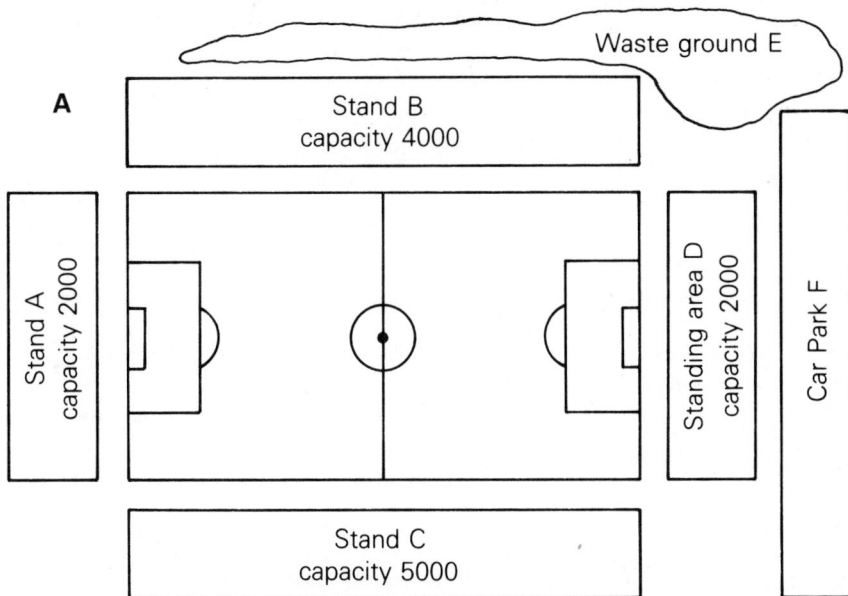

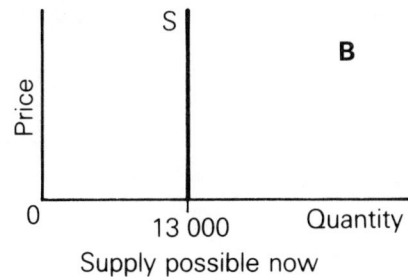

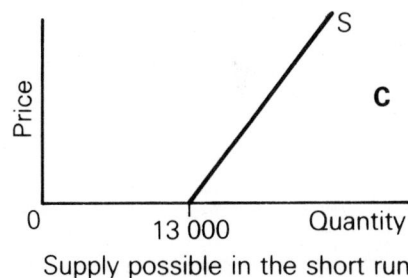

1 It is Saturday tomorrow and the day of the local football final. How many tickets can Melchester FC supply for those wanting to watch the event?

2 Stand B burns down. By how much will the total supply of seats be reduced?

3 Copy graph **B** and construct on it a supply curve that illustrates the new situation. Label the curve **S₂**. What might be the effect on the price of tickets?

4 If over time the price paid for football tickets was to rise, Melchester FC would be willing to expand the supply of seats. Suggest how they could do so.

5 On a graph show:
   a the increased amount of seats they would supply; and
   b a possible price at which they would be willing to supply seats.

Extension 2

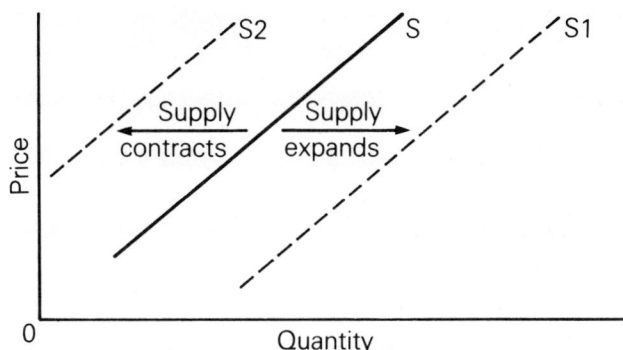

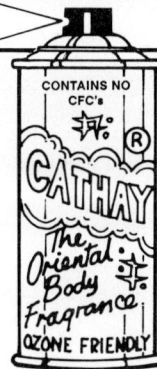

Below are listed some of the determinants of supply. Changes in these determinants can lead to expansions or contractions of the whole supply curve as shown in the diagram:
a changes in taxes/subsidies;
b changes in the supply of raw materials;
c changes in the cost of the factors of production;
d suppliers entering or leaving the market;
e technical innovation/progress.

You are the managing director of an aerosol company and have recently begun to supply the market with an 'ozone-friendly' deodorant.

Look at the situations below and decide whether the supply curve for your product, in each instance, will expand (move to the right) or contract (move to the left).

1 The government subsidises (gives money to) all firms manufacturing aerosols that do not contain fluorocarbons.

2 There is a huge increase in the supply of raw materials used in the manufacture of aerosol cans, making them cheaper to produce.

3 Interest charged on the capital you borrowed to build your new aerosol factory rises sharply.

4 Your research department finds a very cheap and environmentally sound substitute for the expensive product you have used to replace fluorocarbons.

5 Labour unrest increases with reports that your new product involves some risk to workers. You increase wages to compensate for this.

Coursework

Aim: To investigate the supply of leisure facilities within an agreed radius of your school.

1 Make a survey of leisure activities around the school, listing both private and publicly provided services. Examples of such facilities include cinemas, swimming pools, libraries, athletic tracks, football clubs.

2 Find a way of recording and displaying your results.

3 Consider whether the suppliers of leisure facilities have plans to expand the supply of these facilities.

  a What price increases will be involved?

  b How do your findings illustrate a basic principle in economics?

25 Prices and Markets

In many economies the state allocates some of the goods and services produced and consumed, but in most economies the major way in which goods are allocated is by way of the *market mechanism*. There are three stages in the operation of this mechanism:
- buyers and sellers meet;
- a price is agreed;
- the good (or service) is exchanged for some form of payment.

To market, to market

The McDonalds are off to market with a load of potatoes. They deliver their load to the crisp factory in Melchester. Sandy McDonald is very disappointed. "I thought we were going to the Market Square. I was planning to meet my friends there."

"A market," says Mr McDonald, "is any place where a good or service is bought or sold. That means that our market place is the crisp factory."

Decide for yourself

- Which of the following are markets: the Stock Exchange; your local corner shop; your local swimming pool; the hairdressers?
- Buyers and sellers often meet only by telephone. A buyer in Japan wants a ship. He telephones a ship broker in London who has a client in Sweden with a vessel for sale. Why can we say that a market exists even though the buyers and sellers are scattered around the world?

The forces of supply and demand

It is the total demand and the total supply at any one moment that *determines*, or fixes, the price of a good or service.

The equilibrium price

In the market place those who demand, or want, goods (the buyers) and those who supply goods (the sellers) are brought together. The price they agree on is the price at which the same quantity is supplied as is demanded. Because the forces of supply and demand are in balance at this point, the price is called the *equilibrium price*.

You can see this balance if you compare these three graphs.

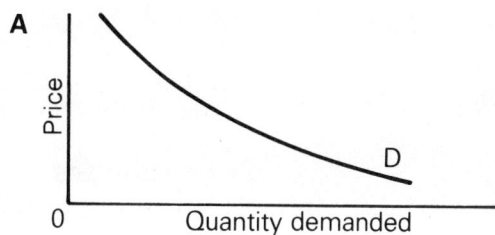

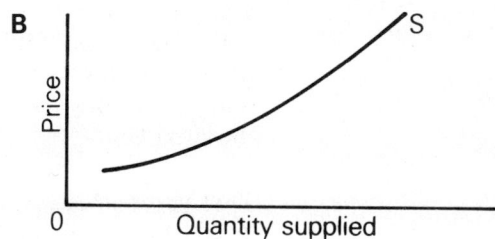

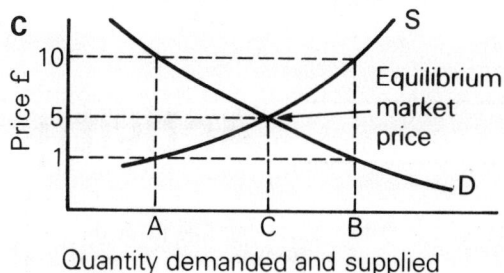

Look at graph **C**. Only at a price of £5 will the amount demanded exactly equal the amount supplied. If the price is higher, say £10, then only the quantity 0–A will be demanded. At this price suppliers would be willing to make available the quantity 0–B.

In this situation we have *excess supply*. There will be an increase in the number of goods stockpiled ready to be sold. In such situations many manufacturers will lower their prices by holding clearance sales. In this way demand is stimulated. Once the excess supply has been cleared, demand and supply will once again be in balance.

D

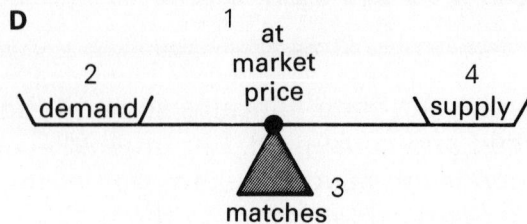

In some situations too much of a product is produced. Even though demand might exist, it would not be at a price that would encourage the supplier to take the goods to market. In these situations we say a *glut* exists.

Look again at graph **C**. In some situations there is an *excess demand*. For example, at a price of £1, O–B will be demanded, but only O–A will be supplied. In these circumstances order books would be full and queues of hopeful customers might develop.

Price changes

Excess demand will lead to an increase in price if it results in an increase in the amount supplied to the market.

Excess supply will lead to a reduction in price in order to clear stocks of goods. We will look more closely at price changes in the next Unit.

Test yourself
1 What do economists mean by equilibrium price?

ECONOMIC TERMS

Price: this is the point at which supply and demand meet. The value of a given quantity of a product at this point is called the price.
Equilibrium: when two forces match or are in balance we have a state of equilibrium.
Market: place where buyers and sellers meet.
Equilibrium market price: the point at which demand and supply balance.
Gluts: when too much of a product has been produced we have a glut of the product.

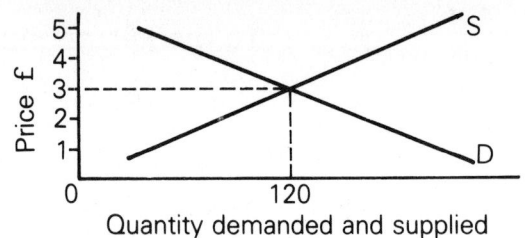

2 What is the equilibrium price in this diagram?
3 At the equilibrium price what must the quantity demanded be?
4 What was the quantity demanded and supplied at the equilibrium price in the diagram?
5 *a* How can situations of excess supply develop?
  b How can the market mechanism remove them?
6 Explain why and how situations of excess demand can lead to shortages and queues.

Activity

WHY PRICES MUST GO UP

PETROL is the most argued-about commodity in the United Kingdom. The latest round of increases in the price of a gallon has sparked-off the usual barrage of protest.

Nobody believes the oil bos-

ses when they say the price "has" to go up. But do they really have a case?

In this article we've given VIV THOMAS, BP Oil's marketing director, the chance to give the oil industry's side of the story.

THERE are few topics likely to raise the blood pressure to boiling point more rapidly than that of petrol prices.

The motorist has yet to be

born who looks forward to running out of petrol so that he can experience the joy of filling up again. A "distress purchase" the market researchers call it.

Poor old petrol. You can't feel it. You can't taste it. You can't see it.

And to make matters worse, the price you pay is up there on the petrol station pole sign in foot high letters hitting you square between the eyes at each turn of the road.

There's no getting away from it – you can't get away from petrol prices.

And because the price paid adds up to a fair slice of most families' weekly outgoings, it is naturally a sensitive topic. So it's important to try to understand the things that affect the price of the most talked-about commodity in the UK.

So what **does** affect the price you pay at the pump?

Five different factors. Three which make up the actual cost of producing a gallon are the price of crude oil from which petrol is made, the exchange rate, and the level of government taxes. Two more which decide if the oil companies can actually charge this price at the pumps are the "spot" market price of petrol and the force of the competition.

Let's take a down-to-earth look at each of these.

The price of crude oil is not, on its own, too difficult to understand. Oil companies use crude oil to make petrol and the price they pay for it obviously affects the cost to the motorist at the pumps. Up go crude oil prices, up go petrol prices, and vice versa. Simple.

"Hold on", you say, "most large oil companies have their own North Sea crude oil, so they don't actually have to buy it do they? That should bring down the price of petrol."

Oh dear, it's already started to get complicated.

The answer is that even though some oil companies have their own crude oil in the North Sea or elsewhere, they must sell it at the prevailing market price if they're to recover the quite colossal investments they have to make. So the refining and selling arms of the big oil companies have to pay the going rate.

On to the Exchange Rate. Crude oil whether we like it or not is sold all over the world in dollars, so our pounds will buy only what they are worth in dollars terms.

If the pound falls in value against the dollar as it did earlier this year we'll need more of them (pounds that is) to buy the crude oil for making petrol. So if the pound takes a dive, petrol prices should rise. If the pound gains in value against the dollar we'll be better off so petrol prices should fall. Everyone experiences these up-down exchange rate effects when they holiday abroad.

As if that itself wasn't enough to cope with, a third and vital petrol pricing factor is likely to jump out of the hat – the "spot" market price of petrol.

This "market", sometimes referred to as the Rotterdam spot market, is where surplus petrol and other oil products are bought and sold. While overall the prices of these products reflect the going price of crude oil, individually they can fluctuate enormously.

For example in the spring it is quite normal for the price of petrol to go up sharply in response to seasonal demand while fuel oil becomes cheaper. In the autumn these trends may well be reversed and at the same time crude oil may be going up or down! The price of petrol on the Rotterdam market is yet another influence on prices right across Western Europe and has a direct bearing on prices charged in the UK. It is, in effect, the "going rate" for petrol.

Contrary to belief in some quarters, the oil companies do not get together to fix petrol prices.

In that case why do companies move so quickly after one another and to precisely the same number? The answer is obvious when you think about it. They all face the same sort of costs.

Then one company moves and the others have to follow. If they don't, price competition will force the price back down immediately. And there's no point in moving to a different number because everyone else will immediately match it, and the slide down to unprofitability will have started again.

To confuse matters even more, petrol prices are always under pressure from the fierce competition that exists.

Petrol promotions which sales figures show that motorists like, cost less than 1p a gallon to run.

It's an economic fact of life that few oil companies have been able consistently to make even a reasonable return on petrol for some years.

Budget hikes in petrol tax are the only price increases that never fail to "stick". It's a sober thought that if the tax on petrol were removed tomorrow, the price at the pumps would be a mere 60 pence a gallon!

Source: *Evening Post*, 10 September 1986

Look at the article, cartoon and graph.

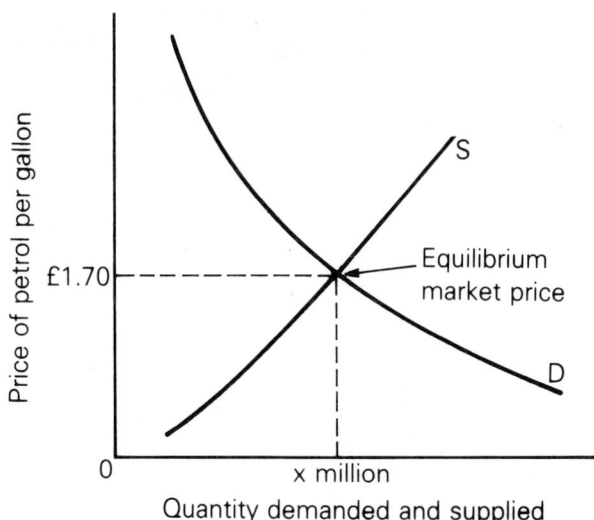

Price of petrol per gallon (vertical axis)

£1.70

Equilibrium market price

S

D

0 — x million

Quantity demanded and supplied

1 **a** What is the price of petrol?
  b Look at the graph. The price of a product is determined by the point at which supply and demand intersect (cross over). What is this point called?
2 Why is the price of petrol of concern to
  a producers;
  b consumers?
3 According to the article, which five factors make up the cost of producing, and therefore the price at which petrol companies are willing to supply their product to the market?
4 Why might the price of petrol rise in spring and the price of fuel oil fall?
5 Why is the price of petrol provided by one petrol company likely to be similar to the price provided by another company?

DATA RESPONSE

Bangers and cash

MR TOAD, of "Wind in the Willows", was inordinately proud of his shiny red motor car. More and more Britons these days share his enthusiasm. The market in classic cars is motoring ahead almost as fast as his parp-parping vehicle did up the country lanes around Toad Hall.

Last October's collapse of world stockmarkets has helped move money out of paper and into tangible assets. Veteran and classic cars have shared the benefits. At the top end of the market especially, prices have roared. Cars costing £250,000 or more—50-year-old Bugattis, Alfa Romeos, Bentleys—have seen their value rise by 30%-50% in the past 12 months, according to Mr Stewart Skilbeck of Sotheby's.

Cars that raced in competitions sell best. Earlier this month Christie's sold a 1936 Alfa Romeo race-winner for the world record price (for a Grand Prix car) of £1.5m. Last year a Bugatti Royale became the most expensive car ever, when it was sold at an auction for £5.5m. The anonymous buyer is rumoured to have sold it on privately already, for around £7m.

Not all classic-car collectors have to be immensely rich. Most of the demand is for cars costing between £10,000 and £15,000, and more of the buyers are people on high salaries, perhaps from the City, who are buying their first classic car. Some are investing their own spare cash; others are taking advantage of the fact that a few companies are waiving the rule that a company car has to be new. Almost all are men; fewer than 5% of buyers at a typical Sotheby's auction are female. Most tend to buy open-top, two-seater sports cars: perhaps an Austin Healey, a Mercedes or an old MG. The value of these cars has gone up by about a quarter in the past year.

Two worries may stall the over-enthusiastic. British classic-car magazines are now full of advertisements from American dealers. The weak dollar has sent a flood of cars to Europe. "Go down to almost any dock, and you will see container-loads of old cars being discharged," says one classic-car auctioneer. The white-walled tyres and chromium-plated wheels are a tell-tale sign of an American restoration. Some were bought by Americans in 1985 when the dollar was strong, and are already streaming back across the Atlantic.

Although the gross profits to be made on resale may look impressive, they ignore the costs involved. Classic cars have to be kept in a garage, and they may cost a lot to insure and maintain. Enthusiasts retort that the rise in prices should make the possession of a classic car self-financing, and that cars have plenty of advantages over stocks and shares. More fun, for a start.

Source: *The Economist*, 28 May 1988

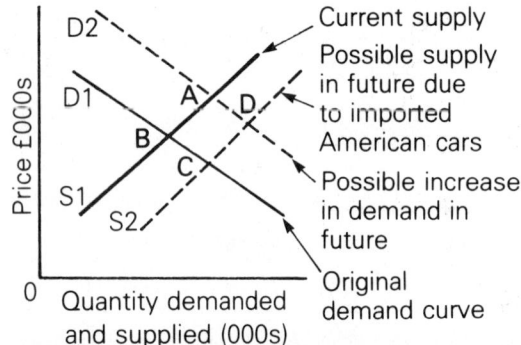

1 Why has demand increased for classic cars?
2 The cars are sold in a market where they go to the highest bidder. What name is given to this sort of market place?
3 One of the laws of demand states that the lower the price of a product the more is demanded. How is this illustrated in the article?
4 You are considering purchasing a classic car as an 'investment'. Why should you be aware of the costs involved?
5 Why might the price you could obtain when re-selling a classic car prove disappointing? Give reasons for your answer.

You may use the diagram and equilibrium points **B**, **A** and **D** to help you provide an answer.

A chrome-edged investment

Extension 1

OWNERSHIP OF TELEVISION EQUIPMENT
% of TV households

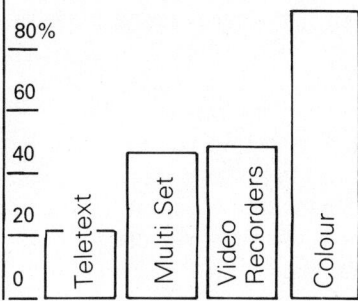

The Broadcasters' Audience Research Board (BARB) commissions and co-ordinates research for the television industry. Its annual survey shows that over 90 per cent of television households in Britain now view in colour. Half have video recorders and nearly a quarter have sets with Teletext – 16 per cent more than last year – and nearly half have more than one set.

1 a What percentage of households with televisions now view in colour?
  b Why might the demand for video recorders continue to expand?
  c What alternative to owning a video recorder exists?

2 Examine diagram A. At a price $0-P_1$ the quantity demanded is $0-Q_1$. What will be the new quantity demanded at the price $0-P_1$, if demand rises from D_1 to D_3?

3 What will happen to total demand if the government reduces taxes?

4 Watching TV is the most popular leisure activity in the UK. What will happen to the demand curve for video recorders if people begin to prefer more active leisure pursuits like golf, gardening or greyhound racing? Give reasons for your answers.

5 What will happen to the total demand for video recorders if:
  a there is an economic boom;
  b there is a rise in the birth rate?

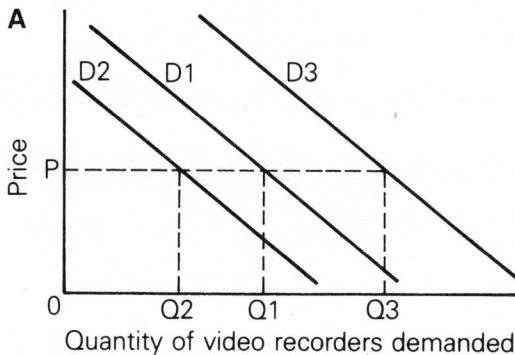

A

Extension 2

1 School meals are often provided at a subsidised price. This means the local council use ratepayers' money to keep the price of the meals they offer below the market price. The meals provided by the school meals service are nutritionally well balanced. At Melchester Comprehensive many pupils prefer instead, however, to buy fish and chips during their lunch hour at the Angel Fish and Chip Shop, opposite the school entrance. Why do you think they prefer to do so?

2 Pocket money given by parents increases. What will happen to the price of chips at the Angel Fish and Chip Shop if the equilibrium price was originally at point E?

3 Potato blight hits this year's potato crop. What will be the new equilibrium price for chips if the former price was point E?

4 A series of school assemblies about the need for a healthy diet results in a decline in demand for chips at the Angel. What will be the new equilibrium price if the former price was at point H?

5 If the demand for chips declined what would be the effect on the demand for fish?

6 Given the information provided discover the new equilibrium position for questions 2–5. First decide how demand and supply will be affected by each change.

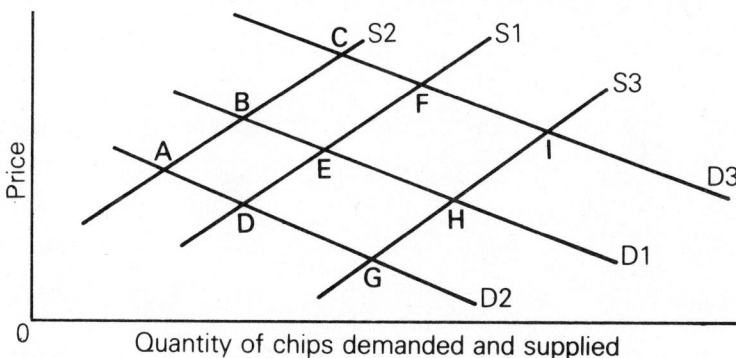

Quantity of chips demanded and supplied

Coursework

Aim: To examine the price variations for petrol at local garages.

1 Identify and collect information about the garages that exist within a three mile radius of your home or school.
2 In particular discover the various prices for a particular grade of petrol. Make sure it is the same grade that you investigate at each petrol station.
3 Describe the differences in price that you have discovered.
4 Isolate one factor, either a demand or a supply condition, that could be responsible.

5 Collect further information to determine whether it is as you suppose by interviewing or writing to petrol companies.
6 Consider what factors determine the price of a product.
7 Use this information to consider what factors, other than the one identified, could be responsible for the variations that you have discovered in petrol prices.
8 In conclusion assess the extent to which the factor you isolated is responsible for the price changes.

26 The Price of Houses

Some form of shelter or accommodation is an example of a basic economic want because:
- it represents something most of us want to have; and
- we are prepared to pay for it.

"But it's a garage not a house!"

Buying your own home is likely to be the most expensive purchase you make in your life.

The majority of people in the UK live in a home that they or their family own outright, or in a home that they are in the process of buying with the help of a building society *mortgage*.

Many other people may want to do so but they lack effective demand. These families have no choice but to rent their home from the local council, a housing association, or a private landlord. A person who rents their home is called a tenant.

Some families find it difficult to enter the housing market at all in any form, and find themselves homeless.

In a mixed economy some accommodation is provided by the public sector whilst other housing is provided by the private sector.

Decide for yourself
- Which sector provides council houses?
- Which sector provides houses for purchase?
- Your Mum and Dad live in a council flat. They have the opportunity to buy it (this is one of the rights of council tenants). Which sector of the economy will the flat be moving from and to?

Advantages of buying a home
Why do many people dream of owning their own home?
- If you can borrow the money to purchase a home, you will eventually have an asset of great value.
- You will get tax relief on the interest you pay on your loan. This helps you with your purchase.
- If you rent a property, you could end up having paid a considerable amount but still having no asset to show for it. There is also a real risk that you will have to face rent increases.
- As you get older, your income usually increases, but your mortgage payments will not vary greatly. The main change will be any variations in the rate of interest you pay on the outstanding loan.
- Because the house is your own property, you can extend it (if planning permission is given), improve it, and you are the one who will benefit.
- The asset you own is likely to increase in value while you are paying for it. If you ever want to move, you will be able to sell your house and have money towards the purchase of a new one.

The demand for and supply of houses
These advantages go a long way to explaining why there has been such a demand for private houses in recent years.

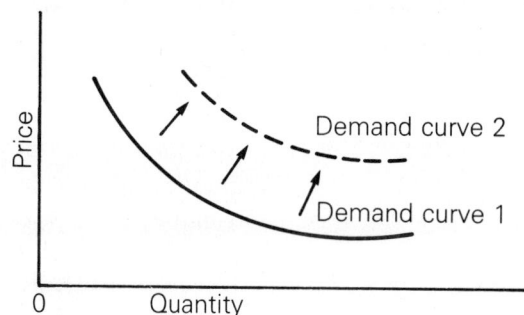

However, there are other reasons, too, for this increased demand:
- More people are living longer in the UK today.
- More people (students, pensioners, divorced couples, etc.) live on their own.
- As living standards have improved some people can afford two or more homes. This leads to a great demand for holiday homes in some parts of the country.
- People's preferences have changed. People are less willing to rent and more willing to make the sacrifices associated with buying a home. The shortage and thus

145

expense of rented accommodation increases this demand.
- An increasing number of people save with building societies. This helps them to provide the deposit for their first home, as well as secure a mortgage to purchase the property.

All these reasons have further swelled the demand to buy houses.

Activity

The average price of houses in Melchester is shown by the equilibrium point **E**. At the price indicated (**p**) the quantity demanded equals the quantity supplied (**q**).

Answer these questions, starting from Point **E** on each occasion.

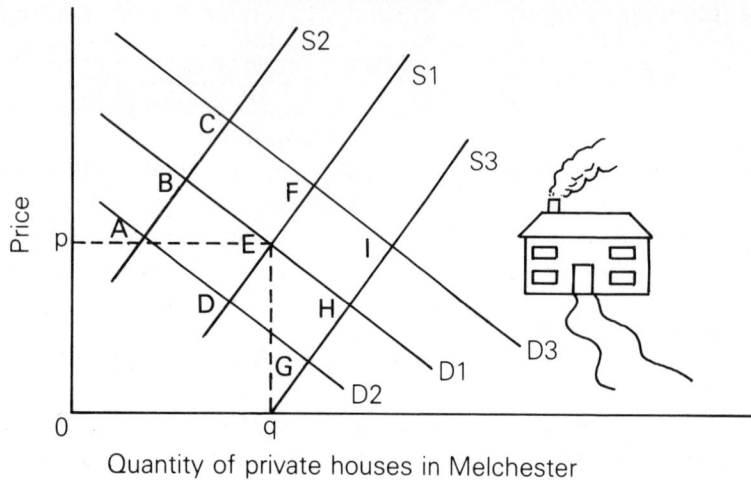

Quantity of private houses in Melchester

1 What will be the new equilibrium point if everyone's income declines dramatically?
2 The banks and building societies of Melchester are competing with each other for business. Both increase the number of advances (loans) made to home buyers. What will be the new equilibrium point?
3 What would be the new equilibrium point if several builders construct private housing estates for sale on the edge of Melchester?
4 What will be the new equilibrium point if it proves necessary to demolish a large number of old dwellings in Melchester in order to make way for multi-storey car parks?
5 The divorce rate in Melchester has begun rising dramatically. At the same time more elderly people demand sheltered accommodation. What will be the new equilibrium point?

Building societies

Building societies are specialist savings institutions. They are usually set up on a mutual basis to provide a means of borrowing money from savers and lending money to potential home buyers.

A loan to buy a home is made in the form of a *mortgage*. Mortgages are of two types: repayment and endowment.
- **Repayment mortgage**: a loan that involves the paying back of a sum borrowed for house purchase that covers the *principal* (the amount borrowed) and the interest on the loan.
- **Endowment mortgage**: the loan is covered by a life insurance policy. The insurance policy matures when the loan has to be repaid and provides a sum of money to cover the payment.

You are usually able to borrow two or three times your annual income. In return for the loan, you surrender (or mortgage) the deeds (or ownership documents) of the property to the building society. When you repay the full loan, the deeds are returned to you and you become the sole owner.

Many other savings institutions now compete with building societies to lend people money for house purchases. These include banks, insurance companies (through the offer of endowment assurance) and local authorities.

Problems of owning your own home

Budgeting very carefully and trying not to over-extend your commitments are very important skills to learn. This is particularly true in the early years of owning your home. You need to make various complex decisions in order to purchase your own home:
- Estate agents help in the initial stages of finding a home. (Normally the seller, not the buyer, pays the estate agent.)
- A surveyor needs to examine the prop-

erty prior to purchase for defects. (The building society's surveyor is only ensuring that the property's value is not less than the loan.)

- Lawyers, called solicitors, can help *convey* the property, that is transfer the legal right to the property from one owner to another.

Even after all these processes have been gone through, an increasing number of people default on their mortgages because they cannot afford to keep up the payments. Some people find themselves trapped by the 'hidden' costs of home ownership: rates, repairs, insurance, etc. If a person defaults on their mortgage, the lender can take over the property.

Housing and supply factors

House prices rise or fall because of changes in total demand. Diagram **A** shows this.

They also rise and fall because of changes in total supply. Diagram **B** shows this.

Some of these supply factors include:

- the cost of land;
- the cost of building homes;
- the rate of interest on loans (this can be important when money is being borrowed to build property).

A

B

Test yourself

1 Why do some people find it difficult to secure a place to live in?
2 What alternatives to house purchase exist? Can you think of any not mentioned in this chapter?
3 Why might you advise someone to consider buying a home rather than renting?
4 Give two reasons why the demand for housing has increased.
5 What is a building society?
6 What possible problems lie ahead if you buy your own home?

ECONOMIC TERM
Mortgage: a loan made against the value of a property.

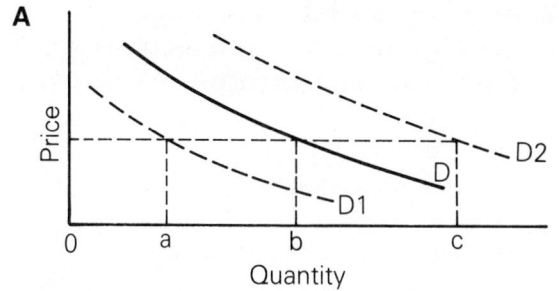

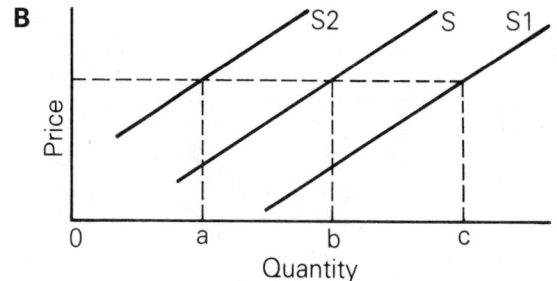

DATA RESPONSE 1

A Stock of dwellings: by tenure

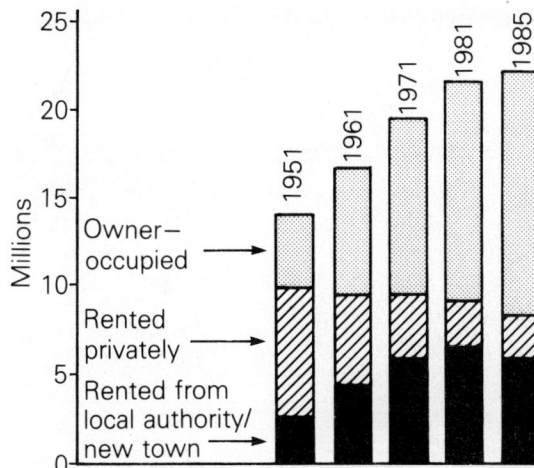

B Building society mortgages: average dwelling prices, mortgage advances, and income of borrowers

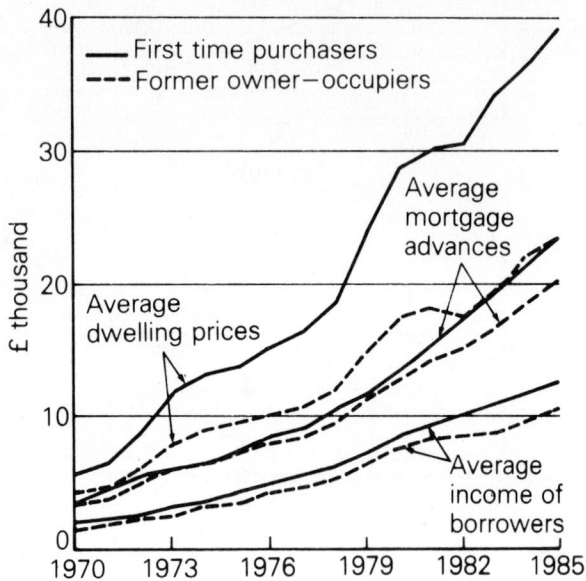

Legend:
— First time purchasers
--- Former owner–occupiers

Average mortgage advances
Average dwelling prices
Average income of borrowers

Y-axis: £ thousand (0, 10, 20, 30, 40)
X-axis: 1970, 1973, 1976, 1979, 1982, 1985

C Building societies: repossessions and mortgage arrears[1]

United Kingdom   Thousands

	Loans at end of period	Loans in arrear at end-period		Properties taken into possession in period
		By 6–12 months	By over 12 months	
1979	5,264	8.4[2]	..	2.5
1980	5,396	13.5[2]	..	3.0
1981	5,505	18.7[2]	..	4.2 [3]
1982	5,664	23.8	4.8	6.0
1983	5,949	25.6	6.5	7.3
1984	6,354	41.9	8.3	10.9
1985	6,707	49.6	11.4	16.8
1985				
1st half	6,530	43.8	9.1	7.4
2nd half	6,707	49.6	11.4	9.4

1 Building Societies Association estimates.
2 Figure should be treated with caution.
3 Change in method of estimation.

Source: *Social Trends* 17

1 Using **A** explain what has happened to the percentage of owner-occupied dwellings since 1951.

2 Over the same period of time which sector of housing, in particular, has declined?

3 Using **B** explain what changes have occurred to the average dwelling price since 1973.

4 What factors have contributed to these changes?

5 Using **C** explain:
  a What has happened to the numbers of mortgage arrears during the 1980s?
  b What has happened to the number of properties that have been re-possessed?

6 What are the benefits and costs of owning your own home?

Extension

Your House 'Earns' More in a Year Than You Do!

"LAST year, my wife and I both worked hard to achieve a joint income of £21,000. During that same period our capital increased by £25,000 for which we did absolutely nothing. It doesn't seem right, somehow."

However

Since the galloping inflationary days of the early seventies, house prices have beaten inflation – but not by much.

Inflation over the period was approximately 330 per cent against 337 per cent for average U.K. house prices.

Source: *Daily Mail*, 9 June 1988

Average Prices & % Increase 1973–87

UK £45,199 (£10,337) + 337%

Scotland £29,920 (£9,289) + 222%

N. Ireland £28,228 (£10,337) + 173%

North £27,542 (£7,874) + 250%

North West £31,106 (8,542) + 264%

Yorkshire & Humberside £28,987 (£7,526) + 285%

W. Midlands £33,572 (£9,298) + 261%

E. Midlands £31,873 (£8,432) + 279%

Wales £31,361 (£9,047) + 247%

East Anglia £43,760 (£10,538) + 315%

South West £45,487 (£11,252) + 304%

G. London £68,329 (£14,774) + 362%

South East £52,234 (£13,582) + 284%

1 What has happened to the average price of houses in the UK over the period 1973–87?
2 According to the map on p 148, in which region of the UK are:
   a house prices currently the highest on average;
   b house prices currently the lowest on average?
3 Imagine a new motorway was built connecting London to East Anglia. Explain how house prices in East Anglia would change and why.

4 What effect is the opening of the Channel Tunnel likely to have on house prices in the South East region?
5 Assume that unemployment increases in the Yorkshire and Humberside region, but falls dramatically in the East Midlands. Explain how house prices in each area might change.

DATA RESPONSE 2

	Average earnings	Average house prices
Northern	£9308	£26 653
Yorks & Humber	£9412	£25 989
East Midlands	£9152	£29 316
East Anglia	£9516	£36 967
Greater London	£12 116	£57 816
South East	£11 128	£50 696
South West	£9308	£40 316
West Midlands	£9630	£29 511
North West	£9620	£28 763
Wales	£9308	£28 667
Scotland	£9880	£29 065

HOUSE PRICES 1974

North £8 400
Yorkshire & Humberside £8 200
Greater London £14 900
South East £13 900

HOUSE PRICES 1986

North £26 600
Yorkshire & Humberside £26 000
Greater London £57 800
South East £50 700

The chart shows average earnings and house prices in various regions of the United Kingdom in 1986; the maps show house prices in 1974 and 1986.

1 Referring to the diagram, in which region in 1986 were house prices:
   a lowest;
   b highest?

2 Using your knowledge of supply and demand, explain what relationship, if any, there is between house prices and earnings.

3 What are the likely effects on the mobility of labour of the differences in house prices between the various regions?

4 Apart from changes in earnings, suggest reasons which might account for the increase in house prices between 1974 and 1986.

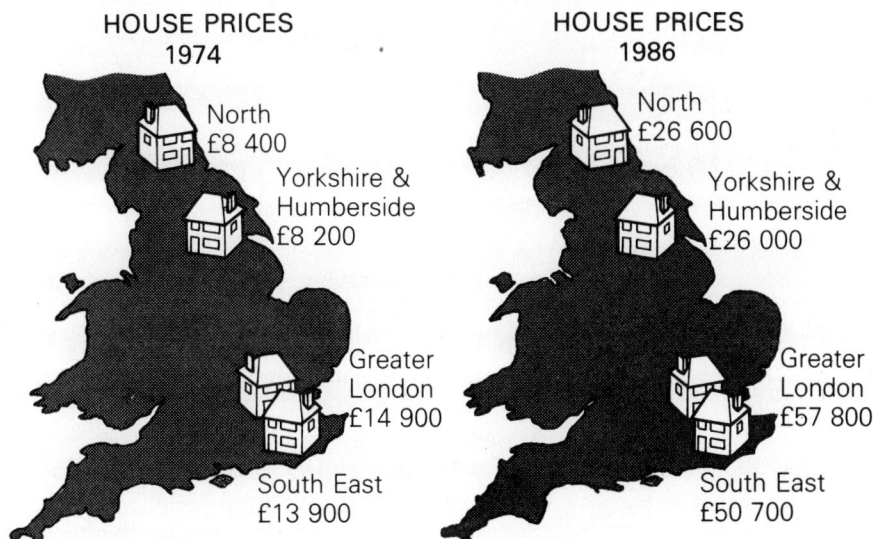

Coursework

Aim: To investigate house price changes.

1 Examine the movement of housing prices in your area in the last year.
2 To what extent could changes in tastes and preferences for housing within your area account for the movements in house prices?

3 What other factors might be responsible?

27 Elasticity

The demand for a good will often change in response to the price of a good. We can measure how demand changes in response to a change in price by examining the shape of the demand curve. If demand is very responsive to a change in price, we describe the demand curve as *elastic*. If demand is not so responsive (and does not change a great deal) to a change in price, then we have an *inelastic* curve. *Elasticity* is the term we use to describe the responsiveness of one factor (either demand or supply) to a change in another factor, for example, price.

Activity

Elasticity

Paper	Average daily sales	
	March	April
Daily Telegraph	1 141 400	1 133 000
The Times	468 000	447 000
The Independent	380 500	372 000

1 a What happened to the price of the three newspapers in April 1988?

b By how much did sales of the *Daily Telegraph* decline as a result, between March and April 1988?

2 Calculate the percentage change in the quantity demanded for the *Daily Telegraph* between March and April 1988.

To work out the percentage change in a figure, place the difference between the original and the new sum over the original sum and multiply by 100/1. (For example, the percentage change between 300 and 200 is 100/200 × 100/1 = 50%.)

3 Why was there only a small decline in the quantity demanded when the price of these papers rose by 20%? Look at the illustration for ideas and then add your own.

Price elasticity of demand

The way demand responds (changes) to a given change in price is called the *price elasticity of demand* (PED). The formula for calculating this is:

$$\text{PED} = \frac{\text{(Percentage change in quantity demanded)}}{\text{(Percentage change in price)}} = \text{Coefficient of price elasticity}$$

If price rose by 5% and demand fell by 20%, then the PED would be 20/5 or 4/1 or 4. Demand in this situation is elastic because the change in quantity demanded is greater than the change in price (the coefficient of demand is greater than 1). If the coefficient of demand is less than 1, demand is said to be inelastic. The curves in diagrams **A** and **B** show some of the situations possible when examining elasticity.

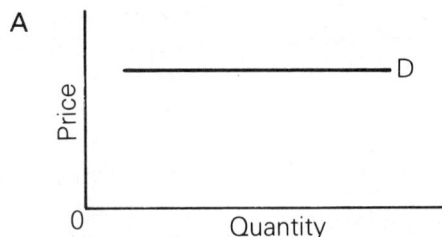

A

- Here the PED value is greater than 1.
- The curve that is shown is relatively flat – and is said to be elastic.
- A large change in quantity is produced by a small change in price. This frequently happens if the good is a luxury or has a close substitute.

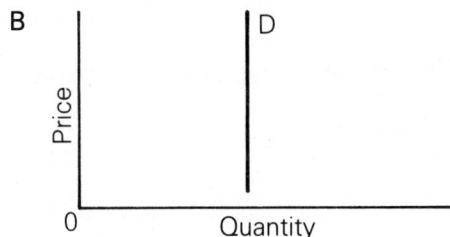

B

- Here the PED value is less than 1.
- The curve is steep – and is said to be inelastic.
- A quite small change in demand is produced by a quite large change in price. In this situation people remain loyal to the product.

The product may be a necessity or comparatively cheap. For example, if you were a car owner and enjoyed driving but hated commuting by train, would you continue to buy petrol if the price rose? If you need matches to light your gas stove, would you stop buying matches because they had doubled in price?

If there are no close *substitutes* or if the percentage of total income spent on an item is very small, then demand for the product will tend to be inelastic.

Decide for yourself

The price of bubblegum rises by 150%, from 2p to 5p. Demand hardly falls at all (by 2% at the most).
- Does this describe an elastic or inelastic situation?

The price of margarine falls by 5%, and demand increases by 30%.
- Is this an elastic or inelastic situation?

The price of chocolate buttons rises by 5% and demand falls by 40%.
- Is this an elastic or an inelastic situation?
- Can you think of a situation where demand is elastic?

Income elasticity

It is not only demand which can be described as having elasticity. Income elasticity or YED is measured as follows:

$$\text{YED} = \frac{\text{(Percentage change in quantity demanded)}}{\text{(Percentage change in income)}} = \text{Coefficient of income elasticity}$$

Usually if income rises, people buy more of a good, but sometimes they buy less. Think about this. If your income rose, would you:
- buy more bread?
- buy more of other items, like steak and fruit?
- not change your spending on food?

In the case of bread, you would probably switch a lot of your extra spending power to a superior item more expensive or luxurious, for example meat. For this reason we can describe bread as an *inferior good*.

Cross elasticity of demand

The change in demand for one good given a change in price of another good is called cross elasticity of demand, or XED. It is measured as follows:

$$XED = \frac{\text{Coffee: percentage change in quantity demanded}}{\text{Percentage change in price of tea}}$$

If, for example, tea rises in price, more people will switch to drinking coffee, as the two are close substitutes.

If, however, the price of tea rose and the quantity demanded of sugar fell, then we would be describing a different relationship, in which the two goods *complement* each other:

- If a price rise produces a fall in demand for a related product, we can assume the goods are complements (for example, tea and sugar).
- If a price rise produces a rise in demand for a related product, then we can assume the goods are substitutes (for example, tea and coffee).

Elasticity of supply

Just as we can talk about the elasticity of demand, so we can talk about the elasticity of supply or PES. It is calculated as follows:

$$PES = \frac{\text{(Percentage change in quantity supplied)}}{\text{(Percentage change in price)}} = \text{Coefficient of supply elasticity}$$

Imagine that computer games become the latest craze, and there is a rush for the limited stock in the shops. Prices of those remaining and for new orders rise sharply. However, there are production problems at the largest supplier of games. Supply can be said to be inelastic in this situation; the price increase has no effect on supply.

Decide for yourself

- Tom Tidy saves everything. He has a warehouse full of last year's Hallowe'en masks. If Hallowe'en parties are all the rage this year, why might the supply of masks be elastic?

ECONOMIC TERMS

Elasticity: the responsiveness of one factor to a change in another. Examples include: price elasticity of supply (PES); price elasticity of demand (PED); income elasticity (YED); cross elasticity (XED).

Substitute: when an item can be purchased in place of another, for example tea instead of coffee.

Complement: when an item is usually purchased alongside another, for example tea and sugar or milk.

Normal good: demand increases as income increases.

Inferior good: demand falls when income rises; consumers can afford more expensive and preferred substitutes.

Superior good: demand increases when income increases but the % change in demand is greater than the % change in income.

Test yourself

1 What is meant by the price elasticity of demand?
2 Your favourite brand of soft drink increases in price by 10%.
   a Will you change how much you buy and by how much?
   b Is, then, the quantity you demand of the drink elastic or inelastic?
3 What is the income elasticity of demand for private homes likely to be if there is a rise in incomes?
4 What is the cross elasticity of demand likely to be for fish and chips?
5 A good rises in price by 200% and demand falls by 20%.
   a Calculate the price elasticity of demand.
   b Is the situation elastic or inelastic?

DATA RESPONSE

Price	Quantity demanded	Percentage change in quantity demanded	Percentage change in price	Elasticity
10	100			
9	200	100	10	10
8	350	A	11·1	B
7	C	200	12·5	D
6	1000	E	F	G
5	H	I	J	2

In calculating elasticities you need to first calculate the percentage change in both quantity demanded and the percentage change in price.

You can see how a percentage change is calculated if you look in the activity section of this chapter.

1. What is the percentage change if the original sum is 10 and the new sum is 8?

2. Using the chart, calculate the percentage change in quantity demanded at point **A**.

3. Now calculate the elasticity of demand at point **B**.

4. Calculate the answers for boxes **C** and **D**.

5. Now calculate the answers for boxes **E**, **F**, and **G**.

6. Finally calculate the answer for **H**, **I** and **J**.

Extension 1

TRANSPORT
(Original price £8)

Before price rise Ben goes to work by bus each day using his weekly travel pass.

After the price rise he continues to buy his travel pass.

NEWSFLASH
Government moves to curb spending boom. Goods to rise in price by 10%

GYM

Before the price rise he went to the gym every day.

After the price rise he goes each day.

Ben Pinfield:
works for British Telecom in Halifax. He is a keen sportsman and is a member of a sports club. He enjoys unwinding after a hard day's work by going to the gym for a workout

SOAP (Original price 40p)

Before price rise Ben buys one bar a month.

After price rise he continues to do so.

BREAD (Original price 70p)

Before the price rise he buys 4 loaves a week.

After price rise he purchases 3 loaves a week.

1. In the case of Ben Pinfield, what will be the price elasticity of demand for his travel pass if the above price rise takes effect?

2. Is Ben's demand for his travel pass elastic or inelastic? Give reasons for your answer.

3. Calculate the price elasticity of demand for bread. Is Ben's response elastic or inelastic?

4. What substitutes might Ben consume instead of bread? Use your answer to help you explain your answer to **3**.

5. Given the rise in the price of Ben's gym admission what is the cross elasticity of demand for bread?

6. Why do you think the rise in the price of soap has not affected the quantity of soap demanded?

Extension 2

NEW POTATOES 400 kg quantity demanded increases to 500 kg

APPLES – quantity demanded falls from 300 kg a week to 100 kg

EXOTIC, EXPENSIVE IMPORTED FRUIT – quantity demanded increases with people's income

KIWIS JUST ARRIVED

KIM LIEUNG – DESIGNER
She:
- leads a hectic life;
- is health conscious
- prefers fresh foods;
- loves summer fruits;
- her income has increased from £15,000 to £20,000

Original price was £2 a punnet. Local strawberries come into season and price falls to 50p a punnet. Quantity demanded increases from 20 punnets to 200 a week

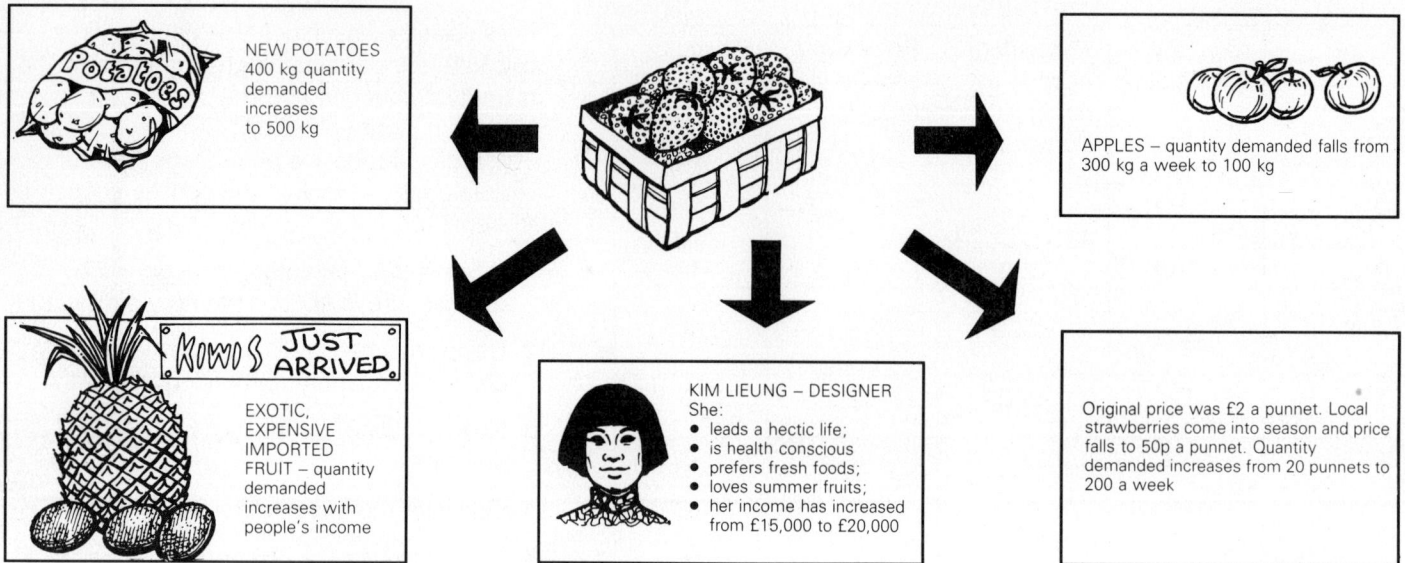

1 Calculate the cross-elasticity of demand for new potatoes if strawberries fall in price by the amount shown.

2 Are new potatoes a substitute for strawberries or are they jointly demanded? Give reasons for your answer, referring to the changes that occur in the quantity demanded for one product when a price changes in the other product.

3 a Calculate the cross-elasticity of demand for apples when strawberries fall in price.
  b Are apples a substitute for strawberries or are they jointly demanded?

4 What is the price elasticity of demand for strawberries?

5 What is the income elasticity of demand with respect to strawberries if income rose by the amount shown for Ms Lieung?

Coursework

Aim: To investigate the elasticity of different products.

1 Identify a number of price changes in a local supermarket.
2 Select a product whose price has changed significantly.
3 Devise an effective way of determining the change that has occurred in the quantity demanded of this product.

4 Examine a range of other products retailed by the supermarket. Consider which of these might be looked on as substitutes for the chosen product.
5 Consider which of your list might be complements for the product in question.
6 a Examine the changes in the quantity demanded of substitutes.
  b Examine the changes in the quantity demanded of complements.
  c What have you discovered?

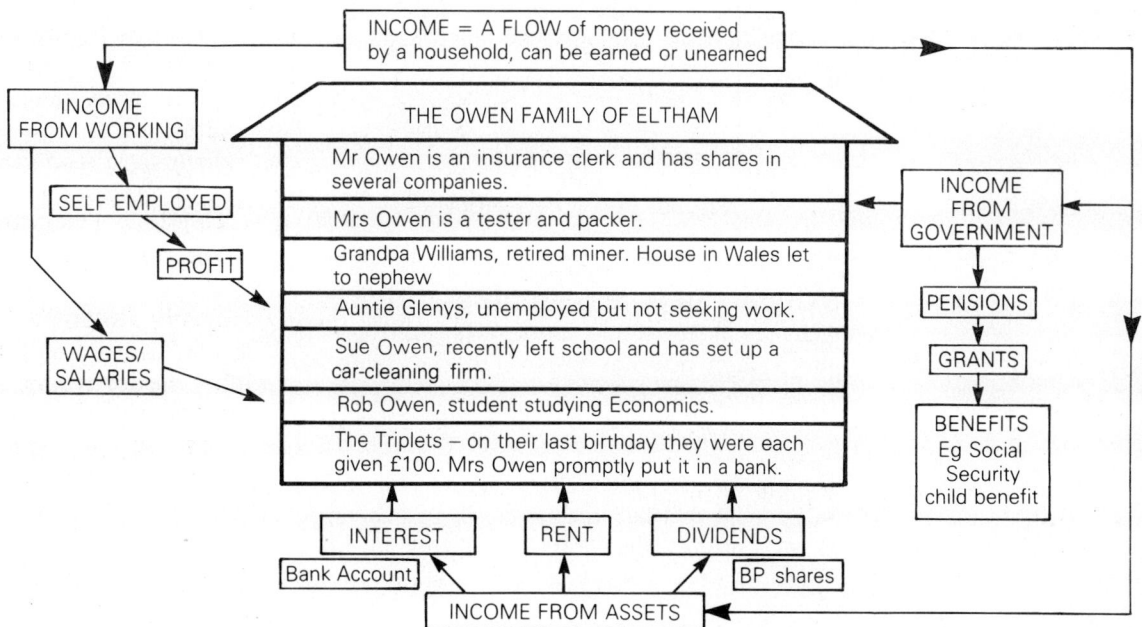

28 Factor Rewards

The various factors of production in an economy receive rewards in different ways:
- Labour earns a wage.
- Businesses earn profits.
- Property let out or hired earns rent.
- Money invested earns interest.

Economists refer to all these rewards as *factor rewards*.

Decide for yourself

Complete each of these sentences using the appropriate factor reward:
- Hugh works as a labourer and receives a . . . .
- Patricia has hired out her car to Ariana in return for . . . .

- Shaheen is delighted with her new business selling furniture. In the first year she has made a healthy . . . .
- Sam put £3000 on deposit in the bank and has just received his first statement showing the . . . .

Activity

```
INCOME = A FLOW of money received
by a household, can be earned or unearned

INCOME FROM WORKING
  SELF EMPLOYED
    PROFIT
  WAGES/SALARIES

THE OWEN FAMILY OF ELTHAM
  Mr Owen is an insurance clerk and has shares in several companies.
  Mrs Owen is a tester and packer.
  Grandpa Williams, retired miner. House in Wales let to nephew
  Auntie Glenys, unemployed but not seeking work.
  Sue Owen, recently left school and has set up a car-cleaning firm.
  Rob Owen, student studying Economics.
  The Triplets – on their last birthday they were each given £100. Mrs Owen promptly put it in a bank.

INCOME FROM GOVERNMENT
  PENSIONS
  GRANTS
  BENEFITS Eg Social Security child benefit

INTEREST        RENT        DIVIDENDS
Bank Account              BP shares
        INCOME FROM ASSETS
```

Factor rewards

1 Which two people in the Owen family are employees and receive a wage or salary?

2 Who is self-employed in the Owen family? What do we call the income made by this person?

3 Who receives income in the form of rent within the family? Where is the property that is rented?

4 What benefits would you imagine are received from the government by the Owen family?

5 What other forms of income are received from the government by the Owen family? Who receives them?

6 Who in the family receives
   a interest;
   b dividends?

Wages and salaries

Probably the best known or most familiar form of return, or reward, for a factor of production is the one received by workers. They sell their labour to employers for either a wage or salary.

- A **salary** is a payment made to non-manual workers and is usually paid on a monthly basis. Salaries are paid on a fixed basis and are not dependent on the number of hours worked.
- **Wages** are paid, usually weekly, to manual workers for either a set number of hours of work completed per week, or the number of items produced. There is usually a *basic wage* (for a standard number of hours worked per week) plus: overtime at a higher rate than the basic wage for any extra hours worked; possibly also a bonus rate linked to the amount produced during the week.

A wage is not only the reward labour receives, but it is also the price paid by the entrepreneur for employing labour.

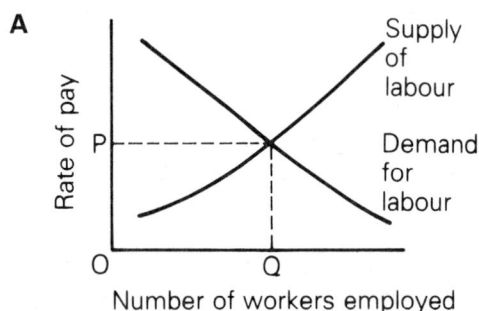

Why are people paid differently?

Why is it that one person is paid much more than another person in the same or other organisations?

Decide for yourself

- Look at this list and sort out, in descending order, the jobs in terms of the amount you think each occupation earns.

architect	teacher	doctor
decorator	shop assistant	nurse
bus driver	road sweeper	home help
mechanic	airline pilot	

- Using this list, decide why some workers might earn more than others. Like all prices, a wage is determined by both the forces of demand and those of supply.

The demand curve for labour

The demand curve for labour slopes down and to the right:

The demand curve is downward sloping because:

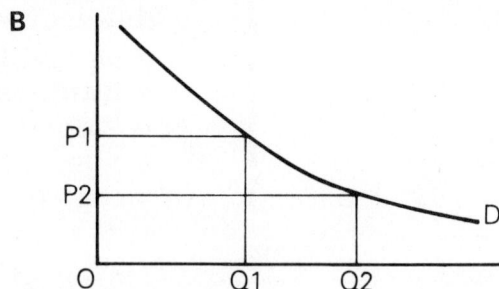

- firms are willing to take on more labour if wage rates fall;
- lower wages lead to a reduction in costs, and in turn an increase in profits, so it becomes worthwhile to hire more workers and expand production;
- the demand curve will shift (to the right or left) if there is a change in the total demand for labour;
- labour is said to be a *derived demand*. This means that the demand for labour depends upon (or is derived from) the demand for the products it produces. If there is an increase in the demand for an item (be it a good or a service), then the firm in question will expand production and increase the number of workers it employs. (The demand curve will shift to the right.)

Supply factors

If you are an employer and are willing to offer higher wages, you are likely to attract more workers.

The supply curve for labour slopes upwards to the right.

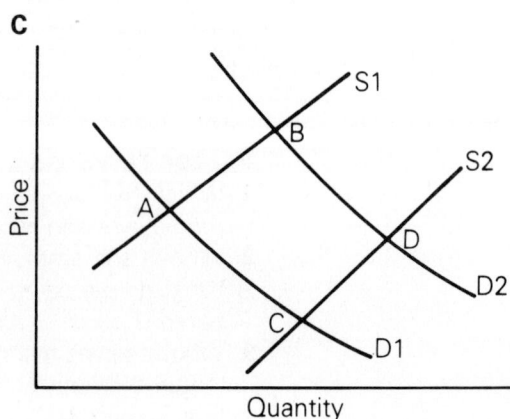

The price of labour

In the boatyard is Mr Boyd able to earn a high salary in comparison to the firm's typist? Why?

One reason is that his skills are in short supply. Not everyone is a talented designer of boats, or has the necessary experience or qualifications. Far more people have the skills of the firm's typist.

At the same time his labour is in demand. However, elsewhere in Shallowford, the closure of several factories has reduced the demand for industrial cleaners.

What is likely to happen to the wage rate for cleaners?

Other factor rewards

Profit: this is the reward an entrepreneur receives for the risks of running a business. It can be calculated by taking total costs away from total revenue.

Some profits will be re-invested in the firm by the entrepreneur; some of the profits will be used to pay taxes on the firm to the government.

Interest: this is the return for loaning a person or a firm capital.

The *rate of interest* charged is calculated as a percentage per annum (each year). Interest rates change according to factors that affect the supply and demand for money. When the interest rate rises, it becomes more expensive to borrow money. When interest rates fall, it becomes less expensive to borrow. If the chance of making a profit is very favourable, then the entrepreneur might be willing to pay a higher rate of interest than normal in order to finance the enterprise.

Rent: this is the return to a person or firm for the use of their land. People also rent property (offices, private houses, factories, etc) and equipment (cars, bulldozers, etc.).

Economic rent

This term is different from the idea of rent as non-economists know it. Economic rent is the surplus a person earns in a job above and beyond the amount needed to keep them continuing to work in that line of business. The amount required to keep a person working in a particular job is called the *transfer earning*. Let us look at the example of your economics teacher. He or she might earn about £12 000 per annum. They might be quite willing to continue to work as a teacher if they were only paid £11 000. It follows that the economic rent in this case is £1 000. Thus the transfer earning is £11 000 for, if their salary were to fall below this point, they would leave teaching for some other work.

Some people, often because they have special skills that are in great demand but who in other respects might not be well qualified, can earn extremely high economic rents.

Decide for yourself

- Why do you think pop stars, footballers, and more recently some athletes earn such huge sums?

When wages rise in an occupation, people are attracted to it by the extra income offered. For example, nurses were offered quite high pay increases in 1988 both to attract them to, and to hold them in, their jobs.

In situations where the supply of labour is elastic, slight increases in pay can result in quite large influxes of workers. This, for example, is true in areas of unskilled work where people can move quite easily from one job to another. For example, when London Transport increased its wage rates in the 1970s there were many applicants for the jobs. A number of these people were clerical workers with a relatively low level of training, and comparatively poor levels of pay.

When a company expands and employers need workers, they often increase the wage they are willing to pay. This can lead to workers quitting their work elsewhere, and their former employers then having to increase wage rates to retain them. This phenomenon is described as *wage drift*.

ECONOMIC TERMS
Wage: the amount of pay a worker receives for a given amount of work.
Economic rent: the payment a factor of production receives above its transfer earnings.
Transfer earnings: the payment a factor of production receives in its next best use.

Test yourself

1 What is the return labour receives?
2 Explain why a headteacher might earn more than:
   a a refuse collector;
   b an ordinary classroom teacher.
3 Labour is said to be a derived demand. What does this mean?
4 Why does Mr Boyd earn a higher wage than the industrial cleaner?
5 What is meant by economic rent? Illustrate your answer by referring to the economic rent likely to be earned by fashion designers. Refer to the term transfer earnings in your answer.
6 Explain how economic rent could apply to your decision to keep your savings in a building society rather than kept at the bank.
7 What is the difference between rent and profit?
8 What is wage drift? Why do you think it can be dangerous for an economy?

DATA RESPONSE

Index of average weekly earnings: industry groups
April 1986

| | All industries and services (Divisions 0 to 9) | | | |
| | Manual employees | | Non-manual employees | |
	Males	Females	Males	Females
Great Britain	174.4	107.5	244.9	145.7
North	173.0	104.6	224.1	136.1
Yorkshire & Humberside	171.2	101.1	226.6	135.3
East Midlands	169.8	103.3	223.9	136.3
East Anglia	169.8	102.9	228.0	135.7
South East	184.7	117.4	270.0	160.8
South West	165.3	101.0	224.3	135.6
West Midlands	169.7	105.8	226.8	134.8
North West	173.1	107.5	231.2	138.0
England	175.0	108.2	246.5	147.0
Wales	167.9	104.7	222.8	134.4
Scotland	173.0	103.2	238.3	139.1
Northern Ireland	149.3	99.2	218.7	140.8

Source: CSO, *Regional Trends 22*, 1987

1 What is the difference between a manual and a non-manual worker?

2 Who earns more on average, manual or non-manual male employees?

3 In which region of England are the highest earnings made by all employees?

4 In which region of the UK are the lowest earnings made by manual employees?

5 Explain why either:
   a regional differences
   b gender differences exist in the distribution of income.

6 You are a superb gardener and also a fairly good financial journalist. Explain why:
   a it is in your interest to be a journalist;
   b non-manual workers on average earn more than manual employees.

Extension 1

The Thomson Twins

Samuel and Samantha Thomson are twins, and very talented ones too. Samuel has just been signed by Melchester Football Club, and is earning £400 a week. Samantha is an up-and-coming pop star. Last year she earned £52 000.

Samuel has very rare football dribbling and shooting skills. He has already scored five goals and the fans love him. Samantha is not only a superb singer but also composes her own songs.

Before they each became successful they worked together in a car wash and each earned £60 a week. Jobs are scarce in Melchester. If they were not in their current jobs they would probably have to return to car washing.

1 What are Samuel and Samantha's transfer earnings?
2 What is the economic rent earned in a week by:
   a Samuel;
   b Samantha?
   Explain why they are able to earn the amounts they do.
3 Which of the two earns the most economic rent?
4 What are the skills that Samuel and Samantha have that allow them to earn the amounts they do?
5 In the long run consider:
   a why in each case their earnings of economic rent could decline;
   b how the economic rent they earn might increase.

Marketing		Advertising revenue		Changes in taste and fashion

Counterfeits, imitations, pirating		Fans switch loyalty		Promotions

Decline in skill levels		Accidents, injuries		Sponsorships

Extension 2

Cathy Cheung. Aged 38. A doctor of medicine and a surgeon. Described by her colleagues as popular and hard working. One friend said of her "She is brilliant in her field. She has very rare talents and skills."
Salary £28 000

Nick Walsh. Aged 29. North sea diver. "It's a skilled and dangerous job. The accident rate is high. I miss my family a lot when I am away."
Salary £21 000

Connie Miller. Aged 23. A machinist in a Bradford clothes factory. Left school with 3 CSEs.
Salary £6000 (including overtime).

Martin Pullin. Aged 24. A porter in a Birmingham hospital. Left school with few qualifications. Likes working with people.
Salary £5500

1 Cathy Cheung could have been a hospital porter or a doctor. Use the information about her and **A** to help you explain why she can earn more as a doctor.

2 **a** Why do you think Nick Walsh is so well paid?
   b Why is the supply of deep sea divers lower than the supply of hospital porters? (Use **A** to help you.)

3 If demand for English-made clothes increases what will happen to the wage rate that Connie receives? (Use **B** to help you.)

4 "I don't understand life. Without hospital workers people would die," says Martin Pullin. "Yet the wage I receive is pitifully low."

   Write Martin a short letter explaining why in spite of this he receives a low wage. (Use **A** to help you.)

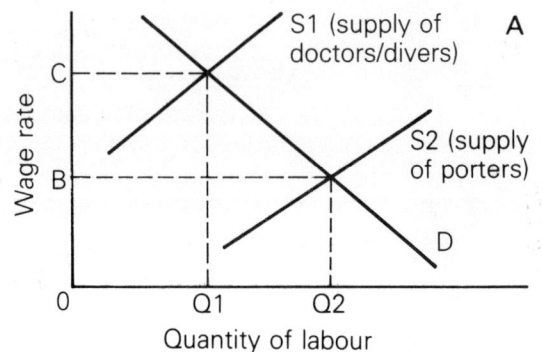

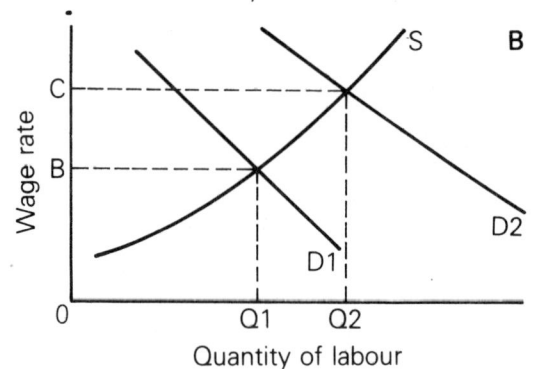

Coursework

Aim: To identify and attempt to calculate the earnings received by a pop star.

1 Investigate the background of a pop star of your choice and endeavour to identify the transfer earnings the star might earn.
2 Consider the factors that might serve to increase the economic rent of the performer: sponsorships, concert tours, record sales, promotions, marketing outlets, new releases.
3 Consider the factors that might serve to reduce the economic rent: changing loyalty of fans, pirating of records, imitation of style.
4 Use your data to test the hypothesis that in the long run the economic rent of pop stars is bound to decline.

29 Trade Unions

Trade unions are organisations which represent workers and try to protect them in their dealings with employers.

This diagram shows how unions organise workers in different areas of employment.

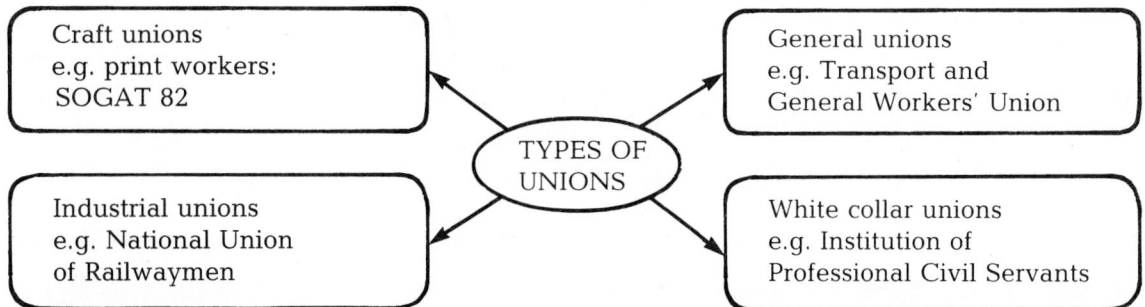

Craft unions
e.g. print workers:
SOGAT 82

General unions
e.g. Transport and
General Workers' Union

TYPES OF
UNIONS

Industrial unions
e.g. National Union
of Railwaymen

White collar unions
e.g. Institution of
Professional Civil Servants

Decide for yourself
- Which type of union represents workers doing a range of different jobs in different industries?
- Which type of union represents skilled workers in a particular occupation?
- Which type of union represents professional workers mainly in service industries?
- Which type of union represents workers in a range of jobs but within the same industry?

In the Activity (see page 162) the Choffee factory workers are in dispute with their management. When individuals feel that their interests are at risk, they often combine together. This is reflected in the trade union motto: "In unity lies strength."

The Choffee factory workers, like other workers, can respond to the demands being made by their employer in a number of ways. They could:
- go on strike, that is withdraw their labour and not work at all;
- work to rule, sometimes called a go slow, when workers work only according to the strict conditions of their employment, refusing to do any tasks over and above those which they would normally do;
- ban all overtime, thus refusing to do any extra work that the employer might want done;
- picket their firm to stop workers crossing the picket line to work when a strike has been agreed;
- boycott or persuade others to boycott the firm's products, that is, not to buy or use them.

Causes of industrial disputes

Disputes do not only occur over pay. They also arise over working conditions, restrictive practices, dismissals and redundancies. This is because unions attempt to help their members on a wide range of issues, for example:
- pay;
- holiday entitlement;
- job security/protection;
- welfare issues;
- industrial tribunal cases;
- hours of work;
- payments if you are sick or on strike;
- problems related to the introduction of machinery.

In the Activity, the Choffee company has decided to talk with their workers about the firm's problems. This is called an attempt at conciliation. If both sides agree to the talks, then they can enter into negotiations. When trade union officials, on behalf of the workers they represent, negotiate with employers over pay or other matters, it is called collective bargaining.

If all attempts at conciliation fail, then both sides in the dispute may turn to an independent third party who acts like a referee and tries to settle the dispute. The government-appointed body, the Advisory and Conciliation Arbitration Service (ACAS), is often called upon when disputes reach this stage.

Activity

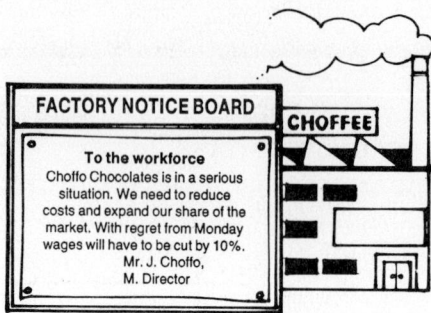

FACTORY NOTICE BOARD

To the workforce
Choffo Chocolates is in a serious situation. We need to reduce costs and expand our share of the market. With regret from Monday wages will have to be cut by 10%.
Mr. J. Choffo,
M. Director

A Joe Smith. Aged 35. Machine worker. Single. Savings of £2,000. He lives with his parents. He doesn't like 'scabs' (people who cross picket lines).

B Penny Collins. Aged 23. Works in quality control. A single parent. She is very loyal to the firm who are very understanding if she has to have time off to look after her daughter. She was recently promoted and needs all the money she can earn.

C Jack Watkins. Aged 45. He was a shop steward in his last firm. Without unions he feels that workers would be terribly exploited. He believes in the motto, "In unity lies strength."

D John Williams. Driver. Aged 28. Married; two children. Would be worried if the strike lasted a long time, but there is plenty of part-time work for drivers in the area, so a short strike would not present problems.

E Sarah Bough. Aged 22. Production line worker. Single. Her mother was the first woman shop steward in the union. She wants to follow in her footsteps and represent the workers in their dealings with the management.

F Tony Boatswain. Aged 18. Single. Apprentice in machine room. If he strikes he is worried that he will lose his apprenticeship.

G Catherine Larrett. Aged 30. Production line worker. Her aged mother needs an urgent operation. Usually Catherine is active in the union, but is currently more interested in saving enough money so that her mother can go to a convalescent home after her operation.

H Lorraine Tiles. Aged 21. Works in the packing department. Recently married and saving for a delayed honeymoon in Majorca. Lorraine believes unions are old-fashioned and would cross a picket line if necessary.

I Paul Fox. Aged 28. Warehouseman. Has lots of ability but it is not always recognised by the firm. He was recently docked pay for being late when there was a bus strike! He is bitter about this. He lives near Mr Choffo, who he knows owns a large detached house, with a swimming pool, and two "Rollers". He also knows that Choffo goes on holiday to the Caribbean twice a year. It's been two years since Paul has been able to afford a holiday. He favours picketing the firm (standing at the entrance and asking other workers to join their strike).

J Claire Bates. Aged 33. Engineer. Has an unemployed husband and four children. Her wage is urgently needed. She can't afford to strike but a cut in pay would be disastrous too.

You are asked to take part in a lunchtime meeting organised by workers in the Choffee Chocolate factory. Before the activity starts everyone is allocated a role from the list of characters **A–J**.

Before the meeting

1 Using the information briefly describe what Mr Choffo is proposing.

2 **a** Which character have you been allocated to play? Decide, using the information you have been given, whether you are likely to be for or against some form of industrial action. Give reasons for your decision.

b Once you have made your decision, write a brief imaginary biography of yourself. Include information on your age, qualifications, family circumstances, standard of living, savings, marital status, attitude to trade unions.

At the meeting

- Elect a chairperson.
- The chairperson is responsible for reading Mr Choffo's notice to the group.
- The chairperson should then ask each person present to introduce themselves to the others.
- Each person should be asked whether they wish to accept or reject Mr Choffo's wages cut and give reasons for their decision.
- After everyone has had their say, a vote for or against industrial action should be taken.
- If as a group you choose industrial action, you should decide the form of the action you will take, and how you plan to make it effective. (Possible action includes: go slows, strikes, picketing, occupation of the site.)
- If you decide against industrial action, you should consider what you could do to protect fellow workers.

3 Record the decision of your group.

4 Write a brief summary of the main arguments presented by your group in reaching their decision.

5 Briefly list the further action your group has proposed.

The TUC is an umbrella organisation

Trade union organisation

Workers usually elect their own representatives at workshop or factory floor level. These are called *shop stewards* (short for workshop stewards). Workers in one plant may form a local *branch* with other workers in their union. Local branches send delegates to the union's annual conference.

Local branches are usually formed into regional groupings with their own full-time paid union officials. Many unions have a national executive elected by the members and a general secretary (employed full time) who are responsible for running the union at the national level.

Most unions are affiliated to (or belong to) the national Trades Union Congress. The TUC is not in itself a union. It acts as an umbrella organisation. Its job is to keep an eye on issues affecting all unions in the country. Once a year it organises a congress (or meeting) with delegates (representatives) attending from all member unions.

Unions and the economy

Unions can affect the economy of a country in a number of ways.

Positive aspects of union activities

- Unions help workers to be fairly paid. Better paid workers can spend more and thus help others who are in work by creating demand.
- Unions help those who are discriminated against by employers, such as women and ethnic groups.
- Unions help individuals with claims for compensation after an accident, or redundancy claims when they lose their jobs.
- Employers often prefer to deal with just one union representing all their workers rather than with the claims of many individuals.
- Workers, through their unions, can make a useful contribution to a firm on matters like health and safety.

Negative aspects of union activities

- Trade unions can limit the supply of labour by:
  a) insisting on demarcation (marking out jobs which only one group can do, for example, *all* electrical work to be done by trained electricians);
  b) proposing or operating a closed shop (where the employer can only employ workers of one particular union);
  c) limiting the entry of new members;
  d) striking.

This can result in the minimum wage rate of workers being higher than the wage rate would be in a 'free market' (0–T, instead of 0–P on the graph, see next page).

However, the employer's demand for labour (unless the wage increase is paid for out of profits) will fall (from $0-Q_2$ to $0-Q_1$) and unemployment will rise.

- If firms give in to wage demands and cannot absorb the cost of doing so, by reducing profits, then they are forced to pass the cost on to customers.
- When strikes occur firms can lose customers, and therefore revenue.
- A strike or other dispute allows rivals to step in and capture a share of the market because of the problems the regular supplier has.
- Customers are upset and may look elsewhere for a supplier. Demand will fall for the product and the firm may be forced to lay off workers.

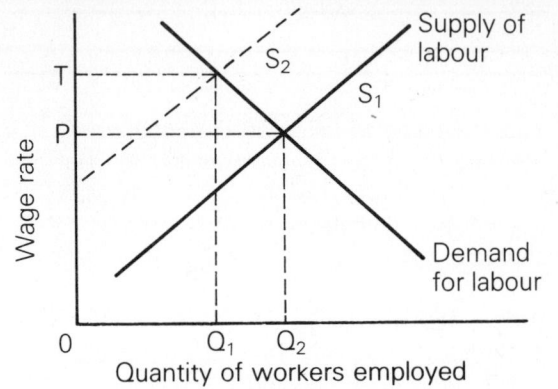

- Other firms that supply products to the affected company may end up having to halt their production and lay off workers.

Activity

LETTER TO SUPPLIERS

Sorry I can't pay you at the moment, I'm in dispute with my workers.

Phone call to Bank Manager: Can you finance my operation during the period of the strike?

CHOFFEE

Rival company: At long last – now we can get ahead of Choffee

Mummy, I want my Choffee bar.

Where are my orders? I need my regular supply of Choffee bars

SHOP AT BLOGGS

Use the situation at Choffee's as above and the points below and write a short description of some of the problems that a union can bring to the running of an economy.

Cocoa importer

CHOFFEE'S CHOCOLATE CHERRIES

Dairies supplying milk

Suppliers of chocolate boxes

Glacé cherries

Unions can also be of benefit to others in an economy.

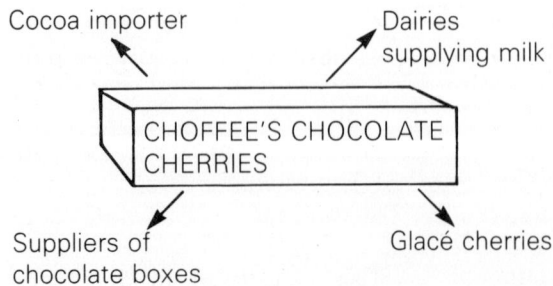

I'm well paid because of my union. I can spend a lot, that's good news for others in work.

If it wasn't for the union I'd never have got my compensation. I'd be very badly off.

I'm glad the union helped us fight our case for equal pay. (Female shop fitter)

It makes sense for me to deal with just one union, representing all my workers. It saves me the time. (Busy employer)

When we built our new supermarket our existing workforce, through their union representatives, were very helpful and made some useful suggestions connected with the health and safety of both workers and customers.

In the 1980s legislation has restricted the rights of unions such that now:

- unions must ballot members on the payment of a political levy (or contribution) to a political party (usually the Labour Party);
- unions must hold a secret ballot and obtain a majority before calling a strike;
- if they fail to do so, the union can be subject to civil action in the courts (where they can be sued for damages);
- picketing (standing at entrance to workplace and discouraging people to enter) in large numbers is illegal;
- a strike must not be spread to firms supplying the firm in question, or to firms purchasing from the firm (this so-called secondary industrial action has been made illegal).
- closed shops are prohibited in line with EC Social Charter. 1990 Employment Bill makes it unlawful to refuse work to someone because they are a union member, or because they are not.

Test yourself

1 A car firm goes on strike. Using this diagram, explain the effects on other firms in the economy.

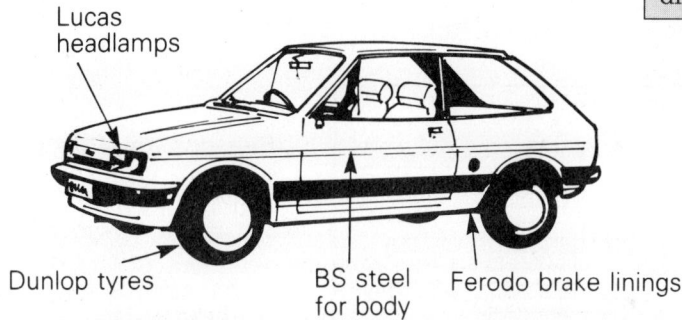

Lucas headlamps

Dunlop tyres

BS steel for body

Ferodo brake linings

2 You are nervous of asking your boss for a pay rise. Given this, explain:
  a why you might join a union;
  b what collective bargaining is.
3 What is the difference between a strike and a lockout?
4 What is the difference between negotiation and arbitration?
5 What are the advantages and disadvantages of trade unions to the economy?
6 How can trade unions by their activity sometimes increase unemployment?

ECONOMIC TERMS

Collective bargaining: when a union negotiates with employers on behalf of all workers in the union rather than leaving it to individuals to negotiate.
Shop steward: trade union representative elected at factory, workshop or office level.
Conciliation: an attempt to reach an agreement in a dispute.
Closed shop: where workers in a production unit have to belong to a particular union in order to work in the unit.
Demarcation: when the trade of one worker is protected and cannot be done by other workers (for example, electricians cannot do joinery or joiners mend fuses).
Restrictive practices: an action that is designed to limit competition. For example, firms might collude to divide the market between them. Unions can protect their members from the competition of other workers by demarcation, closed shops or overmanning (see page 168).
Lock-out: when an employer locks out his workers, usually during a trade dispute.

DATA RESPONSE 1

A

Work stoppages in progress during year (all firms)

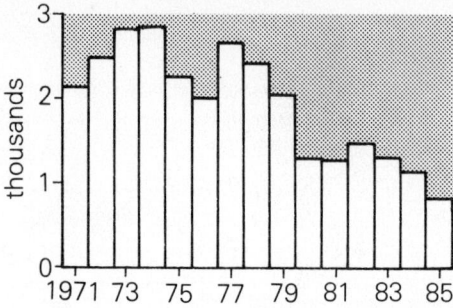

Source: *Social Trends 17*

B

Working days lost during year
(If 20 people strike for 50 days each, 1000 working days are lost.)

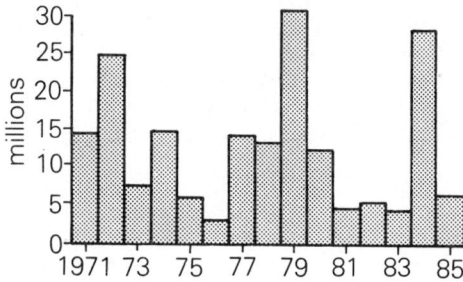

Source: *Social Trends 17*

C

Where the members aren't

Union membership, 1984 as % of total employees
By region

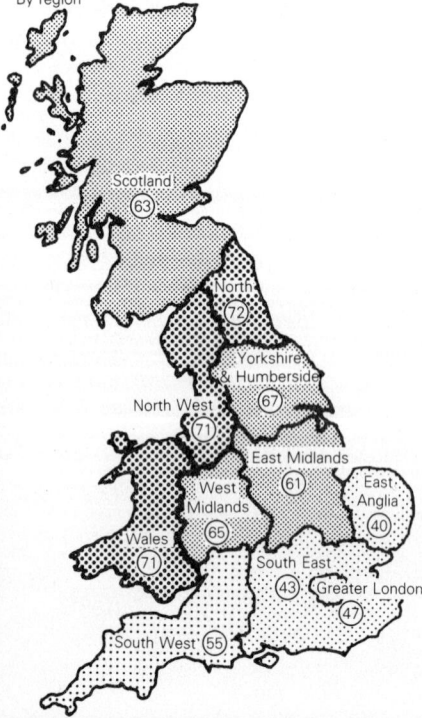

Source: *The Economist*, 7 May 1988

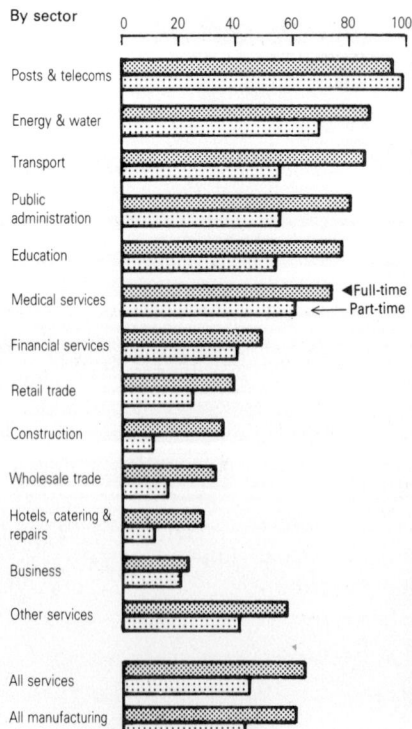

Scotland (63)
North (72)
Yorkshire & Humberside (67)
North West (71)
East Midlands (61)
East Anglia (40)
West Midlands (65)
Wales (71)
South East (43)
Greater London (47)
South West (55)

By sector

| | 0 | 20 | 40 | 60 | 80 | 100 |

Posts & telecoms
Energy & water
Transport
Public administration
Education
Medical services ◀Full-time ← Part-time
Financial services
Retail trade
Construction
Wholesale trade
Hotels, catering & repairs
Business
Other services
All services
All manufacturing

D

USA	130	
UK	440	
Japan	20	
Holland	20	
Italy	780	
Greece	660	
Spain	600	

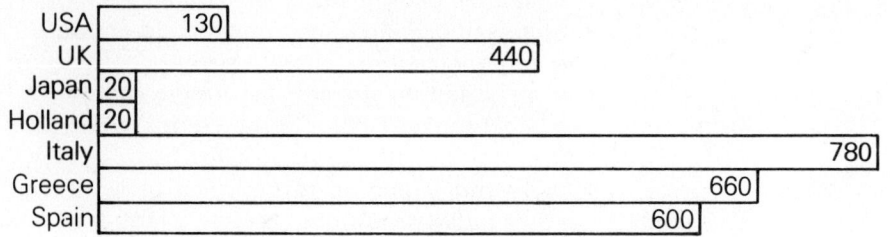

International comparisons of the average number of working days lost per 1000 employees in all industries

Source: *Employment Gazette*, Nov. 1987

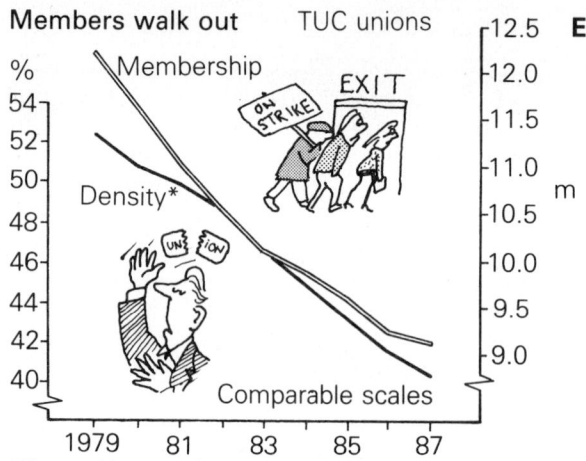

E

Members walk out   TUC unions

Membership
Density*
Comparable scales

*Membership as % of employees in employment

Source: *The Economist*, 20 August 1988

F

Reasons for striking
(October 1986 to October 1987)

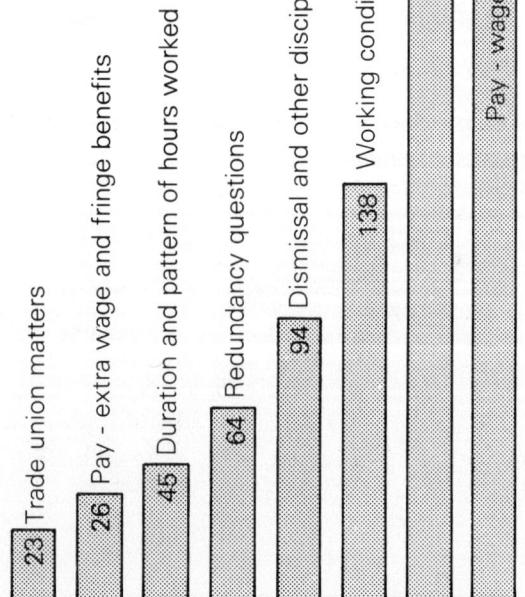

- Trade union matters — 23
- Pay - extra wage and fringe benefits — 26
- Duration and pattern of hours worked — 45
- Redundancy questions — 64
- Dismissal and other disciplinary measures — 94
- Working conditions and supervision — 138
- Manning and work allocation — 217
- Pay - wage rates and earning levels — 323

Source: *New Society*, 26 February 1988

1 a What has happened to union
membership between 1979 and 1986?

b What has happened to work stoppages
between 1977 and 1985?

2 What were the two most common reasons
given for striking in 1986?

3 a Which sector has the largest percentage
of workers in unions?

b Which sector has the smallest
percentage of workers in unions?

4 Which two regions of the UK are the least
unionised?

5 Explain why chart **B** provides a more
accurate picture of the pattern of industrial
unrest than chart **A**.

6 It has been argued that Britain is a strike-
prone country. In what way does the
evidence support or refute this idea?

DATA RESPONSE 2

Workers resist production targets

Jaguar faces all-out strike

By Craig Seton and Daniel Ward

Four thousand manual workers at Jaguar in Coventry have voted by a big majority for an all-out strike in protest at the company's plans to increase production.

The ballot at the Browns Lane factory, where assembly-line workers earn more than £220 a week, showed 2,410 in favour of a strike and 1,312 against when the result was declared yesterday.

Union leaders said that the strike would go ahead after the Easter holiday unless Sir John Egan, Jaguar's chairman, suspended plans to step up production by 92 cars a

day to increase the annual output from 48,000 to 56,000 this year.

The company argues that its workforce of 12,700 is sufficient to produce 1,300 cars a week, or 60,000 a year. It says that improved productivity and more automated machinery will push up output to 80,000 annually by the mid 1990s.

Workers believe it is not possible to increase production enough to earn the additional £12.50 a week bonus offered by the company.

Mr David Boole, Jaguar's director of public relations, said that 1,000 extra workers

had been taken on by the company last year to achieve the new production rate.

Mr Chris Lidell, the local Transport and General Workers' Union official responsible for the motor industry, said there was probably room for more production.

However, he emphasized that "the unions will not tolerate management by diktak. The unions are also saying there is not sufficient time in certain areas to accommodate 92 more cars. They need more hours or more manpower. It is not a question of money."

Jaguar needs to improve

productivity to cut costs at a time when profits are under attack from unfavourable exchange rates. Last week, the company announced that profits for 1987 were down to £97 million from £121 million in 1986.

Sir John aims to push up output per man by 10 to 15 per cent a year and has set a target of matching Mercede's productivity of six cars per man per year by 1990.

Source: *The Times*, 26 March 1988

Jaguar strike caused by 'aggressive' demands

By Craig Seton and Daniel
Ward

Production workers at the Jaguar plant in Coventry yesterday claimed that the company's aggressive demands were to blame for what could be its first big dispute in three years.

"Even if we were given extra money we would still find it difficult to increase production", one worker among a group of three said as he sat against a wall, sip-

ping beer from a can during the 30-minute lunch break.

"On our track we produce 10 cars a day and they want us to produce another one. We would have to find an extra three-quarters-of-an-hour to produce one more car and I do not think that would be possible."

Mr Tony Russell, shop steward for the Amalgamated Engineering Union, claimed that, apart from increasing production. Jaguar was also seeking to eliminate 79 jobs

at the plant through natural wastage and to cut overtime by 7,000 hours a week.

Overtime was required to recover production lost through plant breakdowns and bottlenecks.

He said that although there was an opportunity for manual workers to earn the extra bonus "the lads do not believe it's a good deal to speed up the track and produce 92 more cars and cut available overtime. They are going to work a lot harder

and they do not believe its good for the money.

"We have never had sufficient outside parts coming in on time to do these sort of figures". Mr Russell said.

One worker said that it was possible, after starting work at 7.30am to have completed the 10 cars required from that track by 3.15pm or 3.20pm if there were no hold-ups but, before clocking off at 4pm, they also had to prepare for the next day's work.

continued on next page

Another said: "All the tracks are stretched. I do not think we have any time to do more."

There had been trouble with the paint booths at Castle Bromwich, the plant where Jaguar bodies are produced. "If they cannot supply the bodies we do not get our full week's bonus, but that is not our fault", he said.

A second shift at the Castle Bromwich paint plant was introduced last month to overcome production bottle-necks, but the management has made it clear that bonus payments, now more than £34 a week, will be reduced for all workers if production is slowed down because of problems at any of its factories.

The men also criticized the claim made by Sir John Egan, the Jaguar chairman, that whenever he walked around the assembly hall at about 3.15pm he hardly ever saw anybody working.

One of the three said: "I fit the trim inside cars. I have got to do 10 cars a day and then that is it for the day. I have never seen the chairman walking round. We only ever see him at Christmas when he shakes a few people's hands."

The plant operates an eight-hour day from 7.30am until 4pm on the day shift, with 30 minutes for lunch and a 10-minute break in the morning for coffee.

Most of the manual workers stay inside the plant and take food and drink from vending machines or the canteen, which, Mr Russell pointed out, was not subsidized. Only a few workers who live locally could go home for lunch.

The night shift starts at 7.30pm and operates a 10-hour shift for four days.

Source: *The Times*, 26 March 1988

1 Why did Jaguar workers vote for a strike?

2 What incentives did management offer the workers?

3 Which unions were involved in the dispute?

4 What criticisms did the unions have of management?

5 Why were Jaguar management concerned to increase production?

Extension

Dock-labour scheme*

Quaint seaside customs

THAT infamous relic of post-war trade-unionism, the dock-labour scheme, has survived the 1980s unscathed. It still enjoys the explicit backing of the law. Yet its days may now be numbered.

The scheme was set up in 1947 as a reaction to the way casual dockers were treated before the war. It lets national and local boards (half-

The jobs have gone, the wages risen

168

controlled by the dockers themselves) guarantee minimum dock wages, fix the size of dock labour forces, and stop non-dockers doing dockers' work. A 1967 amendment even provided a near-right to lifetime employment. One measure of the scheme's effect is that a docker in Port Talbot, south Wales (the second-cheapest labour market in Britain) earns an average of £478 a week.

In the four decades of its life, the scheme has fostered a goodly set of abuses: "ghosting", where dockers are paid to watch others do dock work; "bobbing", where twice as many dockers as necessary are given a job, so half of them can "bob off"; "moon-lighting"; and "disappointment money", when an expected ship fails to come in.

All this has made ports covered by the scheme uncompetitive. (Unloading a box of fish in Aberdeen costs £3; non-scheme Peterhead would charge only £1.44 for the same box.) It has also encouraged the growth of ports outside the scheme: their share of Britain's non-fuel port tonnage rose from 8% in 1965 to 32% in 1987. In turn, the number of registered dock workers in the scheme has fallen from over 64,000 to under 10,000. Their average age is 47.

Two years ago the National Association of Port Employers (NAPE), which represents docks in the scheme, decided to lobby against it. NAPE denies that the scheme is needed to prevent the return of casual labour and exploitation in the docks: its members, it says, would be happy to guarantee full-time work to dockers if the scheme were abolished.

A report published last week by the WEFA group, a consultancy commissioned by NAPE, predicts that abolishing the scheme would, simply by increasing efficiency, create 4,200 jobs and extra output of £150m in five years. It might do more, since jobs have increased more slowly in areas with a scheme port in them than those with a non-scheme port. Even after adjusting for different local growth rates, employment rose 5.8% a year on average between 1984 and 1987 in the former and 7.6% in the latter.

Source: *The Economist,* 2 July 1988

*In April 1989 the government announced plans to scrap the dock labour scheme. The unions representing dock workers affected were concerned about what terms and conditions would replace the scheme.

1 Why was the dock labour scheme set up and how does it operate?
2 What effect has the scheme had on a docker's wage in South Wales?
3 What types of practices have made the scheme very expensive to operate and led to the ports involved becoming uncompetitive?
4 You are a ship owner or captain and have to unload a cargo of fish. Peterhead is further away from you than Aberdeen. Explain why you decide to sail to Peterhead rather than unload your fish in Aberdeen.
5 What effects has the scheme had on dock scheme and non-dock scheme docks throughout the UK?
6 Why might abolishing the scheme make sound economic sense:
   a for dockworkers;
   b for producers;
   c for consumers?

Coursework

Aim: To investigate a recent industrial dispute.

1 Describe the nature of the dispute.
2 a What was the position of the employers?
   b What were the views of the employees and their union representatives?
3 What was the result of the action taken by union members?
4 To what extent does your survey prove or disprove that unions are effective organisations in protecting the interests of their members? Give possible reasons for your conclusions.

30 Spending and Advertising

We consume (purchase and use) goods and services in order to satisfy our wants.

In an economy some goods are produced by manufacturers for supply directly to the market (or the consumers). These are called *consumer goods* or *services*. Other goods are produced by manufacturers to help make other goods or services. These are called *capital goods*. In this unit we will examine consumer goods.

Decide for yourself
- Which of the things Matt purchases is a durable good (one that will last for a period of time)?
- Which of his purchases has a relatively short life?
- Which of his purchases is a service?

Satisfying needs and wants
In simple economies people are often concerned with little more than satisfying the basic needs of life. In advanced economies there is more wealth available, partly as a result of mass production. In these conditions, mass consumption is encouraged through advertising and easy credit (borrowing) terms, as a way of maintaining growth of the economy.

As an economy becomes wealthier, there is an increase in spending on goods and services that formerly might be regarded as luxuries. There is a relative decline in spending on necessities. An increased proportion of the population will in such circumstances be either renting or buying more consumer durables: cookers, washing machines, lawn mowers, computers, etc.

The paradox of thrift
A paradox is an apparently contradictory but true statement.
- If we consume less than we have available as income, then we have spare savings available for future emergencies.
- If we consume more than we have available as income, then we are either forced to borrow or find another means of financing our debts.

Many people, at various times, purchase goods on credit because they are short of income and cannot purchase with cash. One such method of purchasing with credit is called *hire purchase*. The borrower hires the use of the goods and gradually pays off the total cost over a period of time. He becomes the owner when the final repayment is made.

Budgeting
Living within one's income is sound economic sense for the individual. We call this budgeting. But the paradox of thrift reminds us that what might be good for an individual, is not necessarily good for others in a community. Industry benefits considerably from the fact that credit exists. It allows firms to increase production to make more profits, and to employ more workers and to sell more goods. This is one reason why firms advertise their products.

Advertising
Other reasons for firms advertising their products are:
- A firm is able to increase its share of the market. This is good news for that firm, but bad news for its rivals, who may have to respond by increasing their advertising.
- Advertising brings information about new products to the attention of potential consumers. Consumers with greater knowledge are better able to make effective choices.

Extension 1

The weekly household spending of the Howard family.

	£
Food	28.00
Clothing	14.00
Housing	29.80
Power/fuel	10.00
Household goods	13.20
Transport	33.60
Recreation	18.40
Other goods and services	31.60
Total	___

A

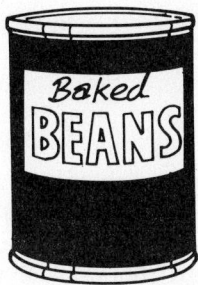

Pattern of household spending

B

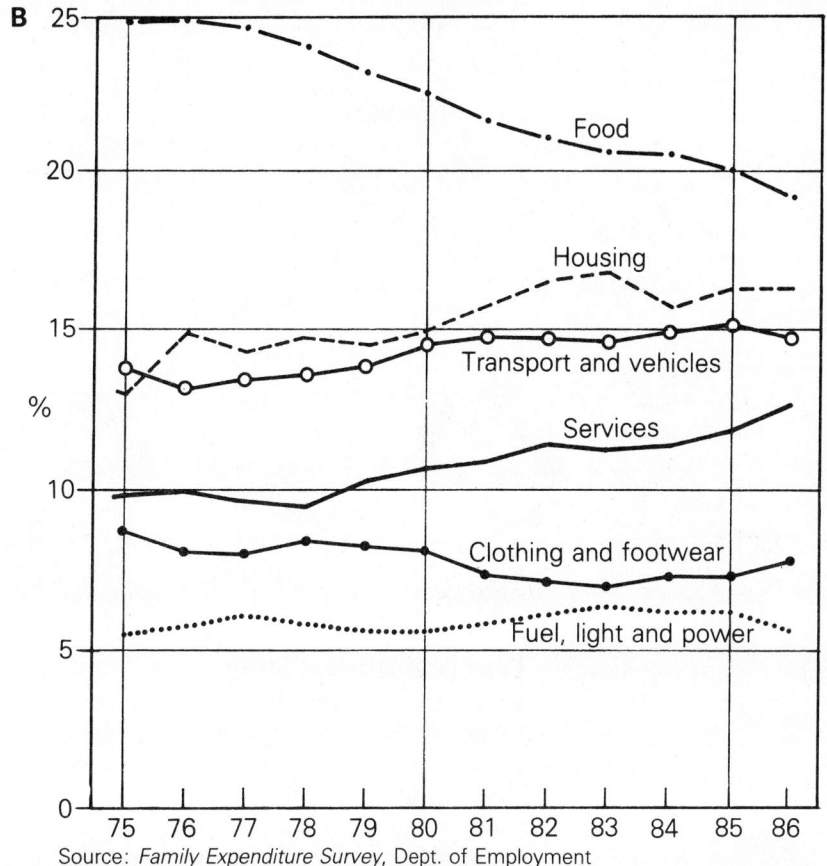

Source: *Family Expenditure Survey*, Dept. of Employment

1 Work out the total weekly household spending of the Howard family (see **A**).
2 Using the information in **A**, construct a pie chart to display the Howard's pattern of spending.
3 During the period shown in **B** real household income has risen. When real income rises in a community a smaller proportion of total spending tends to be devoted to necessities, and a higher proportion of total spending goes on luxuries. What evidence in **B** supports this view?
4 How much does your own household (or how much do you) spend on each of the items shown in **A**? Display your information on a pie chart.

5 What differences in the pattern of spending can you find between the two pie charts that you have constructed for **2** and **4**?
6 You are the advertising manager for a food company marketing baked beans. You are concerned that families are spending too little of their budget on food. Design a poster that more effectively advertises your product. You may include in your poster the following information:
   a the price of the product;
   b a brand name;
   c nutritional information;
   d a slogan;
   e a free offer or other inducement.

ECONOMIC TERMS

Consumption: the purchase of a good or service to satisfy a want.
Advertisement: a public notice or display designed to sell goods.
Budget: a plan of one's income and spending.

Test yourself

1 What is a consumer durable?
2 Which of the following are consumer durables?
   a watch, bread, cabbage, pears, a pen, jewellery, a car, a fridge, frozen peas, shoes

The other side of advertising

Earlier we looked at the advantages of advertising. However, advertising can also bring disadvantages to both consumers and producers.

Types of advertising

There are two main types of advertisement:

- **Informative**: contains information on the purpose, price, or on other relevant matters, like the ingredients of the product advertised.
- **Persuasive**: the aim of the advertiser is to keep demand at a high level by hiding 'persuaders' in the advertisement. Some advertisements make use of famous personalities, 'beautiful' women, 'tough-looking' men, 'experts' and romantic situations. Other advertisements might try to trade on your desires, your secret fears or hidden shames or your sense of loyalty or responsibility.

Decide for yourself

Look at these slogans:

- how are you being persuaded to buy the product in question?

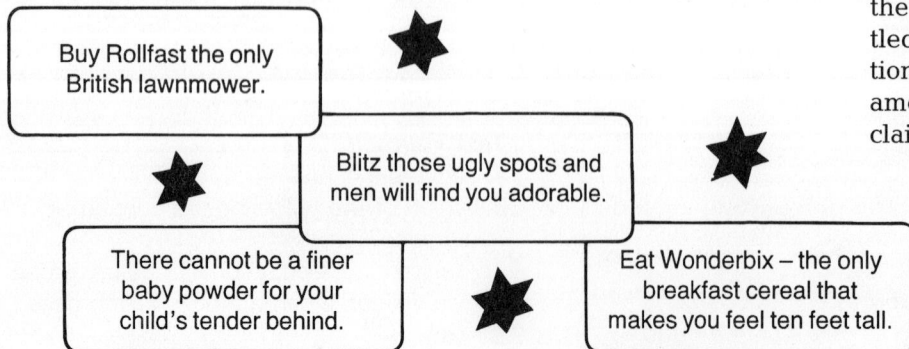

Consumer protection

As some manufacturers might be more concerned to increase sales or to make profits than to worry about the welfare of their customers, governments have increasingly stepped in to provide legislation designed to protect people who purchase products or services. Here are a few examples of such legislation:

- **Weights and Measures acts**: goods must be sold at the correct standard weight or measure to the consumer.
- **The Trade Descriptions Act 1968**: this act makes it an offence to describe goods inaccurately.
- **The Hire Purchase Acts**: these Acts provide consumers with the right to a period when they can change their mind if the good has been purchased at home (the so-called cooling-off period). Some protection is also provided if you fall behind with your payments for the goods and the hire purchase company wish to recover them. This protection depends on the amount that has been paid, and the value of the goods.
- **Consumer Protection Act 1961**: empowers the government to prevent the risk of death or personal injury by making regulations governing the manufacture of goods.
- **The Sale of Goods Act 1893, 1979**: goods must be fit for the purpose for which they are provided, and must meet the description made of them. Most importantly they should be of a 'merchantable quality', that is, in a fit state to be sold.
- **The Supply of Goods (Implied Terms) Act 1973**: consumers' rights are guaranteed and cannot be lost by signing a guarantee or by notices on display in the shop. The Act also says that the person responsible for making amends if a consumer complains about a faulty good is the last person who supplied the good to the consumer. (In most cases this will be the shopkeeper.) The consumer is entitled to their money back in such situations. Once the shopkeeper has made amends to the consumer, they in turn can claim from the manufacturer.

We're just a ha'penny in the pound worse off

ALTHOUGH food prices have increased considerably, they accounted for 19·1 per cent of the average family's spending last year, against 21·8 ten years ago.

ALCOHOL accounted for 8 per cent of the average family's spending, against 6·7 in 1966. The relative price of drink has fallen, so people drink even more.

RENTS and mortgages account for only 14·8 per cent of average spending – an increase of 3 per cent in a decade.

LAST year running a car took 9·2 per cent of average family outgoings.
While clothing and footwear accounted for 8·1 per cent. Fuel and light was 4·9.

TEN years ago people spent 6·2 per cent of their income on cigarettes and tobacco. Last year, with far fewer people smoking, the figure was 4·2.

YOU'VE not been having it so bad as you thought.

Despite all the gloom about inflation and rising prices, the buying power of Mr and Mrs Average Briton fell by just ½ per cent last year, according to official figures today.

The average take-home pay went up by 15 per cent. After allowing for inflation and taxes it was actually worth ½p in the £ less.

The annual analysis of National Income and Expenditure, published by the Central Statistical Office, suggest that many people are cutting back on food but buying more consumer goods. Spending was up by 16 per cent on the year before.

And it shows that people are drinking more – but fewer are smoking.

The statistics –

virtually the annual accounts of United Kingdom Ltd – reveal that Britain's national income last year was a record £110 billion. This represents £1,970 per head of population against £1,680 in 1975.

Of this, 73 per cent was used to pay wages, a 1 per cent drop on the previous year but still 3 per cent up on the average for the last ten years.

Most of the increase, however, was due to higher pay and prices. The real output of goods and services was only 2 per cent up on 1975.

Company profits rose from 6 per cent to 6½ per cent but still compared badly with the average of 11 per cent for the previous decade.

Last year, while wages went up, savings went down – from 15·3 to 14·6 per cent.

The Government limited its rise in spending to 17 per cent last year, against 32 per cent in 1975.

Social security benefits took the lion's share of tax money last year – 19·2 per cent, with education second at 12·5.

Source: *Daily Mail*, September 1977

1 What do you think is meant by the phrase 'the buying power of Mr and Mrs Average Briton fell by just ½ per cent last year'?

2 What changes have occurred to people's pattern of food expenditure?

3 On average how much money did each person have available in 1976 for spending?

4 Use the information in the diagrams to construct a pie chart to show a typical family's spending pattern. You will need to include a category entitled Miscellaneous or other expenditure. Calculate how large this category will have to be.

DATA RESPONSE 2

Money spent in one month
% who spent money on

Age 10–14 ▨   15–19 ◩
20–25 ■

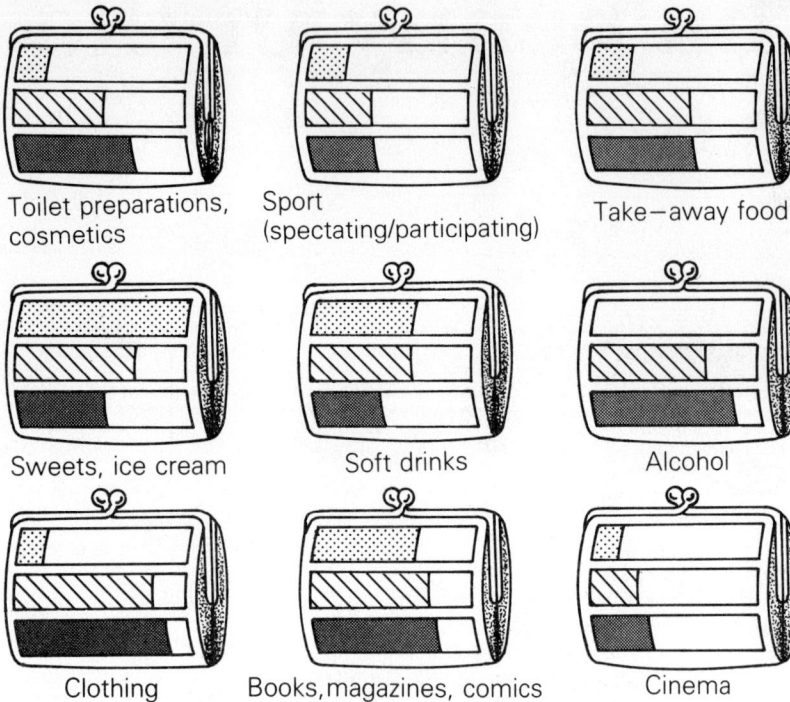

Toilet preparations, cosmetics

Sport (spectating/participating)

Take–away food

Sweets, ice cream

Soft drinks

Alcohol

Clothing

Books, magazines, comics

Cinema

We learn to organise our spending early and become quite experienced consumers at a young age, according to a survey of youth in Britain by the advertising agency, McCann-Erickson. This table shows that young people spend their money on a wide range of goods and services, despite the fact that they only have small sums available.

Source: *New Society*

1 Which age group spent most of their money on sweets and ice cream?

2 Which age group spent least on clothing? Give a reason why.

3 In which area does spending increase most rapidly as a child grows older? Give reasons why.

4 Using the information from the survey construct a list that shows the order of preferred spending for 15–19 year olds.

Extension 2

Availability of durable goods: by household type
Great Britain

Percentages

	Elderly households[1]			Other households without children[2]			Other households with children			All households			
	1973	1979	1984	1973	1979	1984	1973	1979	1984	1973	1979	1984	1985
Percentage of households with:													
Vacuum cleaner	83	90	..	90	93	..	90	95	..	88	93	..	..
Refrigerator[3]	63	85	92	83	93	95	86	96	97	78	92	94	95
Deep-freezer[3]	..	22	43	..	46	66	..	52	75	..	40	61	66
Washing machine	48	56	65	67	76	81	84	91	94	67	74	79	81
Tumble drier	..	9	14	..	19	31	..	28	46	..	19	29	33
Dishwasher	..	1	2	..	3	6	..	5	8	..	3	5	6
Telephone	35	55	73	50	72	81	50	74	80	45	67	78	81
Car	25	30	36	64	70	73	69	71	74	54	57	61	62
Central heating	30	46	59	38	56	67	49	65	74	39	55	66	69
Television	90												
Colour		50	77		70	84		77	89		66	83	86
Black and	}	{	} 95	{	}	}	{	}	}	{	} 95	{		
white only		45	20		26	13		22	10		31	14	11
Video	..	..	5	..	..	32	..	..	38	..	..	24	31
Home computer	..	..	1	..	..	9	..	..	18	..	..	9	13

1 One adult aged 60 or over, or two adults, one or both aged 60 or over.   3 Fridge freezers are included in both Refrigerators and Deep-freezers.
2 Includes households containing three adults with child.

Source: CSO *Social Trends 17*, HMSO 1978

1 List two items that were not included in the durable goods survey in 1973.
2 Identify the two most frequently found items in all households in 1985.
3 Explain why
   a cars
   b tumble driers
   are less likely to be found in elderly households compared to households with children.
4 What items have been added to the survey in recent years and why?

5 Why might, in a modern economy, many items such as cars, telephones, televisions, and washing machines be considered necessities and not luxuries. You can use the ideas below to help you.

| More women in work. | | Society has become more mobile. |

| Relatives may live further away. |

| People have to move or commute further to find work. | | Local facilities, such as bus services and the number of launderettes, have declined. |

| People feel a greater need to keep up with the news. |

Test yourself
1 Design an advertisement for a soap product using persuasive advertising techniques to promote its sale.
2 Which Act protects you in these cases?
   a A 1lb box of chocolates weighs 10oz.
   b A baby suit falls apart after the first wash.
   c A car from a used car showroom is advertised as fitted with a new engine. The engine is later found to be second-hand.
   d The head falls off a new teddy bear, revealing a spike.
3 Your sister buys some shoes, and one heel comes off. Write her a letter advising her what to do.

Coursework

Aim: To investigate consumer complaints.

1 Undertake a survey of students in your economics class who have had problems with goods that they have purchased.
2 Find a way of describing and classifying these problems.
3 Endeavour to establish what each student had done in order to resolve their problem.

4 Establish the major reason why problems were not resolved.
5 Using the information design a poster informing pupils of their rights in the area of consumer protection.

31 Money

'Are you worth your salt?'

In order to spend people have to obtain some form of purchasing power. There was a time when people were paid for their labour in salt!

Over the years many methods have been used to obtain the goods and services people need.

Barter

One way of having purchasing power is to swap or *barter*. For example, Sue wants an LP that Bob has. She is willing to let him have three cassette tapes in return. Sue and Bob have entered into a transaction called an *exchange*.

Swapping goods in this sort of way is described as barter. Barter is the oldest form of exchange and existed before the invention of money. The form of exchange we use more normally is using money.

Barter can be a very compliated means of buying what you want. Sue was lucky. Bob had the LP that Sue wanted and she had something (the three cassettes) that Bob was prepared to accept in return. This is sometimes referred to as a *double coincidence of wants*.

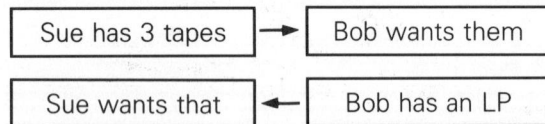

Sue has 3 tapes	→	Bob wants them
Sue wants that	←	Bob has an LP

Usually, however, barter presents problems:
- it is not always possible to find someone willing to swap with you (remember that there has to be a double coincidence of wants);
- it is not always possible to calculate a fair rate of exchange. Jack wants fish and has spears to offer in exchange. What does he do if he cannot determine how many fish one spear is worth?

For these and other reasons people invented other forms of exchange.

Commodity money

All manner of items have at different times been used as money. Crops and other

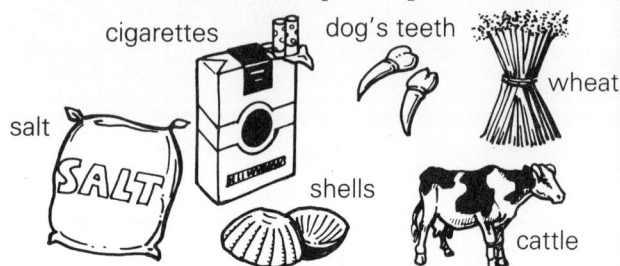

goods were frequently used but these commodity items were unsuitable as money (wheat, for example, rots over time). Precious metals, such as gold and silver, thus became a common form of money as they were durable. In Asia Minor at the time of Croesus* the king's face was stamped on the metal, and coins were made. This stopped people arguing about the value of the piece of metal.

Since those times many governments have controlled the supply of money within their economies. Money approved by the state is called *fiat* money. People who try and copy the state's money are called counterfeiters.

Most of our coins today are only of token value. This means that their face value is more than their full weight in metal value. In the past all coins were 'full bodied' or worth their face value. Sometimes people would try to cheat others by only passing on badly worn (and therefore light) coins or by clipping the edges of the coins to make them smaller. Even today our coins are made in such a way as to prevent this happening. (Look at a coin to see how this is done.)

One of the earliest laws in economics stems from the time of Queen Elizabeth I. Her finance minister, Sir Thomas Gresham,

*Have you heard of the expression 'as rich as Croesus'?

observed that people kept good coins and tried to pass on debased coins (coins that were worn or had been clipped around the edge to remove some of the gold or silver content). "Bad money drives out good money," he noted.

Decide for yourself
- Can you think of a modern way in which Gresham's law applies?

Banknotes

Coins are convenient for small exchanges, but can you imagine paying for a car in pennies? You would need sackfuls! Therefore, for large exchanges people use banknotes. These developed from the receipts goldsmiths issued when people asked them to store valuables in their safes which they kept for their everyday business. People then used these receipts to make purchases and the person who had the receipt could reclaim the valuables.

Banknotes were originally convertible into gold. If you look at a banknote it still carries the message: 'I promise to pay the bearer on demand the sum of . . .'

Today, however, our currency is what we call *fiduciary*. This means that we take it on trust, and hope it will keep its value.

Bank deposits

Many people think cheques are a form of money. They are not. If cheques were accepted by the government as a valid form of money (or legal tender), then what would stop your bank manager taking all the money in your account and fleeing abroad leaving a cheque for you as settlement?

Would the cheque have any value? Why not?

A cheque only has value in that people accept it knowing that it is an instruction to transfer money into their account from the account of the person who has written the cheque. What the person is accepting is the money in your bank account. If you have no money and the cheque 'bounces', you have committed the criminal offence of fraud.

Credit cards

Credit cards are often referred to as 'plastic money', and they are an increasingly accepted form of money. The seller accepts your card knowing they will be paid by the credit card company. You in turn, and at a later date, pay the credit card company for the service they provide.

ECONOMIC TERMS
Money: an item acceptable in an economy as a method of payment.
Exchange: a transaction involving the transfer of ownership of goods or services.
Commodity money: any good (for example, matches) used as a medium of exchange.
Cash: coin or banknotes that are readily available (or 'in hand').
Acceptable: something a person is willing to receive.
Legal tender: money that is officially accepted as a means of payment.

Activity

Qualities money must possess

Forms of Exchange		Acceptable	Durable	Portable	Divisible	Multipliable	Totals
Barter		0			0		
Coins				1			
Notes							
Cheques plus Bankers card	Representing money in bank accounts					3	
Credit Card		1					

1 Copy the table on the previous page.
2 For each quality listed select four forms of exchange that provide these qualities. Score against the most suitable form of exchange 4; against the next 3, then 2, then 1 and 0. (Some squares have already been done for you.)
3 When you have completed the table, total the score for each form of exchange. Which forms of exchange are the most suitable, that is have the highest score?
4 How does your selection compare with other students in your class?

Functions of money

As you have seen, for money to work it has to be able to perform certain functions or jobs:

- It must be a medium of exchange that people are prepared to accept in return for goods and services supplied.
- It must be a unit of account. It must be possible to measure all goods in terms of this common standard of measure or value.
- Money is a store of value so we can save up for the future with it; it is also a means of deferring payment. We can obtain goods on credit now and people will happily accept payment later, in the belief that money will keep its value.

A system for understanding money

	Disadvantages of barter	Functions of money	Qualities money must possess
A	Need for a double coincidence of wants.	Acts as a medium of exchange.	Acceptability
B	Need to determine a fair rate of exchange.	Acts as a unit of account	Divisibility and uniformity
C	Not possible to store wealth over a long period.	A store of value	Scarcity/durability
D	Impossible to plan ahead.	A means of deferred payment	Durability/acceptability

To perform all these jobs, money has to possess certain qualities:

- **portability**: be easy to carry around;
- **durability**: has to last and not disintegrate;
- **scarcity**: pebbles on the beach cannot be used as money because everyone can have as much as they want;
- **divisibility and multipliability**: people must be able to use it for small and large transactions;
- **acceptability**: other people should be prepared to take it in exchange for goods or services.

Test yourself

1 What functions does money perform?
2 What qualities must money possess to perform these functions effectively?
3 You wish to sell a valuable stamp collection you own. Why might you not accept a cheque in payment for the collection?

DATA RESPONSE 1

CUT OUT THE CASH
and keep down the dangers

WE'RE all still carrying far too much cash about.

A recent survey shows that we use cash to settle nine in every ten transactions.

Even where larger sums are involved we still use cash to meet half of all bills between £25 and £50.

Cash may be convenient but it can be lost or stolen – and there's always the chance you could be mugged.

True, you can't dispense with cash altogether. You'd hardly pay your bus fare or buy a box of matches with a cheque.

But there are plenty of ways to cut down your use of cash and the risks you run with it.

Here's a few tips:

- Have your wages paid into a bank account.
- Get the bank to settle all your regular bills for you by standing order.
- Pay all irregular or occasional bills, such as gas, electricity or phone by cheque or bank giro.
- Get yourself a credit card. You can then settle a whole batch of bills with one cheque each month, and you get one or two months free credit thrown in.
- It may be possible to pay your electricity, rates, or even book club subscription on your credit card nowadays.
- Open a monthly account with stores or shop chains you use regularly.
- Forget bus or train fares by buying a season ticket or travel card. It'll save you time queueing and often works out a lot cheaper too.

Paying these ways will help you keep better track of your cash, making it easier to save.

Source: *Daily Mirror*, 10 June 1985

178

1 a What is meant by cash?
  b How often do we use cash when settling a transaction?

2 To what extent is cash used to settle large bills?

3 What are the principal advantages of cash?

4 What disadvantages does cash present to the user?

5 Why despite these disadvantages is it unlikely that society could do away with cash as a form of money?

6 a How can you protect yourself against the dangers of using too much cash?
  b What advantages are there to be gained from this protection?

Extension 1

1 Look at the methods of payment shown on the left. Decide which of these you would be most likely to use when making each of the purchases shown on the right.

2 Which one of the means of payments shown might not be accepted by all sellers of goods or providers of services?

3 What are
   a the advantages
   b the disadvantages
   of using coins to purchase a good?
4 What are
   a the advantages
   b the disadvantages
   of using credit cards to purchase a good?
5 Money is anything that is acceptable to users in an economy when making a purchase. It acts as a medium of exchange – the seller will accept the money from the purchasers of the good for the good being bought.
   a Which two forms of payment above are more likely to be accepted as a medium of exchange, and why?
   b In the past many people used to barter or swap, and some still do so today, to exchange goods. Why are the forms of payment shown here more convenient than barter?
6 Which item is most commonly exchanged in shops?

DATA RESPONSE 2

The tanner is ordered off the decimal stage

Sixpenny pieces will not be legal tender by June 30. Gareth Parry reports

THE SIXPENNY piece will cease to be legal tender on June 30, and even after that, its value will be no more than a numismatic nuisance to thousands of amateur collectors who for years have been pestering dealers with "rare" tanners.

. . . Nigel Lawson, Financial Secretary . . . said that as a result of the review of the future of the sixpence . . . "a Royal Proclamation under the College Act, 1971, was made earlier today calling in all coins of the denomination of 2½ pence by June 30."

. . . Its end was, of course, on the cards since decimalisation – known to many as inflation – broke out on February 15, 1971. The sixpence today has only a third of its then value.

The Treasury said . . . an estimated 200 million sixpences were in circulation, but it was reckoned that if most of these were melted down, the resultant mass of metal would be worth around £3 million.

The most vociferous campaign to save the sixpence was mounted eight years ago by National Consumer Protection. Its members suspected skullduggery at the British Banking Association which, at the Government's request, conducted a detailed survey into the precise status of the coin – how many there were, how many slot machines swallowed them, and how many banks still used them.

The sixpence was preserved after a similar campaign in 1970, but none have been struck since decimalisation day. The coin was first struck during the reign of Edward the Sixth (1547–53), and was until 1920, known in coin dealing as "the 925" – .925 of it was pure silver. After 1946, the "Fifty Fine" was minted – half silver, half alloy.

But after June 30, its value will be nil to collectors, said Mr Mark Rasmussen, an expert in English milled coins, at Spink and Son yesterday. "The only sixpence worth anything will be more than fifty years old and in excellent condition. My advice to people who have been hoarding them as potentially valuable collections is to rush round to the bank, cash them and forget them. It is an offence to do just about anything else to them."

Source: *Guardian*, 14 February 1980

180

1 The article describes a range of money no longer accepted as legal tender. What is legal tender?

2 a What would you have been unable to do beyond 31 May 1979 in the case of the notes referred to, and beyond 30 June 1979 in the case of the sixpence?
  b What is meant by the term denomination?

3 a What was decimalisation?
  b How had the value of the sixpence declined after decimalisation?

4 Why do you think
  a the sixpence
  b the £1 note
were withdrawn from circulation?

5 The £1 note was replaced with a coin. Using some or all of the following ideas explain why it was necessary to do so.

> Currency needs to be durable.

> £1 is like small change nowadays.

> The government needs to pay attention to the number of times a note passes from one person to the next in transactions.

Extension 2

1 The government is considering redesigning the country's money system. Consider what you think is wrong with our existing notes and coins and other forms of money and comment on the faults you have discovered. You may devise a questionnaire to assist you.

2 Using the information devise, design and justify your own new system of currency.

Coursework

Aim: To survey the nature of the medium of exchange.

Undertake a survey of your class.
1 Calculate the average amount of income spent by the class over a period of time, e.g. a week or month.
2 Establish via a questionnaire what proportion of debts are settled using each of the following methods:
  a coins;
  b notes;
  c cheques.

3 Undertake the same survey for a range of adults. What differences do you observe?
4 a To what extent do the differences exist because of the quantity of money/ qualities of money involved?
  b To what extent are other factors considered important? You might find it useful to establish people's view (via a questionnaire) of the advantages and disadvantages involved in using each of the means of payment detailed above.

32 Causes and Costs of Inflation

Decide for yourself

It's a winter's evening and an old man is pushing a wheelbarrow full of banknotes through the street. He is going to the baker's to buy bread. He lives in a country where there is such a rapid rate of inflation that not long ago he needed only a handful of notes to buy bread; now he needs a barrow load. Two boys see the old man and decide to steal from him. What do you think they take? (See bottom of the page for the answer.)

What is inflation?

Inflation can be defined as a persistent rise in prices of goods and services. In some countries inflation produces such rapid and large increases in prices that we talk of hyperinflation. (That is an inflation rate where price rises are so high that money rapidly loses its value. This situation was experienced in Germany in 1923. Prices rose over and over again in a matter of weeks.) When this happens people lose faith in the system of money being used. In Germany this collapse of faith is said to have helped Hitler into power.

Decide for yourself

If you lived in such a country, what might you want your wages paid in?
- banknotes
- diamonds
- gold
- iron bars
- postage stamps
- food

Why would you choose this medium of payment?

Activity

Inflation over one period of time can be compared with inflation in another time period by calculating the annual average rate of inflation for each time period.

You can calculate the annual average rate of inflation by adding up the rate for each year in your time period and then dividing by the number of years. For example:

    1960   5%
    1961   4%
    1962   9%
    = total of 18%

divided by 3 = a.a. inflation rate of 6%

1 Calculate the annual average rate of inflation for
  a 1960–1969
  b 1970–1979
2 During which year on the graph was inflation:
  a at its lowest;
  b at its highest?
3 Estimate the level of inflation in 1980.

4 Describe how the trends in inflation have changed since the 1960s.
5 Suggest reasons why the annual average rate of inflation was higher in the 1970s than in the 1960s.

General index of retail prices 1960–86

% change on a year earlier

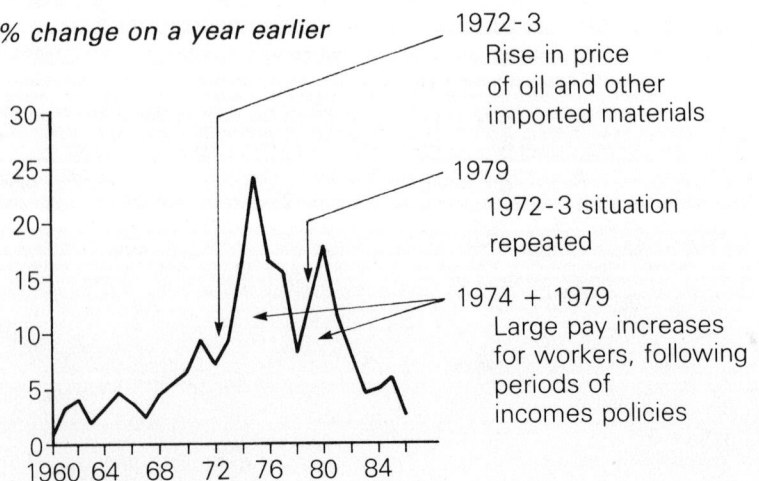

1972-3
Rise in price of oil and other imported materials

1979
1972-3 situation repeated

1974 + 1979
Large pay increases for workers, following periods of incomes policies

Source: *Economic Progress Report*, May–June 1986

*The wheelbarrow.

182

The consequences of inflation

The consequences of inflation and its costs are many.

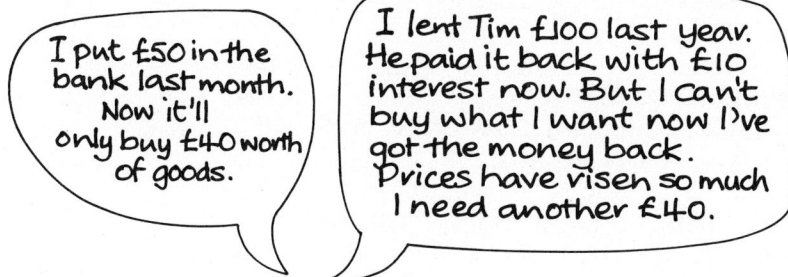

I put £50 in the bank last month. Now it'll only buy £40 worth of goods.

I lent Tim £100 last year. He paid it back with £10 interest now. But I can't buy what I want now I've got the money back. Prices have risen so much I need another £40.

Purchasing power

The most important reason why inflation causes concern to people is that it is seen to erode the purchasing power of money. That means that it eats away at how much we can buy.

Decide for yourself

In 1968 £1 would buy 40 bars of chocolate. How many could you buy today?

However, particular groups of people are especially hard hit by inflation:

- **People on fixed incomes suffer**: for many of us, because our wages rise faster than the increase in prices, we do not suffer greatly from the effects of inflation. However, people on fixed incomes soon cannot buy as much as they did before. Their purchasing power declines. Such people include pensioners, workers in weak trade unions or no unions, and the unemployed and other people on social welfare.
- **Creditors suffer**: people who loan money to others do not like inflation. By the time they have been repaid for loans they have made, they can end up, despite any interest payments charged, worse off.
- **Savers suffer**: if you save money in a bank or building society during a period of high inflation and interest rates are lower than the rate of inflation, you lose out. In such circumstances people tend to stop saving with savings institutions and put their money into gold and jewellery or other precious objects which they think will keep their value.
- **Investors suffer**: people who wish to create new wealth cannot be certain whether or not a new project will turn out to be profitable.

- **Manufacturers suffer**: if inflation is occurring in one economy but not in others, then goods in that economy become more expensive in world markets. Consumers will import cheaper goods from abroad. Manufacturers suffer doubly: they lose their home markets and are not able to export their goods.
- **The unemployed suffer**: it can be argued that many of the people unemployed in the UK today are unemployed because Britain has not been competitive enough in the past. It has priced itself out of world markets by giving in to excessive wage demands.

Not all economists agree with this theory. Some point to our poor record in delivering goods on time as significant; others stress that we need better managers and more investment in British industry.

The benefits of inflation

Inflation can bring some benefits. It can help stimulate economic growth if people have excess money to spend. If you are a borrower, then, during a period of inflation, you gain. The money you are repaying is less valuable than the money you have borrowed to buy goods (like Tim in the example above).

If you are an entrepreneur, you might be able to pass on rising prices to customers, without seeing a reduction in profits. This will depend, of course, on how much your product is wanted and whether people have the necessary purchasing power. If you are in a strong trade union, or in a skilled job which is in demand, you might gain an increase in wages greater than inflation.

ECONOMIC TERMS

Inflation: a persistent rise in prices.
Hyper-inflation: a very high rate of price increases.
Purchasing power: the amount of goods and services that can be bought with a particular amount of money.

What causes inflation?

There is no one cause of inflation; there are in fact many possible causes.

Money and inflation

Some argue that inflation is simply the result of there being too much money chasing too few goods in the economy. Supporters of this view point to the recent competition between banks and other savings institutions to lend money as an important factor in the inflation of the late 1980s. Others blame government for allowing generous pay awards or for overspending.

Demand-pull inflation

When the various factors of production are in full employment in the economy, or when there are supply shortages, there is a tendency for the price of scarce resources to rise. (Wage drift is a factor here, see page 157.) The reason for this rise is that the factors are bid up in price by those who demand them. If consumers have a lot of money, then they will demand goods and, in turn, entrepreneurs will bid up prices in order to meet the demand.

Imagine this . . .

There is a building boom in the London area, but a shortage of joiners and plumbers. As a result building firms in the London area offer higher rates of pay. Plumbers and joiners might be tempted to move from jobs elsewhere to the South East. Employers in the regions find that they have to increase the wages they offer to retain staff. This in turn leads to higher prices to their customers. Meanwhile employers in the South East have to respond by making their rates of pay even more attractive . . .

Cost-push inflation

If wages rise rapidly, then the cost of producing a good will be forced up. If the price of raw materials rises then again the cost of producing a good will rise.

In the early 1970s payment for basic raw materials that the economy required (like oil) led to inflation being "imported" into the British economy. In turn, the price of many finished goods was forced to rise sharply.

The wage-price spiral

If costs rise and these are passed on to consumers, then consumers will, as workers, demand more in wages. As wages are a significant part of costs, prices will be bound to rise. If people get used to price rises, they will demand more in wages. Then the economy becomes locked into a cycle of inflation.

ECONOMIC TERMS

Cost-push inflation: persistent rise in prices caused by a rise in the cost of the factors of production.
Demand-pull inflation: persistent rise in prices caused by an increase in consumer purchasing power.

Test yourself

1 What is inflation?
2 What is hyper-inflation? Name one economy which has experienced hyper-inflation.
3 Describe some of the groups who suffer when there is inflation in an economy. How do they suffer?
4 Why can some groups benefit from inflation?
5 What are the possible causes of inflation?
6 What is an inflationary cycle? Why is this dangerous for an economy?

DATA RESPONSE 1

Loadsa loadsa money for our super nurses

HOW ANGELS PAY GOES UP

Nurse	Wage now	New grade	New scale	Increase
Student	£4,540–5,170		£4,825–5,575	6.3%–7.8%
Auxiliary	£4,565–5,855	Grade A	£5,000–6,300	7.6%–9.5%
		Grade B	£6,075–6,975	19.1%–33.1%
Enlisted	£6,250–7,750	Grade C	£6,975–8,300	7.1%–11.6%
		Grade D	£8,025–9,200	18.7%–28.4%
Staff	£7,300–8,600	Grade D	£8,025–9,200	7%–9.9%
		Grade E	£9,200–10,650	23.8%–26%
Sister	£9,000–12,000	Grade F	£10,200–12,500	4.2%–13.3%
		Grade G	£12,025–13,925	16%–33.6%
		Grade H	£13,340–15,350	27.9%–49.4%

London nurses will also get £930 London Weighting Supplement

NURSES yesterday won their battle for a big pay increase when they were given rises averaging 15.3 per cent.

Senior staff nurses will get an extra £40 a week, as exclusively predicted by The Sun, which has led the fight for a better deal for the hard-pressed angels.

Ward sisters with special skills in intensive care and children's illnesses will get increases of nearly 60 PER CENT.

In inner city areas, their pay will rocket from £9,930 a year to £15,338.

Last night, Britain's 487,000 angels were delighted by the BILLION-POUND deal.

Student nurse Helen Colliver, 19, from St Mary's Hospital in Paddington, West London, said: "Now I can go out and buy a new fridge."

The Government WILL fund the rises in full, after approving the recommendations of a pay review body yesterday.

They will cost an extra £750 million, on top of the £400 million already allocated to health authorities for rises to match inflation.

The new deal – involving wholesale regrading of duties and salaries – is worth more than FOUR TIMES the current cost of living increase.

It could take six months to complete the shake-up but all rises will be backdated to April 1.

The huge award is aimed at ending the annual wrangle over nurses' pay and puts them on a par with police.

The old rate for an ordinary enrolled nurse started at £6,250. Now the top band in that grade goes from £8,025–£9,200.

Royal Free staff nurse Bernie Wong, 29, said last night: "It's great news – I might be about £1,000 a year better off."

Source: *Sun*, 22 April 1988

---

1 What possible increase in pay could a staff nurse transferred to **Grade E** on the New Grade for Nurses pay receive?

2 How much money had been allocated for rises to match inflation, i.e. the increase in the cost of living?

3 Explain what is meant by the term 'cost of living'.

4 What will the student nurse referred to in the article do with part of her pay increase?

5 Explain how pay awards can fuel inflation. Use the article to help you provide an answer.

6 What factors other than increases in pay can fuel inflation?

Extension

Case A:
The effects of inflation on business.

Dilip Patel runs a sportswear firm. Recently the cost of many of the raw materials has been rising rapidly. The market for his goods is very competitive. He is worried that he will lose business if he passes the costs on to his customers. He would like to expand his business, but this would involve borrowing from the bank, and the latest rise in interest rates worries him. If he keeps his prices to customers low, he might win an export order worth £2m.

Case B:
The effects of inflation on creditors and savers.

Howard Jones has £10 000 in savings. His niece Kate has borrowed £200 of this for one year to help pay for a car. She has promised to pay Howard interest at 5%.

The remaining £9 800 is kept by Howard in a building society account and is earning interest at 15% over a year. Howard is wondering why he let Kate have the loan of £200.

Kate's union has just won a £5 a week pay rise for their workers to help offset the increased cost of living.

Case C:
The effects of inflation on consumers and people on fixed incomes.

Jack Hemsley is 67 and retired. He is finding it difficult to manage on his pension. It seems to him that every time he shops yet another item has risen in price. Jack has £300 saved, "for a rainy day" in a tin box under his bed.

DAILY NEWS
INFLATION RATE SET TO RISE TO 18%

1 Explain why Dilip is worried about the inflation rate.
2 How might a rise in inflation lead to an increase in unemployment? (Think of what could happen to Dilip's business and refer to his problems in your answer.)
3 Explain why inflation is particularly damaging for Jack Hemsley.
4 Why was Howard unwise to let his niece borrow £200? Why instead should Howard have added the £200 to the money he has saved in his building society account.
5 "Inflation only produces losers." Explain what this might mean, using the cases above. How true is this as a statement of fact?

DATA RESPONSE 2

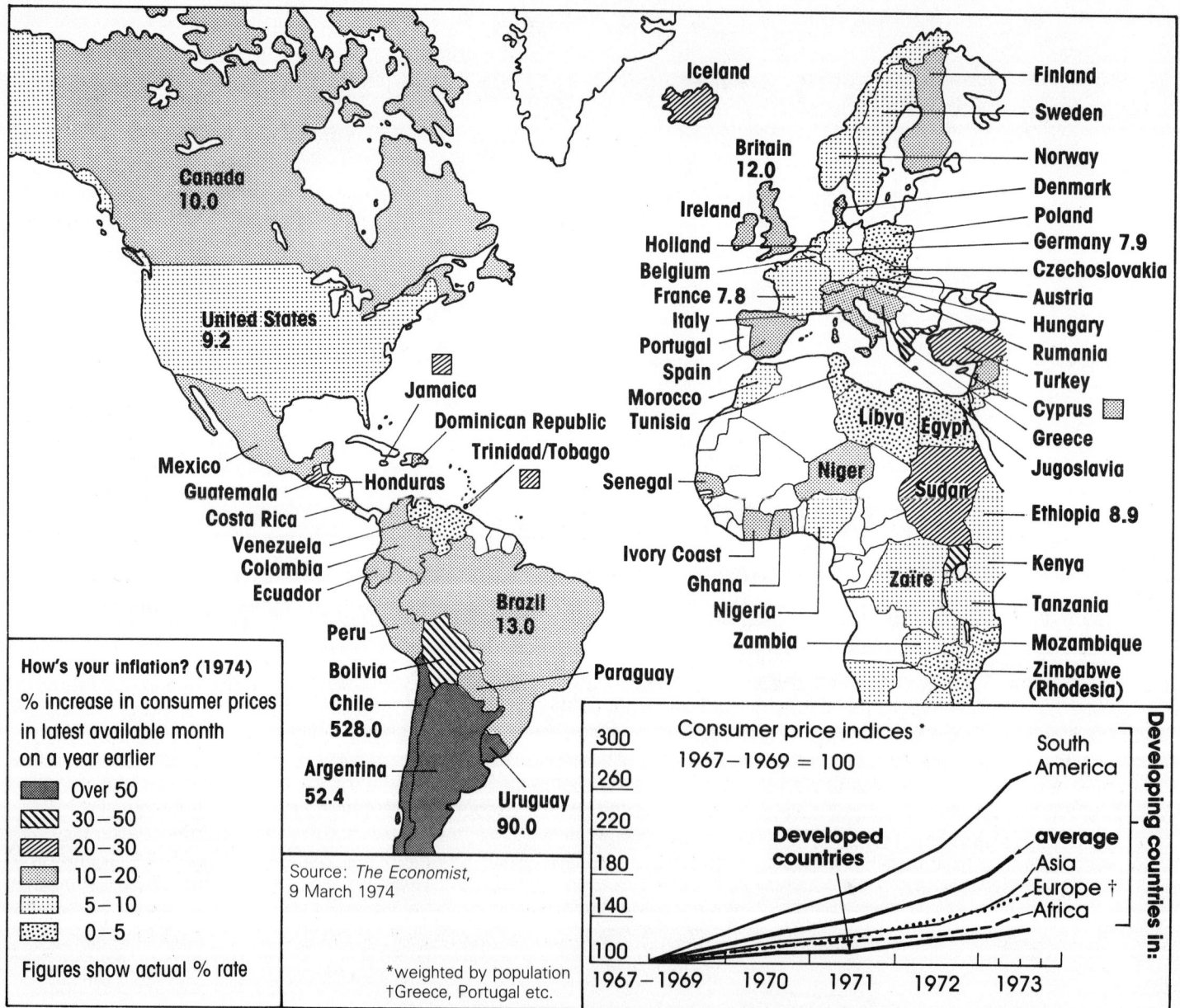

Iceland

Britain 12.0

Ireland
Holland
Belgium
France 7.8
Italy
Portugal
Spain
Morocco
Tunisia

Finland
Sweden
Norway
Denmark
Poland
Germany 7.9
Czechoslovakia
Austria
Hungary
Rumania
Turkey
Cyprus
Greece
Jugoslavia
Ethiopia 8.9
Kenya
Tanzania
Mozambique
Zimbabwe (Rhodesia)

Libya Egypt
Niger
Sudan
Senegal
Ivory Coast
Ghana
Nigeria
Zambia
Zaire

Canada 10.0

United States 9.2

Jamaica
Dominican Republic
Trinidad/Tobago

Mexico
Guatemala
Honduras
Costa Rica
Venezuela
Colombia
Ecuador
Peru
Brazil 13.0
Bolivia
Chile 528.0
Argentina 52.4
Paraguay
Uruguay 90.0

How's your inflation? (1974)

% increase in consumer prices in latest available month on a year earlier

	Over 50
	30–50
	20–30
	10–20
	5–10
	0–5

Figures show actual % rate

Source: *The Economist*, 9 March 1974

*weighted by population
†Greece, Portugal etc.

Consumer price indices *
1967–1969 = 100

Developed countries

South America
average
Asia
Europe †
Africa

Developing countries in:

300
260
220
180
140
100

1967–1969 1970 1971 1972 1973

Argentina

Consumer prices
(% increase on
a year earlier)

1000
800
600
400
200
0

15
10
5
0

Budget deficit
as % of GDP

IMF
plan

1984 85 86 87 88

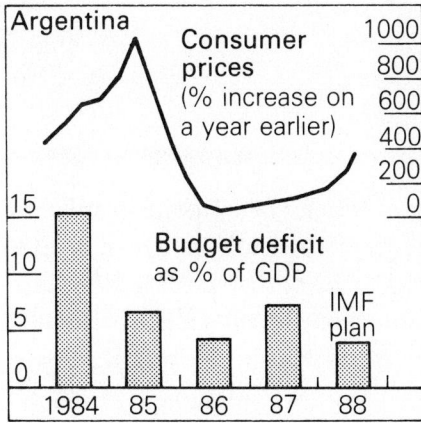

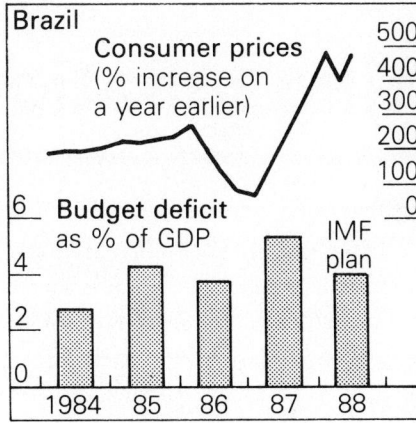

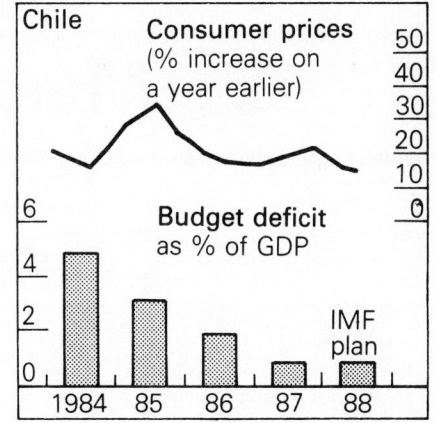

Source: *The Economist*,
6 August 1988

Brazil

Consumer prices
(% increase on
a year earlier)

500
400
300
200
100
0

6
4
2
0

Budget deficit
as % of GDP

IMF
plan

1984 85 86 87 88

Chile

Consumer prices
(% increase on
a year earlier)

50
40
30
20
10
0

6
4
2
0

Budget deficit
as % of GDP

IMF
plan

1984 85 86 87 88

1 What was Chile's inflation rate per annum in 1974 (i.e. over a period of a year).

2 Identify two countries with a low inflation rate in 1974.

3 What happened to the inflation rate throughout the world in the early 1970s? What differences can you detect between the various economies' inflation rates during this time?

4 Why had Chile made a spectacular recovery by 1988?

5 What evidence of hyper-inflation could be seen in Argentina and Brazil in 1988?

Coursework

Aim: To examine inflation in the British economy over the last 20 years.

Use data from sources to be found in local libraries, for example, government publications like *Social Trends*, *Annual Abstract of Statistics*, *Economic Progress Reports*.

Interview people of different age groups to gather information as to the possible causes of inflation during this period. What costs of inflation do your interviews reveal?

To what extent do your findings support or reject the view that there is no one single cause of inflation?

33 Measuring Inflation

Why have rail fares gone up 10%? My wages have only gone up 5%.

Look, it was only 10p last week, now it's 15p.

People complain about inflation but they often forget periods when prices fall. (We call this *deflation*.) They forget too when their wages are going up faster than price rises. If prices were to rise by 5% but our wages were increased by 10%, then we would clearly be better off. There would be a rise not just in our money income but in our *real income.*

However, inflation can have long-term effects on our economy, and our ability to trade and compete with the rest of the world. For this reason it is important to be able to measure the price rises that occur.

The cost of living

When prices rise then we can say that there has been a fall in the value of your money, or a decline in your *purchasing power.* At the same time there is a rise in the *cost of living.* That means that you need more money to purchase a given amount of goods. If during a period of inflation your income does not change, then the fact that you cannot purchase the same amount of goods as you could before means there has been a fall in your *standard of living.*

If, on the other hand, your income rises faster than the cost of living, your standard of living would improve.

The Retail Price Index

There are a number of methods that the government uses to measure inflation. The most widely known is the Retail Price Index (an index, in this sense, is a way of measuring change, in this case change in prices):

- it is used by trade unions when they negotiate pay awards;
- certain benefits (for example, pensions) are linked to the Index (this is called indexation);
- it is used to judge government attempts to manage the economy.

The government constructs the Retail Price Index in the following way:

- a survey of spending is undertaken to discover the average level of spending of households;
- the survey measures the price of a typical "shopping basket" of goods, and how much money the families in its survey spend on these items;

- all price rises are measured from a Base Year – this is currently 1987;
- the price of each item in the Base Year is given the index number of 100;
- a weight is given to each item as well. This allows the relative proportions of each item in the basket of goods to be taken into account. If, for example, 20% of a family's budget is spent on heating, then this needs to be reflected in the index. This is because any rise in heating costs will have a greater impact than a rise in the price of an item like newspapers which are only a very small part of a family's budget;
- the prices for the whole of the basket is then expressed as 100 for the Base Year;
- in future years price changes can be worked out by calculating the percentage change in prices multiplied by their weight. These price changes are measured from the Base Year.

ECONOMIC TERMS

The Retail Price Index: the major measure of price rises in the British economy.

Cost of living: the amount of money required to purchase a given range of goods and services.

The base year: the year from which changes in prices are measured.

The "basket of goods": a term used to describe the typical items families are thought to spend their money on.

The weight: the relative importance of an *item* in a range of goods and services.

1 What is the opposite of inflation?

2 Prices rise by 7%, your wages rise by 11%: has your standard of living fallen or risen?

3 When people talk about the cost of living, what do they mean?

4 What is the Retail Price Index?

5 Here is a prices index for two years:
1978   100
1987   135

  a Which year is probably the base year?

  b What percentage change in prices has occurred?

6 Why do some people think that the Retail Price Index is a poor measure of inflation?

Activity

Measure inflation by constructing a Retail Price Index.

1 The first step is to choose a "basket" of items that accurately reflects a family's spending.

In order to keep our example simple we will only have four items in our basket.

Choose these by selecting four items from this list. Each item that you choose must be one that a typical family might spend their money on:

a Caviar		**f**	Mink coat
b Potatoes		**g**	Soft drinks
c Fish fingers		**h**	Gold necklace
d Video camera		**i**	Milk
e Champagne		**j**	Bread

2 Now we need to compare the changes that occur in the price of our basket of goods over a period of time. To do so we must first have a Base Year Chart. The base year is the year we will measure all changes in prices from, (it's the year we begin with). This one has been completed for you.

The Base Year Chart

	A Item	**B** Price in shop	**C** Price on index	**D** Weight	**E** Price × Weight
1			100	20	2 000
2			100	30	3 000
3			100	40	4 000
4			100	10	1 000
				100	10 000

  a Make a copy of a blank Base Year Chart.

  b List the items you have chosen under column **A**.

  c In column **B** record the average price these items are being sold for currently.

  d The price of each item is represented by an index number. This number in the base year chart is 100; it is shown in column **C**.

  e In column **D** record for each item the percentage of your budget that you would spend on it (assume that you only have the four items selected to think about). Your total must come to 100; this is called the *weight* or *weighting factor*.

  f In column **E** record the index price multiplied by the weight.

  g To work out the final index divide the total in column **E** by the total for column **D**.

3 Now we are going to imagine what the inflation situation might be like in two years' time. Use the following information to help you construct a second index. The first example has been completed for you overleaf.

  a A special European Community subsidy has reduced milk prices by 50%.

  b Following a series of disastrous harvests bread prices have risen by 20p for a standard loaf.

  c The price of potatoes and potato-based products has not altered during the period.

  d Following further declines in the North Sea cod catch the price of fish fingers has risen by 80%.

  e Soft drinks fall by 5p in price for each and every litre sold.

The Current Year Chart

	A	B	C	D	E
	Item	*Price in shop*	*Price on index*	*Weight*	*Price × Weight*
1	Milk	Price in shop	Has fallen by 50%	20%	−1 000

Once you have completed this second table work out the index by dividing the total for column **E** by the total for column **D**.

4 Now calculate the percentage change in prices between the two years given.

Problems with the Retail Price Index

There are a number of problems with using the Retail Price Index to give us an accurate guide to inflation in the economy and its effect on people.

- The Howard family love raspberry ripple ice cream, but the Pathan family dislike it. How can the government find an average family, when tastes are so different?
- How do we assess the effects on individuals? Pensioners suffer from cold, for example, but if the price of heating fuel rises why might their increased costs not be shown up in the Index?

The poor also spend more on food and heating as a proportion of their spending. As these are items that have increased the most in recent years, the Index which shows an average family's consumption, under-estimates the effects of inflation on those who often get help in the form of benefits, which are in turn determined by the RPI!

- Spending patterns change but the basket of goods chosen does not keep pace. More people now eat out, and drink at home; they own videos and play computer games. With such changes, it becomes necessary to revise the items included in the survey's basket.

Extension 1

A

What £1 bought in 1954

(note: 1d = 0·4p, 1/– = 5p)

½ pint beer 10½d.
¼ lb Brooke Bond Tea 1/8d.
½ pt milk 3¾d.
½ lb rice 7½d.
½ lb sugar 3¾d.
½ oz wool 8½d.
5 Woodbines cigarettes 8d.
½ oz tobacco 1/10½d.
¼ lb cheese 5½d.
½ cwt coal 3/6
1 nip Johnny Walker Whisky 1/1d.
1 loaf bread 7½d.
1 pr socks 2/4d.
1 lb shin of beef 1/4d.
1 lb potatoes 2d.
¼ lb chocolate 1/-d.
¼ lb butter 11d.
1 egg 5d.
½ bar soap 5½d.

Total £1. 0. 0.

What £1 could buy in 1954

B **Length of time necessary to work to pay for selected commodities and services**

Great Britain

	Married couple with husband only working							Two-earner couple
	1971	1981	1982	1983	1983	1984	1985	1985
	Hrs mins	Hrs mins	Hrs mins	Hrs mins	Hrs mins	Hrs mins	Hrs mins	Hrs mins
1 large loaf (white sliced)	9	8	8	7	7	7	7	4
1lb of rump steak	54	57	57	52	53	51	47	28
500g of butter (home produced)	20	20	21	19	19	17	17	10
1 pint fresh milk	5	4	4	4	4	4	4	2
1 dozen eggs (medium size)	22	16	16	12	13	16	14	8
100g of coffee (instant)	22	19	17	23	23	22	24	14
125gr of tea (medium priced)	9	7	6	6	6	8	9	5
1 pint of beer	13	12	12	12	12	12	12	7
1 bottle of whisky	4 17	2 24	2 25	2 20	2 21	2 16	2 11	1 18
20 cigarettes	22	20	20	20	21	21	22	13
Weekly gas bill	55	1 00	1 12	1 18	1 19	1 19	1 20	48
Weekly electricity bill	1 04	1 14	1 16	1 14	1 15	1 09	1 06	39
1 gallon of petrol (4 star)	33	36	34	34	34	33	34	20
1 cwt of coal	1 19	1 33	1 28	1 30	1 31	1 28	1 32	55
Weekly telephone bill	50	42	45	39	40	38		
Motor car licence	39 59	26 41	27 59	27 08	27 26	26 45	27 47	16 35
Colour television licence	19 40	13 05	6 05	14 41	14 51	13 40	16 07	0 37
Cinema admission	29	34	34	34	34	34	31	18
Long-playing record (full price)	3 16	1 49	1 45	1 41	1 42	1 38	1 37	58

Source: CSO, *Social Trends 17*, HMSO 1987

1 If you went into a shop today would you be able to buy as many items as you can see on the table in **A**?

2 If with £1 today you are able to purchase less than you could have purchased in 1954, what does this mean has happened:
a to the value of money; and
b to the level of prices?
Choose the correct answer from the list below.
A The value of money and the level of prices has not changed.
B The value of money has risen and the level of prices has fallen.
C The value of money and the level of prices have fallen.
D The value of money has fallen and the level of prices has risen.
E The value of money and the level of prices has risen.

3 Using **B**, identify how many hours and minutes a person had to work in 1971 to be able to afford a motor car licence. What changes had occurred by 1985?

4 Look at the overall changes in time required to purchase goods and services between 1971 and 1985. What do these changes suggest to you about the amount of money people had to spend and what they could do with this money?

5 Were there any items where more working time was required in 1985 than in 1971 in order to be able to afford goods? If so what were these items?

6 If prices rise and all other factors remain the same then economists would point out that the effect would be a decline in living standards. Do you think living standards overall have fallen or risen in Britain since 1954? Give reasons for your answer.

Inflation rate rises to 4.8% with no sign of break in upward trend

By Ralph Atkins,
Economics Staff

BRITAIN'S annual inflation rate last month was the highest for 2½ years and there is no sign of an early break in the upward trend.

Car price rises and higher electricity and gas costs were partly offset by lower prices for fresh foods, clothing and footwear.

Source: *The Financial Times,*
20 August 1988

Prices & Taxes
Change over previous year

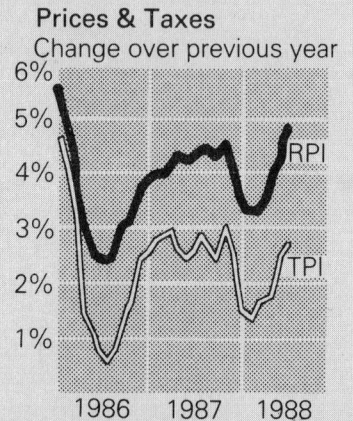

Interest rate fears grow as inflation hits 4.8%

By Richard Thomson

Inflation rose to 4.8 per cent in the 12 months to July and is now certain to rise well above 5 per cent in August as this month's mortgage rate increases are taken into account.

The accelerating rate of inflation is causing fears in the City that interest rates may soon be lifted to 11.5 per cent in a further attempt to dampen demand in the economy.

There is little sign that the last round of interest rate rises has done anything to slow down demand and huge amounts of imports are still being brought in.

The inflation rate in July rose by only 0.1 of a percentage point, in line with expectations, leaving the retail price index at 106.7 (January 1987 = 100).

The increase was mainly caused by higher vehicle and insurance costs as well as further increases in electricity and gas prices. These were offset by seasonal factors such as the summer sales and the lower price of fresh foods.

In the August figures, however, the mortgage rate rises which came into effect this month are likely to push the retail price index up by at least 0.5 of a point. According to some City estimates, the monthly increase could be as much as 0.75, giving an annual inflation rate of 5.5 per cent.

Building society lending figures confirmed the boom in consumer demand with record loans to home buyers of £5.4 billion during July, substantially higher than the £4.9 billion lent in June.

Deposits also continued at a high rate, with £1.3 billion received in July – the highest ever recorded for the month.

The markets are now waiting anxiously for next week's balance of payments figures for July. They are expected to show a rise in the trade deficit of about £1 billion, making a total deficit of some £6.7 billion for the first seven months of this year.

Mr Bill Martin, chief UK economist at Phillips & Drew, the broker, said: "Practically every aspect of the economy is still showing excessive demand. Tax cuts and higher pay awards mean that demand is likely to accelerate.

"This is bad news for pay, because the economy only seems to be speeding up as we go into the next pay round."

Mr Norman Fowler, the Secretary of State for Employment, urged restraint in pay settlements. He said pay bargainers should consider factors other than the position of prices . . . "When taxes are taken into account as well, then today's figures show that gross earnings need only to have risen by 3.7 per cent over the last year to maintain purchasing power," Mr Fowler said.

Source: *The Times,*
20 August 1988

Inflation heads for 5 per cent

Ben Laurance

BRITAIN'S inflation rate is set to top 5 per cent for the first time since the beginning of 1986.

The Government, which has raised interest rates seven times in three months after mounting evidence that inflation is gathering pace, yesterday released figures showing retail prices were up 4.8 per cent in the 12 months to July.

This rise does not include the effect of higher mortgage payments stemming from recent Bank of England base rate hikes, which will only show up when the figures for August are collated.

Average building society rates for borrowers have risen by about 1.75 per cent, bringing the typical mortgage rate to 11.5 per cent, which is likely to add about 0.7 per cent to the Retail Price Index. Mr Bill Martin, an economist with the stockbrokers Phillips and Drew, said: "In August, the full hit from mortgage rates will show up and that could push the figure to 5.5 per cent. With a new pay round coming up, it's hardly surprising that the Government is making worried noises about the need to keep settlements down."

The Employment Secretary, Mr Norman Fowler, insisted that yesterday's figures meant that "the overall position is little changed". Pay bargainers should remember this, he said.

The figures reflected higher car prices, dearer car insurance and higher tariffs for electricity and gas.

Source: *Guardian*, 20 August 1988

1 In August 1988 the newspapers carried reports of a rise in the inflation rate. Provide a brief summary of the reported increase in inflation as your own news report.

2 Describe how the Retail Price Index has changed since 1986.

3 According to the data, what had the government done to slow inflation down? Had this action been successful?

4 What factors had led to the increase in inflation? Why could the news have been worse?

5 What evidence is there in these extracts that inflation will continue to rise (or spiral) upwards?

6 In what way is the Retail Price Index a misleading guide to the effect of inflation in people's purchasing power?

Extension 2

A

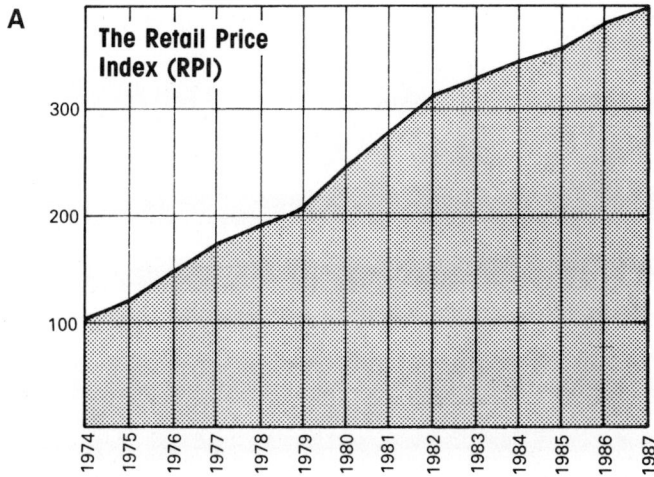

The Retail Price Index (RPI)

Source: *Employment Gazette*

B

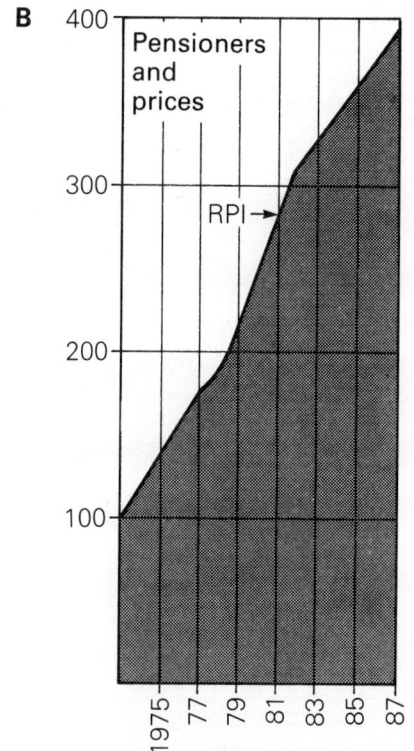

Pensioners and prices

RPI→

Source: *Employment Gazette*

What's in the basket
Components of RPI

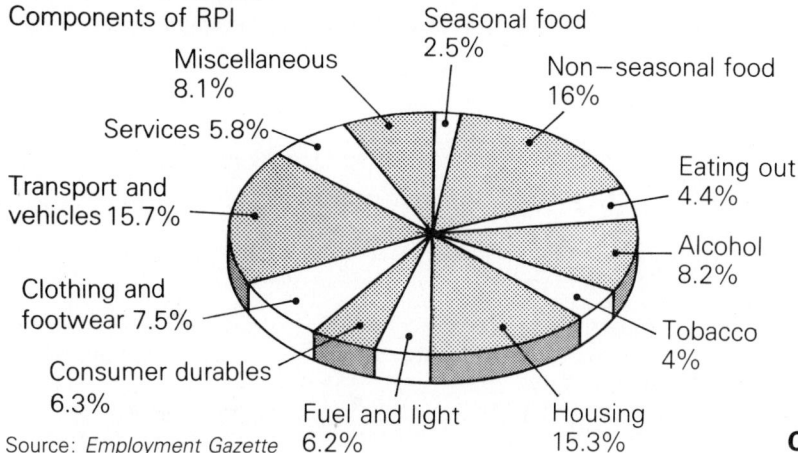

Miscellaneous 8.1%
Services 5.8%
Transport and vehicles 15.7%
Clothing and footwear 7.5%
Consumer durables 6.3%
Fuel and light 6.2%
Housing 15.3%
Seasonal food 2.5%
Non–seasonal food 16%
Eating out 4.4%
Alcohol 8.2%
Tobacco 4%

Source: *Employment Gazette*

C

1 Examine the Retail Price Index in **A**. Compare this to the RPI for Pensioners as shown in **B**.
  a What differences do you notice between the two graphs?
  b What do these differences suggest about the burden of price changes on pensioners in comparison to others?
2 Look at the basket of goods shown in **C**.
  a Which is the smallest item of expenditure?
  b Which is the largest item of expenditure?
3 If fuel costs rise dramatically explain why pensioners might find the rise a greater burden than many others in the economy.

4 **a** Using the categories included in the basket ask a small sample of your friends what they typically spend on each item.
  b Calculate the average amount of spending for each category and express your results as percentages of your friends' average total spending.
5 Compare the information you obtained in **4** with the percentages shown in **C**. What differences can you observe?
6 Why do you think these differences exist? Are teenagers less likely as a result to be concerned about an increase in prices?

Coursework

Aim: To measure inflation.

Construct an index that allows you to compare for a selected range of goods price rises in:
  a a corner store;
  b a local supermarket.
Use a base month from which to undertake your work, and calculate the changes that take place each month from this base month.
1 What do you discover at the end of your survey?

2 Are prices steady or do prices increase, decrease or fluctuate?
3 What differences are there between your two shops?
4 How would you account for these differences?
5 What problems did you have in carrying out your survey?
6 Would you include the same items in a second survey? What other changes might you make?

34 Savings

Financial institutions are organisations that accept money from those who want to save. In turn, they loan this money to those who want to borrow. For this reason they are called *financial intermediaries*. They are the middle links in a chain between lenders and borrowers of money.

Why can't you borrow from another financial intermediary, Dad?

Who are these financial institutions?

The financial intermediaries or institutions that most ordinary people have heard of are:
- Commercial banks
- National Girobank
- Building societies

Commercial banks

There are four large commercial banks in the UK today. They all have branches in most high streets and shopping centres. The Big Four banks, as they are known, are:
- National Westminster;
- Barclays;
- Lloyds;
- Midland.

These banks are Public Limited Companies, owned by shareholders. They are in the business of making profits for these shareholders. They do so by loaning money some of which they in turn have borrowed, and by providing a range of other financial services.

National Girobank

This is a countrywide bank operated by the Post Office. It offers most of the services provided by commercial banks, but is able to provide a larger number of outlets: the post offices scattered up and down the country.

Building societies

These are organisations that help people save money by offering to borrow their money and pay them interest. They in turn lend the money to those who want to buy or improve their homes, offering them mortgages on their property.

We will look at these in more detail later. In this chapter we are taking a close look at banks.

Opening a bank account

If you decide to open a bank account at a bank in your local high street, you will need to provide:
- a sum of money;
- your address;
- a specimen signature;
- a reference.

Decide for yourself

- Why do you need to provide these things?
- Why is it not enough for you just to put money into the bank? What will you need to identify your account?

The functions of banks

- To provide a place of safe keeping for money and other valuables.
- To provide the facility for people to use this money.
- To lend money.

To keep assets safe, banks provide safes (where cash is kept) and safe deposit boxes (used for people's valuables). Shopkeepers can use a bank's night safe facility to deposit their takings at the end of each working day.

You can keep your money in a bank in two main kinds of *account*: a *deposit account* or a *current account*.

You can draw (or take) money out of a current account by writing a cheque or by using a cash dispensing card. To draw

Activity

Banks are financial institutions. Financial institutions act as intermediaries and allow savers' money to be used by borrowers.

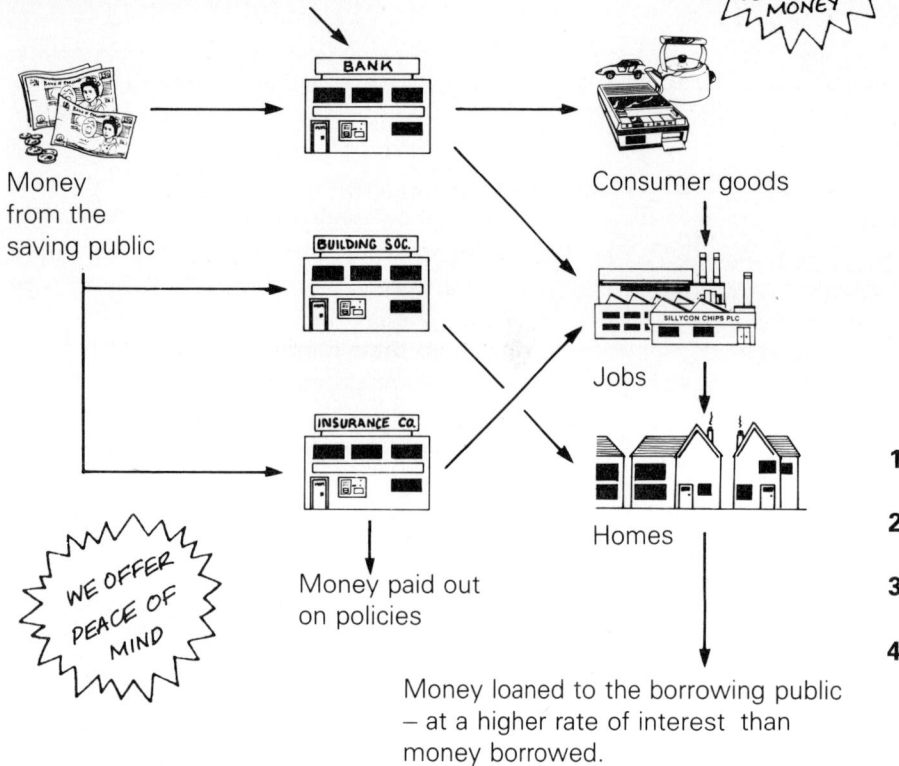

WE OFFER HIGH RATES OF INTEREST AND A SECURE PLACE TO SAVE YOUR MONEY

BANK

Money from the saving public

BUILDING SOC.

INSURANCE CO.

WE OFFER PEACE OF MIND

Money paid out on policies

Consumer goods

Jobs

SILLYCON CHIPS PLC

Homes

Money loaned to the borrowing public – at a higher rate of interest than money borrowed.

1 Which three types of financial institution are shown?
2 List two reasons for saving with a financial institution.
3 Name three groups of people that might wish to borrow from a financial institution.
4 The ACY Commercial Bank increases the rate of interest that it offers to its depositors. Explain why the BT Building Society might also have to increase their interest rates.
5 Financial institutions have to pay interest on money they borrow from the public, and pay a dividend to their shareholders. Explain how banks finance (pay for) these commitments.

---

bank giro credit

Date	Paid in by Address	Counter Credit	
		Notes £50	
		£20	
		£10	
		£5	
	Destination Branch Code Number	Coins £1	
Cashier's stamp and initials	Bank	50p	
		20p	
	Branch (where account is held)	Silver	
		Bronze	
	Account (in Block Letters)	Total Cash £	
		Cheques etc. (see over)	
		No of Cheques	
Fee	Account Number	For Bank Use Only	£

NWB1450 Rev Apr 87-1

bank giro credit

Date
Cashier's stamp and initials

Paid in by
60-01-04
Bank Use Only
490103491

National Westminster Bank
ADDISCOMBE BRANCH

Notes £50	
£20	
£10	
£5	
£1	
Coins £	
Total Cash £	
Cheques	

A/c
Cashier's stamp and initials

Date

MRS T M C BETT

Fee Box
No of Ch's
70

X £

Cash

Please do not write or mark below this line

Cheques, etc

£

⑈100006 ⑈⑈100006⑈ 60⑈01041: 39983714⑈ 84

money from a deposit account, you have to give notice to the bank, but in return the bank pays you interest on the money in your deposit account. However, increasingly, banks (and other financial intermediaries) are offering to pay interest on current accounts too.

When you open an account with a bank you are provided with a *cheque book* and a *paying-in* book. You use the paying-in book to *deposit* (or put) money into your account and to keep a record of this transaction. This is called *crediting* your account (or adding to it). You can also pay money into your account using a credit slip which you obtain at your own branch or at any bank with a bank giro credit slip.

The second main function of a bank, as we have said, is to provide the facility for you to use the money in your account. You can use this money to help you settle your debts. The bank helps you to do this in various ways:

- **With a cheque**: a cheque book contains slips which, when you fill them out, instruct the bank to transfer money from your account (that is the account of the *drawer*, who has written out the cheque) to the person the cheque is made out to (known as the *payee*).

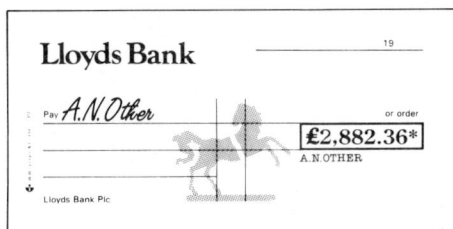

Many banks provide a *cheque guarantee card*. This helps to identify you as the person who wishes to settle their debts with a cheque on that account. Providing the person receiving the cheque writes the number of your guarantee card on the back of the cheque, the bank guarantees to meet their customer's debt up to a certain amount (shown on the card). This amount is often limited to £50. Why do you think this might be a problem?

- **With a standing order**: you may have some regular bills to pay: a subscription to a magazine, membership of your trade union or of a club, your rates bill or a quarterly insurance premium. The bank can help you settle these debts. All you have to do is complete a standing order form. This tells the bank who to pay, how often to pay them and when to make the payments. The bank then undertakes to make the payments on your behalf and *debit* your account (take the money from it).

- **By direct debit**: sometimes you are not sure how much you are going to be charged for even a regular payment. You can instruct the bank with a direct debit form to let the person you owe money to take the money from your account as and when they need to. You might use this method of payment for gas and electricity bills which vary from one quarter to another.

- **Budget accounts**: some people prefer to use a budget account to settle such debts. With this sort of account a regular sum is saved within the bank to meet debts. As long as a regular saving of a given amount takes place, the bank will honour these debts as and when they occur, even if at times this account is overdrawn. In this way the management of debts can be spread.

- **Personal cheques**: of course it is not only other people you want to pay from your bank account. You also want cash for yourself. To do this you write a cheque made out to 'Pay cash' or 'Pay self'. Alternatively you can take money from your account through a *cash dispensing machine*, using the card provided by the bank and keying in your personal number. This identifies you as the account holder. These machines give you access to the money in your account even when the bank is closed.

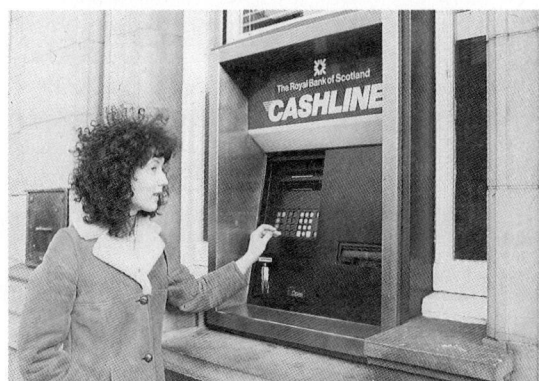

Other bank services to customers

If you have a bank account, the bank will offer you other services, too:

- **Bank statements**: to help you keep track of your financial commitments, the bank will send you a statement at regular intervals. This will show what has been paid into (credited) and what has been paid out (debited) from your account. You can tell from this how much money you have in your account after all transactions have been made.

- **Traveller's cheques** and **foreign currency**: when you travel, your bank will provide you with foreign currency or traveller's cheques in the currency of the area you are going to. They will debit your account accordingly and charge a small fee for this service.

- **Financial advice**: banks offer financial

and tax advice to both individuals and businesses. Again they may charge for this service.

- **Other services**: increasingly banks are offering services such as mortgages (once only offered by building societies) and building societies are offering services once only offered by banks.

The third main function of banks is to lend money. As we have seen banks pay interest to those of their depositors who lend them money as long as they provide notice of withdrawal, or keep their accounts substantially in credit. In turn banks charge those who borrow from them at a higher rate of interest. The difference between what they collect and what they pay out is used to finance their business and to pay their shareholders a dividend, or share of the profits.

There are two main ways by which you can borrow money if you have a bank account:

- **An overdraft**: If you have the agreement of the bank, you can run your account into debit (so you owe the bank money) and the bank will charge you interest on this amount.
- **A personal loan**: to finance a larger than usual item of spending (for example, the purchase of a new car, a special holiday, or an improvement to your home) you might ask for a personal loan. The bank agrees to lend you the money and in return you pay back a regular sum (say an amount each month) over a fixed period of time (for example, a year). The money you repay covers both the capital sum borrowed and the interest charged by the bank.

A personal loan is usually more expensive than an overdraft. Banks, just like their customers, have to keep their eye on their finances. If they lend money for a long period, they charge a high rate of interest because of the risks involved. This long-term business is the most profitable part of their activities.

However, assets lent for a long period become *illiquid* (very hard to turn quickly into cash). For this reason, banks keep a reserve of money in *liquid assets*. These are assets that, while not earning a lot or any interest, can be turned quickly into cash. This allows banks to meet the needs of customers who want cash or transactions settled (not all customers want their cash at any one moment!).

Clearing cheques

You pay cheques in and out of your account, but what happens to them then? Cheques you receive will often have to be sent to other banks to be *cleared*. This is the process of making sure that the person who has written the cheque has sufficient funds in their account to settle their debt in this way. If they have, then the cheque is *honoured* by the person's bank and the money deducted from their account. If there are insufficient funds in their account, the cheque is sent back to your bank – we say it has *bounced*. You are then left with an unsettled debt.

The Big Four commercial banks have a clearing house organisation that allows them to sort out cheques drawn on each other's banks. For this reason they are often known as the *clearing banks*. They settle up any differences in monies owing to each other at the end of each day of clearing. They use balances of cash they hold for this purpose with the Bank of England.

ECONOMIC TERMS

Banks: financial organisations that help people to save, borrow and use money.
A cheque: a way of settling debts by writing an instruction authorising the payment of money from a bank account.
Overdraft and loans: ways of borrowing money from a bank.
Liquid assets: wealth a bank controls and keeps in a form that can easily be converted into cash.

Test yourself

1 What is a financial intermediary?
2 What is the difference between a current and a deposit account?
3 Describe two ways in which you can use a bank account to settle your debts.
4 Why do banks keep some of their assets in holdings that may not earn interest?
5 Banks help you to settle your debts. Name two other functions they perform.
6 Why is it dangerous to accept a cheque in payment for a good or service? What might you insist on if you are taking a cheque?

DATA RESPONSE

A bank's balance sheet

Liabilities What the bank owes people who have lent the bank their money for safekeeping		Assets What the bank owns and can use to pay its creditors – the people who have lent it money		
Deposits	100	Cash in the till	2	⎫
		Balance held at the Bank of England	4	⎬ Liquid
		Money at call	7	⎭
		Treasury bills	5	⎫ Illiquid
		Special deposits	10	⎬ (longer-term lending)
		Investments	16	
		Advances (e.g. 5-year loan to J Bloggs)	56	⎭
Total	100		100	

I need some money from my account.

No problem Madam. We can let you have it straight away.

Thank goodness we kept some of our assets liquid. (A liquid asset is any item that can be turned into cash quickly). I'm glad that not everyone wants their cash all at the same time.

1 You have £100 deposited with the bank at 4% interest. Explain how the bank will be able to pay you interest.

2 **a** Why does the bank keep some of its assets as cash in the till?
 b Why does it only need to keep such a small amount of assets in this form?

3 Why is money kept in the Bank of England?

4 **a** What do you think is meant by the term a liquid asset?
 b Why are the assets (as labelled) good examples of liquid assets?

5 Explain why an illiquid asset is illiquid.

6 Banks have to be both profitable and at the same time must make money available to their deposit holders. Explain why this can cause a conflict.

Extension 1

I'm sure we can arrange a loan for you. It'll cost 15%

NIGHT SAFE

ARMED DELIVERY

LEWIS BANK

Interest Rate Now 9% For New Savers

Bank with us – We'll settle your debts

CHEQUES
DIRECT DEBITS
BANK GIROS
STANDING ORDERS
CREDIT CARDS
CASH DISPENSER

When you bank with us we'll let you have a monthly statement too. You can see what you pay in and what you're paying out.

Oh, your money is safe with us.

1 List two reasons for having a bank account.
2 When a bank is closed for business how can someone pay money in and take money out of their account?
3 List four ways in which you could use a bank to settle your debts.
4 If this particular bank is planning to offer interest at 9% to new savers, explain how it will be able to make a profit for its shareholders.
5 Your aunt has recently been burgled. She has lost her life savings which she kept hidden in a mattress. Write a short letter to her explaining to her the advantage of saving with a financial intermediary such as a bank or a building society.

Mr A

LLOYDS

Mr B

BARCLAYS

HOME BRANCH

PAYING IN BRANCH

BANK HEAD OFFICE

BANK HEAD OFFICE

CLEARING HOUSE

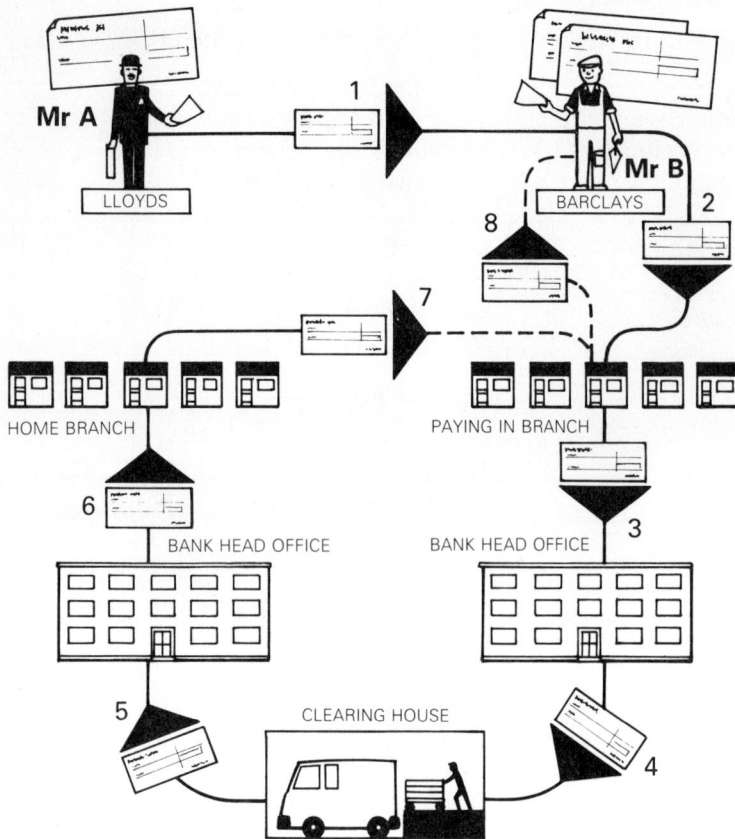

1. How does Mr A plan to settle this debt with Mr B?
2. When Mr B receives payment from Mr A and pays the sum received into the Paying in Branch of his bank, what will happen to Mr B's account?
3. Why is it necessary for payments to be forwarded to the Clearing House?
4. What will happen eventually to Mr A's account?
5. Assume that Mr A has no money in his account and no agreement to run an overdraft on his account. Explain what will happen now. What is this process called?

Coursework

Aim: To investigate the similarities of the services offered by banks and building societies.

Select a local branch of a building society and a local branch of one of the clearing banks.

Gather information about the services each organisation provides.

Use the information to test the hypothesis that banks and building societies are becoming very similar in the range of services they each provide.

35 Savings and Interest

Saving is an act of not spending. When we save we forgo (or give up) the right to spend our income now. We do this in return for a future benefit.

Shaheen opens a bank account in order to safeguard her money. People have lots of other reasons too for saving with a savings institution.

Decide for yourself

Look at each of these situations.

Mamoud Taheri. Aged 28. Not married. No dependents.

Sue and Jim Evans. In their 50s. Their only son is planning to marry but has nowhere to live.

Tim and Kate Mitchell. Early 20s. Last year their washing machine broke down. This year it could be the fridge's turn!

Ellen Cohen. Aged 21. Planning to go on holiday to Yugoslavia.

- Why might each of these people be interested in saving?
  Use the following ideas to help you.

Reasons for saving
- Saving allows you to buy an expensive item at a future time.
- Saving is useful for a 'rainy day', in other words to meet an unforeseen expense that might occur in the future.
- Saving is a way of providing for the future needs and wants of any children you may have.
- Saving now allows you to provide for your needs when you retire.

Test yourself
Rosie has won £2500 with a Premium Bond. She is considering using the money to buy a new car, but after a lot of thought she decides instead to place the money in a deposit account in her local bank. What is the opportunity cost involved for Rosie in making this decision?

What people consider when they save
People have to weigh up a lot of factors when they consider where and how much to save. Here are some of these factors:
- **Safety**: many ways of saving are very reliable, but not all of them. If you invest in shares, for example, you have to bear in mind that there is no guarantee that your savings will rise in value. You could even end up losing all your money.
- **Access**: people need to have access (be able to get at) their savings in the event of needing cash to meet an unforeseen need.

  Three important factors that influence the ease of access are:
  a the number of branches of the savings institution that exist;
  b the opening times of the branches;
  c the amount of notice (or time) you are asked to give in order to withdraw your savings.

Banks, for example, are a convenient place to save because there are many branches up and down the country, but some people prefer building societies because they are more likely to be open on a Saturday, a day when many people go shopping and might need access to their savings.
- **Liquidity**: when we talk about liquidity, we are referring to the speed at which we can convert our savings back into cash, or some form of purchasing power.

  Many people save with the National Savings Bank at the Post Office. But this is sometimes an inconvenient form of saving as it is not always possible to have the sum you want on demand (as we shall see later).
- **Interest**: this is the return or reward a person receives for saving. The rate of

interest can vary from one savings institution to another.

If you are a small saver and wish to earn some interest, but also want to get your money out on demand, then you cannot expect to earn a great deal of money. If, on the other hand, you are prepared to save a large sum of money on a regular basis and are also prepared to give plenty of notice (that is, to say in advance when you want your money back) before withdrawing all or part of your savings, then the savings institution will probably be prepared to pay you a higher rate of interest for the use of your money.

Test yourself
Why do you think a person or institution would be more prepared to pay you a high rate of interest if you lent them a large sum of money for a considerable period of time?

Activity

A Mrs Johnson
Aged 55. Wants to save her money where it can earn interest. Would like to be able to withdraw money on Saturdays to buy any bargains she sees in Melchester market.

B Mr Harris
Aged 60. Wants a secure place to save. His mother lost all her savings when a savings club she belonged to went bankrupt.

C Shaheen Pathan
Aged 23. Has recently been left a house and some capital when her parents died. Is thinking of saving in the long run. Is not too worried in the short run if her savings decline in value.

1. Make a list of the different ways in which these people can save their money.
2. Match each saver with an appropriate savings institution.
3. Which of these forms of savings could in the long run bring the best rate of return? What risk is involved?
4. Liquidity is the term used to describe assets that can be withdrawn easily from a savings institution and converted into immediate purchasing power.
   a Which of the above forms of saving is the most liquid?
   b Which is least liquid?
5. What risk might be involved in saving with a building society?
6. Assume that you consider it to be too much of a risk to purchase shares. Do some research to identify other ways in which you could save your money. (You could get some ideas from Data Response 1 on page 204.)

1 The Stock Exchange
A market for the sale and purchase of stocks and shares. Shares can increase considerably in value, but there is also a risk that share prices will fall.

2 Commercial banks
Melchester has branches of two banks. Both are open Monday–Friday and have cash dispenser facilities too. These are very heavily used on Saturday and Sunday and sometimes run out of cash.

3 Building societies
Melchester has branches of three building societies. Two are open Monday–Saturday.

Additions to savings and deductions from savings

Interest is an example of an addition you can make to your savings if you do not keep your money idle.

Let us look at the sad tale of Grandma Hawkins and the happy story of her grandson, Tony.

Grandma Hawkins has never trusted the local bank. She keeps her savings stuffed in a mattress instead! On 1 January 1989 she had £500 in her mattress: her total life savings.

Decide for yourself
- Assume that Grandma Hawkins did not add to her total life savings. How much would she have had on 31 December 1989?
- How and why did she risk losing all her savings during the year?

Grandma Hawkins' grandson, Tony, also has £500. But he chose to place the money for a year on a deposit account at the bank. The account paid interest at 8% a year.

Decide for yourself
- How much more money did Tony have than his grandmother when the year ended?

Tony also has £1000 invested in a building society account. By the end of the year Tony had a total of £1700 (including interest) saved in the building society and his bank account. This amount is called his *gross savings*.

A percentage of the interest Tony earned during the year has to be paid to the government in tax. When the amount of tax has been deducted, he is left with the final amount he saved during the year. This is called his *net savings*.

Tax and savings

The amount of tax you have to pay depends, upon the form of your savings. Some types of savings are free of tax on the interest you receive. If your income is low you may be exempt from (not have to pay) tax anyway but some forms of interest are taxed at source regardless of your income.

Both these factors have to be borne in mind when you decide where to save.

Where the Owen family save

The Owen family, who we met in Unit 10, save with a number of institutions. Mr and Mrs Owen have a joint current account in a bank. They do not use this for saving, but for settling their debts. They also share a deposit account (see Unit 34). Auntie Glenys has a savings account at the bank. This pays a higher rate of interest than the deposit account but she has to commit herself to saving a regular sum of money. Like the deposit account she has to give notice of withdrawal or lose some of her interest.

The triplets have money in a share account with a building society. Originally Mrs Owen had placed this money for them in bank accounts but she has moved it into share accounts. Each of the triplets gets a pass book and can deposit or withdraw money on demand. Mrs Owen found this more convenient than a deposit account and prefers that they get the higher rate of interest, even though this is taxed at source.

The Owens' son, Rob, is also saving when he can, in a building society account. He has an account designed for someone with larger amounts of savings.

With some of these accounts a saver has

to make a large initial deposit (for example, £500); with others the deposit can be as little as £1. These accounts can be termed "tiered" accounts, as they share the feature that the more you save, the higher the rate of interest earned.

Access to your savings is usually immediate, but with some accounts you lose some interest unless you give notice. With others, if your balance falls below a given amount, you lose your higher rate of interest. Some tiered accounts are linked to cash dispensing facilities.

Saving at the Post Office

Grandpa Williams saves with the Post Office. This is convenient as the local Post Office is near where he lives and he calls in once a week to collect his pension there.

Grandpa has £30 saved in Premium Bonds and £2000 in a National Savings Investment Account. The Premium Bonds do not offer any interest but last year Grandpa won £25 on one of his bonds. The Investment Account offers a high rate of interest and no tax is taken off at source. This is, therefore, attractive for non-taxpayers (like Grandpa Williams), but he has to give a month's notice to withdraw any of his savings.

A National Savings Ordinary Account is a simpler way of saving at the Post Office. You get a bank book and can take out up to £100 a day on demand but if you take out more than £50 your book is retained for checking. The interest rate is lower, but the first £70 of interest is paid free of tax. The minimum initial deposit is £5.

Other forms of National Saving through the Post Office (that is saving in government financial institutions) include:
- income bonds;
- yearly plan savings;
- savings certificates;
- government stock;
- capital bonds

Information about all these forms of savings is available free from any Post Office.

The major ways in which people saved in the early 1980s

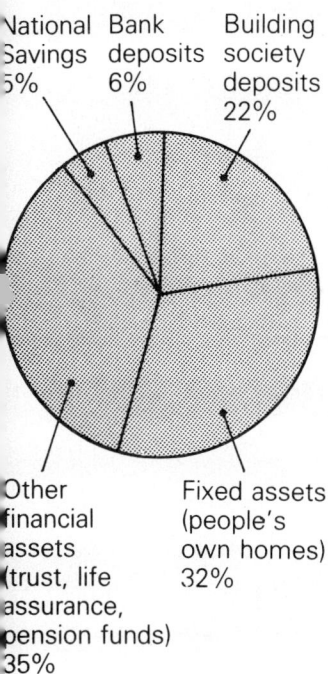

National Savings 5%
Bank deposits 6%
Building society deposits 22%
Other financial assets (trust, life assurance, pension funds) 35%
Fixed assets (people's own homes) 32%

Test yourself _____

1 Why is there a difference between a person's gross and net savings?

2 Mr and Mrs Owen often have to buy new clothes for the triplets on a Saturday. Explain why this made them decide to move the triplets' accounts from a bank to a building society.

3 What is the common feature of a tiered account?

4 Name advantages and disadvantages of National Savings accounts as a method of saving.

DATA RESPONSE 1

Type of savings: by social class[1], age, and sex, 1986[2]

Great Britain   Percentages and numbers

	Social class				Age					All
	AB	C1	C2	DE	16–34	35–64	65 or over	Males	Females	All adults
Percentage of adults[3] holding:										
Bank current account	86	75	59	39	57	68	46	63	57	60
Bank deposit account										
With cheque book	15	13	10	6	9	12	7	11	10	10
Other	35	29	22	18	25	24	23	26	23	24
National Savings Bank account	10	9	8	4	6	7	10	6	8	7
Trustee Savings Bank account	10	11	15	10	10	14	12	13	11	12
Building society account	81	73	66	49	67	65	55	65	63	64
Premium Savings Bonds	50	41	36	26	25	43	38	35	37	36
National Savings Certificates										
Index linked	12	9	6	7	4	7	16	7	8	8
Other	12	8	4	3	2	6	11	6	5	6
Unit trusts	19	7	4	3	3	9	7	8	5	6
Shares	34	19	10	4	9	18	13	15	12	13
Government/Local authority securities	5	1	–	1	–	1	3	2	1	1
Sample size (numbers)	328	588	671	868	868	1,135	452	1,174	1,281	2,455

[1] Social class: IPA definition.
[2] Fieldwork took place in February and March 1986.
[3] Aged 16 or over.
Source: CSO, *Social Trends 17*, HMSO 1987

1 According to this table, what is the commonest way of saving for all adults?

2 What percentage of social class C1 had
  a Premium Bonds;
  b Unit trusts?

3 Describe the pattern of savings:
  a by people of different ages;
  b by people of different social classes.

4 Examine more closely the pattern of savings by age, and give reasons for the differences that you have detected.

Test yourself _____

Why do you think that building societies and banks are more popular than other forms of saving?

Battle for £1bn teenage market

YOUNG savers are worth more than £1bn, and this week Lloyds Bank joins the battle for a share of the lucrative teenage market.

According to a recent survey by McCann Erikson, the teenagers in France desire love, in Finland they hanker after peace of mind, but in Britain they want money.

Ten per cent of 15–19 year-old teenage boys want money even above health. And teenagers generally like the image of an upwardly mobile job in the City.

The emergence of the young Yuppies in the classrooms, is also revealed in Lloyds Bank research for its new teenage banking package. In the 13–18 age group, the favourite car is a Porsche and the prerequisite of City life – socialising – is one of the most popular hobbies.

Image is all important. Youngsters regard current accounts as boring, so the banks have an uphill struggle to attract them. For the 13–15 age group, the new Lloyds teenage Headway account pays 3.5 per cent interest on credit balances, and with parental consent the youngsters can have a Cashpoint card.

But the teenagers need £10 to open the account. The 16–18 year olds have to deposit an initial £20 for their goodies, and they get the same rate of interest. But in true Yuppie fashion, the freebie is a personal organiser, and the account also has a cheque book and Cashpoint card.

For today's teenagers, the plastic card which allows them to get money at midnight, is the big selling point.

Most of the banks offer teenagers plastic access to instant money, together with a range of freebies. Midland Bank has one of the best range of incentives, which includes a camera for those with more than £15 in the account.

The Trustee Savings Bank has no special account for teenagers. The TSB deposit account is passbook based, offers no freebies, and pays a dismal 2.5 per cent interest. A new teenage package is under review.

The most tax-efficient account for teenagers is the National Savings Investment Account, which requires a minimum deposit of £5. The NS investment account is a good bet as it pays 8.5 per cent interest without deduction of tax.

But there are no freebies, and queueing at the Post Office with the pensioners does not appeal for today's teenagers. Moreover, fast cash for the 14 year-olds is not on offer, as there is a one month's notice of withdrawal.

But despite the drawbacks, the young Yuppies use the accounts to amass their fortunes. "We are the only major financial institution to pay interest in full," said a NS spokesman.

LINDA KRISMAN AND ARKADI NACHIMOWSKI

LINDA and her Russian boyfriend Arkadi, are sixth-formers at a co-educational boarding school. Linda is planning to take a year off before university, and work for a London estate agent. Arkadi has an offer from Cambridge University to study Economics, and he wants to go into merchant banking.

"I opened a bank account about two years ago when I first started boarding," said Linda. "I chose Barclays because it had a cash point outside.

"Teenagers are influenced by image. I have just opened a building society account in the town near school. I walked past the Portman Building Society. It looked so drab, and I took one look at the animals in the window, and did not fancy it. So I went to the Abbey National instead."

Some of the sixth-formers dabble on the Stock Exchange. Arkadi is an avid share buyer, and has an account with a stockbroker.

"About six sixth formers here have their own accounts with stockbrokers. We are trying to make money in every possible way," said Arkadi. "Some of my friends lost a lot of money in the crash. I was lucky."

Sue Fieldman

"In the 7–16 age group we have 650,000 accounts, and the average balance is £610.85. Presents from grandparents and friends of the family bump up the balances."

The building societies also want to attract the schoolroom tycoons. But generally they do not offer special teenage accounts. "We are looking at a teenage package at the moment," said a spokesman from the Halifax.

"Normally we offer the teenagers the Cardcash account. From the age of fourteen they can have a card, and the main attraction is that they can draw out £5 and £10 straight away."

The Abbey National does not provide a teenage package. However, youngsters can get their fast cash using a plastic card.

Bradford and Bingley has a Money Manager account which is geared to young people. However, it admits it has not been a hit. "The account pays the same rate of interest, 3.5 per cent, and on top offers a money advice kit," said a Bradford spokesman.

Source: *The Independent*, 11 June 1988

---

1 According to the article, how much are young savers worth as a market to the savings institutions?

2 What evidence is given that young people are money conscious?

3 a How much did teenagers need to deposit to open a Headway account?
   b What immediate benefits were there from doing so?
   c Why do parents have to give permission?

4 a Why might a young person not be attracted by the TSB offer?
   b Why did Linda choose to save with
      i Barclays;
      ii Abbey National?

5 Copy the table below and complete it using the information in the article.

Savings institutions mentioned	Initial deposit	Interest rate quoted	Free offers	If cash card available

6 a Analyse the table you have constructed and come to a conclusion as to where you would like to open an account.
b Give reasons for your choice.

7 a Do your friends agree with your decision? If not, why not?

Extension

Interest is an amount of money paid to someone as a reward for lending a person or firm a sum of money. The *rate of interest* is usually expressed as a percentage of the sum (principal) being lent.

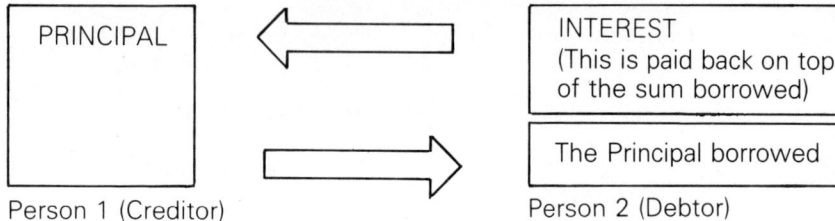

PRINCIPAL

INTEREST
(This is paid back on top of the sum borrowed)

The Principal borrowed

Person 1 (Creditor)

Person 2 (Debtor)

Principal	Amount of interest	Total amount to repay
300	–	324
–	8	108
–	16	–
400	–	–

1 If you borrowed £100 over 12 months at an interest rate of 12% of the principal sum per annum (meaning for each year), how much would you have to pay back after one year?

2 Now assume that you loan someone £300 at 12% per annum.
a How much would you expect to receive in repayment if the loan was for a year?
b How much more would you expect to receive if the loan was for a period of 18 months?

3 Complete the table, above right. Assume that interest is paid at a rate of 8% per annum. All loans shown run for a period of one year.

4 Alex, a friend of yours, has saved £500. He could:
a spend it all by throwing a party;
b buy a hi-fi system;
c go on holiday to Tunisia;
d continue to save;
e lend you the £500.
What is the opportunity cost for Alex if he lends you the money? Write a letter to Alex asking him to lend you the money so that you can start up a small business enterprise. Words to use in your letter include: safety – interest – guaranteed repayment – sound investment – worthwhile risk – business opportunity.

Coursework

Aim: To investigate what people look for in a savings institution.
1 Select one factor that a person might consider important when deciding where to save, using the following to guide you: interest, risk, liquidity, access.
2 Collect information from a range of people, of different ages and backgrounds on their amount of savings by type of savings institution.

3 Using interviews, collect as much information as you can from these same people as to why they save where they do, as opposed to somewhere else.
4 To what extent has the factor you originally selected proved to be the most important factor to bear in mind when people consider where to save?
5 What other factors have you discovered to be important?

36 Credit and Debt

Many people at some point in their lives live on credit. Credit exists when a person purchases goods and services or borrows money and is given time to repay the amount they owe. The sum owed is called the *debt*.

When a person borrows money, they usually have to pay a charge. Most of this is interest, but there may be an amount included to cover administrative costs.

Ways of obtaining credit

There are many ways to obtain credit.

Decide for yourself
- Which organisation from the following list will offer each of the types of credit outlined below?

        banks
        finance companies/money lenders
        mail order companies
        building societies

Types of credit available
- **Mortgages**: a popular form of long-term credit used when buying a home;
- **Cheques**: an interest free way of obtaining credit until the cheque is cleared through the drawer's account. Loans, overdrafts and credit cards are also available through this source.
- **Loans of last resort**: a personal loan but not one provided by the commercial banks. The interest rate charged for such a service can be very high.
- **Postal shopping**: a popular way of shopping from home with repayment allowed over an extended period like 30 weeks.

Hire purchase

This is another form of credit, usually provided by finance companies. Hire purchase is different from other forms of credit in that you are not the owner of the item until you have made the final payment. You are only hiring it.

When you buy a good on hire purchase, you pay an initial deposit in return for the hire, or borrowing, of the item. This is followed by further payments called *instalments*. Once the final instalment is paid the item is legally yours. The final price of all the money you pay will be greater than the price if you had "bought for cash", as there

is a charge for the service and interest on the money owing too.

If you fall behind with the repayments, the finance company can claim the goods back. If you have repaid at least one third of the debt, the company will need to get a court order to repossess the goods. You cannot sell your purchase, which might, for example, be a car, until you have repaid the whole debt.

Comparing forms of credit

As the law now stands a trader must tell you the true cost of credit. They should do this by displaying the annual percentage rate of charge (or APR). This helps you to shop around for the best credit deal.

£300 APR 5%

£200 APR 60%

Which would you buy?

The APR shows the true rate of interest because it is based not on the total you owed at the beginning of the loan, but on the average amount owed during the life of the loan. This amount declines during the loan period (as you make repayments). Therefore the true rate of interest may often be higher than the flat rate quoted.

Test yourself
1 What is the difference between credit and debt?
2 List two ways in which you can live on credit.
3 What is the most important thing to remember about hire purchase?
4 What does APR stand for? What does it allow you to do?

Activity

1 Look at this advertisement. Then read the following information which summarises your rights when you obtain credit.

2 What is misleading about the advertisement?

3 What is missing that should be prominently displayed?

4 Jan is in debt. She points out this advertisement to you saying, "Look at this! It's the answer to all my problems, isn't it?" Explain to her why she should be careful. What advice would you give her?

5 Working in groups redesign the advertisement so that it falls within the law.

6 Examine each of the redesigned advertisements and ask an independent observer to judge which is the best at providing the borrower with information on their rights in the area of credit.

Checklist for legal information and consumer advice on credit

An advertisement offering credit should contain:

1 A *reference to the APR* clearly and prominently displayed.
   - There is no point having fast financial help available if it puts you faster into debt!
   - A 'consolidation' loan is often not going to be at a rate that will help you get out of debt but at a rate that will increase the size of debt repayments.

2 Reference must be made to the fee being charged. Such services are not provided free of charge.

3 Reference should be made to the period the loan will be for or the total amount you will have to pay. The repayment terms should be displayed in a table giving the number and the amount and frequency of repayments.
   - The rate says it's competitive – but what is it competitive with?
   - It is clear from the advertisement, "Home owners only", "Sorry no tenants", that the loan is secured against your property. You would risk losing your house.

The advantages of credit

Many people like using credit because they are able to have the use of the goods and services they want straight away. They do not have to wait and save up.

If you are using a credit card, you can borrow for a short period without any cost at all if you repay the credit card company in the time they allow you.

At a time when prices are rising rapidly all creditors gain, but of course all lenders lose.

The dangers of credit

There has been a considerable boom in the amount of credit available in recent years. This has often been matched by an increase in the number of people who cannot pay their debts:

- In 1986 there were 2 million debt claims presented in the civil courts.
- In 1987 more than 145 000 families were disconnected for failure to pay their gas or electricity bills.
- An increasing number of people each year are behind with rent or mortgage repayments.

Credit can be dangerous because:
- you can be tempted to live beyond your means;
- there are often cheaper ways of meeting your needs than buying on credit. Renting or hiring an item as and when you need it might be a better alternative;
- you not only have the capital sum you borrow to repay, but also the interest on the loan;

208

> When you have a credit card you just buy and don't think. I don't have any savings. If the money is there I just spend it

- once in debt you can be tempted to borrow even more to get out of debt (the "debt trap").

The debt trap

A survey undertaken in 1988 by the Office of Fair Trading (the government's watchdog on consumer matters) noted that many young people fall into the debt trap.

Think about Penniless Penny. She had a bank account at 17. When she was 20 she was offered a credit card with a £700 credit limit by her bank and a bank overdraft limit of £800. She soon found that she made use of both and ran up debts of £1500.

Many people are refused credit facilities each year. If you are refused credit because of the activity of a credit reference agency, then you have the right to investigate and challenge the basis for the decision under the Data Protection Act.

Budgeting

Managing your expenditure by relating it to your income is a sensible precaution when you see the problems debt can bring. We call this management *budgeting*.

Adam earned £80 this week but he has nothing in his savings account.

"If I have any money I spend it," he says.

Decide for yourself

Adam has regular weekly expenses which are listed below.

- What would you recommend that Adam does to save £15 a week to go on holiday?
- Try and ensure that Adam meets all his immediate needs and yet has money to save.

Adam's expenses	
Rent to parents	£15
Put aside for clothes	£10
Bus fares to work	£8
Drink	£12
Entertainment (disco, cinema, etc.)	£20
Food (his family give him one meal a day)	£15

Test yourself

1 What can be dangerous about credit?
2 What is a budget?

DATA RESPONSE 1

Bank lending rises to record £9bn

By Ralph Atkins,
Economics Staff

BRITISH BANK and building society lending continued to expand rapidly in July, highlighting inflationary pressures in the economy, according to official figures yesterday.

The Bank of England said lending totalled a record £9bn last month. This was higher than expected by most City analysts and compared with a revised £8.8bn in June.

The rise suggests there has been no let-up in Britain's fast pace of economic growth. It reinforced fears that excessive expansion in lending is leading to upward pressure on prices.

The figures show that M0, one of the Government's key measures of the money supply, was again growing outside its target range. In the 12 months to July, M0 increased by 7.0 per cent against 7.7 per cent in the 12 months to June. In March, Mr Nigel Lawson, the Chancellor, set a target for M0 growth of 1 per cent to 5 per cent in 1988–89.

The Treasury said the figures were broadly in line with its assessment of monetary conditions which lay behind the 3½ point rise in base rates since the end of May.

Although July's statistics suggest a slowdown in the growth of M0, figures for the last six months expressed at an annual rate show an 8.5 per cent rise against an annualised figure of 6.0 per cent for the six months to June.

The Treasury said the six-month figures were volatile and did not represent a worsening trend. It pointed out that they excluded January when M0 showed a fall.

The latest figures show that M3, the broad measure of money supply, increased by 20.6 per cent in the 12 months to July. M4, which includes building society deposits, rose by 17.4 per cent.

The increase in bank and building society lending is explained partly by a rush for mortgages to beat the August 1 introduction of tax changes announced in the Budget.

Lending could have been pushed higher by early financing of car purchases by people keen to get 'F' registration numbers this month.

The Banking Information Service said personal borrowing accounted for an unusually large proportion of lending by leading UK banks in July. Lending for house purchases, excluding bridging finance, was a record.

However, corporate lending remains strong, suggesting that industry continued to increase investment spending.

Tom Lynch writes: Mr John Smith, the shadow Chancellor, said the surge in the money supply figures was "further proof that Mr Lawson's irresponsible Budget has accelerated a credit boom that is now so out of control that he has had to increase interest rates seven times."

Industry and those regions which had not benefited from

continued on next page

Total consumer credit given
(£ million)

20 000

15 000

10 000

5000

1977 1978 1979 1980 1981 1982 1983 1984 1985 1986

Inflation: 1976 = 100

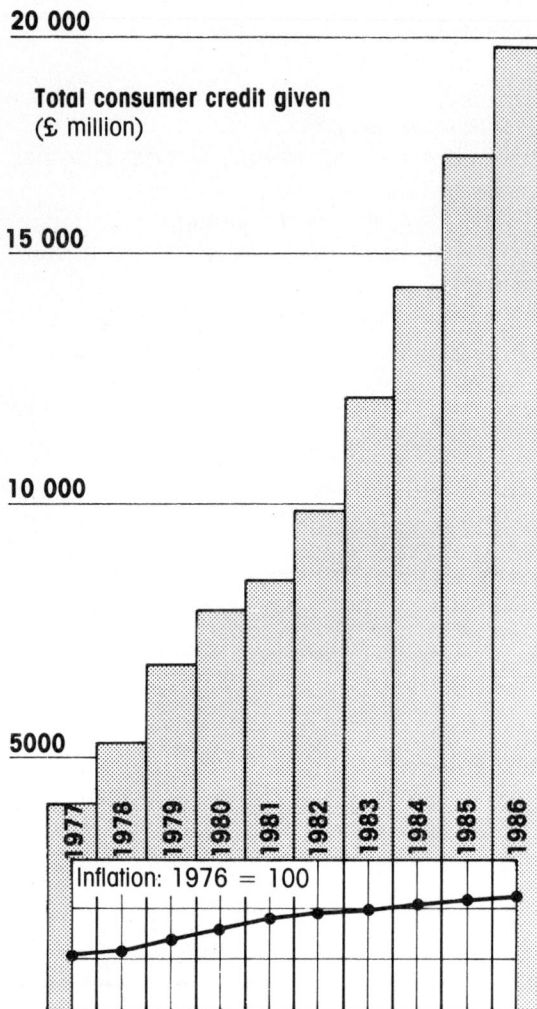

the growth generated by the credit boom would pay the price for that strategy, he said.

"The economy is badly out of balance. Escalating private expenditure on imported consumer goods is driving our balance of payments into serious deficit and the increases in interest rates will place a severe burden on British industry."

M0: Narrow measure of money – rates, coins and bankers' cash held at Bank of England.

Source: *New Society*, 6 November 1987

Money Supply

Percentage change over previous 12 months

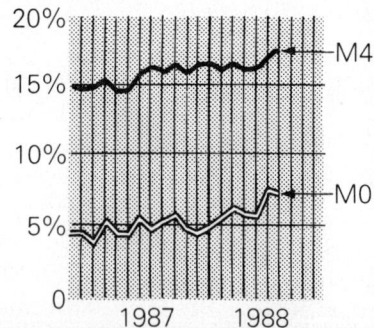

20%

15% — M4

10%

5% — M0

0

1987 1988

1 What level did bank lending rise to in July 1988?

2 What level did consumer credit reach in 1986?

3 Explain what is meant by the phrase "all bank lending is a form of credit, not all credit stems from bank lending."

4 List two factors that may have accounted for the demand for credit in July.

5 What is the difference between M0 and M4 as a measure of the supply of money in the economy?

6 Why was the Shadow Chancellor critical of the Chancellor?

DATA RESPONSE 2

**Credit cards are a part of daily life.
SIMON MOUNTFORD, Money Post Editor, and STEPHEN WALSH look at the costs and the consequences.**

What price the plastic revolution?

By STEPHEN WALSH

THE AFFLUENT advance of Britain's credit card revolution hides a mounting tide of casualties who bought now and paid dearly later — sometimes with their lives.

For while business continues to boom for the credit barons, thousands of their customers have found paying by plastic is a route to debt, depress-ion, and even suicidal despair.

A bewildered battalion of half a million borrowers with debts amounting to £500m walked into Citizens' Advice Bureaux last year — and about 15 per cent of that figure was owed to credit cards of one sort or another.

Many more people are reckoned to be coping alone with personal debt, too embarrassed or afraid of the stigma it carries.

Almost everyone now has some credit, even if it is under control. Every family in Britain is estimated to owe an average of £1,000 without counting mortgage and rent commitments.

The growing crisis of consumer debt is spawning a whole new profession of specialist debt advisers who are struggling to cope with an ever-expanding list of clients — with young people accounting for a growing part of it.

□CASE No 1: Mr G is an intelligent, unmarried, 40-year-old medical representative who was driven to plan his own death after becoming caught on a helter-skelter of mounting credit — now standing at almost £25,000.

The spiral of borrowing from one company to pay another began about ten years ago with modest use of credit to buy household items for his home in the Bradford area.

But he gradually found interest payments were becoming too much for his salary — he now earns £135 a week — and began taking further loans to finance even further borrowing.

His creditors include eight credit cards from finance companies, banks, and stores who, he says, were more than happy to help him out with extended loans when the crisis began to bite.

He said: "I never thought I could get into this situation. I don't think I am reckless — it just seemed to gradually creep up on me.

"I must have been getting good credit references. Everyone was only too happy to supply me with whatever I liked. I didn't have to tell any lies about anything.

"Eventually, all the debts piled up in a sort of domino effect and I realised I had problems.

"Before I went to the CAB, I thought suicide was the only solution. I had drawn up plans in my mind of how to do it."

Mr G, a trained nurse, had planned to give himself a lethal injection of insulin in an attempt to disguise his death as a heart attack.

He added: "I was extremely depressed, and I couldn't see any other way.

"The only thing that stopped me was the realisation that it would be leaving the problems for my parents to deal with."

Finally Mr G went to the debt counselling unit at the Bradford CAB, which, he says, has enabled him to face life again.

A counsellor offered a shoulder to cry on, then quickly contacted the 18 creditors, each owed between £34 and £10,000, to arrange a freeze on interest and a pro rata repayment plan.

The unit now pays the debts on his behalf through a special clients' account. It will be many years before his finances return to normal — and he will never use credit again.

Source: *Yorkshire Post*, 1 September 1987

1 a How many borrowers with debts sought help from the Citizens' Advice Bureau in 1986?

b How much of this debt was related to credit cards?

2 How much on average does each family in Britain owe according to the report?

3 In case number 1, why did the spiral of borrowing get out of hand?

4 Who were Mr G's creditors? Why was he able to obtain credit?

5 How did he plan to solve his debt problem?

6 How did the CAB debt counselling unit help Mr G to solve his problems?

DATA RESPONSE 3

HOW TO WIN THE HEARTS OF CREDITORS
Place your debts

NEXT time a nasty bill drops on your doormat, don't tear it up and hope it will go away.

Because it won't. Ignore a debt and you could end up with a County Court order against you and your name on a national credit blacklist.

Malcolm Hurlston, chairman of Registry Trust which keeps the list, tells me that more than TWO MILLION names figure on it – half a million of them were added last year alone.

Malcolm says: "Many people later paid off their debts. They could have kept their names off the register if only they had settled up within 31 days of the judgement."

Problem

So if you can't pay all your month's bills you need a plan of action.

At very least you should offer to pay something towards each one. *Never ignore them.*

If creditors know you are trying to tackle the problem, they are more likely to treat you as a "can't pay" rather than a "won't pay".

● SOME missed payments are more serious than others. Motor insurance is one. If your policy runs out you must move the car *off* the street. It is not enough just to stop driving.

● FAILURE to pay the local council rates can land you behind bars.

● PAYING the rent or mortgage is also important. But building societies are reluctant to throw you out of your home. They prefer to try and help

people in genuine trouble.

- BRITISH Telecom will pull out the plug after two months. Then it costs more than £100 to have it reconnected.

Telecom is kinder to the sick or elderly. As long as you let them know in advance, they are unlikely to cut off anyone who needs the telephone for safety's sake.

Cover

- ELECTRICITY and gas boards promise not to disconnect elderly customers between October and March if they can't pay their bills.

But other electricity users can be switched off if their first bill is not paid within 70 days.

Then it costs at least £15 to be plugged in again and a £100 deposit may also be demanded.

Gas costs about £12.60 to reconnect if the meter is left behind – but £30 if they've taken it away.

- LIFE insurance cover stops if you don't pay the premiums. The company will send back any money owing to you. But you'll get little or nothing back if you have been running the policy for only a year or two.
- INSURANCE cover for house contents stops if you fail to pay, which leaves your belongings at risk.

So if trouble strikes, keep your head, get your priorities right and talk to your creditors.

Source: *Daily Mirror*, 13 April 1988

How old are the debtors
Proportion of age group with debts

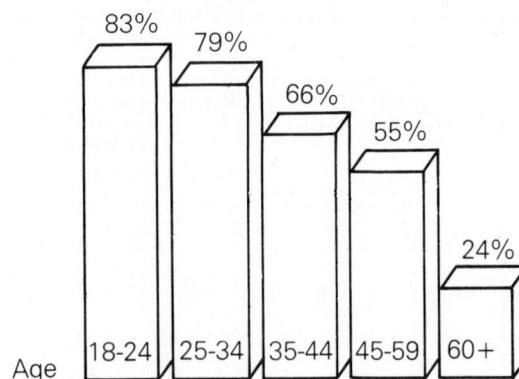

| Age | 18-24 | 25-34 | 35-44 | 45-59 | 60+ |

83% 79% 66% 55% 24%

Debtors in the courts
Legal actions for the recovery of money and goods

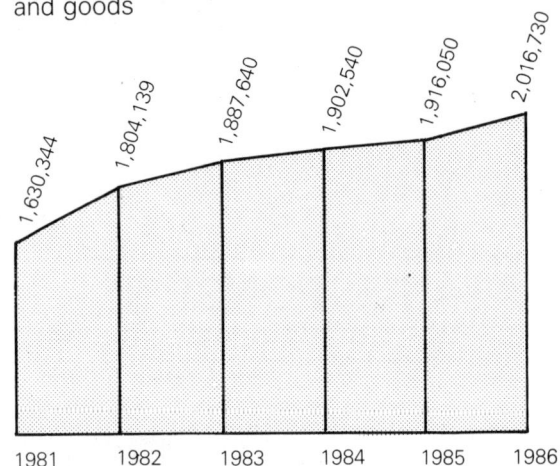

1,630,344 1,804,139 1,887,640 1,902,540 1,916,050 2,016,730

1981 1982 1983 1984 1985 1986

Source: *New Society*, 6 November 1987

1 The younger a person is the more likely they are to be in debt: true or false? Give a reason for your answer.

2 Look at the graph. What do you notice about the change in the number of debtors being taken to court?

3 Why is it important not to ignore a debt?

4 Use the information provided to write a letter of advice to a person who has fallen in debt.

Coursework

Aim: To investigate debt.

1 Undertake a survey of people in your school on the subject of debt.
2 Investigate the extent to which debt exists amongst people in the fourth and fifth year at school. Compare this to the amount of debt amongst 18 to 20 year olds.

3 Identify and investigate possible reasons for the differences in the debt patterns you find. Using the information you have managed to gather, design an advertising campaign warning young people of the problems of debts.

37 Business Finance and Investment

Donna loves skating, but recently the local authority has had to close the town's only skating rink. Her parents decide to build their daughter a skating rink in the back garden.

When Donna bought a pair of skates and first went skating, it was because of the utility (immediate satisfaction) that she obtained. Donna's skates were thus an example of a *consumer good*. As soon as she had purchased her skates she was able to use them.

However, Donna won't be able to benefit immediately from her parents' decision to build an ice rink. An ice rink can be described as a *capital good* or item. The benefit from having it will come some time in the future.

Investment is the growth taking place in the amount (stock) of capital goods in a particular economy. Investment now will allow the production and consumption of goods but at a future date.

There is a trade-off between the amount of investment (or gross domestic fixed capital formation as economists call it) and the amount of consumption. If we allocate our resources in an economy to the production of consumer goods, then in the future, as machines and other equipment wear out (depreciate), the economy will not be able to enjoy having such a large number of consumer goods as it now has.

On the other hand, if we invest in the production of capital goods, then there will be less consumer goods available now because of the diversion (re-allocation) that has occurred with the nation's resources. Once again we can see how important the concept of choice is for the study of economics.

Public investment

Much of an economy's investment is public investment undertaken by the government. This includes investment in the country's infrastructure and in its social capital.

Public investment in an area can, by improving the infrastructure, allow local firms to gain benefits from operating their businesses in an improved environment. Costs for the firms will be lower if there is

---

ECONOMIC TERMS

Investment: growth (or gross domestic fixed capital formation) in the stock of capital in an economy.
Depreciation: the wearing out of capital stock.
Retained profit: profits kept by a firm and ploughed back into the business rather than given to the firm's shareholders.
Sources of finance: ways in which a business can obtain money to expand its capital.

---

an effective infrastructure that allows, for example, the easy distribution of raw materials and goods. Firms gain from these so-called external economies of scale.

Private sector investment

Firms can finance their own plans for growth. By expanding investment now a firm can reduce costs in the future, and improve on its future share of the market and profits. Firms can raise the finance to do this by:

- Keeping or **retaining past profits** and ploughing them back into the business.
- **Selling share certificates** which entitle people to a share in the profits. When a firm does this it adds to the firm's equity (value in money terms).
- **Issuing (selling) stocks**. The holder of the stock certificate, in return for making the firm a loan, is entitled to receive an annual amount of interest.
- **Securing a debenture** which is a special kind of loan to a firm. It is made for a fixed period of time and for a fixed and guaranteed amount of interest.
- **Asking for trade credit**. Firms often give each other time to pay for the raw materials and finished goods they purchase from each other. This amounts to an interest free loan.
- **Leasing and renting.** A firm that cannot afford to purchase capital equipment can finance its activities by leasing or renting the items it needs. It can also approach a finance company to purchase goods on hire purchase terms.

Activity

The Business Game

Here is a game to be played in pairs. You have just started up in business, but so has your rival. See how many times you can go round the board. You will need dice and counters.

You must throw a six to accumulate enough finance to leave the start.

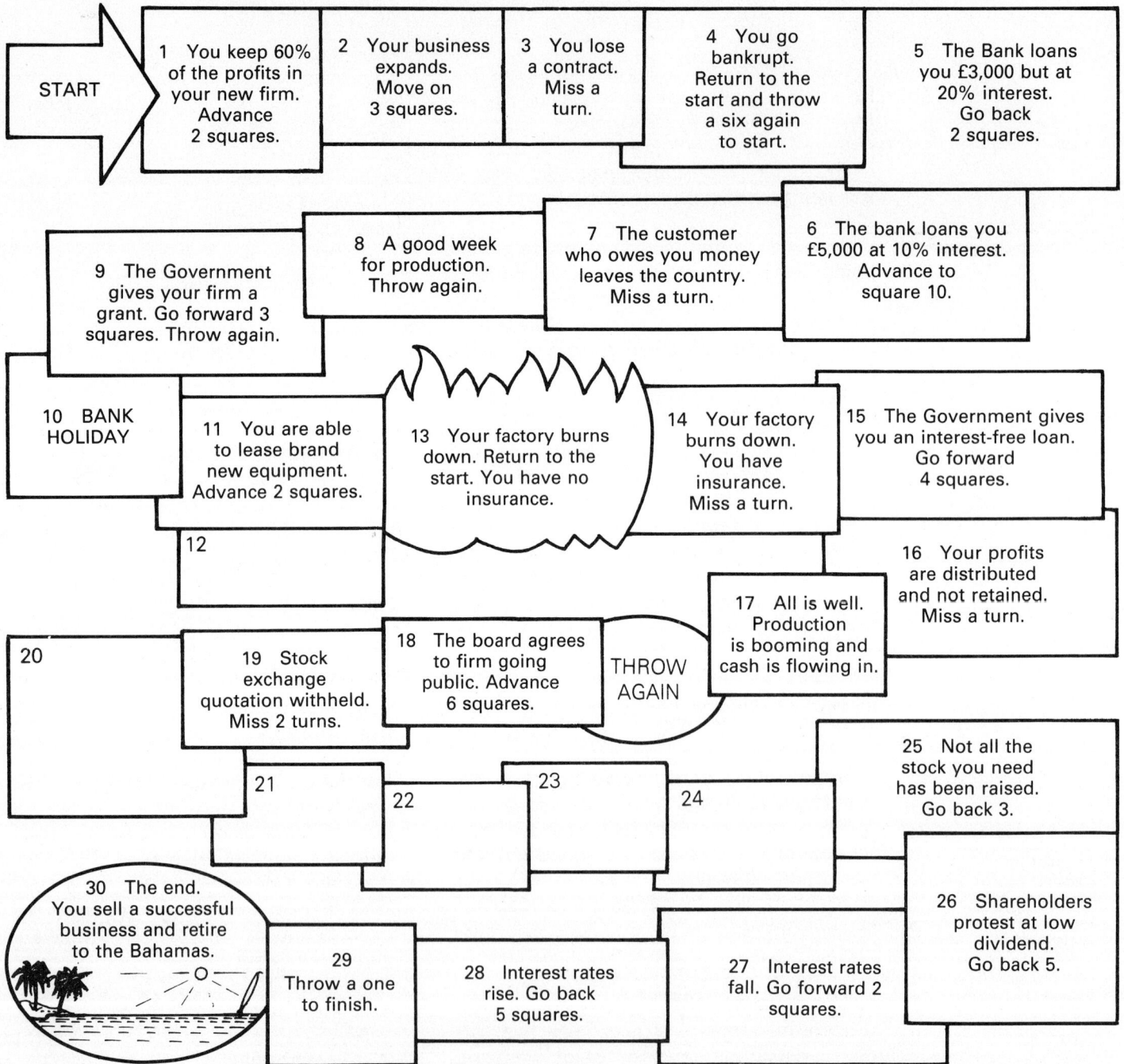

START

1 You keep 60% of the profits in your new firm. Advance 2 squares.

2 Your business expands. Move on 3 squares.

3 You lose a contract. Miss a turn.

4 You go bankrupt. Return to the start and throw a six again to start.

5 The Bank loans you £3,000 but at 20% interest. Go back 2 squares.

6 The bank loans you £5,000 at 10% interest. Advance to square 10.

7 The customer who owes you money leaves the country. Miss a turn.

8 A good week for production. Throw again.

9 The Government gives your firm a grant. Go forward 3 squares. Throw again.

10 BANK HOLIDAY

11 You are able to lease brand new equipment. Advance 2 squares.

12

13 Your factory burns down. Return to the start. You have no insurance.

14 Your factory burns down. You have insurance. Miss a turn.

15 The Government gives you an interest-free loan. Go forward 4 squares.

16 Your profits are distributed and not retained. Miss a turn.

17 All is well. Production is booming and cash is flowing in.

THROW AGAIN

18 The board agrees to firm going public. Advance 6 squares.

19 Stock exchange quotation withheld. Miss 2 turns.

20

21

22

23

24

25 Not all the stock you need has been raised. Go back 3.

26 Shareholders protest at low dividend. Go back 5.

27 Interest rates fall. Go forward 2 squares.

28 Interest rates rise. Go back 5 squares.

29 Throw a one to finish.

30 The end. You sell a successful business and retire to the Bahamas.

1 Who won the game? Explain why you think they did so.

2 What advantages did you discover there were in obtaining finance for your business?

3 What problems did you encounter in trying to obtain (raise) finance?

214

- **Mortgaging property.** Firms can always mortgage (raise a loan on) their property. This can be an important source of finance for the small business. Firms have to approach special companies for such mortgages. They cannot use the building societies as an individual does.
- **Borrowing from commercial banks.** Some firms borrow from banks or run up overdrafts with them. Other firms go to special banks for help. The Industrial and Commercial Finance Corporation is an example of one of these special banks. It was formed by the Bank of England and some of the major commercial banks for this purpose.

Test yourself

1 What is the difference between consumer goods and capital goods?
2 What is investment?
3 Why is a good infrastructure important for private firms?
4 What is a debenture?
5 Why can leasing help a firm to finance its business?
6 List four sources of finance for a firm.

DATA RESPONSE 1

They want you to dig deep for Eurotunnel

Martin Baker

THE BEATING of the Eurotunnel drum has begun. A glossy corporate brochure and a sheet with answers to basic questions about Europe's favourite hole in the ground are now available for the price of a telephone call.

You will not be able to miss the media drive for what is – because of its pursuit of the small investor – an honorary privatisation.

The first television commercials of the £7m campaign were transmitted last night and the Share Information Office is already describing response, somewhat vaguely, as "good".

Although Eurotunnel may want the public to respond it should not be assumed that the issue is a "buy" for everyone.

"Issues like British Gas and British Telecom were boring and tired utilities. This is a thrusting potential utility," says Richard Hannah, of stockbrokers Phillips & Drew. "Eurotunnel is a virtual company, a company on paper, not an actual company."

A cynic might say that Eurotunnel is pointing to a hole in the ground and crying: "Investment opportunity!" And of course the company will be right if enough people believe in the viability of a share which broker Charles Williams, of James Capel, describes as having "inherent risks." Mr Williams is waiting to see further forecasts and the first prospectus – to be published early next month – before making up his mind. He describes his attitude as "a cautiously optimistic wait and see".

The forecasts to which Mr Williams refers concern the cost of construction and the expected revenues when the tunnel is operational.

"What they're doing is tweaking up the estimated traffic numbers and making it look attractive," says Bob Cowell, of Hoare Govett. His position is decidedly reserved. "The company defeats analysis on the information available at present."

Malcolm Roberts, of Montagu Loebl Stanley, is marginally more sanguine: "The projections for the next 10 years are rather more optimistic than before, as you'd expect near the launch. This is close to the old-style equity investment, where one paid for a ship's voyage and reaped the benefits a year later if and when the ship returned."

So forget the BT and British Gas-style certainty of making a small but quick profit. "You might make a fortune on Eurotunnel," says Mr Hannah. "If not, you'll lose your shirt."

What then is the identikit picture of a Eurotunnel investor? Mr Roberts believes: "It is not a widows' and orphans' stock. They want immediate income, and this is deferred for a several years. It is a share for people who have a relatively large amount invested in shares and can afford to wait.

Eurotunnel is a risk, and opinion is sharply divided. "It shouldn't be a bloody public company at all. It's a venture capital company," says one broker.

"It just could be like the M25," says Malcolm Roberts. "They started building it years ago, and the underestimate of its use was massive. We may not be so xenophobic in a few years' time."

Investors wanting to register with the share information office should write to: Eurotunnel Share Information Office, PO Box 501 Bristol, BS99 1ET. Tel: 0272 277 007

Source: *The Independent*, 3 October 1987

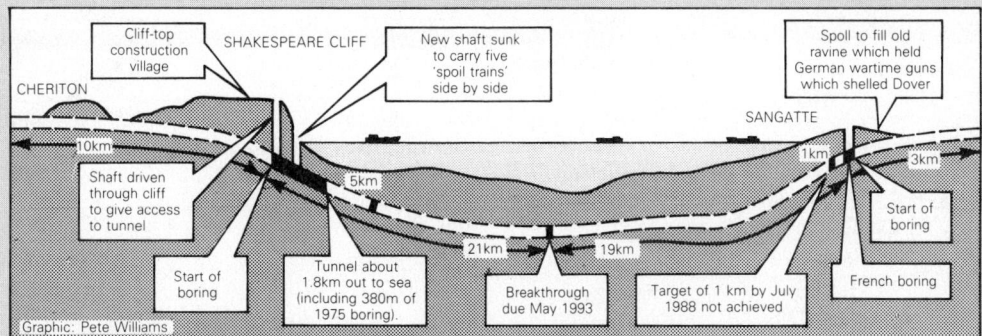

Graphic: Pete Williams

215

1 What company has been launched to build the Channel Tunnel?

2 Explain why investing in this company could make sound economic sense:
  a for the economy;
  b for ordinary savers.

3 What risks are there in providing the capital for this business venture?

4 What type of investor is mentioned as being interested in investing money in the company?

DATA RESPONSE 2

Queen bee Irene is set to buzz to market

by GARETH DAVID

THE USM may not always be good for your financial health but when Regina Health & Beauty Products makes its debut there should be no doubt that its products will be good for your physical health.

Quite how good its curious range of pills and potions are for you is something which neither the Stock Exchange nor the Advertising Standards Authority will allow the company to reveal, so it is a case of nudge-nudge, wink-wink.

Chairwoman Irene Stein discovered Royal Jelly in 1978 and pioneered a way of preserving the substance, which is produced by young adult female bees to nourish the queen bee in the hive.

Today the range of her products includes capsules, a skin cream and phials of Regina Royal Concorde, a potent blend of royal jelly, ginseng and other herbs, which help the user to "achieve peak performance during times of particular stress and exertion".

Profits

Profits took off last year, reaching £224,000 pre-tax in the 12 months to June on sales of £924,000, and now Mrs Stein sees the USM as a way of raising the company's profile and providing finance for possible acquisitions.

Brokers Le Mare, Martin are placing 4.5 million shaes at 20p apiece to raise a net £400,000 in new money for the company, and value the group at £3.35 million. On the basis of a profits jump to £300,000 this year, the prospective p/e is 17.1.

Source: *London Daily News,* 3 March 1987

BICC raises £35m from sale to ITT

BICC, the cables and construction group, has taken time off from its acquisition programme to dispose of its Sealectro companies and the connector business of BICC-Vero Group for £35m cash, including £3.8m of intercompany debt.

ITT Corporation is taking over the interests which have net assets of £27.6m, and which produced taxable profits of £2.3m in the year to 31 December 1987 on sales of slightly more than £50m.

Robin Biggam, chief executive of BICC, said: "This move is part of the reshaping of the BICC Technologies group to concentrate on the long-term growth businesses of electronic packaging and communications and control systems for industrial, building and energy applications."

The money raised from the disposals will be used to finance the development of BICC's remaining businesses.

BICC recently added to its cables business through the acquisition of Ceat Cavi, Italy's second largest cable maker for £90.4m, and Continental Wire and Cables of the US for £15m.

BICC's shares gained 2p to 355p on the disposal announcement.

Source: *The Independent,* 13 August 1988

Irene Stein: looking to the USM for finance

216

1 Describe the business idea discovered and developed by Irene Stein in 1978.

2 What evidence is there in the article that she has been economically successful in developing her business idea?

3 How does she plan to raise the finance she needs to expand and how will her brokers assist her?

4 BICC also wishes to obtain more finance. What alternative method have they used to do so?

5 What are BICC planning to do with the money they raise?

Extension

1. ELSA'S BUSINESS NOW

2. WITH INVESTMENT WHAT IT COULD GROW TO BE

3. HOW ELSA THE ENTREPRENEUR CAN FINANCE THE EXPANSION OF HER BUSINESS

SHE CAN USE OTHER PEOPLE'S RESOURCES

SHE CAN USE HER OWN SOURCES OF MONEY

Methods of raising Finance

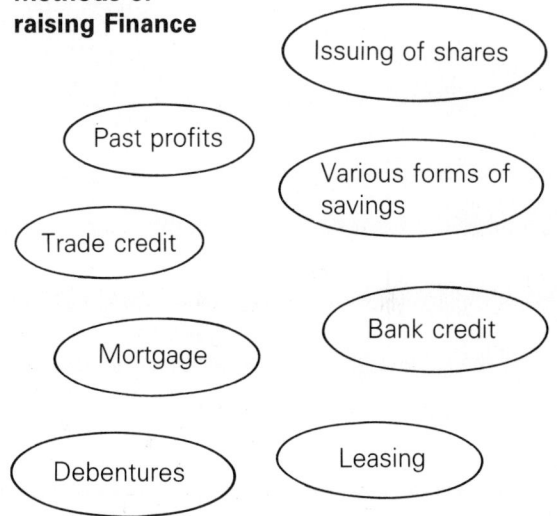

Issuing of shares

Past profits

Various forms of savings

Trade credit

Mortgage

Bank credit

Debentures

Leasing

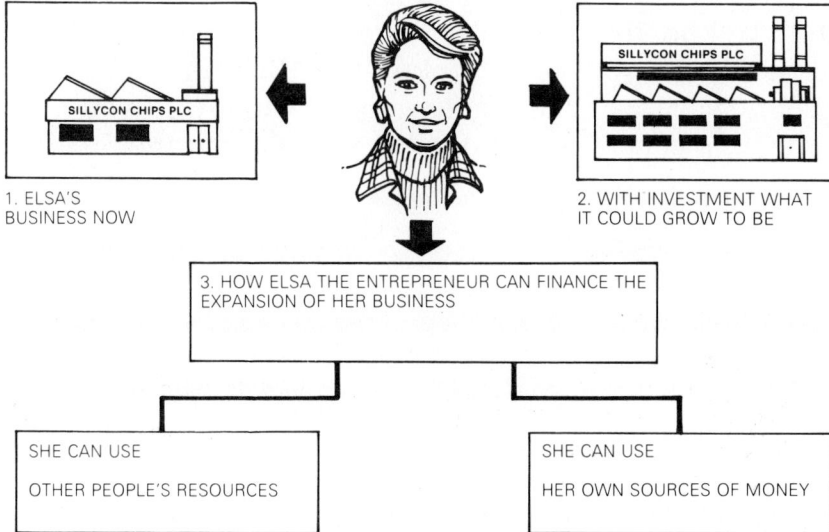

1 If Elsa successfully expands her business explain what will probably happen to:
   a Elsa's profits;
   b Elsa's competitors;
   c Elsa's share of the market.

2 As you will see in the exercise there are two general ways in which Elsa can expand her business. What are these?

3 Using the two ways you have identified, group the various sources of finance under the appropriate heading.

4 Explain what is meant by a bank mortgage. Why is this a comparatively safe way for a bank to lend money?

5 What advantages are there for Elsa in borrowing from a bank rather than issuing shares?

Coursework

Aim: To investigate how a firm should finance its growth.

Select a local firm and consider what its prospects for expansion and growth might be and what limits or obstacles lie in its way. Identify one possible improvement that could be made to the running of the firm that would involve the injection of capital.

Investigate the possible methods available for raising the necessary capital.

Once identified, produce a report for the firm setting out the possible sources of finance that they could use.

Identify one of these sources as the best possible option for the firm giving reasons for your answer.

38 The Stock Exchange

Jill and Peter are thinking of buying a brand new bike as a Christmas present for their small daughter. Peter is rather concerned about the price.

"It's a lot of money for something she'll grow out of within a year," he says.

"That's all right," says Jill. "There's always someone wanting a child's second-hand bike. We'll sell it easily."

In a similar way people buy shares in a joint stock company (a plc) knowing that they will be able to resell to a ready buyer. If you want to buy a second-hand bike you would look in the "Buy-and-Sell" columns of a local newspaper or in a newsagent's window. If you want to buy shares in a company you need to know about the Stock Exchange.

What is the Stock Exchange?
- The Stock Exchange is the market place where people buy and sell *securities*.
- Securities are documents that show that a person is the owner of shares in a company, and is entitled to a dividend (share of the profits), or holds the title on a loan to a private firm or public body and is entitled to interest on the loan.
- The Stock Exchange plays a role in ensuring that any firm wishing to become a public limited company (plc) is suitable to have its shares advertised to the public. When a company is set up in this way, or launched, it is said to be *floated*. Organisations such as merchant banks specialise in *flotations*.
- Most Stock Exchange business does not centre around flotations. It is connected with the purchase and sale of existing securities. In this sense the Stock Exchange acts as a market place for dealings in second-hand securities.

How to invest in shares
Stephanie has come into a small inheritance on the death of her aunt. Her family want her to take them on holiday, but she has decided to place the money on the Stock Exchange.

Stephanie discovers that she cannot buy shares directly herself. There are rules about who is allowed to trade "on the floor" of the Exchange which make this impossible.

The Rules
1 Members of the Stock Exchange are allowed to trade in their own right in shares.
2 They must settle up any debts at the end of each account period. (My *word* is *my bond*: the motto of the Stock Exchange.)

Decide for yourself
- Given these rules and, remembering that shares can fall in price, would you let an "outsider" trade?

To place your money on the Stock Exchange this is what you have to do:
- First, you contact a *broker/dealer.*
- The broker/dealer is in touch with all the others in the market because each member of the market is linked by computer in a system called *SEAQ* (Stock Exchange Automated Quotation System). The broker/dealer can locate on his or her screen the name of the *market maker* willing to sell the shares you want at the current lowest price. This gives the client (in this example, Stephanie) the best value for money.

  If Stephanie (or you) wished to sell shares, the broker/dealer would have chosen the market maker willing to offer the highest price.
- Stephanie purchases *ordinary shares* in a company of her choice. An ordinary share (sometimes called *equity*) entitles her to vote at the company's annual general meeting and to share in any pro-

fits that the company makes. (Profits distributed to shareholders are referred to as the *dividends*. They are the reward you receive for owning part of the company.)

- Stephanie's brother, Jack, has securities too. He has *government stock*. This entitles him to the payment of interest, as the document he holds means that someone at some stage has lent the government money. However, Jack is not entitled to an extra vote at the General Election when it is next held!

How does a broker/dealer earn a living?

Imagine that you are the broker/dealer who has purchased shares for Stephanie. You make your living by charging clients a *commission* for arranging the purchase or sale of their shares.

The market maker makes a living by buying shares at a low price and selling them at a higher price; the difference is their profit.

What are speculators on the Stock Exchange?

Many people who save by buying shares on the Stock Exchange are interested in the income that the dividend will bring to them. Others are more interested in making money by dealing in the market and anticipating the rise and fall of share prices. These people are called *speculators*. There are three kinds of speculators:

- **Bulls**: buy shares when prices are low and sell when the price has risen. Aim: profit.
- **Bears**: sell shares when prices are high and buy up a greater quantity when prices are low. Aim: control of the company.
- **Stags**: buy new shares and sell when trading in them starts. Aim: quick profit.

Beware of shares!

Shares can be a very useful way for an individual to save, but it is worth remembering that shares can fall in value as well as rise. To help you understand this read the sad tale of Bill and Ben.

Bill bought shares in the Flowerpot Company when the shares were first sold to the public. Their *nominal price* (the price on the certificate) was £1 each.

Flowerpot shares traded very well, given an increase in the interest consumers showed in garden activities. The company developed a range of new products and marketed a very effective weedkiller. The dividend at the end of the financial year was very high and, as a result, shares in the Flowerpot Company were wanted by everyone. The market price on the Stock Exchange rose. Bill sold his shares at a handsome profit. Ben bought them.

Then came the bad news. The weedkiller was found to have harmful side effects on its users. Profits in the company slumped. Share prices fell to below the nominal price.

Ben now hates Bill . . .

Test yourself

1 What is the Stock Exchange?
2 Why do you have to contact a broker/dealer when you want to buy or sell shares?
3 What is SEAQ?
4 What does an ordinary share entitle you to?
5 What is a speculator?
6 Explain the difference between a stock and a share.
7 Why is the Stock Exchange important for the survival of joint stock companies?
8 Why could the market price of a share differ from its nominal price?
9 How does:
   a a market maker;
   b a broker-dealer
   earn a living?

ECONOMIC TERMS

Equity: another term for an ordinary share.
Dividend: the portion of profits distributed to a shareholder.
Nominal price: price of shares when originally issued to the public.
Market price: the price as determined by the forces of supply and demand.
Stocks and shares: forms of securities that can be bought and sold.

Summary

The main Stock Exchange market deals with the purchase and sale of shares in public limited companies.

Government and local authority stock is dealt in on the Gilt Edged Securities market. There also exists the Unlisted Securities Market, and the Third Market. The former is a market for shares on the Exchange, the latter is a special market for companies which are even riskier to invest in.

Activity

THE S.E.A.Q. SCREEN

SHARES
A way of saving for your future

TREACLE TOPS PLC
SHARES FOR SALE

Market maker A	50p
Market maker B	49p
Market maker C	45p

TREACLE TOPS PLC
SHARES FOR PURCHASE

Market maker A	48p
Market maker B	46p
Market maker C	44p

RETIRE IN PARADISE HAVEN

And I don't have to worry about unlimited liability.

THE STOCK EXCHANGE

BROKER/DEALER — MARKET MAKERS — BROKER/DEALER

HAWKINS

Of course the broker/dealer will charge me a commission.

MARKET MAKERS WILL BUY AT A LOW PRICE AND SELL AT A HIGH PRICE. MARKET MAKERS & BROKER/DEALERS ARE ALLOWED TO BUY AND SELL SHARES ON 'ACCOUNT' BUT MUST SETTLE BY ACCOUNT DAY

Share Certificate
Mrs. Ramsbottom

KEY:
⇨ money
➡ Share Certificate

1 Why does Mrs Ramsbottom want to sell her shares?
2 Who wants to buy shares and why?
3 What name is given to the place where buyers and sellers of stocks and shares meet?
4 Buyers and sellers of stocks and shares are not allowed to deal directly with each other. Who do they have to deal through?
5 Why is account day important?
6 Examine the SEAQ screen information:
  a Which market maker should Mr Hawkins' broker approach when buying shares?
  b Which market maker should Mrs Ramsbottom's broker approach when selling her shares?
7 If Mrs Ramsbottom sold 500 shares to Market Maker A and he in turn sold them to Mr Hawkins, how much profit would Market Maker A gain?

DATA RESPONSE 1

Stock markets struggle to exorcize the ghost of 1929

Graham Searjeant
Financial Editor

Share prices fell by a seventh on the London Stock Exchange on Black Monday. At the end of the working day, dealers and investors knew the long 1980s bull market in shares was over. By the end of the evening, that was old hat.

As New York's day unfolded, Wall Street's slide of the previous week accelerated crazily as each further fall triggered computers programmed to sell stock and share index futures to protect big portfolios from further losses.

When the market closed, share prices had dropped by almost a quarter in a single day. By then, the talk was only of 1929, when a stock market collapse, apparently out of the blue, transformed US prosperity into the Thirties slump.

On Tuesday, October 20, 1987, Hong Kong closed its market for the week and City bookshops ran out of copies of Professor JK Galbraith's classic book on the Great Crash. Ever since, fear of the "1929 scenario" has lurked at the back of the markets' collective consciousness.

That was one reason why New York dealers in particular were nervous about today's semi-anniversary of Black Monday. In 1929, share prices quickly lost 40 per cent of their value, jumped back, then spent the spring recovering half their losses.

But in April 1930, just when confidence was returning, the recovery petered out and prices started falling again. They did not stop for another two years. By then, shares had lost four-fifths of their value.

By last Wednesday, the Dow had regained half the 30 per cent drop in the week culminating in Black Monday. The recovery had to survive this nervy period before its participants could finally exorcize the ghost of 1929.

Share prices in London have been chained by an anchor to Wall Street this year. As long as the shadow of 1929 persists, therefore, it is just as important to spot the differences as to dwell on the similarities.

Changed market structures, which put big institutions to the fore instead of individual speculators, have been much remarked on.

As the Chancellor said last week, however, the biggest difference is that the October crash has, thus far, proved to be a "non-economic event." After October, forecasters prudently cut their predictions for economic growth. But, outside the securities business and the financial district, nothing untoward happened.

Consumers did not stop buying, business did not halt expansion plans and, thanks to the authorities' swift and intelligent response, there was no string of failures among securities firms, banks or their customers. By March, financial analysis and international organizations had restored their economic growth forecasts and even raised them.

The share price recovery of 1930 was reversed by the economic effects of 1929, rather than by some mysterious force. Few such effects have appeared in 1988.

Big investors, having been reassured by the swift international action last autumn, including the crucial deal over the US budget deficit between the White House and Congress, now worry that nothing has really changed.

In New York and Washington great inquests were held, blame apportioned and measures proposed. In Tokyo, where the stock markets are seen as part of Japan Inc. support was organized and regulations adjusted to help demand for shares and obviate any need for sales.

Everywhere except Tokyo, confidence remains severely dented. Sentiment has changed a bull market into a bear market. Instead of viewing price falls as an opportunity to buy, investors see rises as a chance to take their profits or recoup their losses. Investors fear losing money by holding shares instead of missing profits by holding cash.

Source: *The Times*, 18 April 1988

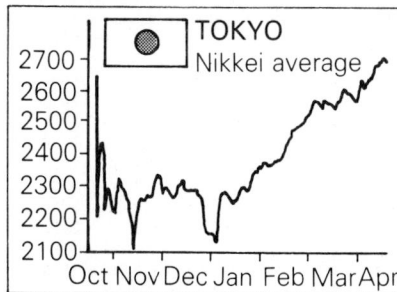

TOKYO Nikkei average

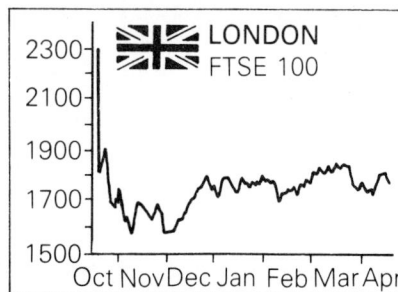

LONDON FTSE 100

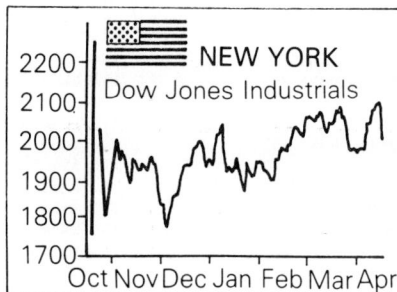

NEW YORK Dow Jones Industrials

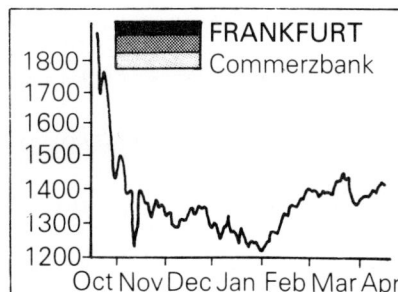

FRANKFURT Commerzbank

1 Describe what happened on 19 October 1987 to the prices of shares on the world's stock markets.

2 What is Wall Street?

3 What name is given to the indexes used to measure share price changes in:
a London;
b New York?

4 Why were comparisons made between the 1987 stock market situation and the position in 1929?

5 What differences exist between the 1929 and 1987 stock market situations?

6 What has been different about the situation on the Tokyo stock exchange since October 1987 when compared to other world stock markets?

DATA RESPONSE 2

Bad news ahead for hamburger lovers

ONE man's meat is another man's poison, as last Thursday's US Government crop report amply demonstrated.

There was plenty of glum reading in it for Big Mac and Butterkist lovers, as well as for the American taxpayer. But European producers and taxpayers have been quick to conclude that what is bad for the US must be good for the Community.

According to the report, the drought which has ravaged the US Midwest will cut American production of corn by 37 per cent, soyabeans by 26 per cent and wheat by 13 per cent this year.

Tighter supplies will mean higher prices for – among others – the hamburger munchers of the world, since to make a respectable hamburger you need wheat for the buns and soyabeans to feed the cattle.

American nibblers look set to lose out all round because the dismal harvests will mean that the US taxpayer will have to stump up a $3.9bn support package for the beleagured US farmers.

The report's prognosis was rather worse than expected, and US prices for grains and beans duly opened on Friday at the top of their permitted range.

Admittedly the sight of the magic words "showers" in the weather reports did cause traders some nervousness and prices slipped back during the day – the average commodity dealer has a truly British obsession with the weather.

However, the market for fundamentals, the grain and soyabean crops, remain strong, and the outlook for prices is bullish.

Stocks, for example, continue to shrink. The crop report reduced estimates of ending soyabean stocks by 45m bushels to just 100m bushels, a figure considered critically low – last year ending stocks of this essential animal feedstock were considered to be "tight" at 250m bushels.

Vultures thrive in arid conditions, however, and European producers are gleefully looking at the positive side to the worst US drought in 50 years. The problems in the US should mean not only higher prices for the Europeans but also the chance to regain markets previously lost to the Americans.

This year Europe is expecting good grain yields. According to COCERAL, the EC cereal traders' association, the Community's cereal harvest is expected to reach 160.5m tonnes this year, compared with only 154.4m last year.

continued on next page

221

The French, the biggest agricultural power in the 12-member EC, have long been annoyed about what they see as unjustified American penetration of markets in North Africa and parts of Latin America which should rightfully be theirs. Other voices are arguing that the drought will be a golden opportunity to cut EC grain surpluses by exporting to the Soviet Union and Saudi Arabia.

European traders calculate the EC could capture 18 per cent of the world grain market this year, up from around 14 per cent last year. Rising prices for US maize and soyabeans could also give European farmers a chance to regain the animal feed market, where cheaper US products have been squeezing out domestic grains.

Source: *The Independent*, 15 August 1988

Key to columns:

1 The highest price that the share has reached in the last year.
2 The lowest price that the share has reached during last year.
3 The name under which trading in the share takes place.
4 The actual price that you will currently have to pay. (In practice the price shown is the price that is halfway between the price at which the share is bought and the price at which it is sold.)
5 The yield (the dividend divided by the share price).
6 The price earnings ratio (how much an investor has to pay for a share of the company's profits).
7 The number of the share in the Stock Exchange index.

FOOD MANUFACTURING

1	2	3	4			5	6	7
503	375	Acatos&H	375			3.2	15.1	1513
322	274	Ass Br Fd	316	xd	+1	3.5	10.5	1674
191	151	Ass Fish	166		+1	4.0	16.5	1678
220	185	Bank Syd C	205			4.6	9.5	1747
153	129	Barker&Dob	140		+3	3.4	13.8	1758
281	195	Bassett	280		+5	3.7	11.9	1773
103	68	Benson Crp	88		+2	1.2	17.3	1807
400	274	Berisford	400		+16	4.8	16.1	1809
220	159	Bibby (J)	170			6.7	7.8	1823
417	347	Booker	393	xr		5.4	14.0	1872
74	42	Borthwick	65			1.0	–	1880
236	163	Brake Bros	232		–1	1.6	20.5	1936
429	231	Cadbury-S	375		+3	2.9	20.9	2030
253	188	Carrs Mill	253			3.8	8.9	2075
107	92	Chamb&Ferg	94			4.0	10.1	2101
120	73	Cranswck M	93			8.0	12.3	2270
100	77	Dalepack	82	xd		4.4	12.4	2303
368	272	Dalgety	339		+4	5.7	13.6	2304
117	76	Daniels S	78			5.7	16.3	2310
83	39	England JE	68		+5	0.0	–	2478
118	92	Fisher A	105		+2	2.4	21.3	2581
300	253	Fitch Lvll	280	xd	+2	5.7	11.2	2583
165	90	Freshbake	160	xd		2.3	23.8	2634
298	220	Geest	263			2.1	21.1	2669
97	68	Global Grp	83			5.0	10.9	2705
437	370	Greggs	435			2.5	18.3	2774
260	215	Hazlewood	230	xd	–2	1.5	17.6	2859
308	266	Hillsdown	285		+8	2.3	13.8	2898
198	158	Hunter Sap	181			3.0	15.9	2937
27¾	21	Israel Jk	24¼	xd		3.3	14.2	3008
263	203	Jacob W R	263		+2	–	–	1450
120	65	Lees Jon T	120	xd		2.1	19.2	3148
153	120	Lovell G F	148			1.8	21.2	3223
98	76	Matthews B	81		–1	3.0	11.3	3306
333	198	Meat Trade	303			1.7	86.3	3324
318	243	Nthn Foods	293	xd		4.5	11.8	3536
113	81	Nrthmbrn F	110	xd		2.4	13.2	3517
247	158	Park Foods	187		+2	3.5	11.5	3598
103	66	Perkins Fd	90			2.8	25.7	3638
105	78	Ptarmigan	86			0.0	–	3734
480	303	Ranks Hov	451		+2	2.7	18.7	3777
10$^{25/32}$	411	Rowntree	£10$^{47/64}$			1.9	27.3	3870
87	72	Sheldon J	72			8.8	12.3	4001
64	38	Sutherland	62		+3	2.4	24.5	4146
890	730	Tate&Lyle	852		+3	4.3	11.8	4173
100	85	Tavener R	95	xd		1.8	12.0	4175
345	252	Unigate	312		+4	5.4	12.4	4344
320	248	Utd Bisc	298			5.1	12.7	4370
230	185	Watson & P	210	xd		5.3	15.4	4445

Look at the information here about shares in food manufacturing.

1 What was the highest price at which Freshbake shares sold during the year referred to?

2 Look at the yield column. Explain why shares in Sheldon during the period in question were a good investment.

3 In the article how will the drought referred to affect:
   a American producers;
   b American consumers?

4 a What effect will the American situation have on a European food company's profits?
   b Explain how this will be reflected in terms of the demand for and price of shares of European food firms.

Extension

1 Choose five food manufacturing companies.
2 Imagine you have purchased 100 shares in each company. Calculate their total value to you using the shares page of a newspaper.
3 At four regular intervals over the next month (once a week) you may sell these shares for shares in any other company. (It does not have to be a food company.) Use the shares column in your newspaper to help you. Keep a careful record of all your 'transactions' (sales and purchases).
4 At the end of the month work out the total value of your shares. Have you "made" a profit or loss over the period you have been dealing?

TELL SID . .

He's still on a high-speed gas winner!

PLEASE tell Sid not to worry about his British Gas shares. I've been flooded with letters and calls from angry investors.

They are anxious about shares they bought when Mrs Thatcher sold off the State-owned gasworks back in 1986.

Nearly three million people have paid £1.35 for each British Gas share. They have just been sent a share certificate.

But thousands of them are horrified to see it says the shares are 25p each.

A typical Sid from Plymouth writes: "I bought 400 shares at £1.35, which cost me £540. But I got a share certificate for 400 shares of 25p each which is £100. So I reckon £440 has been fiddled!"

Well Sid *hasn't* been diddled. And here's why.

All companies put a face value on their shares. Most, like British Gas, call them 25p shares.

Others have shares with a face value of £1 each, or even 5p. But it *doesn't matter* what the face value is. It's what the shares are *really worth* that counts.

And this depends on what the company's assets are worth.

These include the land, gas-works, pipelines, showrooms and vans it owns. Plus the profits they bring in.

When British Gas was sold off it had a share capital of about £1,000 million. But the Government reckoned the company was in fact worth £5,400 million.

Split

British Gas could have split its capital into 1,000 million £1 shares and offered them to investors at £5.40 each.

Then Sid would have 100 shares for his £540.

● OR it could have split its capital into 5,000 million 5p shares and flogged them at 27p each. Sid would then have 2,000 shares for £540.

● INSTEAD British Gas chose to sell 4,000 million 25p shares at £1.35 each. So Sid got 400 shares for his £540.

British Gas shares are now being bought and sold on the Stock Exchange at around £1.80 each. Not 25p. Not £1.35p. I repeat: £1.80.

So for Heaven's sake Sid, relax. You're winning!.

Source: *Daily Mirror,* 20 July 1988

---

1 Why are people worried about the share certificates they had purchased from British Gas?

2 Why hadn't they been "fiddled" (cheated)?

3 What is:
   a the face value of a share?
   b the real value of a share?

4 What was the difference between the face or nominal value of British Gas shares and the real or market price of British Gas shares
   a when first issued
   b when the article was written?

5 Assuming you had purchased British Gas when they were sold off, how much profit would you have made by the time the article was written?

Coursework

Aim: To investigate share price fluctuations.

Select up to twenty companies and from a newspaper monitor the share price fluctuations (movements up and down in price) that take place, over an extended period, e.g. a term. Display your results using graphs.

Using information about the companies you have chosen (again use the financial sections of newspapers), analyse why the changes have taken place.

Imagine that you are a broker/dealer and a client is interested in purchasing some shares. Write a letter to your client explaining the advantages and disadvantages of each of the above companies you have chosen to monitor, and present three of them for the client to make a final choice from. In choosing your final three give well-argued reasons for your choices.

39 Exports and Imports

Tracey's British-made bike gleams because it has a chrome finish. However, the UK does not have large deposits of chromium, the mineral used to make chromium plating. The cycle manufacturers therefore have to import the raw material for their bikes. (When we *import* goods we bring them into the country. When we export goods we send them out.)

Decide for yourself
- Look at this list of countries:
  France Switzerland Japan Saudi Arabia Italy Malaysia Australia
- From which of the countries would the UK obtain the following products:
  wine compact disc players pasta rubber wool chocolates petrol

Reasons for trade

It would be quite possible for Britain to grow its own bananas but to do so would be very expensive. Greenhouses and vast supplies of heat would be needed. Can you think why?

For this reason Britain finds it cheaper to import its bananas from countries in the tropics.

In the nineteenth century Britain was "the workshop of the world" and Britain imported raw materials that it could not provide for itself, or which would have been very expensive to produce. It used these raw materials to make manufactured goods which were then supplied to the world.

More recently Britain's imports have included an increasing number of goods that are already manufactured. Why do you think this is so?

Choosing a washing machine

The Khanom family wish to buy a washing machine. They have a choice of four machines. They can only afford to spend £500.

Washing machine 1
Built in Leeds where they live. As an engineer Mrs Khanom is very keen to keep jobs in Britain. It's an expensive model (price £520), but reliable.

Washing machine 2
Made in South Wales. The price is £500, but they will have to wait three months for delivery.

Washing machine 3
Made elsewhere in the north of England. The firm is currently on strike. The price when the machine is available is £480.

Washing machine 4
Made in Italy. Price £480. Available from stock now and guaranteed delivery when the Khanom's cheque clears through the bank.

Which machine do you think the Khanom family will decide to buy?

Test yourself
1 Suggest as many reasons as you can to explain why we import:
   a raw materials;
   b finished goods.
2 Why was Britain once called the "workshop of the world"?
3 Write a short letter to the Khanom family who you have heard are deciding to buy an Italian-made washing machine. Put a case for 'Buying British'.
4 Imagine you are either Mr or Mrs Khanom and have received such a letter. Write a reply.

Britain's trading figures

Britain has to pay its way in the world. When Britain imports an item it has to export goods to other countries to pay for the import.

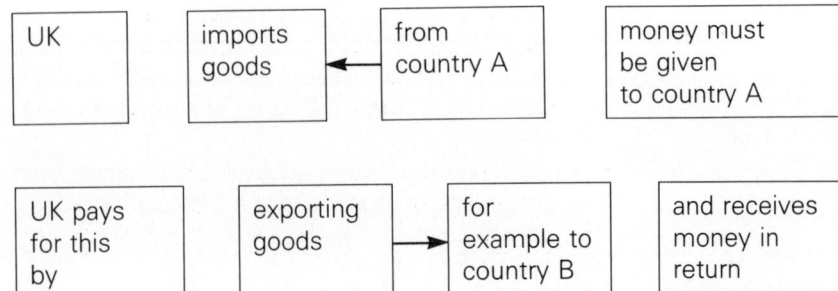

UK	imports goods	← from country A	money must be given to country A

| UK pays for this by | exporting goods | → for example to country B | and receives money in return |

224

For this reason economists pay particular attention to our trading figures or *Balance of Payments*. A country's Balance of Payments is made up of two parts: *visible* items and *invisible* items.

The visible items

The first part of a balance of payments that economists look at is called the *visible trade balance* (or balance of trade). This is made up of all the goods that can be physically seen coming into Britain as imports, or leaving Britain as exports. If we export more than we import in physical (visible) goods, then we have a *balance of trade surplus*. But if we import more than we export, then we have a *balance of trade deficit*.

Hi Fi from Japan

IMPORTS

Scotch whisky to USA

EXPORTS

Test yourself
- If we import £200 of goods and export £200 of goods, the balance of trade is £0.
- If we import a car worth £5000 and export a washing machine worth £500, the balance of trade is a minus or deficit figure of £4500.

1 Now calculate the balance of trade if:
- *a* we import cars worth £70 000 and export aircraft worth £300 000;
- *b* we import diamonds worth £50 million and export £2 million worth of machine tools.

2 Explain which of these transactions puts our accounts in surplus and which puts our accounts in deficit.

The invisible items

Goods can be seen entering and leaving a country but services are not so easily seen. For this reason they are called *invisibles*. The next part of a country's Balance of Payments to consider is the invisible trade balance. Invisible items are payments made for services. We earn money by exporting services as well as goods, and we owe money if we import services. Invisible items include:
- tourism;
- defence spending (for example, maintaining a garrison in the Falklands costs the UK a lot of money, but we earn money by having American bases in this country);
- interest, profit and dividends;
- insurance;
- shipping;
- air transport.

When we put these two balances together we get the *current balance*.

Activity

A

Balance of payments Current account

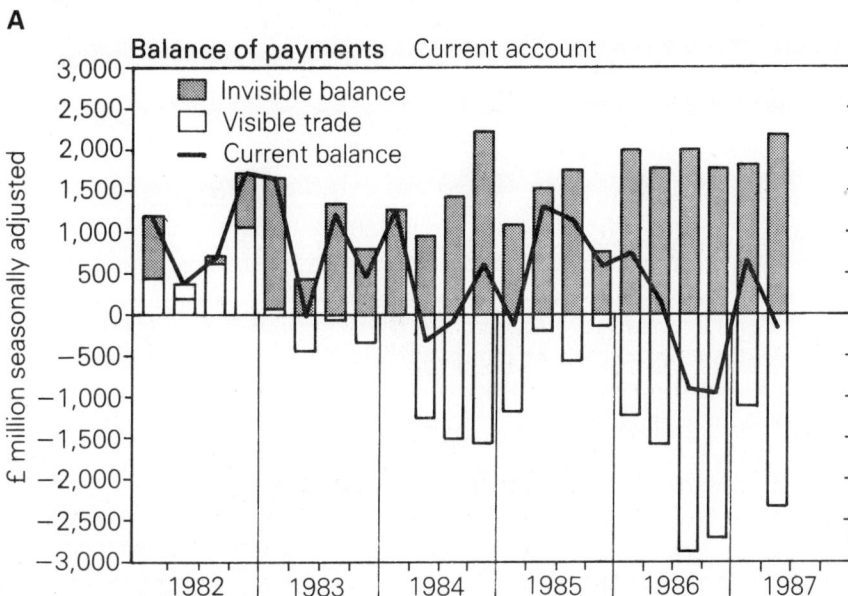

Source: CSO *Economic Trends*, 1987

Look at **A**.

1 In which year was the visible trade balance last in surplus?
2 Describe the overall trend in the visible trade balance since 1984.

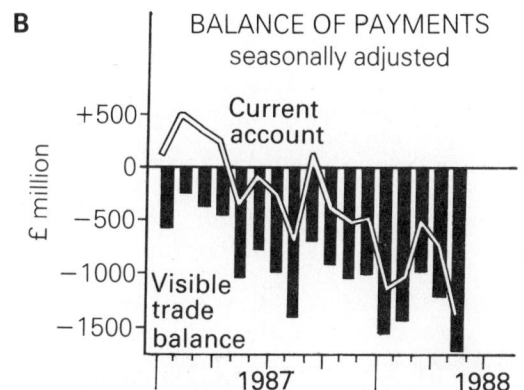

B

BALANCE OF PAYMENTS
seasonally adjusted

Source: *The Independent*, 28 June 1988

3 What trends occurred in the invisible trade balance between 1985 and 1987?

4 Remembering that the current balance combines the invisible and visible balances: why is it fortunate that Britain has had a surplus in the invisible trade balance?

5 In which year between 1984 and 1987 do you think Britain was most successful in trading with the rest of the world?

Now look at **B**.

6 The visible trade balance has continued to remain in deficit, but the current account balance has slipped even further into deficit. What does this suggest has started to happen to our invisible earnings?

ECONOMIC TERMS
Imports: goods and services brought into an economy.
Exports: goods and services sent to other economies.
Visible items: physical goods.
Invisible items: services.
Visible balance of trade: the export of goods less the import of goods. If there is a surplus, this is shown as a plus figure. If there is a deficit of exports (more imports than exports) then this is shown as a minus figure.
Invisible balance of trade: the export of services less the import of services. Like the visible trade balance, there can be a surplus or a deficit.
Current Balance: the combination of the visible and invisible balance of trade.

Invisible exports

An American comes to London

Horace P. Stonefeller, the well known American millionaire, has always wanted to visit "little old England", the birthplace of his ancestors.

At last his dream has come true. He flies from New York by British Airways Concorde to Paris (price of ticket £1000). He then catches an Air France flight to Heathrow London (price £100). He stays in the largest suite he can find at the Dorchester Hotel and has a very busy and hectic fortnight visiting Shakespeare's birthplace, other tourist spots and, the home of his ancestors, Liverpool. He spends a total of £15 000 on hotel bills, meals, theatre tickets, hire cars and postcards. He decides to sail back to New York by the Cunard Line from Southampton. The cost of his ticket in the best cabin is £3000.

Decide for yourself
- How much money has Britain earned from Horace P. Stonefeller's visit?*

Invisible imports

Britain earns money from invisible exports, but increasingly it has had to pay money out for a range of invisible imports. These include the costs incurred when holidaymakers go abroad, and when businesses insure their goods with foreign insurance firms, or export them on foreign owned ships. When we subtract or take away the invisible imports from the invisible exports, we get the *invisible balance.*

We have to add this balance to the balance of trade. When we add the balance of trade (or visible balance) and the invisible balance together we get a total called the *balance of payments on current account.*

Visible imports	£100	Visible exports	£50	
		Balance of trade (deficit)	£50	**A**
Invisible imports	£200	Invisible exports	£300	
net invisibles	£100 (surplus)			**B**
Current account balance	**B–A**	= £100–£50	= £50 (surplus)	

Capital/investment flows

The balance of payments on current account is not the end of the story. To this

*£19,000

226

current figure has to be added *capital/investment flows.*

Such flows occur when any one country invests in another country. For example, when Japan invests in a car firm in South Wales this is an investment flow from Japan to Britain.

The difference between the flows in and out of the country gives us the *balance of payments on capital account.*

Balancing the balance

The balance of payments must always balance. To achieve this the government allows for an item called the *balancing item.* Adding the current and capital accounts together plus the balancing item, we arrive at the *official financing figure.* This is covered by borrowing from other countries or by lending or taking from official reserves (the moneys kept by government to meet emergencies).

Test yourself

Which of the following transactions are:

a visible imports;

b invisible imports;

c visible exports;

d invisible exports?

1 A Japanese transistor radio sold to a Welsh student.

2 A bottle of Scotch whisky sent from Glasgow to New York.

3 A cheque for £10 from your brother serving in the army in Germany.

4 A meal purchased by British tourists in Majorca.

Exchange Rates

When you go abroad on holiday, you need to use the money (or currency) of the country you are visiting.

Decide for yourself

- Which currency would you need for each of these countries?
  Eire/West Germany/France/USSR/Saudi Arabia/USA/Italy/Japan

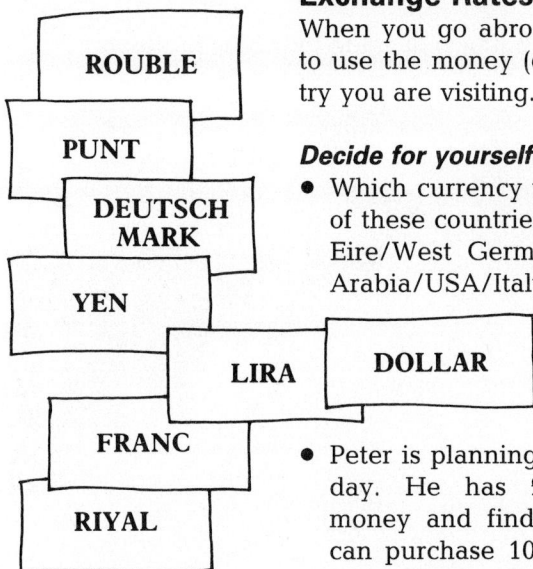

ROUBLE

PUNT

DEUTSCH MARK

YEN

LIRA

DOLLAR

FRANC

RIYAL

- Peter is planning to go to France on holiday. He has £100 sterling spending money and finds that with each £1 he can purchase 10 francs. If Peter decides to buy £90 worth of francs, how many francs will he get?

The rate at which one currency trades against another currency is called the *exchange rate.* It is the price of that country's currency measured in terms of the other country's currency.

Decide for yourself

When Peter returns to England, he has 200 francs left to convert back into pounds. He finds the rate of exchange has altered. The pound is now worth only 5 francs.

- Is Peter pleased or not pleased?
- Why?
- Has the pound appreciated or depreciated while Peter was in France?

ECONOMIC TERMS
Appreciates: when a currency rises in value, it appreciates. **Depreciates**: when a currency falls in value, it depreciates.

Currencies and supply and demand

The price of a country's currency rises and falls according to the laws of supply and demand.

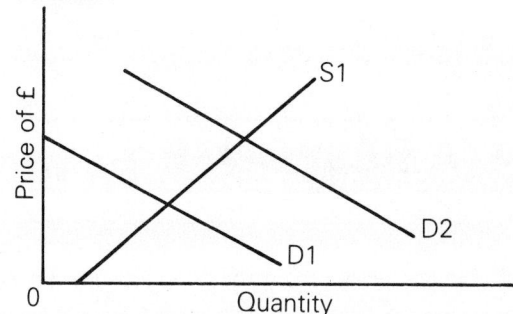

The pound will rise in value or appreciate if:

- more people want to come to Britain as tourists;
- more people buy British exports;
- people think the pound will rise in value soon. (People who buy and sell currency in the hope of making a profit from future changes in value are called *speculators.*)

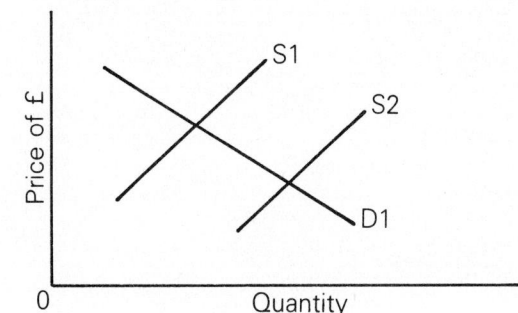

However, the pound will fall in value if:

- more people want to get rid of their pounds;
- British people import goods rather than export;
- speculators are worried about the British economy.

It is not always possible to compare the UK's performance against other countries accurately. The pound may rise against the dollar but fall against the yen. To overcome this problem the average value of the pound is compared against a range (or basket) of currencies of the countries we trade with using the *Sterling Exchange Rate* or *Index*.

In recent years high interest rates have encouraged people to invest in Britain, and the Sterling Exchange Index has been quite high. However, not everyone supports such a policy. If sterling is priced high, then our exports become expensive, although it is easier for us to pay for our imports.

Heine Riekenbacker wants a Rolls Royce. At 2 DM (Deutchmark) = £1 he's happy to buy one, but if the pound rises in value and he now needs 4 DM to £1, he might think again.

Decide for yourself

If the pound is low in value against other currencies, our exports become attractive to other countries and our exports should increase. But we have to work harder to pay for imports

- Can you see why?

> When £1 = $2 it bought one box of popcorn.
> When £1 = $1 it only buys ½ box of popcorn.

A rise in the exchange rate leads to:

- a fall in the price of imports and a rise in their demand; and
- a rise in the price of exports and a fall in their demand (if such demand is not inelastic);

A fall in the exchange rate leads to:

- a rise in the price of imports and a fall in their demand;
- a fall in the price of exports and a rise in their demand.

Test yourself

On 20 January £1 = $2 and a British sports car exporter is very happy. Explain why he is furious when he reads the next day that the pound has risen in value and is now worth $3. Would he favour a policy of depreciating or appreciating the pound?

DATA RESPONSE 1

Car makers gearing up to turn import tide

This much-improved balance of trade in built-up vehicles was mainly responsible for the relatively small increase in the UK's trade deficit on all motor products last year, to £3.99m from £3.89m in 1986.

With exports continuing to grow, there are hopes that next year they may at last more than offset one particularly negative factor – surging imports of replacements parts.

SMMT economists say they believe "the prospects for 1988 are encouraging, although British-produced vehicles will have to be com-petitive without the advantage of the very low pound which prevailed during the early part of 1987."

The number of car imports – 1,047,413 – remained far higher than exports. But this was 2 per cent less than in 1986 as the UK-based multi-nationals sought to provide more of their UK sales with cars actually built in British plants. Imports of light commercials fell 14 per cent in unit terms to 71,683 and other commercials fell 5 per cent to 36,986.

Source: *The Financial Times*, 7 March 1988

Britain's balance of trade in motor products

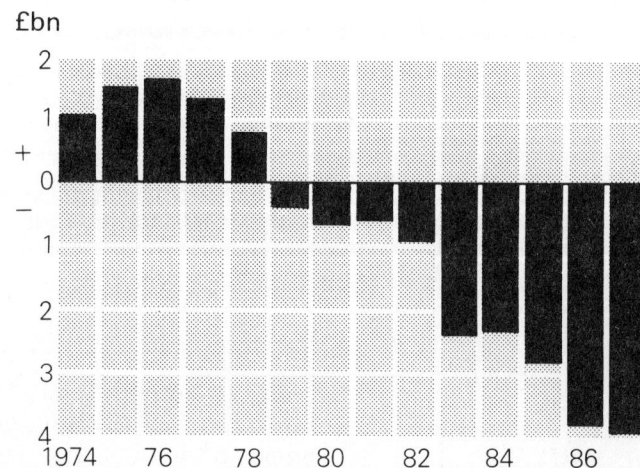

UK motor trade £m

| | Fourth Quarter | | Full year | |
	1987	**1986**	**1987**	**1986**
Exports(fob)				
Cars	529	378	1,901	1,312
CVs<3tonnes gvw	26	18	110	55
Other Cvs	68	59	278	260
Parts and accessories	862	756	2,998	2,750
Other products	279	236	936	850
Imports(cif)				
Cars	1,182	1,084	4,995	4,791
CVs<3tonnes gvw	81	66	299	296
Other CVs	186	143	603	553
Parts and accessories	1,084	919	3,874	3,098
Other products	128	98	443	399
Trade balance				
Cars	−653	−706	−3,094	−3,479
CVs<3tonnes gvw	−55	−48	−189	−241
Other CVs	−118	−84	−325	−293
Parts and accessories	−222	−163	−876	−346
Other products	151	138	493	451
Total	−897	−867	−3,991	−3,887

UK vehicle production

	1987	**1986**
Cars		
Rover*	471,504	404,454
Ford	386,698	346,267
Vauxhall	183, 857	161,857
Jaguar	47,960	41,437
Peug./Tal.	45,549	58,426
R–R	2,570	2,531
Carbodies	2,128	2,231
Lotus	798	704
TVR	550	521
Reliant	225	269
Ast. Mart.#	222	–
Panther	209	237
Others	413	585
Total	1,142,985	1,019,519
Commercial vehicles		
Ford	101,237	93,805
Bedford§	46,595	51,201
Rover	36,746	31,976
Ley. Daf§§	32,264	29,360
Iveco Ford	14,805	15,802
Renault	5,104	4,133
ERF	2,983	1,991
Seddon A.	1,861	1,626
AWD	1,821	–
Ley. Bus	862	–
Hestair	833	683
Foden	829	533
MCW	664	278
Reliant	8	22
Others	115	155
Total	246,727	228,685

*Includes Range Rover #Formerly in Others §Car-based vans and panel vans now built by IBC §§Includes Freight Rover

1 What can you notice about the Balance of Trade in motor products between 1974 and 1978?

2 How had the situation changed after 1978?

3 Calculate the improvement in the production of cars between 1986 and 1987.

4 What motor products other than cars are included in the exports and imports of the UK motor trade?

5 Explain the different effects on the balance of trade in motor products of:
   a industrial unrest in France, Germany, and Japan's motor car production plants;
   b a 6 month strike in the major UK-based factory of Britain's largest supplier of headlights for motor vehicles.

6 Describe how British car makers are beginning to improve the Balance of Trade figures in motor products.

Extension

KEY

▨▷ Flow of goods and services

▷ Flow of money

Visible exports

£200

🕐 £50

Invisible exports

Having a swell time in little old ENGLAND – wish you were here.

£500

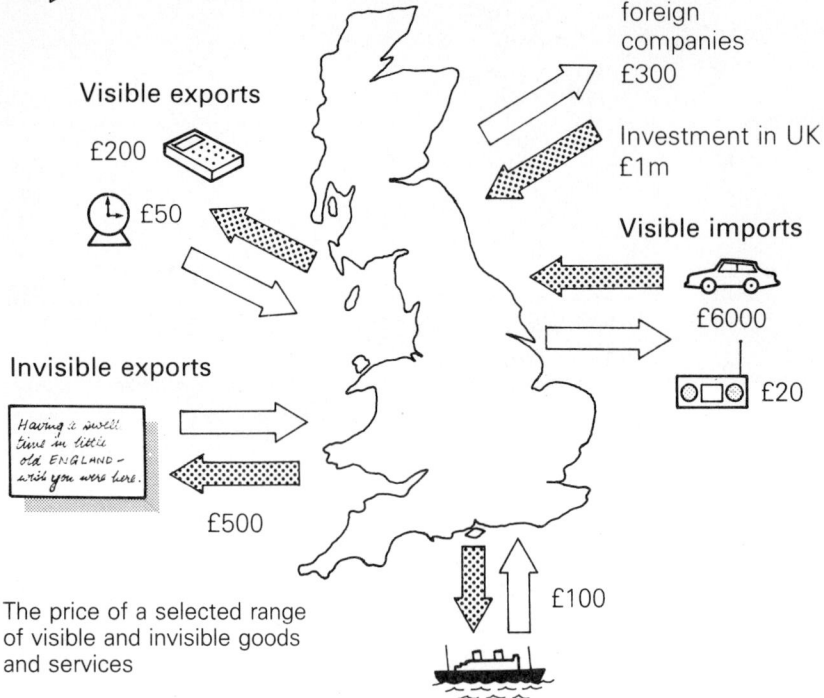

The price of a selected range of visible and invisible goods and services

Invisible imports

Dividends paid to foreign companies £300

Investment in UK £1m

Visible imports

🚗

£6000

📻 £20

£100

🚢

1 Make a list of:
  a the visible imports in the picture;
  b the visible exports.
2 The Balance of Trade is the difference between the price of visible imports and visible exports. What would the Balance of Trade be in this example? Is it a surplus or deficit figure?
3 a What is meant by the term invisible balance?
  b Calculate the invisible balance.
4 Add the invisible balance to the Balance of Trade. This will give you the Current Balance. What was this?
5 What other factors would you have to think about to arrive at the Balance of Payments on Capital Account?

DATA RESPONSE 2

UK shipbuilding orders fall again

By Edward Townsend, Industrial Correspondent

Britain's state-owned merchant shipbuilding yards are continuing to struggle against fierce foreign competition and suffered another fall in order books in the second quarter of this year.

Latest figures from Lloyd's Register of Merchant Shipping show the volume of ships on order at the end of June was 213,822 gross tons against 262,407 tons a year earlier. The British share of the world order book was just 1 per cent.

The new figures underline the continuing dominance by the South Korean and Japa-nese shipyards of the world merchant shipbuilding scene. Despite the British Government's shipbuilding intervention fund, designed to help bridge the gap been British and Far Eastern prices, British Shipbuilders has been unable to pare its prices enough and is concentrating on more specialized, high technology vessels including research and refrigeration ships. It hopes to re-enter the luxury cruise ferry market.

In the second quarter the world order book rose to 21.35 million tons from 20.9 million tons in the previous three months – the first reversal of the decline in shipbuilding since 1983. But most of the increase came from the Korean yards' additional intake of orders and the country's total order book stands at 146 ships representing 5.07 million tons.

Japan has 290 vessels on order amounting to 5.29 million tons, a big dip from the 8.69 million tons of a year earlier.

Tankers remain the world industry's mainstay. At the end of June there were 238 on order – none of them in Britain – with a total of 14.7 million deadweight tonnes, against 127 ore and bulk carriers representing 7.97 million tonnes.

Japan is building 48 of the tankers but South Korean yards are building 59 crude and product carriers.

Significantly, China is steadily increasing its shipbuilding position with an order book up by more than 100,000 tons up to the middle of the year to 790,399 tons. Taiwan has an order book of almost 700,000 tons – up by 81,400 tons on the previous quarter.

Source: The Times,
8 September 1987

1 What has happened to Britain's chances of winning new orders to build merchant ships?

2 In the nineteenth century the UK produced the majority of the world's ships. What share of the world market does the UK now hold?

3 Which countries are increasing their share of the world market for orders?

4 How has the British government tried to help the British shipbuilding industry?

5 How is the British shipbuilding industry responding to the competition from abroad?

Coursework

Aim: To investigate reasons for importing finished goods.

1 Select any one room in a family home (for example, the kitchen) and make a list of the domestic appliances to be found in this room.

2 Use this list to help you construct a questionnaire to find out how much people had to pay for each item, what problems they have experienced with the appliance, whether there were any other problems (e.g. delays in delivering the item).

3 Make sure you discover the brand name of each item and the country of origin.

4 What percentage of each type of appliance was imported from abroad?

5 Use the results and any other information you can obtain to comment on why the UK imports finished goods that could be made in this country.

40 Protectionism and the European Community

I'm sorry, but only 5000 and a half cars are allowed from Japan according to our list.

Free trade exists when there are no barriers between countries to prevent them exchanging goods and services.

Protectionism is the opposite of a policy of free trade. It is the promotion of government policies that restrict the import of goods into an economy.

Free trade or not?

Alex likes to buy the latest fashions to sell in her chain of dress shops. Under a system of free trade she can buy an expensive range of clothes from the best British designers or she can buy the cheapest range of clothes at a similar level of quality supplied by a Korean firm.

Alex supports free trade. She argues that firms that compete with each other are able to be more efficient, seize markets, employ more workers, and make the best use of scarce resources. (See the idea of comparative advantage on page 235–6.) Alex is sure that such firms are in the best position to capture export markets and create jobs at home.

Rob is not so sure. He works as a tailor in a small firm making fashion garments. He has to work quite long hours for relatively low pay. Many of the friends he went to college with who went into the clothing business are now out of work. This, he argues, is because consumers are not buying British goods but spending their money on cheaper imported products.

Rob says to Alex, "It's bad of you not to buy British. If you don't, more workers in this town will be unemployed. It won't just be in tailoring either. There's all the other industries that rely on us too. Why should we put our own workers out of business? I don't mind competing fairly with other countries, but some make their workers work 60 hours or more a week and others pay starvation wages. I don't think that's right."

Rob thinks the government should do something to protect British jobs by stopping imports coming into Britain.

There are a number of ways that a government can prevent imports coming into the economy:

- **Quota**: placing a fixed limit (or quota) on the number of goods allowed to enter.
- **Tariff**: imposing a tax known as a tariff (or customs duty) on goods entering the country.
- **Regulations**: imposing restrictions in the form of regulations (or rules) about how goods enter the country and how they are made.

Test yourself

1 If British clocks cost £50 to make and sell and Swiss clocks only £30, what level of tax might the government impose on Swiss clocks to protect our own clockmakers?

2 You are in charge of a government department faced with a flood of cheap imported cars. Working in groups, decide what regulations you could impose to limit their import.

Reasons for protection

There are many reasons why countries try to protect their economies:

- To prevent import penetration and encourage the maximisation of exports. A country concerned about its balance of payments will do all it can to prevent too many goods being imported. It will often subsidise exports so that foreign currency can be earned.
- To protect levels of employment and provide more jobs within their economy. If a British car firm closes, then not only are the car workers unemployed but so are others working in subsidiary industries that supplied the firm. This leads to an increase in government benefits being paid out and a loss of revenue from

taxes. In such circumstances there might be an economic case for subsidising the car firm.

- To protect a new industry. While it is still in its infancy and needs protection from a strong overseas competitor there might be a strong argument to provide subsidies.
- To protect home industries against unfair competition from abroad. Some countries sell their goods at a high price in their own markets which they protect with a range of regulations. Using the profits obtained, they subsidise the sale of the same goods abroad and sell them at a price well below the price at which a foreign country is able to compete. When goods are sold below the market price in this way in order to capture foreign markets the term *dumping* is applied.
- To protect strategic interests. Recently the British army had to choose between buying a British or an American tank. If we had bought American, Britain would no longer have had its own tank industry and would have had to rely on the Americans in future to equip its army.

The European Community: a protectionist grouping

The European Community or EC (often called the EEC or European Economic Community) was founded by the Treaty of Rome in 1957 to encourage post-war European unity.

The first step in the creation of this body was the setting up of a Customs Union. All the countries involved agreed to remove any tariffs between them. Under this agreement, a German clock can enter the UK at a price below a British made clock and the UK must not impose or levy a tariff. By 1992 there can be no restrictions on the movement of people, capital and trade between the members of the Community. The EC will truly become a single market. Alongside the customs union a Common External Tariff wall (CET) was set up. The CET acts as a barrier not to other European Community (or Common Market) countries but to countries elsewhere in the world. Countries outside the EC who want to export to EC countries are placed at an unfair advantage by such an arrangement.

So the European Community is a body that in one way encourages free trade (among its members) but in other ways is protectionist.

ECONOMIC TERMS
Quota: a fixed limit on goods entering a country.
Tariff: a tax in the form of a customs duty levied on goods entering a country.
Dumping: selling goods below their market price in order to capture a foreign market.
Subsidy: financial help from the government that allows an item to be sold at below cost price.
Import penetration: the ability of one country to increase its percentage of exports to another economy which then substitutes for domestically produced goods.
Customs union: any group of countries that allows free trade between its members.

Other policies of the European Community

A customs union is only the first step towards creating a free trade region. The EC has also set up a range of other policies designed to encourage more than just free trade among its members. These include common agreements and laws on trading, food regulations, health and safety, and business activity.

It has special funds to help areas, particularly in matters of regional and social policy, that do not gain as much benefit from being part of the Community as others. Funds also help families who move to find work and assist areas that are very economically depressed.

Another feature of the EC is its policy on agriculture. This Common Agricultural Policy (or CAP) aims to guarantee that farmers receive a minimum price for the food they produce. This has guaranteed that there are plentiful supplies of food in the Community. (See Extension 2.)

Britain and the EC

Many people argue that Britain does not benefit from its membership of the European Community. They argue that the CAP is very expensive and only a few people in the country benefit as Britain has very few workers involved in agriculture. Our consumers, on the other hand, they say, have to pay high prices for their food. The surpluses stockpiled to prevent prices to farmers falling are seen to be a waste of a nation's resources.

Activity

The growth of the European Community

1958 6 members

France

Italy

Luxemburg

Netherlands

Belgium

West
Germany

1973 9 members

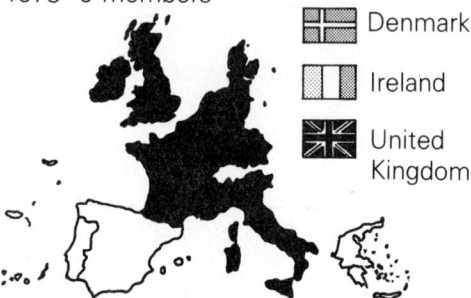

Denmark

Ireland

United
Kingdom

1981 10 members

Greece

1986 12 members

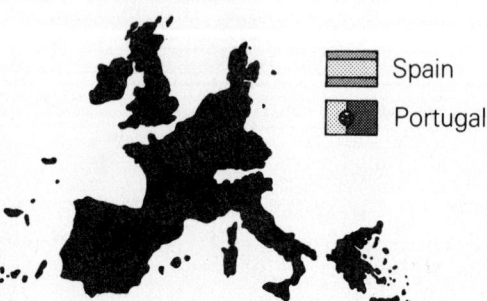

Spain

Portugal

General Community budget: 1985

Receipts			Expenditure	
VAT	55.5%		Agriculture and fisheries	72.9%
Customs duties	29.6%		Regional policy	5.9%
Non–repayable advances	5.9%		Social policy	5.7%
Agricultural levies	4.0%		Development cooperation	3.9%
Sugar levies	3.8%		Research, energy, industry and transport	2.6%
Miscellaneous	1.2%		Administrative costs	4.6%
			Miscellaneous	4.4%

28 000 million European Currency Units

Unemployment rate (%)

	EUR 12	USA	JAPAN
1975	2,9	8,5	1,9
1981	7,8	7,6	2,2
1985	10,6	7,2	2,6
1986	10,7	7,0	2,0

Population growth 1985 - 2005

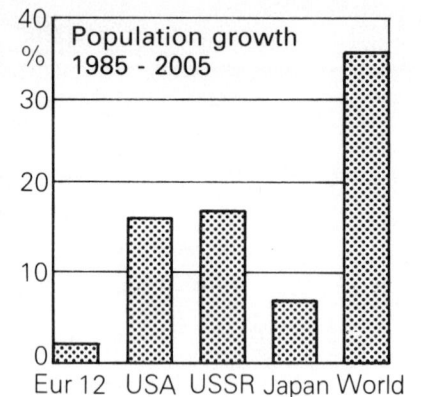

Eur 12 USA USSR Japan World

Gross domestic product 1985 ('000 million European Currency Units)

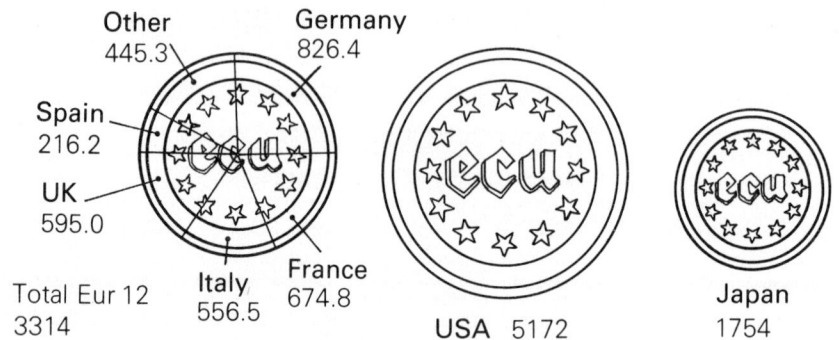

Other 445.3
Germany 826.4
Spain 216.2
UK 595.0
Total Eur 12 3314
Italy 556.5
France 674.8
USA 5172
Japan 1754

Growth in GDP (volume)   (1960 = 100)

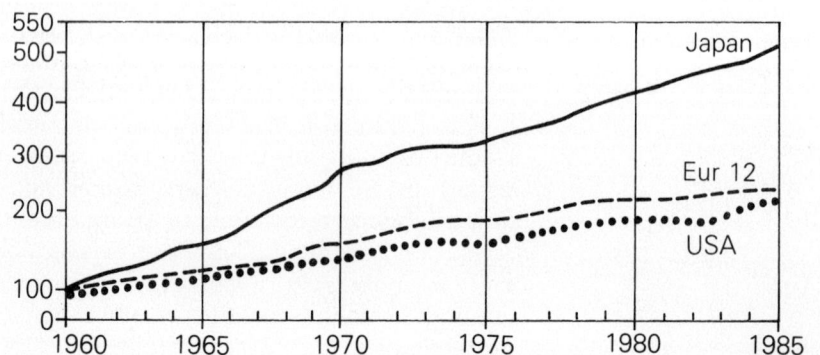

Japan

Eur 12

USA

1960 1965 1970 1975 1980 1985

Industry: the challenge to Europe
Trend of industrial production (1980 = 100)

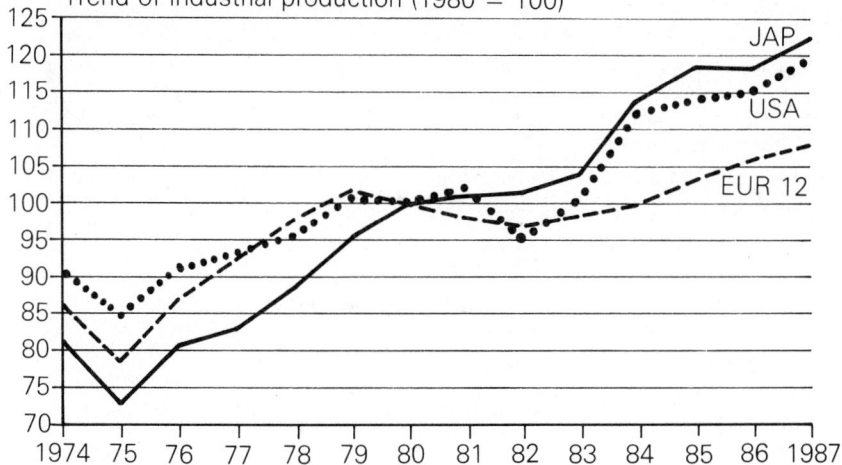

1 **a** Which countries were the original members of the European Community (EC)?
  b When did the United Kingdom become a member of the European Community?
  c Name the last two countries to have joined the European Community.
2 Briefly describe how the Community finances its activities.
3 Which two countries in the Community have a greater Gross Domestic Product than the United Kingdom?
4 Where does most of the EC's money go?
5 Compare the performance and prospects of the European Community with the performance and prospects of the economies of: **a** the USA; **b** Japan.

The UK still has many strong trading links with countries outside the Community. It imports goods from them (like lamb from New Zealand) and in doing so CET has to be paid by British consumers. This means that British consumers end up contributing more than others (in proportionate terms) to Community funds.

Against these arguments is the very powerful point that, as members of the EC, it is easier for us to trade with our nearest neighbours (the countries of Western Europe) as we do not have to face the CET as a barrier. Also many people argue that Britain has not taken full advantage of the much larger consumer market that the total EC population offers.

Test yourself

1 What is the difference between free trade and protectionism?
2 What does free trade allow an economy to do?
3 Why can free trade cause an economy problems?
4 How can an economy be protected from imports?
5 Explain in detail why economies sometimes need protection.
6 What is the EC? How does it protect itself?
7 What are some of the advantages and disadvantages of Britain belonging to the European Community?

Absolute and comparative advantage

Although protectionism as a policy presents advantages, in the long run the principle of absolute and comparative advantage would suggest that protectionism encourages inefficiency by discouraging specialisation.

Absolute advantage

Let us imagine that the world has only two countries and produces only two products: wellington boots and umbrellas.

- Country A with half its resources can make 500 pairs of wellingtons and with the other half 100 umbrellas.
- Country B with half its resources can make 50 pairs of wellingtons and with the other half 600 umbrellas.

In this example it is clear that country A should make wellingtons. It could produce 1000 (the world would have 450 more pairs as a result). Country B could make 1200 umbrellas (the world would have 500 more umbrellas as a result).

Country A has the absolute advantage in making wellingtons and Country B in making umbrellas. A clear case for trade exists.

However, even in a situation where a country has the absolute advantage in making both products, a case for trade can still exist.

Comparative advantage

- Country A can make 100 pairs of wellingtons or 50 umbrellas.

- Country B can make 60 pairs of wellingtons or 10 umbrellas.

Here country A has an absolute advantage in making both.

The opportunity cost for country A of making umbrellas is that it could make wellingtons twice as fast. The opportunity cost for country B of making umbrellas is that it could make wellingtons six times faster. Country B is relatively better equipped to make wellingtons than umbrellas, and can be said to have a comparative advantage in wellington boot production. It makes sense for Country B to export wellingtons and import umbrellas and for country A to export umbrellas and import wellingtons.

Test yourself

Look at this table.

Hours it takes	UK	USSR
A to make a pair of shoes	4	10
B to make a pair of jeans	1	3

Which country has the comparative advantage in making:

a shoes;
b jeans?

DATA RESPONSE

SINGLE EUROPEAN MARKET
Creating awareness of 1992

IT IS nearly three years since the 1992 campaign was launched. A recent survey by Ernst and Whinney revealed a low – but growing – level of British business appreciation of the enormous changes, opportunities, and potential pitfalls, involved.

The Community's aim over the next five years is to complete the original prospectus of the common market. This means flattening visible barriers to internal EC trade, such as tax, immigration and police checks at frontiers. It also means removing all the invisible barriers, created by the jumble of differing technical standards, legal restrictions on crossborder trade in services and national preferences for the public purchases of goods.

In the words of Lord Cockfield, the European Commission vice-president in charge of the barrier-flattening campaign, the aim is to create a "community in which traders could do business with customers in other member states just as they do with customers in the next street or the next town".

But who will be the winners and losers from the progressive dissolution of EC barriers? The first answer is everyone. A European Commission study is expected next month on the economic benefits of flattening barriers. There should also be direct benefits to consumers in reduced prices and increased choice.

But there will be pain as well as pleasure. Many firms, exposed to direct competition for the first time, could find themselves in difficulties.

They say the present barriers are highest and toughest in areas where Britain is strong, especially in financial service industries and high-tech and telecommunications manufacturing. In the areas where Britain does relatively badly the borders are already relatively low.

Source: *The Times,*
16 February 1988

Comparative Prices in the EC (100 = cheapest)

	B	D	DK	E	F	UK	GR	I	IRL	NL	P
Records	159	147	182	134	170	132	100	161	139	161	136
Video cassettes	121	115	235	150	137	100	162	135	120	117	135
Sports shoes	157	147	168	147	117	106	165*	142	100	161	130
Tennis racquets	192	161	225	186	118	140	100*	168	148	211	161

*small sample of makes

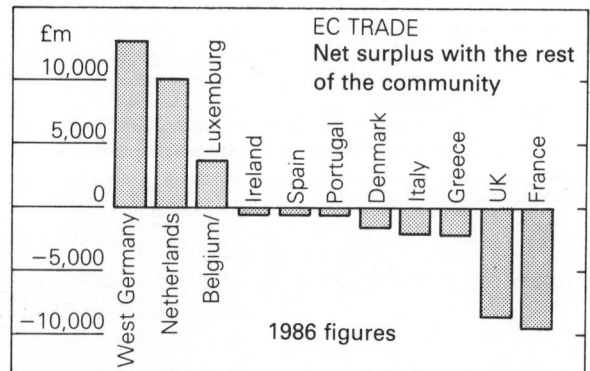

EC TRADE
Net surplus with the rest of the community

1986 figures

1 What do the initials EC stand for?

2 What is the Community planning to do by 1992?

3 Imagine you are a consumer wishing to buy cassettes. Which country would you wish to live in? In which country are tennis racquets the most expensive?

4 Compare Britain's trading performance with that of other EC economies.

5 Explain how consumers will benefit from the changes to be made in 1992.

6 How will the British economy benefit from the changes to be made in 1992?

Extension 1

Country A, B and C have set up their own customs union or common market. They have abolished (removed) all charges on goods traded between them and set up an external tariff barrier. All goods entering countries A, B, or C from any country outside their union (say country 1, 2, or 3) have a charge placed on them that raises their price by 10%.

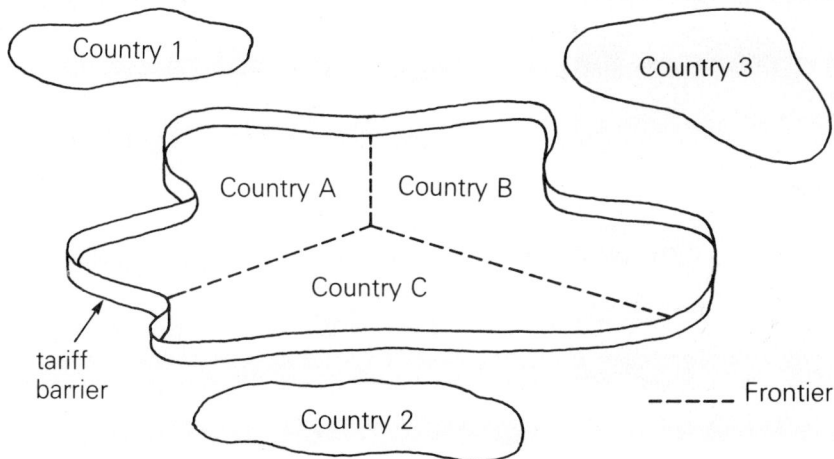

Country 1

Country 3

Country A | Country B

Country C

tariff barrier

Country 2

- - - - - Frontier

1 a Country A wishes to export goods to country B. Will it have to pay the tariff charge?

b Country A wishes to send country 1 goods. Will it have to pay the tariff charge?

c Country 3 wishes to send goods to country B. Will it have to pay the charge?

d Country B wishes to send goods to country 3. Will it have to pay a charge?

2 If country 2 sends shoes worth £20 to country C, how much will the shoes eventually be sold for in the shoe shops of country C?

3 If country A sends shoes valued at £21, how much will they eventually be sold for in country C?

4 Explain how the tariff barrier protects country A's economy, but does not help country 2's economy.

5 What arguments can be used for and against establishing customs unions?

Extension 2

Most of the EC's funds are spent supporting the CAP (Common Agricultural Policy). Demand for food throughout the Community does not alter very much but the supply of food can change. This could result in wild fluctuations in price, making planning for farmers very difficult. In order to support farmers and the stable production of crops the EC has established a system of intervention designed to moderate movements in prices. This is how the system works . . .

In a good harvest the supply of crops increases.

Demand does not alter greatly. Price falls to clear supplies.

Reverse this process if there is a bad harvest.

The EC buys up the surplus crops at an *intervention price*. These surpluses are stored, sold off outside the EC or destroyed.

237

Monitoring the quality of grain in storage

1 If the olive harvest was exceptionally good, what would the EC do?
2 Now assume that, instead of there being a good harvest, fires have swept through many of Europe's olive groves. What would the Community now do?
3 There is a very large 'wine lake' (or surplus), but the Community has run out of storage facilities. What other options are available?
4 Imagine that in 1989 the apple crop was a failure. Why might you:
   a as a consumer be happy with the Community's CAP scheme?
   b as a farmer, with a successful apple crop, be unhappy with the CAP scheme?
5 "The CAP makes the price of all European food expensive. Farmers may benefit but it's a tax on us poor consumers," says an angry shopper.
   Discuss his/her reasons for saying this.

Coursework

Aim: To investigate the effects of trade barriers.

Beet or cane?

Sugar can be produced from sugar cane or sugar beet.

Sugar beet production occurs largely within Common Market countries and is protected by tariff walls. Sugar cane production takes place largely in tropical countries.

1 Collect information on the production of sugar by each method. Consider the advantages and disadvantages of using various forms of protection to protect each of these methods of production.

2 Write a letter to the government asking for their support in either:

   a subsidising the production of cane sugar; or
   b protecting the position of beet producers.

In your letter you should clearly show how your investigations/arguments would benefit:
   a the consumer;
   b the producer;
   c others in the Common Market.

3 Discuss the drawbacks of following the route that you have chosen.

4 Consider the impact on Third World countries of a policy of subsidising beet sugar. (You can obtain information on this subject from a range of development agencies.)

41 Developing Economies

All countries depend on each other in some way or other. Economists refer to this fact as *interdependence*.

"No *country* is an island, entire of itself . . ."

Decide for yourself

Imagine a three country world:

- Country A produces cocoa and sells it to country B in return for sugar.
- Country C produces milk and imports sugar and cocoa from A and B to make chocolate, which in turn it supplies to them.
- Can you see how the countries need each other?

The relationships between the countries of the world are not equal ones, however. When examining trading patterns, economists have divided the world into three broad groupings: the First World, the Second World and the Third World.

The First World is better known as the *developed world*. It is composed largely of western countries situated in the Northern Hemisphere. These countries are highly developed and industrialised. They have affluent populations who largely enjoy high standards of living.

The Second World is better known as the *Communist World* or the *Eastern Bloc*. It is largely made up of the Soviet Union, her Warsaw Pact allies, and other East European countries.

The Third World is composed largely of countries in the Southern Hemisphere. Most of the world's population lives in the Third World. This group is also known as the *developing world*. Most of the developing countries are very poor, although it is always dangerous to generalise. Sometimes Third World countries are referred to as LDCs (less developed countries).

Over the last two decades the Brandt Reports have drawn the world's attention to the needs of Third World countries. They describe the world as divided into a rich North with a quarter of the world's population but with four-fifths of its income, and a hungry, poor South with only a fifth of the world's income but three quarters of the population. This description has given rise to the term the North/South divide.

Features of the developing world

In comparison with the developed world, the developing world has many problems.

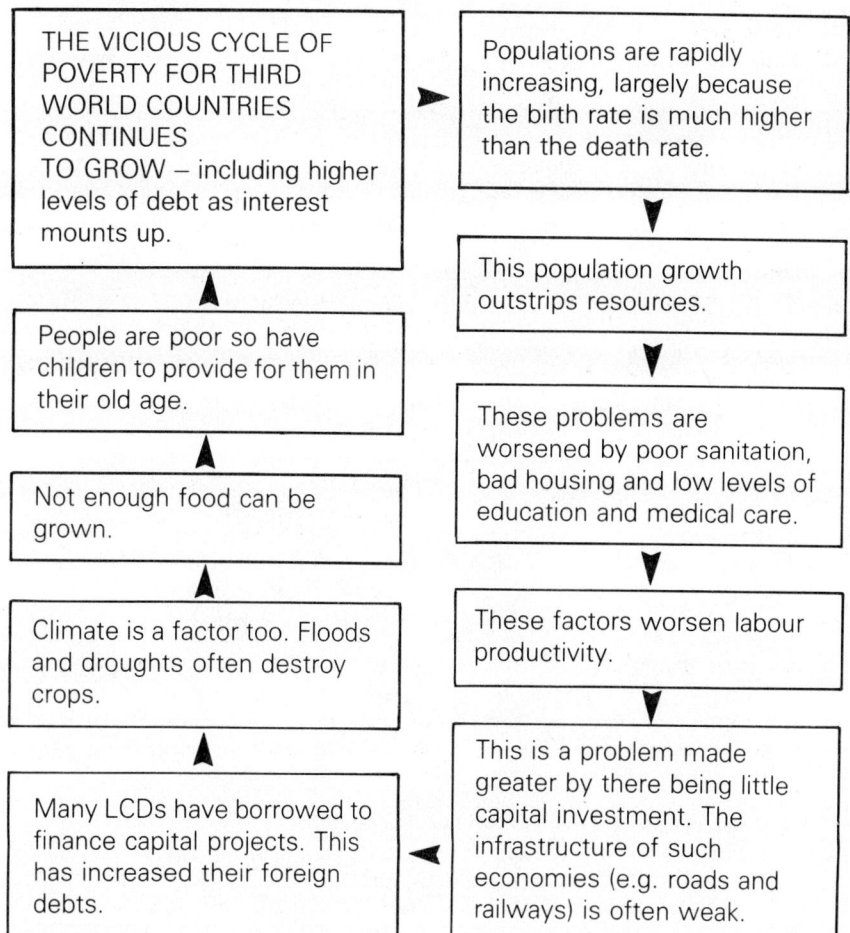

THE VICIOUS CYCLE OF POVERTY FOR THIRD WORLD COUNTRIES CONTINUES TO GROW – including higher levels of debt as interest mounts up.

Populations are rapidly increasing, largely because the birth rate is much higher than the death rate.

This population growth outstrips resources.

These problems are worsened by poor sanitation, bad housing and low levels of education and medical care.

These factors worsen labour productivity.

This is a problem made greater by there being little capital investment. The infrastructure of such economies (e.g. roads and railways) is often weak.

People are poor so have children to provide for them in their old age.

Not enough food can be grown.

Climate is a factor too. Floods and droughts often destroy crops.

Many LCDs have borrowed to finance capital projects. This has increased their foreign debts.

TIME TO BREAK THE CYCLE OF THIRD WORLD DEBT

by Robert Harvey

LIKE THAT tiresome man on the stair who wasn't there, the issue of the world debt has not gone away, in spite of earnest wishes to the contrary expressed by creditor countries herding grumbling bankers into yet another emergency package of loans to stave off a threatened Third-World default.

Recently it has been Brazil's turn; soon it will be Argentina's; and after that Mexico's. As the overall debt burden grows inexorably, and as living standards in the debtor nations continue to sink, the first serious political consequences of the crisis are beginning to make themselves felt.

Concern over the debt is being expressed not just at street level. Sir Douglas Wass, the former Permanent Secretary at the Treasury, is not a man normally associated with voodoo economics; nor indeed are Mr Paulo Baffi, an austere former governor of the Bank of Italy, or Mr Bob Hormats, the respected vice-president of Goldman Sachs. Yet all three have just signed a UN report, Financing Africa's Recovery, which adds up to a hair-raising account of Africa's economic predicament.

That continent — whose aggregate economy is smaller than Britain's — is now suffering from a reversal in its terms of trade to the tune of some $3 billion a year, from interest payments increased by more than $2 billion a year; from a decline in bank lending adding up to $2.4 billion a year; and from reduced direct investment of some 200 million a year. Thus the continent, around $1 billion worse off per year than a decade ago, is today an undeveloping, rather than a developing one.

A more partisan view of the Latin American debt mountain has been issued by a group of authors under the auspices of the Latin American Bureau. The conclusion and language is more predictable. But the statistics suggest that something has gone badly wrong with the world financial system. Between 1980 and 1986 the Third World transferred to the developed world around $325 billion worth of principal and $325 billion in interest payments, roughly 5 per cent of their annual GDP. For Latin America the total flow between 1982 and 1986 was $121 billion ($20 billion more than the total of original lending that was the root of the problem between 1974 and 1981).

The price of all this has been a reduction in living standards in some African countries by up to half and in some Latin American countries by up to a third, accompanied by a doubling in unemployment. Neither in Africa nor Latin America has there been any easing of the debt burden, which has now climbed to more than $1 trillion.

Source: *The Daily Telegraph*, 30 August 1988

Debt burden on developing countries grows

Developing Countries' Debt

Total public and private long-term debt and financial flows
US$ billions

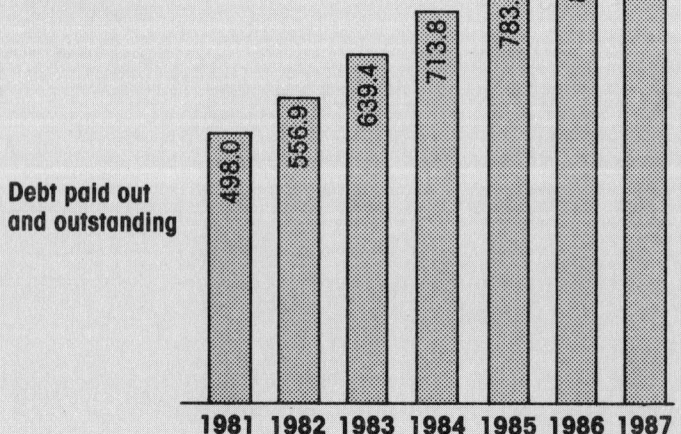

Debt paid out and outstanding

1981	1982	1983	1984	1985	1986	1987
498.0	556.9	639.4	713.8	783.6	870.7	930.5

Source: *The Independent*, 19 January 1988

240

1 What evidence can you discover in the photograph that might indicate that the little girl's family has a low standard of living?

2 Describe what has happened to the debt burden of developing countries between 1981 and 1987.

3 What effect do you think a growing debt burden is likely to have on the living standards of nations in debt?

4 a What is an undeveloping economy?
  b Why is Africa now an undeveloping continent?

5 How has the developed world benefited from the debt of the south?

6 A friend of yours suggests to you that countries of the Third World are poor because the people are lazy and backward. Working in groups consider what alternative reasons could be advanced to account for Third World poverty. Remember that the southern countries with the highest levels of debt are in South America.

Criticisms of the developed world

It is often argued that the developed world does not do enough to help the Third World. Many of the Third World countries' problems date from the days when large numbers of them were colonies of the countries in the developed world. Other problems go back beyond this period. Some of the arguments centre around the terms of trade:

● Developed countries could do more to encourage the import of manufactured goods from the Third World. This would allow Third World countries to develop their infant industries. Too many Third World countries, it is said, are tied to serving the needs of the developed world by supplying raw materials, as and when required, in return for the manufactured goods their consumers demand.

  The terms of trade between the North and South have worsened over the years, with the South losing out.

● When the North does help the South it often gives aid tied to special deals that benefit the developed world. This might be, for example, building prestige projects such as airports and motorways using technicians imported from the developed world and Western companies. Local labour and local companies lose out.

● Many companies in the developing world are owned by companies that have their headquarters in a developed country (the so-called multinational companies). If the developing country objects to such a company's labour record or trading policy, the multinational can always move its operations elsewhere . . . or threaten to do so.

Problems of the developing world for the developed world

In many ways the developed world benefits from having the LDCs. This is particularly true for consumers who can purchase the cheaper products of the LDCs.

Although this is a clear benefit for the consumers of the developed world, those who are workers in the developed world do not necessarily gain. If they are unable to compete, they may find themselves out of work. This is an example of a cost involved in trading with LDCs and has led to many countries of the North imposing import controls.

The banking system of the north has benefited a great deal from the loans it has made to the south. However, the interest payments have become so great that some southern countries have, at times, refused to pay any more interest which threatens the world's banking system and all economies. All countries benefit from trade and this trading is made possible by the flow of money and credit organised by the banks.

ECONOMIC TERMS
Less developed countries (LDCs): countries of the Third World with relatively poorer economies compared to the developed world. **Interdependence**: the fact that economies need each other.

Test yourself

1 What is interdependence?
2 What differences exist between the First and Third Worlds?

3 Explain how Third World countries are caught in a vicious cycle of poverty.

4 How could developed economies provide better help for LDCs?

Helping the South

Help for the LDCs comes from many organisations in the world. The private sector of the developed countries have charities which send relief workers and other forms of aid, financed by voluntary donations. Examples include Oxfam, War on Want, and the Save the Children Fund.

The governments of the developed world also provide aid either in the form of *bilateral aid* (an arrangement between two countries: one giving aid, one receiving it) or as part of multilateral aid programmes (where several developed countries work together to help an LDC).

Multilateral aid is often provided through world organisations that have been established (often by the United Nations) to promote world economic freedom, aid and assistance. Such organisations include:

- The **IMF** or **International Monetary Fund**: the IMF provides short term aid to countries which run into balance of payments problems, and cannot find the money to pay for the goods they have imported.

- **GATT** or the **General Agreement on Tariffs and Trade**: GATT is a body that meets every so often and tries to reduce the barriers between countries that limit trade. This can be very helpful for LDCs trying to export goods into those developed countries that have imposed barriers to protect their own industries.

- **The World Bank**: like the IMF, the World Bank tries to finance world trade. It provides assistance through long-term loans and funding.

- **UNCTAD** or the **United Nations Commission on Trade and Development**: UNCTAD, unlike GATT, meets regularly every four years. It brings together developed countries and LDCs in a forum or body that can secure a better deal for the goods provided by the Third World and supplied to the First World.

Test yourself
List and briefly describe the major international organisations that try to help the Third World.

DATA RESPONSE

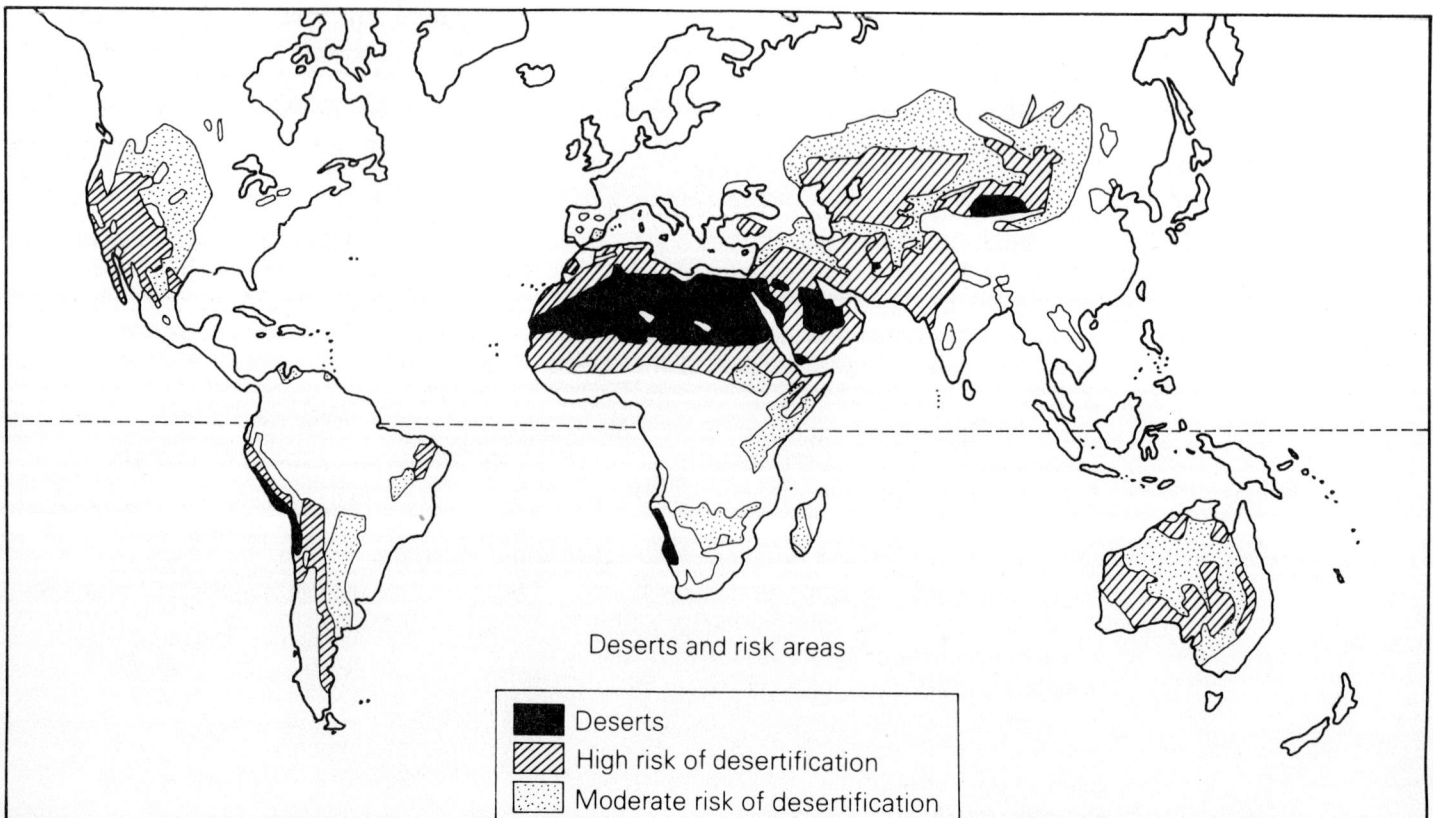

Deserts and risk areas

■ Deserts
▨ High risk of desertification
░ Moderate risk of desertification

ECONOMICS

Christopher Huhne

A COMMON refrain of the government is that you cannot solve all problems by throwing money at them – a useful slogan if only because it is incontrovertible. However, it is equally incontrovertible that you can solve some problems by throwing money at them, and that you do not always make solutions easier by cutting the money available.

Yet that is exactly what the government has done in the case of overseas aid to the Third World. In real terms, this aid is planned to be about one fifth lower this year than it was in 1978–79. Inevitably, the effectiveness of the aid programme has been reduced.

The latest United Nations Conference on Trade and Development report on the least developed countries shows that Britain has not been alone (though certainly an extreme case). Concessional flows of resources even to these countries – the 36 around the world with the lowest standard of life – were lower in dollar terms in 1983 than in 1980.

It is very hard to argue that the problems of drought and famine have been made any easier by throwing less money at them.

Over the same period, the two other main sources of foreign exchange with which to buy imports have also been hard hit. Remittances from foreign workers and direct investment are down as the recession hit, while the prices of the nearly 90 per cent of the LDCs' total exports, which are basic commodities, dropped by around 12 per cent.

The result has been to compound a series of natural and man-made disasters within the countries, and to leave their overall output growing by 1.6 per cent a year, their food output growing by 1.4 per cent a year, while their populations have grown by 2.6 per cent a year.

In other words, living standards have been dropping.

There are various reasons why these countries are poor, the most important of which is the poverty of their land. Most of the 36 countries – with some notable exceptions in Asia like cyclone-prone Bangladesh – are situated in the arid sub-Saharan belt across Africa.

The traditional methods of food production have been slash and burn cultivation or nomadic grazing, both of which relied on using the land for a while before moving on, simply because it was not rich enough to support even a regular cycle of cultivation and leaving land fallow.

The pressure of population growth as infant mortality has fallen and life expectancy has been lengthened by basic medicine, is one factor causing over-use of the land, and a vicious spiral of deforestation and desertification: the dust bowl of the United States between the wars writ large.

Their development problems are enormous. If the literacy rate of about one third is to be improved, clearly education is required, and in turn needs some sort of villagisation. But that puts even more pressure on the arid soil.

The smallness of their national markets, and the increasing protectionism of the industrial countries against even their basic goods (for example, in the case of Bangladesh textile exports) hampers the possibilities of developing manufacturing, which has declined as a share of their output to only 8 per cent.

In addition to these long-standing problems, the sub-Saharan countries have suffered 17 years of drought, broken only by years of still below average rainfall in 1974 and 1975.

Wars in Ethiopia and Chad, and civil disturbances elsewhere have severely disrupted crop output.

Clearly no one would be so foolish as to argue that the problems of these countries, or the deterioration of their economies during the 80s, have been principally due to the influence of the industrial countries, or that much of the task of improvement does not lie with themselves.

There have been clear policy errors. Though food prices have risen faster than domestic costs and prices overall – thus providing an increasing incentive to crop production – some governments have insisted on hitting production for export, already hit by depressed commodity markets, with overvalued exchange rates.

In other cases, LDC governments have connived with the interests of the advanced countries in buying machinery for factories which has proved clearly too sophisticated to be serviced once in place. Poor management and skills have been compounded by corruption.

Yet it is increasingly obvious that few of these problems are going to be resolved in the long term unless substantially more support is given by the industrial countries not only in food aid (which UNCTAD defends), cash transfers, and debt write-offs, but also through trained people who can extend basic agricultural techniques.

Unless there is a much greater international effort to help these countries create the economic capacity to feed themselves, the intermitent pictures of starvation and famine will become a torrent. Sub-Saharan Africa is facing a human calamity on a terrifying scale.

The Least Developed Countries: 1985 Report; United Nations Conference on Trade and Development, Geneva.

Source: *Guardian*, 19 September 1985

---

1 a What does LDC stand for?
  b What does UNCTAD stand for?

2 Where are most of the LDCs situated?

3 Using the world map to help you, explain why there is a risk that the problems of these economies will worsen rather than improve.

4 Other than changes in climate, what factors have made life difficult for the people of the LDCs?

5 Explain how the position of the LDCs could be improved by:
  a the LDCs themselves;
  b help from industrialised economies.

A Farmer to ginger up farming

by David Pallister

NEW season's crop of yams from Onitsha in the East and Middle belt states to the North have begun arriving in markets of Lagos. Agricultural experts say this has been a good harvest and next year should be even better. A combination of good farmgate prices, adequate rains, and a relatively efficient distribution of fertilisers have all helped. But in Nigeria one can never be too sure.

Since the great dams of the river basin development authorities were first begun in the North in the late seventies, an estimated two billion naira has been spent on them. But there has been no Government report of any form on their efficacy. The authorities have been notorious sources of corruption and according to development experts few have been successful.

The drop in oil revenues has meant that feeder channels have not been built, that the machinery regularly malfunctions because of lack of imported spares, and in some cases dams have actually taken out of cultivation more land than has been made available for cropping. One estimate suggests that just over a quarter of the designated land of 57,000 hectares has been irrigated. The trends in agriculture are, however, well established. The oil boom of the seventies had a disastrous effect on the land. People migrated to the cities and those that remained were guaranteed minimum wages that forced down productivity. Development was neglected and from 1975 cheap imports of rice and maize to cater for changing urban tastes were a severe disincentive to domestic production.

Cash crops for export plummeted. From 1970 to 1982 cocoa, rubber, cotton and groundnuts declined by 43 per cent, 29 per cent, 65 per cent and 64 per cent. From being the world's largest exporter of palm oil, it became an importer – primarily from Malaysia, which had learned the techniques from the Nigerian Institute for Palm Oil Research.

Dr Ishrat Husain, the World Bank representative in Nigeria, says that the country's agricultural problems stem from "poor design and planning, poor implementation, and resistance to modern methods."

The World Bank has pumped $1 billion into Nigeria's agricultural development programmes (ADP) for which it provides 66 per cent of the costs. The Federal and State Governments pay the rest.

As with all World Bank loans Nigeria has never defaulted. They run for 20 years with an interest rate of 8.8 per cent which still makes the Bank a huge profit. After their successes in several northern states the ADPs are being extended to all of the states by next year. The guiding principle is to help the small farmer with feeder roads, clean drinking water bore holes, small-scale irrigation, and service centres.

An evaluation of the ADPs suggests that production rose by 5 per cent compared to a national food production rise of 1 per cent.

Source: *Guardian*, 20 September 1985

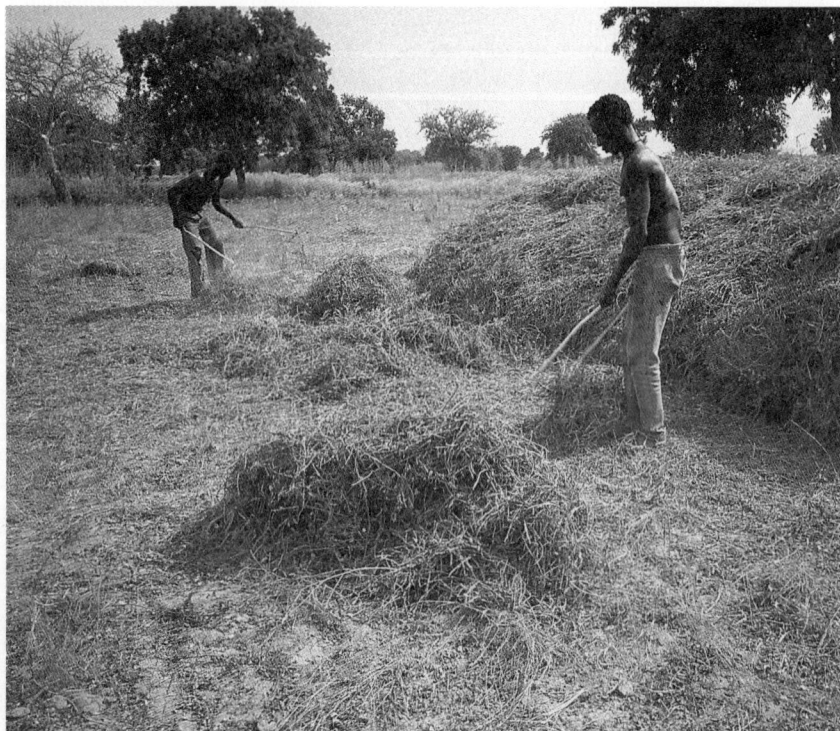

Groundnut threshing in Sapu, Gambia.

1 What criticisms of the authorities have been made by development experts?
2 What effects did the oil boom have on Nigeria's economy?
3 Explain how the drop in oil revenues has made matters worse.
4 a What is meant by the phrase "resistance to modern methods"?
  b How has this resistance affected Nigeria?
5 Describe how the Agricultural Development Programme has helped improve matters.
6 If you were put in charge how would you help improve Nigeria's agricultural economy?

MANCHESTER TRACTORS

The firm has recently won an order for 100 tractors from Zambia. This will keep the firm's 250 workers employed for the rest of the year.

ZAMBIA IMPORTERS LTD

It imports a range of agricultural and industrial machinery. Employs 10 people.

MANCHESTER SUPERMARKET

Imports fresh fruit from all over the world. Employs 50 people. Supplies Manchester Tractors' works canteen.

ZAMBIAN FARMER

Employs 30 workers. Grows cash crops of sugar cane and maize, as well as pawpaws and mangoes for export.

1 Explain how the Zambian farmer relies for his or her livelihood on the other firms shown.
2 Imagine that a serious drought hits Zambia. Explain how this might affect Manchester Tractors.
3 The cost of growing fruit in Central Africa increases dramatically. Explain how this will affect:
   a the spending decisions of Manchester Supermarket;
   b the livelihood of the two Zambian based firms.
4 "When world trade increases, so too does world interdependence." Explain what is meant by this statement.

Coursework

Aim: To consider the needs of a Third World country.

You have been appointed to the staff of a well-known relief charity providing aid to countries in the Third World.

Collect information from relief charities so that you brief yourself on the nature of their problems.

The charity asks you as your first assignment to design an advertising campaign relating to the pressing needs of one of the countries in which they work.

Select a country to use for this campaign. Design a poster and leaflet and an advertising slogan in order to raise the public's awareness of the needs of the country in question.

Assume that the advertising campaign is a great success and brings in £56 million. Explain how you would advise the charity to allocate the money. In your report remember to refer to the alternatives that will have to be sacrificed (the opportunity costs).

42 Public Spending

In the private sector goods and services are allocated through the market place. If you can afford an item, you can become its owner. If you cannot afford an item, you cannot have it.

In the public sector goods are allocated on the basis of need. They can be allocated by central government or local government.

Allocation

Political decision-makers decide how to allocate spending in the public sector. Some items are distributed to individuals universally, for example medical care and education. Some items are distributed to the community as a whole, for example roads, the fire brigade and safety inspection. Other items are allocated on the basis of a person being entitled to receive help. This is done by testing their lack of "means" or ability to provide for themselves.

At regular intervals decisions are made about the amount and type of government expenditure there will be and from where the money for it will come.

Merit goods

Ben is not doing very well at school. He frequently loses books, arrives late and misplaces school equipment.

Is Ben right in what he says?

Education is an example of what economists call a *merit good*. This is an item provided by the state because its consumption is considered desirable, but if it were left to market forces many would not consume the item given at the price involved.

The government finances education for all who want it because it recognises the costs to the economy of a large number of illiterate, unskilled workers. It does not leave such items to be provided solely by the private sector as many citizens would not be able, or willing, to pay the price.

Decide for yourself

● Everyone benefits from children and young people being in schools and colleges. Can you think why?

Other examples of merit goods include libraries and health services. People are considered to need access to information in order to run their lives. Babies are provided with free inoculations against diseases, for example, irrespective of whether their parents can afford the course of injections. This is done to help prevent the spread of illnesses that could be dangerous to others in society, both adults and children.

The state also provides a range of goods that are of benefit to a range of people but are difficult to charge to any one person. These are called *public goods* which were defined in Unit 6.

The government, nationally or locally, has to make choices in the same way as ordinary citizens. If it decides to build a hospital, the opportunity cost might be that a new school cannot be built or an old one repaired. Governments try to consider both the costs and the benefits of a major spending decision before proceeding with it. They particularly bear in mind all the factors that could affect, or be affected by, the decision.

Test yourself

Consider what the external factors, both benefits and costs, might be, given the government's approval of a high-speed rail-link from London to Paris.

Why worry? No one has to pay for it – it's free.

Activity

A fire has broken out on the seventh floor of a block of flats and occupants of a flat on the eighth floor are trapped. Look closely at the picture.

1 **a** What groups can you identify who might be affected by the fire?

   b Using these headings construct a chart listing some of the costs of the fire to the groups you have identified.

Time costs	Money costs	Other costs

DO'S AND DON'TS ON FIRE SAFETY

Never leave a chip pan unattended

Don't rewire property if you're not trained.

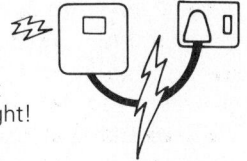

Smell gas? Don't switch on that light!

In bed

Guard open fires

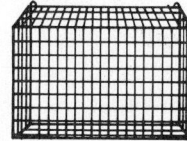

Foam filled furniture can kill in seconds.

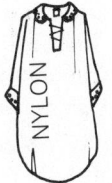

NYLON

2 Now make a list of:

   a the private costs; and

   b the social costs;

   that might arise from a fire.

3 Using the Fire Safety picture:

   a make a list of some of the possible causes of the fire;

   b explain how the actions of individuals not directly responsible for the fire may have hampered the possibility of rescuing the occupants of the flats.

4 The occupant of a ground-floor flat tells the local press that he thought the Fire Brigade arrived too late. He feels that the Brigade should be privatised, with everyone paying for the service through fire insurance policies.

   Why might his next door neighbour not bother to have his flat insured if such a scheme was introduced and she knew that her neighbour was heavily insured?

5 What new spending costs could the local authority find itself facing if a block of flats was destroyed?

Extension 1

Is it possible to eliminate all public spending by privatising all services?

Crowding out or crowding in?

Until recently the size of the public sector grew each year. The Conservative governments of the 1980s made efforts to reduce the role of the state and the amount of public spending. They did this because they believed in two central ideas.

First, if the state is expanding its activities, then, to finance its plans, it has to borrow money. This it does through the London money market. If it borrows money either at a central or a local level, it is competing with other potential borrowers. The government can print money (or increase the *money supply*), and thus it can always pay the interest rates charged and therefore obtain any funds it needs. In effect, the government increases the demand for limited funds and this pushes up the price of borrowing money (or the rate of interest). This means that private sector firms cannot afford the new prices for borrowing money and are priced out of the market by the demand created by government activity: the *crowding out* effect. It is argued that this is bad for private investment which is seen as creating most of the new wealth in the economy.

Secondly, ordinary individuals should have more control over their own spending. This can be achieved by reducing income tax in particular, and leaving individuals with more of their own money to spend in their own way.

The argument states that if workers know they are going to be taxed less, there is a greater incentive to produce more because they will be keeping more of the money they earn.

This will, of course, only work if all forms of government taxation are reduced. If income tax falls but other taxes and contributions increase the burden the government places on the public could be higher.

Advantages from government spending

Spending is needed because:

- The environment and infrastructure of the economy have to be protected. Regular repairs of public buildings prevent very costly repairs caused by neglect at a later date.
- Cutting government spending can lead to more state benefits having to be provided if workers are laid off; at the same time tax receipts fall. This could result in public expenditure rising merely to finance dole queues.
- The government can stimulate the economy and create jobs using public spending programmes.

This is important if spending in the economy's private sector is depressed and needs to be stimulated. The government can play a valuable role in "priming the pump" of the economy. This is often known as the *crowding in* argument.

Test yourself

1 List three public goods or services and three merit goods or services that either central or local government provide.
2 Look at one area of your school. Consider a list of improvements that can be made. Write a letter to the chair of the local education committee requesting these improvements. Explain how the local economy will benefit.
3 What is meant by the "crowding out" effect?

DATA RESPONSE

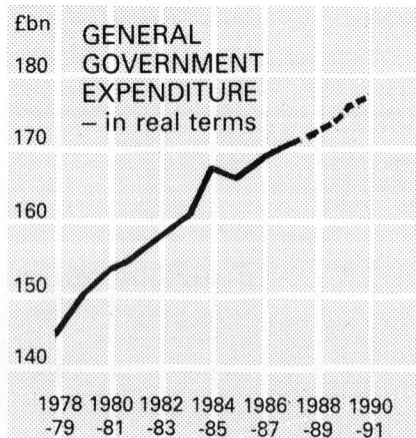

£bn
GENERAL GOVERNMENT EXPENDITURE – in real terms

180
170
160
150
140

1978 1980 1982 1984 1986 1988 1990
-79 -81 -83 -85 -87 -89 -91

Excluding privatisation proceeds
Cash figures adjusted to 86/87 levels by GDP deflator

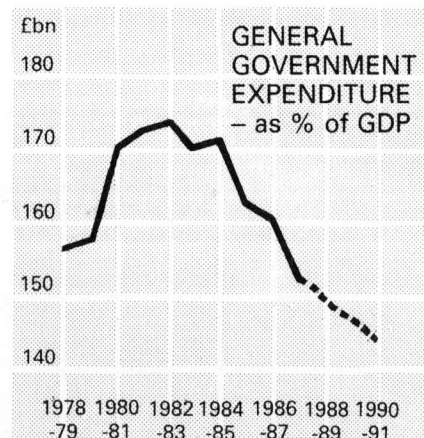

£bn
GENERAL GOVERNMENT EXPENDITURE – as % of GDP

180
170
160
150
140

1978 1980 1982 1984 1986 1988 1990
-79 -81 -83 -85 -87 -89 -91

Excluding privatisation proceeds

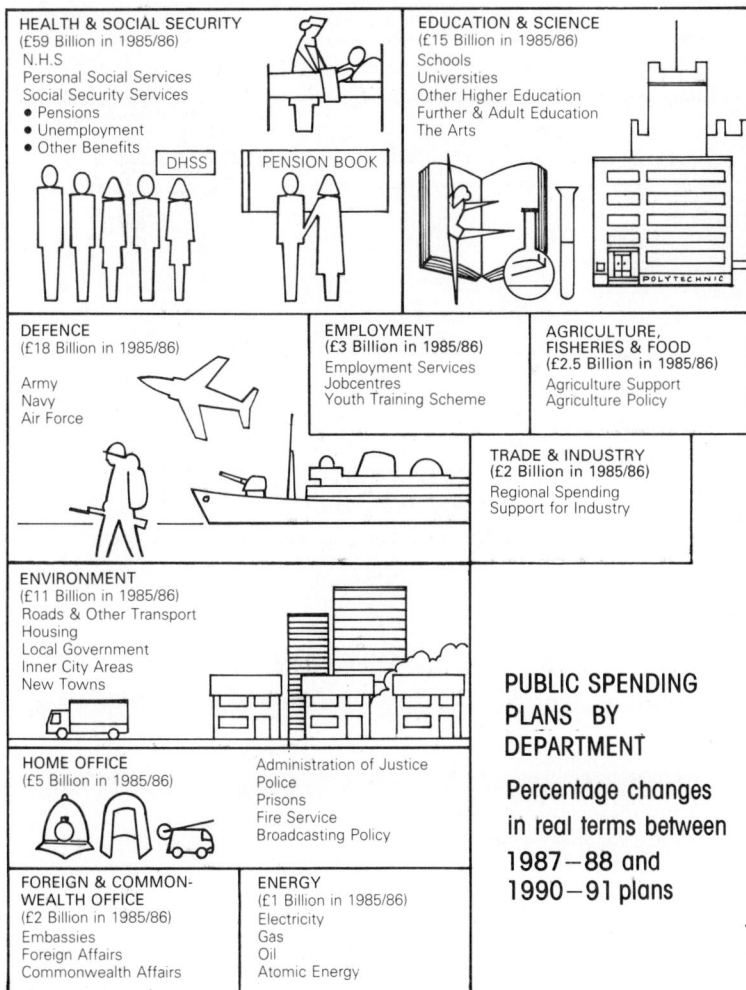

HEALTH & SOCIAL SECURITY
(£59 Billion in 1985/86)
N.H.S
Personal Social Services
Social Security Services
● Pensions
● Unemployment
● Other Benefits

DHSS
PENSION BOOK

EDUCATION & SCIENCE
(£15 Billion in 1985/86)
Schools
Universities
Other Higher Education
Further & Adult Education
The Arts

POLYTECHNIC

DEFENCE
(£18 Billion in 1985/86)
Army
Navy
Air Force

EMPLOYMENT
(£3 Billion in 1985/86)
Employment Services
Jobcentres
Youth Training Scheme

AGRICULTURE, FISHERIES & FOOD
(£2.5 Billion in 1985/86)
Agriculture Support
Agriculture Policy

TRADE & INDUSTRY
(£2 Billion in 1985/86)
Regional Spending
Support for Industry

ENVIRONMENT
(£11 Billion in 1985/86)
Roads & Other Transport
Housing
Local Government
Inner City Areas
New Towns

HOME OFFICE
(£5 Billion in 1985/86)
Administration of Justice
Police
Prisons
Fire Service
Broadcasting Policy

FOREIGN & COMMONWEALTH OFFICE
(£2 Billion in 1985/86)
Embassies
Foreign Affairs
Commonwealth Affairs

ENERGY
(£1 Billion in 1985/86)
Electricity
Gas
Oil
Atomic Energy

Source: Stock Exchange *Spectrum*, September 1986

PUBLIC SPENDING PLANS BY DEPARTMENT

Percentage changes in real terms between 1987−88 and 1990−91 plans

£bn
0 10 20 30 40 50

The width of each bar represents each department's spending in 1987−88

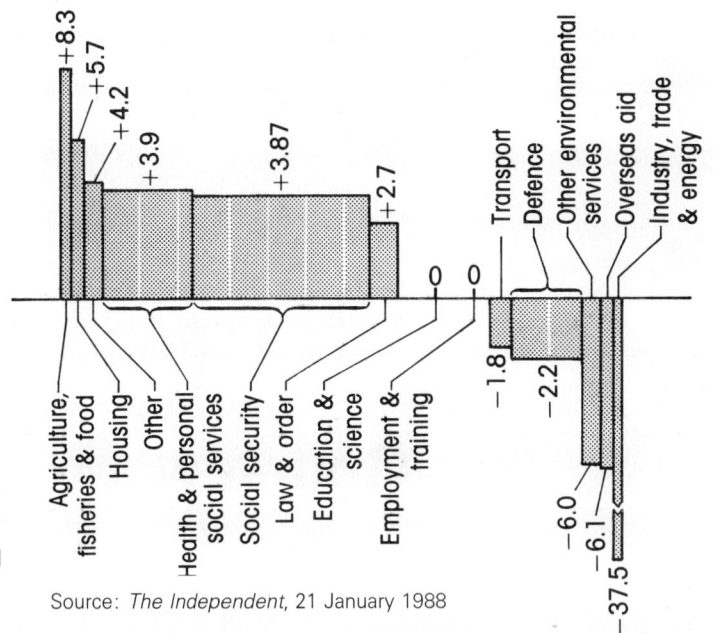

+8.3 Agriculture, fisheries & food
+5.7 Housing
+4.2 Other
+3.9 Health & personal social services
+3.87 Social security
Law & order
+2.7 Education & science
0 Employment & training
0
−1.8 Transport
−2.2 Defence
−6.0 Other environmental services
−6.1 Overseas aid
−37.5 Industry, trade & energy

Source: *The Independent*, 21 January 1988

1 a Which area of central government spending was largest in 1985/86?
  b Which area of public spending was the smallest?

2 What might be the cost in the future of spending so little on research into alternative sources of power?

3 a Which departments are planning to increase their spending between 1987 and 1991?
  b Explain why they need to do so.

5 Using the information provided, construct a pie chart to illustrate the different types of government spending.

6 Explain why in real terms government spending is rising but as a percentage of the country's GDP it is falling.

Extension 2

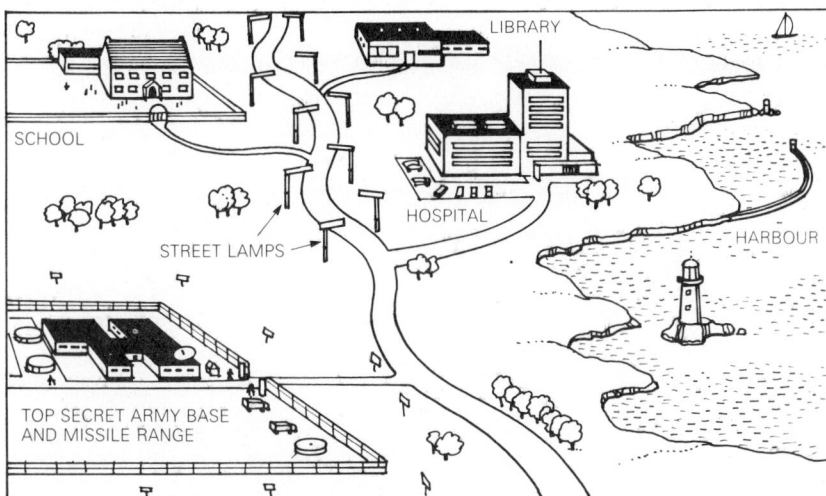

SCHOOL
LIBRARY
STREET LAMPS
HOSPITAL
HARBOUR
TOP SECRET ARMY BASE AND MISSILE RANGE

1 Locate and identify eight items on the map that are frequently provided by central government or other public bodies.

2 Sort the eight items into two columns. Those that are:
  a public goods;
  b merit goods.

3 What would happen to the level of consumption of books if the local council was forced to close the local library? Give reasons for your answer.

4 Why would it be difficult for a private body to provide street lamps and still make a profit?

5 Using the examples listed in **2a** explain what public goods have in common.

Extension 3

Let us look at four committees of a local council. They have been told that central government wishes to see a reduction in spending by the council of at least £5 million. Each committee has been asked to put forward ways in which they could limit their spending in order to save this sum. Their decisions are given here.

RECREATION
Can save by cutting all lawns in parks only twice instead of seven times a year. It can increase charges in libraries, swimming pools and car parks by 50%.

EDUCATION
Can save by halting the removal of asbestos from all educational premises and by doubling the cost of school dinners.

SOCIAL SERVICES
Could save by limiting the Meals on Wheels service to over-80s only. All home help would have to be cut.

HOUSING
Can save by building no new council houses this year. Repairs to all council properties would be cut by 50%.

Divide yourselves into four groups. Each group becomes members of one committee.

1 Working with your other committee members, write a speech to plead why your area of spending is too important to be cut.
   a Explain how the spending cut would damage both the consumers and producers of the service you provide.
   b Choose another committee and explain why it should bear the burden of any proposed cut in spending.
2 When you have prepared your arguments, meet as a full council. A spokesperson for each committee should present points a and b in a speech.
3 When you have heard each person's speech, vote as to which committee should bear the full cost of the spending cuts.
4 Briefly record the decision of the full council, giving reasons why they reached their final decision.

Coursework

Aim: To investigate the costs of merit goods.

1 Identify as best as you can the benefits and costs of educating a child at a state school. Include real costs and benefits and not just money costs and benefits. Your account should refer to the opportunity cost of educating a child, and the social benefits schooling can bring, to name just two.
2 Imagine that you have read a recent government proposal arguing that parents should be made to pay the true cost of educating their child at school – a system of loans would be available for those in real need. Use the information you have collected to write a letter to the Minister for Education either supporting the proposal or attacking it.
3 How has your coursework helped you to understand what economists mean by merit goods?

43 Taxation

Taxation represents a compulsory contribution from a citizen's income made to the government. People who try to evade this obligation can end up by being prosecuted.

where's all my money gone?

I have to take off these deductions. Some of them are voluntary, like Trade Union subscription. Others are compulsory. There's Income Tax, National Insurance contributions. They're paid to the government.

BOSS

GROSS PAY

£400

NET PAY (AFTER TAX)

£300

You don't have to tell the government about me, do you?

Decide for yourself
- What do you think the boss will answer? Why?

The Chancellor and the Budget
Each year the government decides how much will be raised in *revenue* (money coming in to the government) to pay for the *expenditure* (spending) it undertakes. The expenditure will include such items as the army, social security, law and order, grants to local authorities.

The government's financial plans are announced by the Chancellor of the Exchequer in the Budget Speech to Parliament usually in March or April. If the government runs a *budget surplus* then it takes more money out of the economy than it puts back through spending. On the other hand, if the government runs a *budget deficit*, then it puts more money into the economy than it takes out in taxes. If the government decides to run a budget deficit, it has to borrow the extra money to finance its spending. If the revenue raised is designed to match exactly the level of government spending, this is called a *balanced budget*.

The total amount that central and local government and the nationalised industries borrow is referred to as the *Public Sector Borrowing Requirement* or *PSBR*.

More recently the government has been using surpluses of the income over expenditure to repay past loans. They thus reduce the size of the country's National Debt. This process has been called *Public Sector Debt Repayment* or *PSDR*.

Activity

INCOME TAX AFTER THE BUDGET

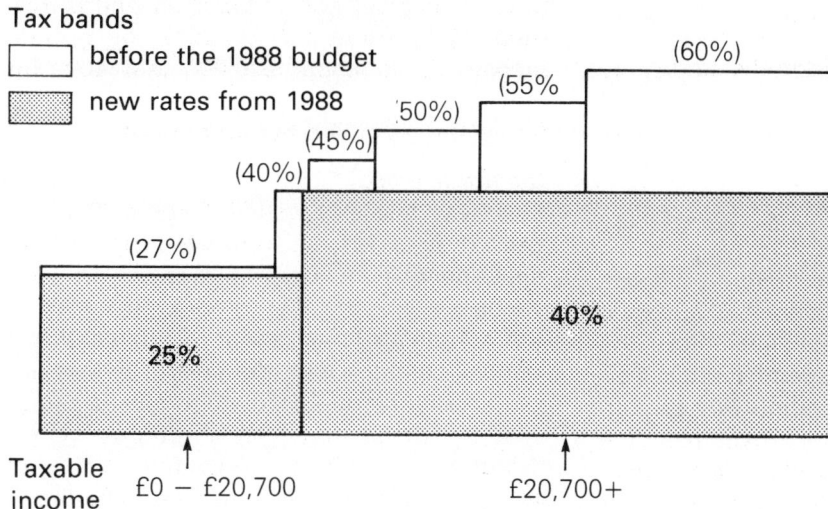

Tax bands
- before the 1988 budget
- new rates from 1988

(27%) (40%) (45%) (50%) (55%) (60%)

25%

40%

Taxable income   £0 − £20,700   £20,700+

Source: *The Independent*, 16 March 1988

PERSONAL TAX ALLOWANCES

	1990-91 £	1989-90 £
Basic rate income tax	25%	25%
Higher rate income tax	40%	40%
Basic rate limit	20,700	20,700
Single person's allowance	3,005	2,785
Married man's allowance	–	4,375
Married couple's allowance	1,720	–
Additional relief for children	1,720	1,590
Age allowances (age 65-74)		
Single	3,670	3,400
Married	5,815	5,385
Age allowances (75+)		
Single	3,820	3,540
Married	6,005	5,565
Age allowance withdrawn by £1 for every £2 of income over	12,300	11,400
Mortgage interest rate (approx)	15%	14%
Top national insurance rate	9%	9%
up to a minimum income per week	350	325
Initial band of national insurance at 2% up to weekly earnings of	46	43
Child benefit (2 children)	754	754

Source: *The Times*, 21 March 1990

1 List two ways in which a government can raise income.

2 Assume you are a single person, and entitled to the single person's allowance. In 1988/9 you earned £10,605 before tax. Calculate how much of your income was taken in tax.

3 If someone smokes 100 cigarettes a week, how much more would they have had to pay after the 1988 budget?

4 If your taxable income was more than £19,300 at what rate would your income above this level be taxed?

5 Mamoud Taheri drives a car which uses leaded petrol. He uses 2 gallons a week.
   a How will the budget affect him?
   b If his car used unleaded petrol what would the affects be then?
   c Should he consider changing or converting his car?

6 Here is information about two families. Identify which family will suffer the most from the budget changes. Explain your answer.

Excise duties before and after 1990 budget			
	Pre-budget excise duty	Price change	Excise duty after Budget
20 cigarettes	98.1p	10p	108.1
Pint of beer	18.9p	2p	20.9
70cl table wine	76.8p	7p	83.8
Bottle of whisky	£4.73	54p	£5.27
Litre of petrol	20.44p	2.04p	22.48p
Litre of unleaded petrol	17.72p	1.77p	19.49

The Hamiltons Ken, aged 40, engineer. Smokes 10 cigarettes a day and drinks 4 pints of beer a week.
June likes a bottle of wine with the Sunday meal.
June drives a car and uses 10 gallons of petrol a week.
Ken also has a car and drives about twice as far as June.

The Cheungs Anita is a sales executive. Trevor looks after Thomas. They are both non-smokers.
Trevor likes whisky and Anita is fond of vodka.
They are very concerned about the environment and last year had their car converted to run on unleaded petrol.
Anita's salary has just been increased to £19,500.

Forms of taxation

There are a number of forms of taxation, some based on an individual's ability to pay, some based on what they spend, and some based on neither.

Direct taxation

Income tax

A major way in which the government can raise the money it needs is to take it directly from a person's income before the person has a chance to spend it. It is collected through a system called *Pay-as-you-Earn* (or *PAYE*) which is an example of a method of tax collection called *direct taxation*. Income tax is deducted according to a person's income. Each person is allowed certain tax free allowances. Any income, either earned or unearned, above this allowance limit (or *threshold*) is termed taxable pay, or income, and is taxed at one of two rates. At present this is 25% for taxable income up to about £20,000 and 40% for that part of taxable income above this figure (the so called marginal rate).

Inheritance tax

This was formerly called Capital Transfer Tax. It is a tax on gifts you transfer to someone else in your lifetime or on your death.

Amounts up to about £120,000 (this amount changes with the cost of living) are not taxed. If you leave a greater amount, then it will be taxed on a progressive (or rising) scale. The percentage of tax involved rises from 30% to 60%. The tax is designed to reduce the inequality that exists in the distribution of wealth. There are, however, a number of exemptions granted, like wedding gifts.

Capital Gains Tax

This is a tax on income when you have profited (gained) from selling certain assets. These might be property, such as a second home or company shares.

Corporation Tax

This is a direct tax levied not on the income of individuals but instead on the income of a company. The current rate of tax is 35% of the profits of a company.

Indirect taxation

These are taxes that are taken from you indirectly when you spend.

Customs

If you go abroad and spend more than a certain amount on goods you bring back into Britain, you have to pay customs duty on them. This duty (or tax) is collected for the government by HM Customs and Excise.

Excise Duties

These are not taxes on goods entering the country but on certain goods currently on sale in Britain. The major examples are wines and spirits, petrol, cigarettes and tobacco.

Value Added Tax (VAT)

When you purchase goods as a consumer you have to pay a tax on most items at a rate of 15%. Certain items (for example, food, newspapers, books and children's clothes and shoes) are *zero rated* so no tax is paid on them.

Producers also pay the tax on goods they purchase but can claim back any money paid. The burden (weight) of the tax thus falls on consumers.

Local taxes

Rates are a local tax paid by homeowners to local councils to finance local services (like pavements, roads, schools). Rates are being replaced by a tax called the Community Charge, better known as the Poll Tax.

The leaflet describes the Poll Tax.

Poll tax. Each and every adult pays, irrespective of size of property.

Rates. The occupant of house A pays the same as the owner of house B. Each house is similar and therefore of similar rateable value.

From *In Touch*, the newsletter of Gravesham Conservative Party

THE POLL TAX AND YOU

WE HAVE grumbled for years about the unfair rates system. Now it is to be replaced by the COMMUNITY CHARGE.

Local Government will in the future be financed half by government taxation, a quarter by business rates, and a quarter by PEOPLE through Community Charge.

The Facts:
* Every adult will be liable to pay Community Charge.
* Exemptions will apply to elderly people in homes and hospitals, the severely mentally handicapped, those still at school, those in prison, and visiting servicemen.
* The least well-off will only pay 20% with a tapering scale of rebates for others on low incomes.
* Full-time students will only pay 20%.
* Everyone will pay something and will have a vested interest in their council's spending.

What will it cost? The Community Charge last year would have been £180 per adult in Gravesham.

The purpose of taxes

Taxes are levied by government for many reasons:

- **To finance spending by government**: government uses taxes to finance their own activities, for example, building motorways, frigates and submarines, paying civil servants, and maintaining the National Health Service.
- **To redistribute income**: a system of taxation can be used to redistribute income by taking money from one group of income earners and giving it to another group.

Taxes can be either *progressive* or *regressive*. A progressive tax is one where the taxation rate increases as income levels rise (like income tax). The burden of tax falls on the rich. With a regressive tax (like VAT) the burden falls hardest on the poor as they consume

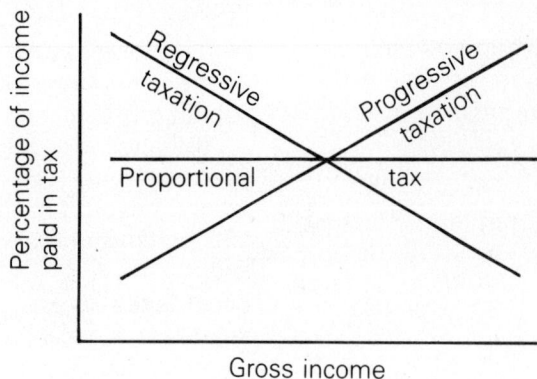

Gross income

Sometimes the real incidence falls partly on the producer or shopkeeper (this is the *producer's burden*) and partly on the consumer (the *consumer's burden*).

Decide for yourself
If the demand for the product is inelastic, then the shopkeeper may be able to pass the whole of this burden over to the consumer.

- Can you think of inelastic goods where this applies?

more of their income. Therefore the amount of tax paid increases proportionately on the low paid. The Community Charge is also a regressive tax in that poorer people pay a larger proportion of their income when everyone pays the same charge.

- **To control the economy**: the level of taxation can be used to shape the level of spending. High taxation can increase unemployment but lower inflation; low levels of taxation can reduce unemployment but the extra spending power available to the consumer might boost the inflation rate.

- **Influence spending**: governments like to promote certain spending (public goods and merit goods like education). Such goods might be subsidised (provided at a price below the real cost). Subsidies are provided for public transport, for example, partly to prevent congestion caused by motor cars. Alternatively governments can penalise spending on economic "bads" because of their cost to the community. (Economic bads include such goods as cigarettes, alcohol, and items that cause pollution, like petrol with a high lead content.)

Incidence of tax
The *formal* incidence of tax is the burden that falls on the person who initially pays the tax. The *real* incidence is the burden that falls on the person who eventually pays the tax.

The shopkeeper has all the worry and inconvenience of collecting a tax like VAT and making sure the government receives the money. This burden is the formal incidence.

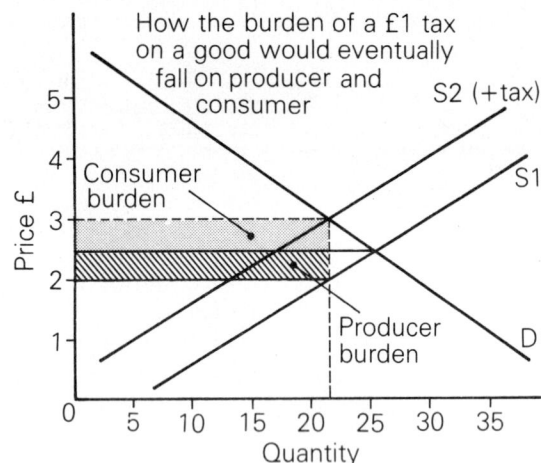

How the burden of a £1 tax on a good would eventually fall on producer and consumer

ECONOMIC TERMS

Taxation: a compulsory contribution by citizens to government. It can be *direct* (from income) or *indirect* (from goods and services purchased).
Threshold: the level at which income begins to be taxed.
Incidence of taxation: a measure of the burden of a tax as it affects the person who pays the tax to government (formal) or the person it eventually affects (real).

Test yourself
1 What is:
   a tax;
   b the Budget?
2 What is the difference between a budget surplus and a budget deficit?
3 What is direct taxation? Give one example of a direct tax.
4 An economy taxes its citizens at two rates: 20% of taxable income for low

earners and 30% of income earned above a certain level for high earners. What is the marginal rate of tax?

5 How does an indirect tax affect you?

6 What is the difference between Inheritance Tax and Capital Gains Tax?

7 You have just purchased a newspaper and a pair of children's shoes. Will you have paid VAT? Give reasons for your answer.

8 Explain briefly why we have to pay taxes.

9 What is the difference between a progressive tax and a regressive tax?

10 What is meant by the real incidence of a tax?

11 What is a subsidy?

DATA RESPONSE 1

Lower rate of duty to be applied to 'coolers'

Distillers expect boost for sales

ALCOHOL

By Rosemary Unsworth and Jill Sherman

The Chancellor's decision to increase excise duties, including Value Added Tax by 4p for table wine, 6p for fortified wine and 1p on a pint of beer or cider was expected and in line with the rate of inflation.

His deviation from a totally neutral Budget was his decision to leave unchanged duty on spirits, delighting the Scotch Whisky Association. It said the move should give sales a much-needed boost.

A lower rate of duty will be applied to "coolers", the alcoholic mixture of wine, fruit juice and soda that originated in California and was introduced to this country about five years ago, to encourage young people to imbibe weaker drinks.

With an alcohol strength of about 4 to 5 per cent – the same as strong beer – coolers are less than half the strength of table wine. Fears that Britain's youth is turning to strong drink are part of the Chancellor's thinking.

Manufacturers welcomed the change, which will also apply to lower strength beers, due to take place on October 1 as it will enable them to make the product under bond and pay the lower duty after that.

The Wine and Spirit Association said yesterday that it did not believe the lowering of the rate of duty would reduce the retail price of coolers.

The decision to increase the excise duty by 1p on a pint of beer or cider as forecast was regarded as "not too bad" by the Brewers' Society.

"It is the first beer tax increase for three years but is the seventh increase in 10 years. Total tax on a typical pint will now be about 29p to 30p. Duty accounts for 19p and VAT 10.5p. In 1979 it was 9.5p."

A neutral Budget would have meant a 20p increase in duty on spirits but the Chancellor left them unchanged.

The Scotch Whisky Association said: "It will further narrow the differential between duties levied on spirits and those on wine and beer.

"This is in line with the representations we made to the Chancellor and is a positive step along the way towards a system of taxing all alcoholic drinks according to their alcohol content – the only fair and logical way in which to treat them."

However, the voluntary organization Action against Alcohol Abuse said: "We are very disappointed that the Chancellor has done nothing for the nation's health with these proposals on alcohol duty".

The association was sceptical about Mr Lawson's gesture of reduced taxes for low-alcohol drinks and said that the Government should have levied much steeper taxes on potent ciders and lagers.

Cereal bar manufacturers were surprised by Mr Lawson's decision to apply VAT to their products. These had previously escaped the tax by being classed as food.

The 3p to 4p increase in duty on a packet of 20 cigarettes and the 2p rise in the price of five small cigars, effective from midnight on Thursday, was in line with economic forecasts but brought a stinging reaction from the anti-smoking lobby, including Action on Smoking and Health. "Consumption will not fall and our epidemic of smoking diseases will be perpetuated", it said.

The Pharmaceutical Society of Great Britain, the professional governing body for all 37,000 pharmacists in the country, said it was "disappointed" that the Chancellor had not imposed higher increases on tobacco duty to discourage cigarette smoking.

The Tobacco Advisory Council said: "A rise on cigarettes only to compensate for inflation seems level-headed and reflects sensible moderation."

Source: *The Times*, 16 March 1988

1 Why was the Scotch Whisky Association pleased with the budget in 1988? Why were beer and wine drinkers not so pleased?

2 a What is a 'cooler'?
  b Why was a lower rate of duty placed on 'coolers'?

3 What changes had occurred to taxes on beer between 1979 and 1988?

4 Why was the organisation Action against Alcohol Abuse unhappy with the Chancellor's budget?

5 What item previously escaped tax by being zero rated for VAT purposes?

6 What differences of opinion does the article reveal on the issue of taxing cigarette and cigar smoking?

7 The British Medical Association described this budget as "a bad day for health". Explain why doctors might take this view.

DATA RESPONSE 2

Price at the pumps to rise 5p

By David Young
Energy Correspondent

PETROL

The rise in duty on petrol prices at a rate higher than inflation means Britain's motorists are still paying less for petrol than drivers on the Continent and considerably less than they were three years ago when Mr Lawson's Budget increase took the pump price to more than £2 a gallon for the first time.

Since then fierce competition on the forecourts and the fall in the world oil price to less than half its 1985 level – North Sea crude is now changing hands at about $15 a barrel – have kept prices hovering about 164p a gallon. The lowest price yesterday was 145.5p a gallon in the Manchester area and prices of about 150p were widespread.

The increase in duty will add between 5p and 6p to a gallon. It will mean that most motorists will still be paying less than 170p for a gallon of four star petrol. But the leading oil companies still believe pump prices are not providing an adequate return on refining costs and would like to increase prices further, but they admit that competitive pressure will continue to keep down the price.

The decision not to increase duty on low-lead petrol widens the differential between the two grades of petrol first introduced last year. The oil companies and their trade body, the Petroleum Industry Association, have argued that the tax gap should be widened even further if motorists are to be persuaded to use low-lead petrol. They reacted favourably to the Budget move.

At present only 700 filling stations out of the 20,600 countrywide sell low-lead petrol and the rate of expansion is being limited by low demand. The oil companies estimate that only one in every 2,000 motorists is buying low-lead petrol, although about 25 per cent of cars on the roads could be modified to use it.

The industry has asked that any duty increase on low-lead petrol should be delayed for three months after the Budget so that the differential between the two fuels could be further emphasized but the Chancellor's decision has met their expectations.

The differential in duty means unleaded petrol will be about 5p a gallon cheaper than normal four star, where previously the price differential was limited to 0.5p because it cost about 5p a gallon more to produce low-lead petrol.

The oil companies argued that Britain should follow the lead shown on the Continent where taxation has been cut on low-lead petrol to encourage its use. In Denmark the differential is 18p, in Luxembourg 15p, in Switzerland 11p and in West Germany 5p.

● The road haulage industry estimated that the increase in duty of about 5p on a gallon of derv would add about £55 million to industry's costs

(Rodney Cowton writes).

The Freight Transport Association and the Road Haulage Association expressed disappointment at this increase and at the rise in the rate of vehicle excise duty on the heaviest rigid commercial vehicles.

The FTA said the Chancellor's move would raise the price of derv at filling stations from about £1.50 a gallon to about £1.55, and that the increase on the duty was about 2 per cent above the rate of inflation.

The RHA said the increase in duty on derv would add just under 1.5 per cent to average operating costs, while increases in vehicle excise duty for rigid vehicles could amount to an increase of more than 10 per cent for four-axle vehicles of 29 to 30.5 tonnes.

The Chancellor said the aim was to bring treatment of rigid vehicles into line with that of articulated lorries, but the FTA complained that he was "clobbering the work-horses".

● The RAC last night warned motorists not to be tempted to fill up with cheaper, unleaded fuel unless they were certain their cars could take it.

Mr John Wood, the RAC's chief engineer, said a car's engine could be seriously damaged if the unsuitable fuel was used.

"The use of unleaded fuel in engines not designed or adapted for it can result in 'pinking', leading to serious damage to pistons, valves and valve seats because the lead in fuel has a secondary role as a lubricant," Mr Wood said.

Source: *The Times*, 16 March 1988

1 How much did the increase on duty add to the price of a gallon of petrol?

2 Why, despite this, are Britain's motorists paying less for petrol than they were three years previously?

3 Explain why it was in the motorists' interest to consider purchasing low-lead/unleaded petrol.

4 Why would industry's costs rise because of this budget?

5 a Why did the budget lead to the oil companies arguing for an increase in petrol prices?

   b What prevented them from increasing prices?

Coursework

Aim: To consider how tax can influence spending.

Imagine that you have recently been appointed to head the Government's Advisory Committee on Health Matters.

The committee has recently been considering the arguments that lead in petrol is damaging the nation's children and their future. Collect and present information on this issue.

The Government asks you to consider ways in which the system of taxation could be used to increase the consumption of lead-free petrol by consumers and reduce the use of lead-based petrols. In your answer refer to:
   a grants;
   b subsidies;
   c direct taxation;
   d indirect taxation.
Consider the wider costs to the government and economy of eliminating all lead in petrol.

44 Economic Growth and National Income

I reckon if I work hard enough I can afford to pay someone to decorate the house. It's a job I hate.

When economists talk about an economy growing, or about economic growth, they are referring to the increase in that economy's productive capacity. This means the country's ability to produce the goods and services that its citizens demand. This is measured over a period, usually a year.

In economics we have learnt about choices. If our economy spends all its money on consumer goods this year, it will not have enough resources to replace the capital goods that will produce the consumer goods of the future. If, on the other hand, the country invests in re-equipping all its factories, not enough consumer goods will be produced in the short run. Then consumers will have to look elsewhere to satisfy their wants. This could lead to a rise in imports of consumer goods. There is a trade off between these two aims: providing consumer goods now, or in the future.

This year I want to go on holiday to Spain.

Why economic growth has advantages

Most people like the idea that their economy is growing. If the economy is producing more goods everyone should be able to benefit and living standards should rise. The improvement in your living standard need not just be in terms of money. If you can earn enough in four days instead of five to meet your needs, you could take more time off and work a four day week. Alternatively you might take longer holidays. You might, on the other hand, decide to use your increased resources to improve the quality of your life in other ways.

I'd like to buy a new car.

I'm not just going to have a new car: I'm going to have a customized one.

When more is produced the living standards of the poorest can rise, too.

My pension has gone up this year. I'll buy a new coat.

Decide for yourself

Economic growth can bring costs as well as benefits. Here are some questions that illustrate this fact.

- Would you be happy to have five more burgers a week if it meant that beef production was boosted by factory farming methods or by cutting down more of the Amazon jungle for pasture land?
- Would you be happy to have five more burgers a week if it meant that the high street was even more littered with plastic cartons whose production helps destroy the ozone layer?
- Would you leave the lights on so often if you realised that pollution from power stations has produced clouds of acid rain that are poisoning many of the lakes and rivers of Europe?
- Would you leave the lights on so often if you realised that electricity produced by nuclear power stations has been linked by some people to a rising incidence of cancer in children?

I'm not just going to have the house redecorated; I'm going to have it insulated to save on the heating bills.

Economic growth and conflict

A new factory or industrial estate is planned for the edge of Melchester. It is very good news for locally unemployed people, but residents nearby are up in arms.

> There'll be more lorries on local roads.

> There's bound to be more pollution.

> They'll cut down part of the woods. Another beauty spot destroyed in the name of progress.

> Whose progress? That's what I'd like to know.

The new railway link from London to the Channel Tunnel would bring jobs to parts of Kent, but this is how the proposals were greeted.

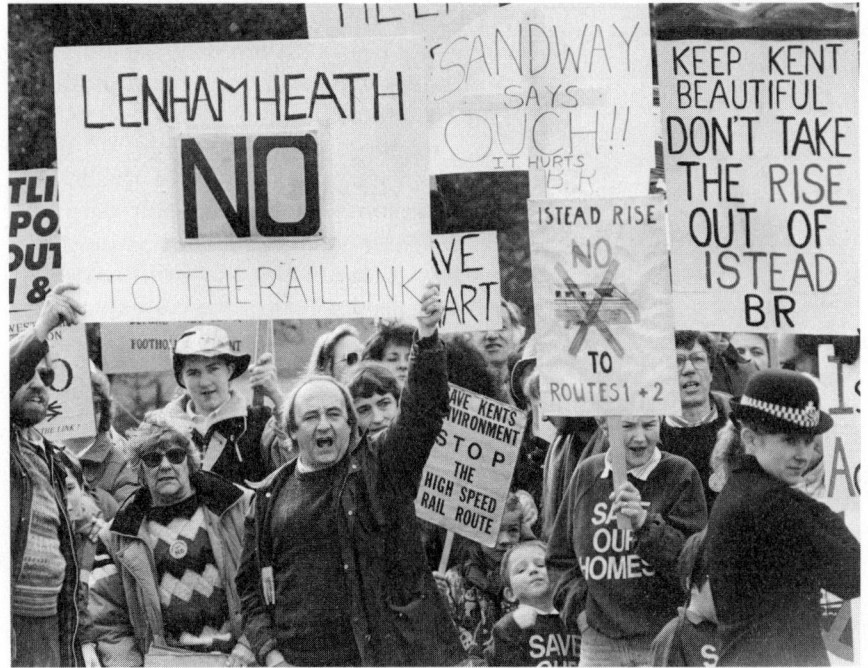

Activity

Pollution of land and sea	Noise

Pollution of land and sea

Noise

Waste of resources

Acid rain

Increased opportunity to travel

Lead poisoning

Increased leisure time

Advances in medical science reduce death rate

Shorter working hours

Greater educational opportunities

Consumer goods for all

An easier life due to inventions such as the car, electricity

'Economic growth does not bring happiness.'

Greater social upheaval

Improved living standards

'We don't care for other people. We just want to make money.'

1 Economic growth is said to bring both economic costs and benefits to an economy. Briefly explain what you understand by the phrase "economic costs and benefits".

2 Working as a group look at these examples of the consequences of economic growth for those living in an economy. Sort the examples into two columns: in the first column put the possible costs of economic growth; in the second put the possible benefits of economic growth.

3 Using your group's knowledge of the British economy, write a brief description of how economic growth has brought benefits to:
a consumers;
b producers;
c government.

4 Now repeat the same exercise but this time consider the costs of growth for:
a consumers;
b producers;
c government.

5 In what ways do people in the UK today have a better standard of living than people had in the past?

6 What possible costs might future generations have to pay given the problems economic growth can bring?

Growth and the national income

Growth can bring positive side effects or negative ones. These are the externalities or wider costs and benefits of an economic proposal. In measuring economic growth itself, economists use changes in the level of national income as an indicator of progress. The *national income* can be measured in terms of the amount of goods and services produced in an economy over a given period of time.

When measuring the national income economists try to arrive at a total figure. They measure it by:

Totalling up all incomes
or
Totalling up all the output
these incomes have created
or
Totalling up all expenditure
(and savings) people
could engage in to purchase
the output.

The total figure reached by one of these methods is called the *Gross Domestic Product* or *GDP*; another is the *GNP* or *Gross National Product*.

ECONOMIC TERMS

Gross Domestic Product: the total product or value of all goods and services produced within an economy in a given time.
Gross National Product: this is the GDP figure but also includes investments earned from abroad (for example, from a British firm in Zambia) less any investments earning money for foreign citizens in the UK (for example, from a Japanese electrical firm in Scotland).

Britain and economic growth

Some people argue that Britain's economy has not grown fast enough. In 1950 Britain was one of the richest countries in Europe, now it is amongst the poorest.

Decide for yourself

- Is it important to have the material possessions that other countries can afford?
- If the price for this was increased pollution, longer hours of work, greater stress, and more families breaking up would this be a price worth paying?

Those who are critical of Britain's relative rate of growth try and find explanations. A day in the life of a firm will illustrate this.

The Sonic Co.: makers of transistor radios

The owner, Mr Hall, is not happy with the level of profits. "The workers aren't working hard enough for the money I give them. I can't see the point in investing in more machines if I can't make a profit out of my investment."

A worker is unhappy when she hears this. "Old Hall is a skinflint. Our wages are far too low. If he increased our wages I could afford to buy one of the radios I make. Others would as well. Orders would roll in and we'd all be better off."

Whenever the managers and unions in the firm meet they blame each other. The production manager says the unions are always stopping production and this holds up orders. The union blames the management, saying they don't know how to care for their workers.

Meanwhile one of the workers has asked Hall for a pay rise: "It's inflation. That's the problem," he says. "I can't afford to buy the basics I need any more."

"But if I give you a rise," growls Hall, "I'll price my product out of the market. Then where will we all be?"

Who is wrong? Who is right?

If the government cannot be certain of the causes of Britain's poor economic growth, it makes it harder to apply the right policies to cure the problem of low economic growth (we'll see this later in Unit 47).

ECONOMIC TERMS

Economic growth: the change in productive potential or capacity of a country as measured over a period of time usually by changes in GDP or GNP.
National income: the value of goods and services earned or produced in an economy over a given period of time.

Test yourself

1 What is meant by economic growth? How is it measured?
2 Give one advantage of an economy increasing economic output.
3 Give one disadvantage of an economy increasing economic output.

4 Why might GNP give a better measure of economic growth than GDP?

5 Why do you think the British economy has not grown as fast as the economies of other European countries?

The trade cycle

Economic growth when achieved by an economy is not often balanced. There are periods of excessive growth (overheating of the economy with rising prices and labour and product shortages) followed by periods when there is a slump in economic activity (with workers laid off as goods and services are stockpiled because they cannot be sold and prices falling until demand improves).

These booms and slumps occur as an economy grows as shown on page 276. The government tries to manage growth so progress is steady. They do this because fluctuations can destroy business confidence.

DATA RESPONSE

UK economy continues to expand

By Steve Levinson
Economics Correspondent

THE British economy continued to grow steadily in the second quarter of this year, showing a rise in output of 0.9 per cent, according to preliminary estimates published by the Central Statistical Office yesterday.

The growth represented the seventh successive quarter of rising output, but the pace of expansion was slightly lower than in the first quarter, and should help ease fears that the economy is overheating. In the year to the second quarter the rise in gross domestic product based on measuring industrial output was 4 per cent, slightly lower than the 4.2 per cent recorded in the year to the first quarter.

The output measure of GDP is one of three such methods of calculation – the others being changes in incomes and spending – and according to the CSO is the most reliable short-term guide. It is also the first measure available for the second quarter.

Increased output was spread through most industrial sectors, apart from energy, where oil rig maintenance depressed production. Output of services is estimated to have grown 1.5 per cent in the quarter, including a 2 per cent increase in distribution and a smaller rise in transport. Figures published last week and incorporated into yesterday's showed that manufacturing output grew by 1.6 per cent in the quarter, but energy output fell 2.2 per cent, leaving the rise for all production industries at 0.5 per cent.

The second quarter growth was in line with City expectations, and was seen as confirmation that the economy is still benefiting from the boost to competitiveness after last year's decline in sterling. Those analysts worried about too rapid growth and industry's ability to meet the demands placed upon it will point out that non-oil growth is running at more than 4 per cent a year. But others expect the growth rate to slip back to a more sustainable 3 per cent in the second half of the year, as the pound's gains in the first half bite into profit margins.

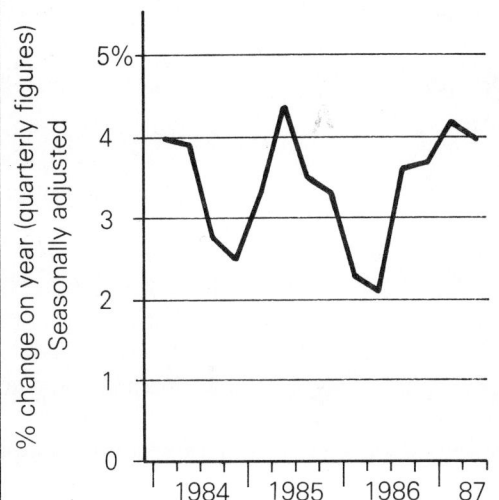

REAL GDP GROWTH
Output measure

% change on year (quarterly figures)
Seasonally adjusted

1984   1985   1986   87

1 What change occurred in GDP between 1986 and 1987?

2 List three methods that can be used when calculating GDP.

3 Briefly describe the expansion in the economy referred to in the article.

4 What reason is given in the article to account for the continued growth in the UK economy?

261

① Major firm in area closes → ② Unemployment rises

The Vicious Cycle of Decline

② → ③ Sales of other firms decline

③ → ④ Further firms close or shed labour

④ → ⑤ Unemployment rises again

⑤ → ①

---

① Large firm arrives in area → ② Employment rises

The Virtuous Cycle of Growth

② → ③ Sales of other firms increase

③ → ④ New firms open and existing firms prosper

④ → ⑤ Employment rises again

⑤ → ①

The North–South divide

SHETLAND

ORKNEYS.

▨ Deprived areas

☐ Growth areas

Source: *Guardian*, 6 January 1988

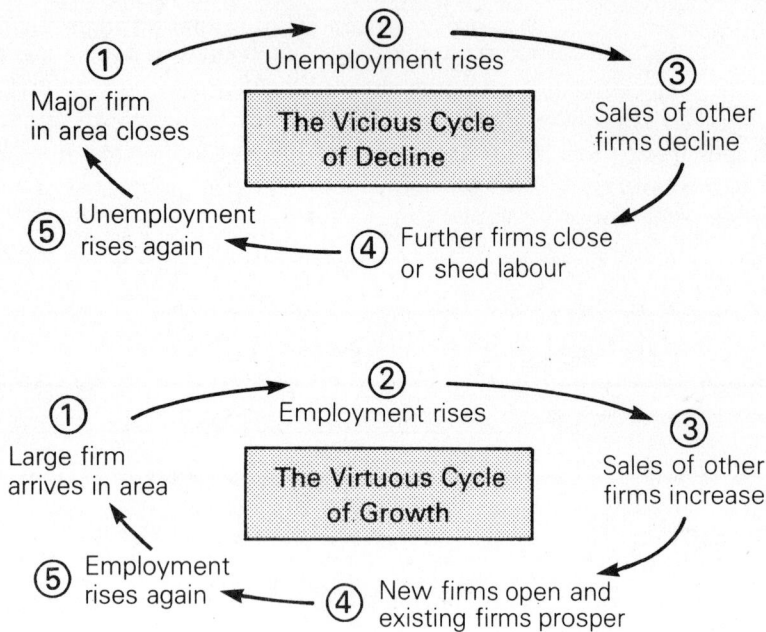

1 The 'North-South divide' is a phrase sometimes used to describe the distribution of prosperity in the UK. Using the map explain what is meant by the phrase.

2 In which area (North or South) would you be more likely to find the cycle of economic decline operating?

3 Imagine you are the economic adviser for a council in North Wales. Recently the largest firm in the area (in terms of employment) has been experiencing problems. It may be forced to close. The council are considering subsidising the firm. What are the arguments that could be used for and against this proposal?

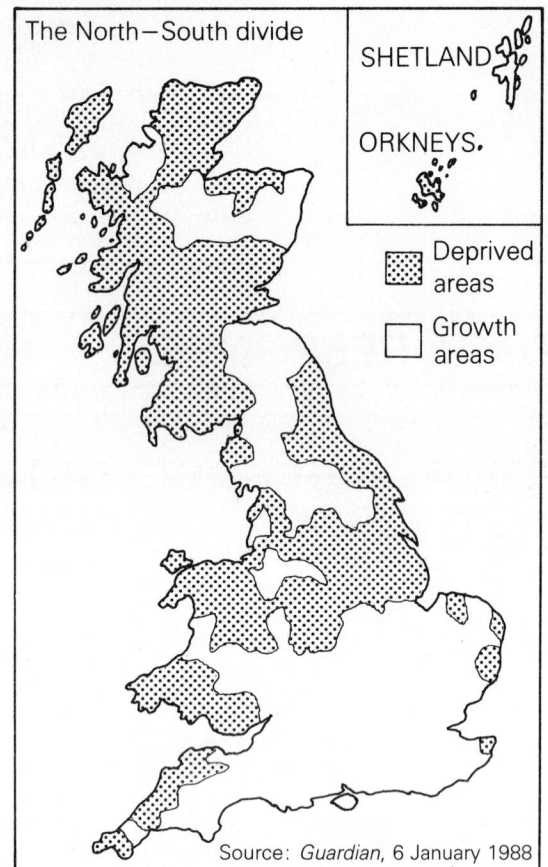

4 What problems have been created by the current rate of economic growth for people living in the South? Do these problems justify continued government aid for depressed regions?

Extension 2

Britain turns into nation of long-lived and languid fat cats

By Peter Murtagh

People in Britain are living longer and are better off, with the result that more and more money is being spent on consumer goods, according to the latest profile of the nation, Britain 1988, a government publication out today.

But while people in general appear to be healthier and wealthier, an analysis of leisure activities suggests they are also lazier. By far the most popular pastime is watching television, with 98 per cent of homes having at least one set and over a third having a video recorder. The average person over the age of four watches about 27 hours of television a week.

The handbook says that while Gross Domestic Product fell in the early 1980s, Britain is experiencing its seventh successive year of economic growth – higher than any of its Common Market rivals. In the first quarter of last year, GDP rose by 4 per cent in real terms.

Employment has been increasing since 1983 – the longest period of growth for almost 30 years – although 10.5 per cent of the United Kingdom (about 2.8 million people) remain unemployed.

Disposable incomes of those in work rose by 4.3 per cent in 1986 and an increasingly significant contribution to household incomes is being made by women. Forty two per cent of the British workforce is comprised of women and over 60 per cent of married women between the ages of 16 and 60 now work outside the home.

Home-owning is increasing with more than 60 per cent of people now owning or buying their home – 14 million in 1985 compared with 13.5 million in 1984 and a mere four million in 1951.

In 1979 when Mrs Thatcher took office, 7 per cent of people owned shares. By the middle of last year (and before the October stock market crash), the number had jumped to almost 20 per cent.

Sixty nine per cent of homes now have central heating, 81 per cent have washing machines, 95 per cent refrigerators, 81 per cent telephones and 62 per cent of people own a car.

Britons are also taking more foreign holidays. United Kingdom residents took over 17 million holidays overseas in 1986, compared with 15.75 million in 1985, and the most popular destinations were unchanged – Spain, France and Greece.

More people are eating meals out and as lifestyles have changed, the consumption of take-away meals, convenience foods and so-called fast food has also risen. Over the past 25 years, consumption of poultry, instant coffee, processed foods, fruit and vegetables has risen while home consumption of beef, veal, mutton, lamb, bread, potatoes, butter, sugar and tea has fallen.

Alcohol consumption is continuing its rise since the 1950s but the type of drinks taken has changed. Beer remains the most popular, but lager now accounts for more than half of beer sales and there has been a switch from whisky and gin to other spirits.

Source: *Guardian*, 6 January 1988

Living in Britain today

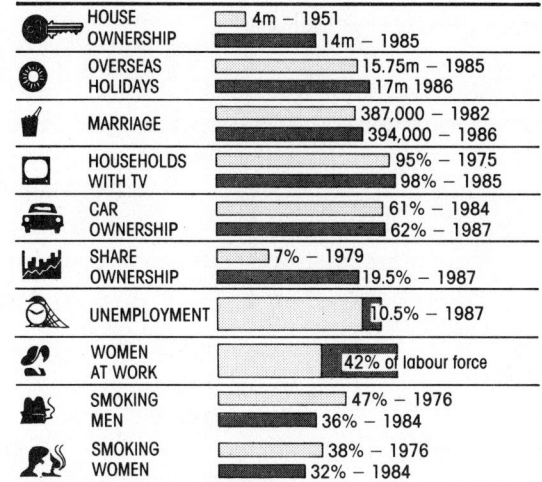

HOUSE OWNERSHIP	4m – 1951	14m – 1985
OVERSEAS HOLIDAYS	15.75m – 1985	17m 1986
MARRIAGE	387,000 – 1982	394,000 – 1986
HOUSEHOLDS WITH TV	95% – 1975	98% – 1985
CAR OWNERSHIP	61% – 1984	62% – 1987
SHARE OWNERSHIP	7% – 1979	19.5% – 1987
UNEMPLOYMENT	10.5% – 1987	
WOMEN AT WORK	42% of labour force	
SMOKING MEN	47% – 1976	36% – 1984
SMOKING WOMEN	38% – 1976	32% – 1984

PETS   Over 6 million dogs in Britain

1 When people are better off what do they spend more of their money on?
2 a What figure is used to measure economic growth?
  b How can we tell, using this figure, that the British economy is growing?
3 a What has happened to employment during this period?
  b Explain why unemployment has remained high.
4 a Describe the changes that have taken place in the following areas (you may use bar charts to help you):
    i   car ownership;
    ii home ownership;
    iii share ownership.
  b Briefly account for the changes you have described.
5 Using the information in the chart and article, write a brief description of the benefits economic growth has brought to the economy.

Coursework

Aim: To evaluate an economic project.

1 Identify any one national or local economic project that is likely to bring increased economic growth to the United Kingdom. Examples of national projects might include the Channel Tunnel or the construction or development of a new town or business area like Docklands.
  Describe your chosen project as fully as you can:
  a consider who might benefit from the project and what the benefits are that the project will bring;
  b consider who will lose from the project and what the costs might be if the government gave permission for the project to proceed.
2 The government appoints you sole director of the project. Write a report to the government summarising and evaluating the case for and against proceeding.

You may present data, such as maps or projections of the income that will be generated, as appendices to your report.

45 Unemployment

Unemployment exists in an economy when people want to work but cannot find jobs. One of the aims of most governments' policies is a commitment to provide jobs or encourage the development of job opportunities.

Whatever the unemployment figure is, and in recent years it has been considerably higher than the post-war average although more recently it has begun to fall again, some will argue that the true figure is higher. Those who argue this, point out that:

- Many who are unemployed do not register as unemployed and are not counted in the unemployment statistics.
- Others do not qualify for unemployment benefit. This is particularly the case with married women who have not made insurance contributions. Nonetheless, if they were offered work they would take it.
- Between 1979 and 1987 the basis on which unemployment figures are calculated in the United Kingdom was changed more than 20 times! If old methods were used the unemployment (jobless) figure would be higher than the current figure.

Others argue that the true rate of unemployment is really lower than the current figure would suggest. They point out that:

- many people who are registered as unemployed live in the wrong place to find work but are not willing to move;
- others are unemployed because they are incapable of working through ill health, or some other reason;
- some people are between jobs (so called *search unemployment*) and eventually they will disappear from the figures when they find work;
- some people are part of the population described by some as *work shy*: they register for unemployment pay but do not intend to take jobs.

Such arguments, of course, are difficult to apply when unemployment is rising and job vacancies are falling or when the real level of unemployment and other benefits is being eroded or lowered.

Let us look at Jeff. He's been unemployed for two years. This is how he describes his situation: "I hate being out of work. People think you're a scrounger, but I've really tried. The trouble is I'm fifty. When my firm made me redundant I knew it was going to be difficult to find another job. I'm a skilled engineer so it's a real waste of my training that no one wants to use it. I'm just left idle. I feel like society has rejected me. It's hard not being able to buy things for my grandchildren. One bloke I know couldn't take it any more. He committed suicide. My wife and I argue a lot because I'm at home so much. Unless I find a job, we'll probably end up getting divorced after more than twenty years of marriage."

Test yourself

Use Jeff's account to make a list of some of the consequences of being unemployed.

ECONOMIC TERMS

Unemployment: when people are available or wanting to work but are not being used.
Types of unemployment include: structural, regional, cyclical, technological, demand deficient, seasonal and search/frictional.
Deindustrialisation: the progressive loss of jobs from the secondary stage of the economy (the manufacturing sector).

Causes of unemployment

Jeff and some friends are sitting in a café discussing the unemployment in their local area.

"It says in the local paper that unemployment is running at 25% of the Melchester area's working population," Jeff says.

"I'm unemployed because they closed the steel works," Bob says. "They built a smaller modern works and my skills weren't needed there."

"With me it was different," says Jeff. "I used to work in the boatyard building ships, but they all seem to be built abroad these days."

"It's the youngsters I feel sorry for," says Patricia. "How are our Sheila and Barry ever going to find work?"

"I blame this deindustrialisation economists go on about," says Norman. "We're losing the really important jobs the rest of the economy depends on. Once they shut the old textile mill down the town wasn't the same. Everyone's trade suffered."

Deindustrialisation is, in fact, a consequence of losing jobs in the manufacturing sector, *not* a cause. Some economists believe it has been caused by allowing import penetration.

"It's all those goods they buy from abroad," growls Jeff.

Some economists believe governments are to blame as they have responded in the wrong way by expanding public sector jobs. These do not always create the wealth an economy needs to grow, it is argued.

In fact there are as many reasons for unemployment as there can be suspects in a murder story.

- **Seasonal unemployment**: this is the unemployment that occurs at particular times of year. In mid July there is no room in the high street for Father Christmases; in December not many people want to buy ice-cream. Building workers often find that their work is affected by seasonal variations. However, this cannot account for more than a minute amount of the total out of work.

- **Frictional unemployment**: this describes those unemployed who are in the process of moving from one job to another. In a modern complex economy old jobs disappear or move location and others arise. There will always be some people who will fall into this category, but this explanation does not account for why there has been such a large increase in unemployment in the 1970s and 80s.

The types of unemployment which have particularly affected Britain include:

- **Structural unemployment**: when workers in a particular industry are no longer wanted (for example, the cinema or textiles). Many of our old industries were concentrated in a particular area, therefore:

- **Regional unemployment**: has a large structural element. The North West has lost much of its textile industry given the rise of cheap Third World manufactured imports.

- **Technological unemployment**: this is unemployment caused by our ability to produce more using fewer people. Computers can replace bank workers; robots can replace car workers. In the long run technology can create more new jobs than the ones lost.

- **Cyclical unemployment**: this is unemployment that varies with activity levels in the economy. If producers find that they have produced more goods than people want, they may lay off workers or reduce overtime. Workers have less money and can purchase less goods as a result. The employer has a greater stockpile of goods that cannot be sold. As a result more workers are laid off. If this process continues, the economy can become depressed.

- **Demand deficient unemployment**: when there is not enough demand in an economy, we say there is a demand deficiency. In these circumstances, many economists argue, the government needs to put money into the economy to make up for the demand taken out by those consumers who are not spending or employees who are not working. Economists who think along these lines call themselves *Keynesians* after the economist J.M. Keynes who first fully described this problem and solution.

- **The natural level of unemployment**: some economist claim there is a natural level of unemployment. Here inflation is seen to be the villain that causes the problem. It is suggested by these economists (known as *monetarists*) that too much money in an economy is the root cause of unemployment. Governments cannot create jobs by spending because this can make future inflation worse. As a result of rising prices, people will not buy British goods but buy cheaper goods produced abroad instead. This puts more British workers out of work. Increasing money in the economy has not solved the fact that British goods are often overpriced, such economists would argue.

Test yourself

1 Suggest some possible reasons why unemployment has increased in Britain through the 1970s and early 1980s.
2 Make a list of different reasons for

265

unemployment. Select from the list the most likely causes of Britain's recent high unemployment and give reasons for your answer.

3 Find out the rate of unemployment in your area and compare this to the national average. If the two figures are different, explain why the difference exists.

Activity

Connie Raine. Aged 48. Textile worker. Lives in Manchester. Unemployed because of the decline in textile industry.

Helen Smith of Newcastle. Aged 59. Too ill to work but registered. Her brother, Robert, is 61 and a shipbuilder. He is out of work, willing to work but not registered.

Jack Kennedy. Aged 30. Car worker in Birmingham. Currently unemployed due to spare capacity in the industry. Demand may pick up soon.

John Williams. Aged 17. Lives in Swansea. Currently on a YTS placement. His father, Peter, is also unemployed. Jobs are hard to find in South Wales.

Will Allen of Coventry. Aged 26. Married with three children. Believes he can earn more in benefit than from working.

Catherine Penhaligon from Cornwall. Aged 29. There is little work available in her area. She does not qualify for unemployment benefit. Would take a job if she was offered one.

Marie Christie. Aged 23. Lives in Southampton. Works as a carpenter on building sites. Currently out of work because of bad weather.

Bill Pyle from London. Aged 46. Currently retraining. Used to be a printer but new processes made him redundant.

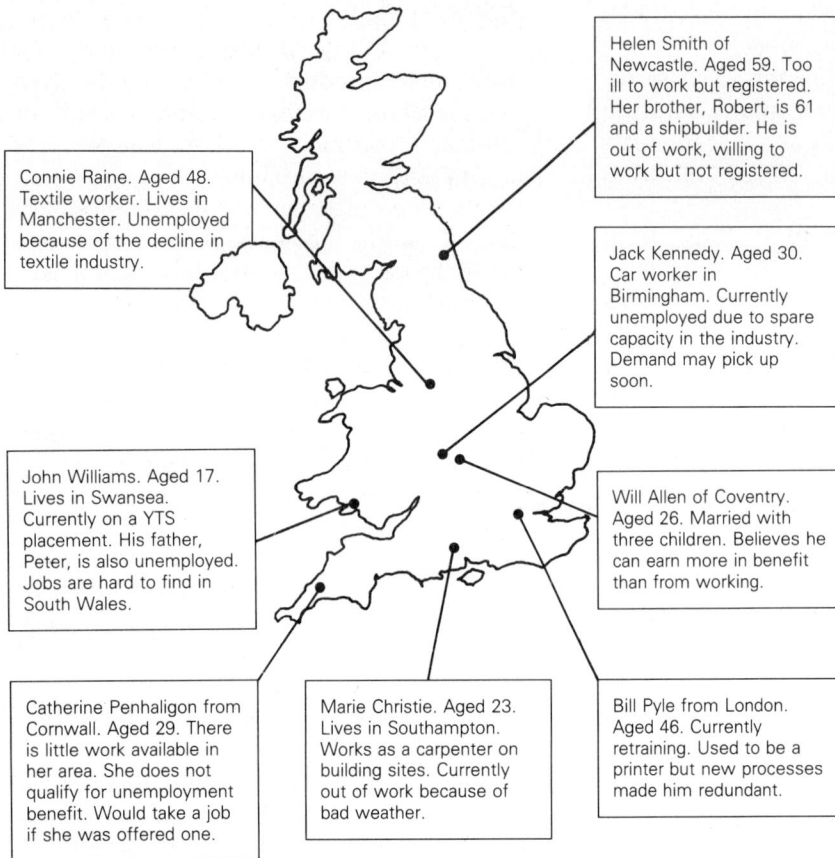

Look at the information and then answer these questions.

1 Who is regionally unemployed?
2 Who is frictionally unemployed?
3 Who is seasonally unemployed?
4 Find two examples of people who are structurally unemployed.
5 Find an example of:
   a someone who is cyclically unemployed;
   b someone who is technologically unemployed.
6 Who is:
   a officially unemployed;
   b officially not available for work?
7 If you were to make a list of the two categories given in question 5 what differences would there be between your list and the one shown here?

DATA RESPONSE

Sharp drop in jobless rate

Christopher Huhne
Economics Editor

UNEMPLOYMENT fell at its sharpest rate for seven months in July though the drop may have been exaggerated by a sharp rise in young people joining the Youth Training Scheme (YTS).

The Department of Employment said yesterday that the 24th consecutive seasonally-adjusted decline was 58,500, the largest fall since November. The unadjusted total dropped by 14,086 to 2,326,703.

The better-than-expected fall is not necessarily an indication that the underlying drop is quickening since the number involved in YTS rose by 22,500 on the month and vacancies reported to Job Centres fell by 5,800 to 249,400.

The best guide to the underlying trend is the six-monthly average change, which shows a monthly fall of 42,000.

The total drop in unemployment since its peak two years ago is 896,400. Most of the fall has been due to fast economic growth and more jobs, although tougher availability for work tests have weeded out people not entitled to benefit – the basis for counting unemployment.

. . . YTS has also expanded from 269,600 to 392,500. However, the impact of special job measures is said to have fallen by around 30,000 to 255,000.

. . . the Unemployment Unit, said the pre-1982 basis

of counting anyone who registered as unemployed would show a total 779,800 higher than the official figure, though it would have dipped below three million for the first time.

Employment Secretary . . . said prospects for a further fall were good, and that the 8.2 per cent jobless rate was lower than many other European countries.

Source: *Guardian*, 19 August 1988

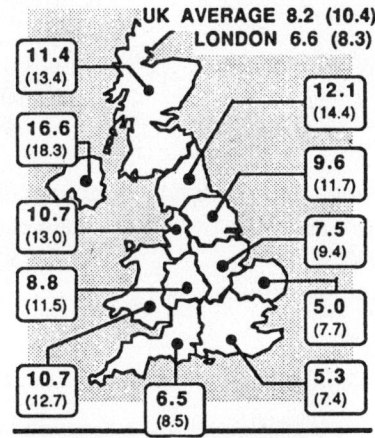

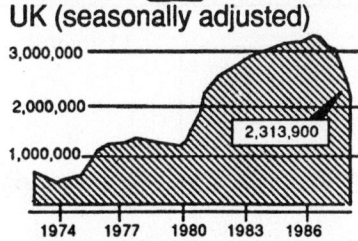

UNEMPLOYMENT

Percentage unemployed last month.
Figures for one year ago in brackets.

UK AVERAGE 8.2 (10.4)
LONDON 6.6 (8.3)

11.4 (13.4)
12.1 (14.4)
16.6 (18.3)
9.6 (11.7)
10.7 (13.0)
7.5 (9.4)
8.8 (11.5)
5.0 (7.7)
10.7 (12.7)
6.5 (8.5)
5.3 (7.4)

UK (seasonally adjusted)

2,313,900

1974 1977 1980 1983 1986

1 What happened to unemployment in July 1988?

2 What was the UK average rate of unemployment in July 1988?

3 What was the level of unemployment in 1984?

4 What special measures have been introduced that have helped reduce the level of unemployment as it appears in economic statistics?

5 Explain why the real level of unemployment is considered by some to be higher than the official figure.

Extension 1

A

Employees in Employment
Figures in millions
21.3
21.2
21.1
21

UK Unemployment
Figures in millions
4
3
2
1
0

Restart Interviews (cumulative)

Dec   Mar   Jun   Sep   Dec   Mar   Jun
      1986   1987

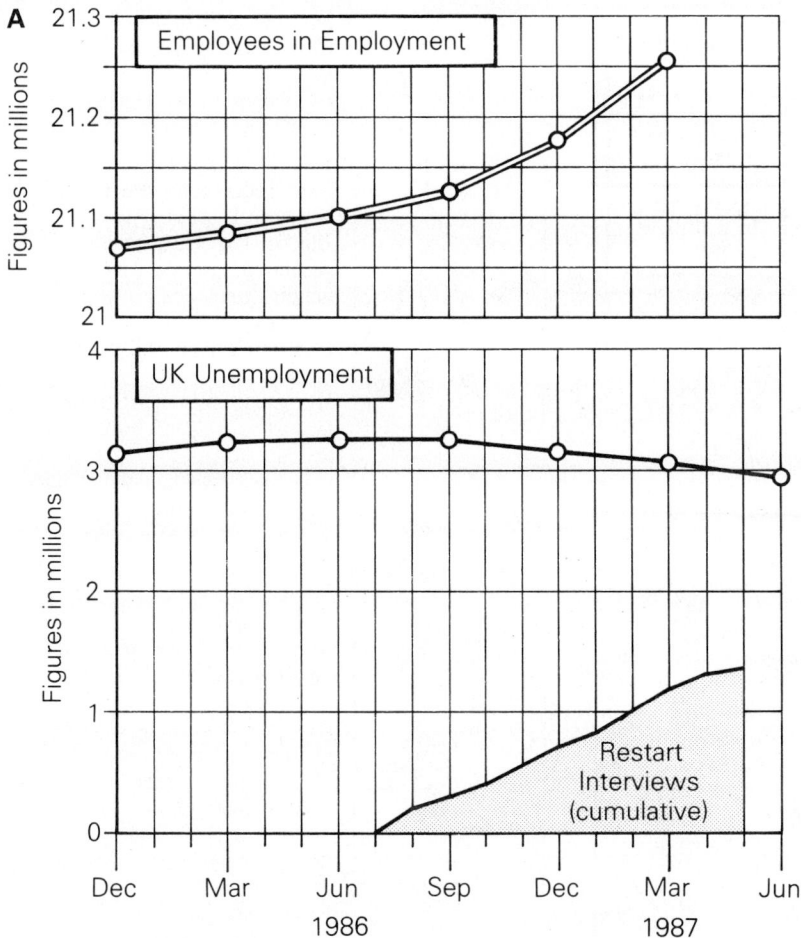

Source: *The Independent*, 3 August 1987

There are different ways of looking at unemployment. Using the graphs answer these questions:

1 a How many people in the UK were unemployed in March 1987?

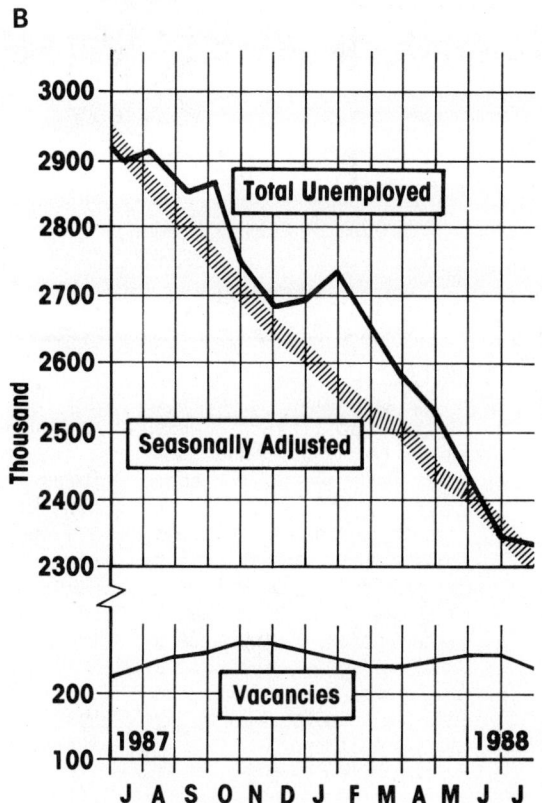

B

Thousand
3000
2900
2800
2700
2600
2500
2400
2300

Total Unemployed
Seasonally Adjusted

200
100

Vacancies

1987   1988
J A S O N D J F M A M J J

Source: *Daily Telegraph*, 19 August 1988

b What changes had taken place by the end of May 1988?

2 a What had occurred to the level of unemployment by June 1988?

b Give some reasons why this had occurred.

3 Examine the fall in UK unemployment as shown in **A**. Now look at the rise in the number of employees in employment. What do you notice about the difference between UK unemployment and the number of employees in employment? How would you account for this apparent discrepancy? (Clue: who else could enter the working population?)

4 "It's a person's own fault if they are unemployed," a friend of yours tells you. Using the vacancies and unemployed figures in **B** prepare a short reply.

Extension 2

REGIONAL UNEMPLOYMENT

UK 10.4%

N. Ireland 18.3%

North West 13.0%

W. Midlands 11.5%

Wales 12.7%

South West 8.5%

Scotland 13.4%

North 14.4%

Yorkshire & Humberside 11.7%

E. Midlands 9.4%

East Anglia 7.7%

G. London 8.3%

South East 7.4%

BRITAIN IS a nation with an ageing population, a widening affluence gap between London and the rest of the country, and an insatiable appetite for home appliances.

It is also a nation where illegitimacy rates have doubled in the past decade, church marriages are going out of fashion, and families are moving south in search of work. At the same time, there is a move from urban areas to the suburbs and rural areas. Crime is highest and clear-up rates lowest in urban conurbations.

The industrial character of Britain is also changing. In the past decade the fastest growth has been in finance and business, distribution, hotels and catering and repairs. Agriculture is in decline in every region, except East Anglia, as is manufacturing.

Source: *Independent*, 14 August 1987

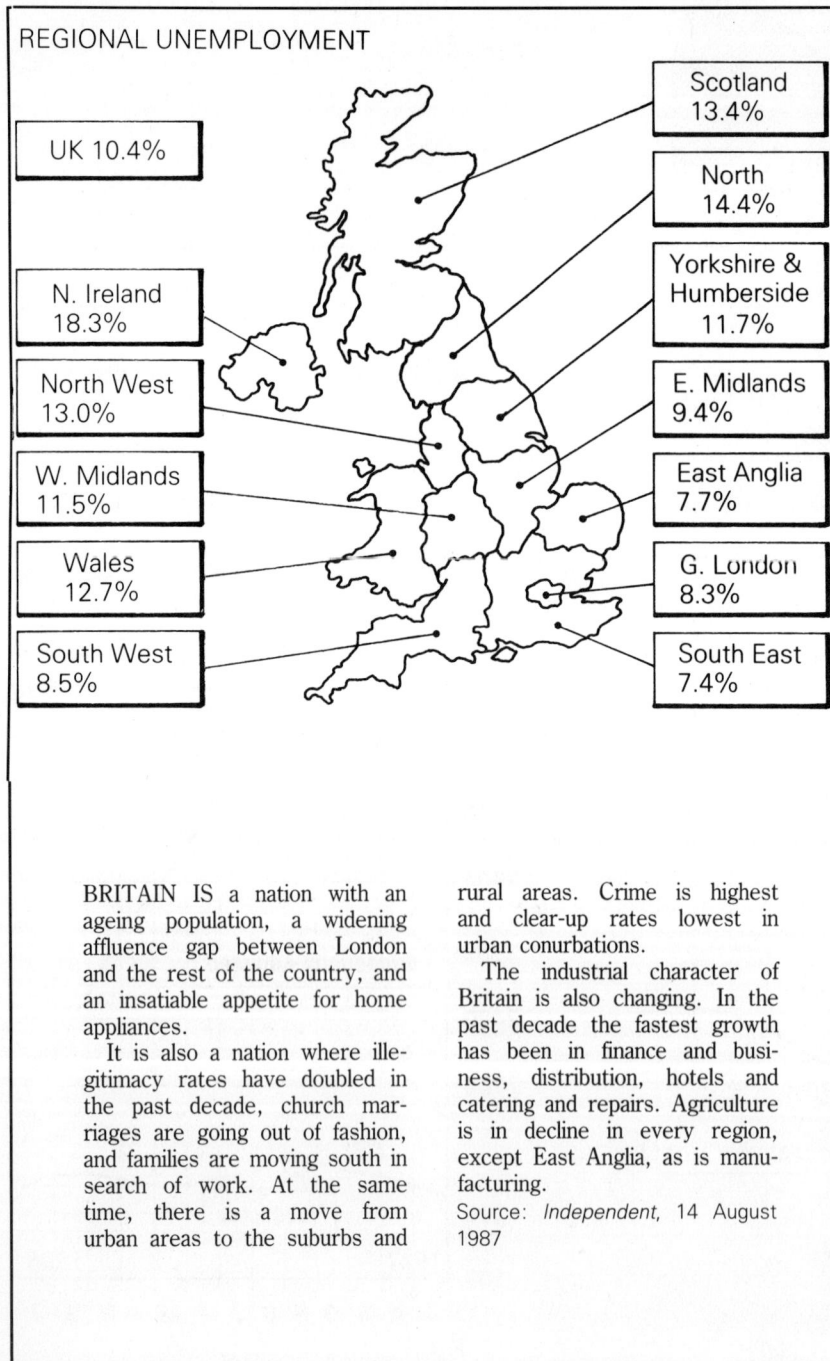

Examples of UK regions

NORTH
Highest crime rate, in particular for burglary and handling stolen goods.
Highest death rate from cancer among males.
Second highest unemployment rate (17 per cent).
Lowest priced housing (average 1985 price £22,800).
Population fell by 1 per cent between 1961 and 1985 (down 8 per cent in Tyne and Wear).
More washing machines, but fewer tumble driers or telephones than other regions.

SOUTH-EAST
Most prosperous region (GDP per head £5,831).
Highest regional output accounting for one third of national total.
Most expensive housing.
Lowest clear-up rate for serious crimes.
Highest proportion of school-leavers in England with A levels.
Civil marriages commoner than any other region.
Fewest homes with washing machines.

WEST MIDLANDS
Most stillbirths and death in new-born babies (12.1 per thousand).
One in five workers employed in engineering, metals and cars.
Highest concentration of Pakistani and Indian households.
More teenage marriages than any other region.
Fewest foreign-owned firms.
Most black and white televisions.

Source: *Independent*, 2 July 1987

1 Which region in England had the highest level of unemployment?
2 Which region in the UK had:
  a the lowest level of unemployment?
  b the highest level of unemployment?
3 What evidence is presented here that could be used by you to demonstrate that the South East of England is a prosperous region?

4 Which region would be most affected by a collapse of demand for motor cars? Give reasons for your answer.
5 What evidence can you find to support the view that as far as unemployment is concerned Britain is a nation divided?

Coursework

Aim: To investigate problems of unemployment.

1 a Collect information on the national percentage of people unemployed. Use this information to argue that the present government has solved, or is solving, unemployment as a problem.
2 Collect information on unemployment in:
  a your own region;
  b the immediate area.
  c Contrast the information gathered in **a** and **b**. What are your findings?

3 a What alternative perspectives could be advanced to account for the level of unemployment in the UK?
  or
  b Test the hypothesis that the only form of unemployment that is of a level to worry about in the United Kingdom is frictional unemployment.

46 Poverty and Wealth

Economists refer to wealth as a stock of goods. Wealth can appreciate (increase in value) or depreciate (decrease in value).

Each year a person can receive income (a flow of money) that can, through the purchase of goods and services, add to that person's wealth. Sometimes this income is earned. Julian earns part of his income by making two LPs a year and going on a world tour every three years.

Income can also be unearned. Julian has savings in a variety of building societies, banks, as well as in shares in a number of companies. Each year he receives income in the form of interest and dividends from these.

Decide for yourself

You live in a small village not far from Dover. Your cottage is worth £65 000. A plan for a rail link is published which shows that the track for a high-speed rail-link from London to Paris will run at the end of your garden.

- Will your property appreciate or depreciate in value?
- Give reasons for your answer.

Test yourself

Take the following and sort them into two columns. In Column 1 place all the examples of earned income and in Column 2 place all the examples of unearned income.

wages received from working in a mine · interest on a bank account · bonus on money held in a building society · dividend paid on shares in the Sonic Co. · salary received from working as an economics teacher

DATA RESPONSE 1

Distribution of Income

Original income		Bottom fifth	Next fifth	Middle fifth	Next fifth	Top fifth
Percentages	1976	0.8	9.4	18.8	26.6	44.4
	1981	0.6	8.1	18.0	26.9	46.4
	1983	0.3	6.7	17.1	27.2	48.0
	1984	0.3	6.1	17.5	27.5	48.6

Disposable income (after direct taxes)

	1976	7.0	12.6	18.2	24.1	38.1
	1981	6.7	12.1	17.7	24.1	39.4
	1983	6.9	11.9	17.6	24.0	39.6
	1984	6.7	11.7	17.5	24.4	39.7

Final income (after all taxes)

	1976	7.4	12.7	18.0	24.0	37.9
	1981	7.1	12.4	17.9	24.0	38.6
	1983	6.9	12.1	17.6	24.0	39.3
	1984	7.1	12.1	17.5	24.0	39.0

Distribution of wealth

Wealth owned by:	1976	1981	1983	1984
Most wealthy 1%	31	24	21	21
Most wealthy 5%	52	45	40	39
Most wealthy 10%	65	60	54	52
Most wealthy 25%	86	84	77	75
Most wealthy 50%	97	95	94	93
Total marketable wealth (£s billion)	140	263	546	762

Source: *Guardian*, 29 January 1987

Distribution of wealth

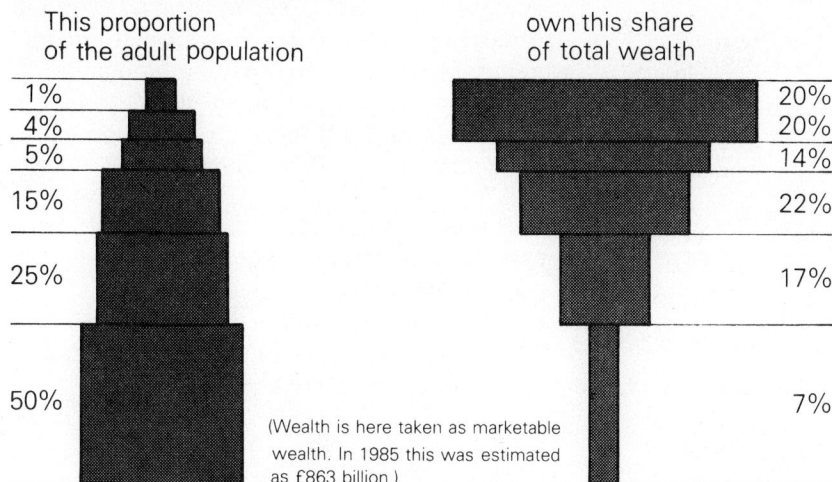

This proportion of the adult population — own this share of total wealth

Proportion of adult population	Share of total wealth
1%	20%
4%	20%
5%	14%
15%	22%
25%	17%
50%	7%

(Wealth is here taken as marketable wealth. In 1985 this was estimated as £863 billion.)

Source: *Social Studies Review*, September 1988

1 According to the data, what has happened to the share of income earned by the top fifth and the bottom fifth of the population between 1976 and 1984?

2 What happened to the share of wealth owned by the top 10% of the population between 1976 and 1984?

3 a What proportion of wealth do the top 10% of the population now own?
   b What has happened to the amount of wealth owned by the top most wealthy 10% of the population since 1984?

4 Why do you think the income and wealth is increasingly unevenly distributed?

The distribution of income and wealth

Wealth and income is unevenly distributed in Britain today. Some people have more than others:

- the wealthiest 5% in 1984 owned 39% of the country's wealth;
- the bottom 50% had to share only 7% of the country's wealth;
- the top 20% of income earners earned 48.6% of all original income in 1984.

Some of this income and wealth is redistributed to others through the tax system, but recently the post-war trend which reduced differences between rich and poor has been reversed. More people are now living in poverty, as measured in terms of those below the official poverty line, than at any other time since the end of the Second World War.

A major reason why some people are poor and others are rich is that ownership of wealth is inherited from one generation to another.

Other reasons are important too. Those who are successful in business can become millionaires. Richard Branson became a millionaire as a successful businessman. If, of course, your business becomes very much less successful, then you can end up with nothing (you might even be made bankrupt).

Another source of wealth comes from having special skills. Not everyone can play football in the First Division or has a singing voice like our pop star Julian.

One of the most important differences between rich and poor is made by the ability to acquire training and qualifications from education. We call this the acquisition of *human capital*. Not everyone who is rich has a high level of qualifications, but generally speaking the better you do at school, the greater the opportunities you have to increase your income later in life.

There are, of course, lots of other reasons why some people are poor and some are wealthy, including age and even luck.

The Welfare State

After the Second World War a system of housing and welfare benefits was developed which became known as the Welfare State. Its purpose was to provide "a safety net" for the less fortunate in society. The Welfare State included the National Health Service, unemployment and supplementary benefits (the latter now replaced by family income support). Both universal and means-tested benefits were created to help the poor and others thought to be in need of help, like families with children. Taxation was designed to be progressive; that is the more you earned the higher the rate of tax you paid.

The system was developed on the theory that all of us run the risk some time of being ill, unemployed, or in need of some form of basic help, like shelter. It was designed to provide for people at the point of need, that is when help was most required by the individual.

Thatcherism

Under the Conservative governments of the 1980s efforts have been made to reduce people's reliance on this Welfare State. An increasing number of benefits have become means-tested (given only when your means, or level of income and wealth, has been assessed); others have been reduced in terms of overall purchasing power.

The role of local government in the provision of personal social services has been reduced by tighter spending controls. Privatisation of public sector firms has been introduced in the hope that all will become members of a "share owning democracy". Council houses have been sold off in the hope that all will become members of a "property owning democracy".

Test yourself

1 What evidence exists of an uneven distribution of wealth in the UK?
2 Why are some people wealthy?
3 Your Dad may fill out the football pools. How could luck make you wealthy?
4 If your Dad won on the football pools, how could he lose it all again?
5 What is the Welfare State?
6 How has Thatcherism changed the Welfare State?

DATA RESPONSE 2

46% of workers 'below decency pay threshold'

LOW PAID workers are now further behind the average wage than they were more than 100 years ago and the divide between rich and poor has widened significantly over the last decade, according to a report published today.

The study by the Low Pay Unit calculates that the poorest fifth of workers earned only 64 per cent of the average income in 1987, compared with 69 per cent in 1886. The highest paid now earn more relative to the average than at any time since 1906.

The report, *The Poor Decade – Wage Inequalities in the 1980s*, also shows that since Margaret Thatcher came to power in 1979, the number of workers falling below the "decency threshold" as specified by the European Social Charter has increased from just under eight million – 38 per cent of the workforce, to 9.4 million – 46 per cent.

Pay rises for the highest paid fifth of men have been 42 per cent greater than those for the lowest paid fifth.

Progress towards equality for women has also stalled: women working full-time still earn on average only two-thirds as much as men. The pay gap between adults and young people has also widened.

The study also points to regional inequalities in pay. Even in the South-east, nearly one in four adults earn low wages, under the social charter definition, despite working full-time. Throughout most of the rest of Britain the proportion is one in three.

One reason for this increasing divide is that the poorest were hit hard by the recession in the early Eighties and have benefited less from the subsequent recovery.

However, the booklet also attributes much of the blame to deliberate Government policy, including the abolition in 1983 of the Fair Wages Resolution, which dates back to 1981 and the weakening in 1986 of the wages council minimum wage system established in 1909. The study claims that some workers have experienced actual cuts in their pay.

Chris Pond, director of the Low Pay Unit, said the report showed that the low paid are slipping behind the standards established as necessary in Victorian times. The Budget and the social security changes will leave many of the lowest paid workers worse off.

"By the end of the 1980s Britain's poorest workers may come to share the Prime Minister's nostalgia for the 1980s. When she promised a return to Victorian values, few expected she might provide the lowest paid with wages to match," he said.

Source: *The Independent*, 18 April 1988

1 What percentage of average income did the poorest fifth of workers earn in 1987?

2 How does this situation compare with the earnings of the poorest fifth of workers in 1886?

3 What has happened to the percentage of workers below the "decency threshold" since 1979?

4 Identify some of the other forms of inequality that have increased since 1979.

5 What aspects of government policy have, according to the article, contributed to an increase in poverty?

Extension 1

Income is a flow that can add to a family's stock of wealth.

If the value of the stock of wealth increases, then the family's assets have appreciated.

CONSUMER DURABLES

PROPERTY

REAL ASSETS

Financial assets include: bank account deposits, shares, stocks, cash in hand, insurance policies, pension rights.

FINANCIAL ASSETS

WEALTH

Expenditure is a flow that can reduce a family's stock of wealth. Depreciation of assets can also reduce a family's stock of wealth. (Depreciation occurs when goods wear out or lose value.)

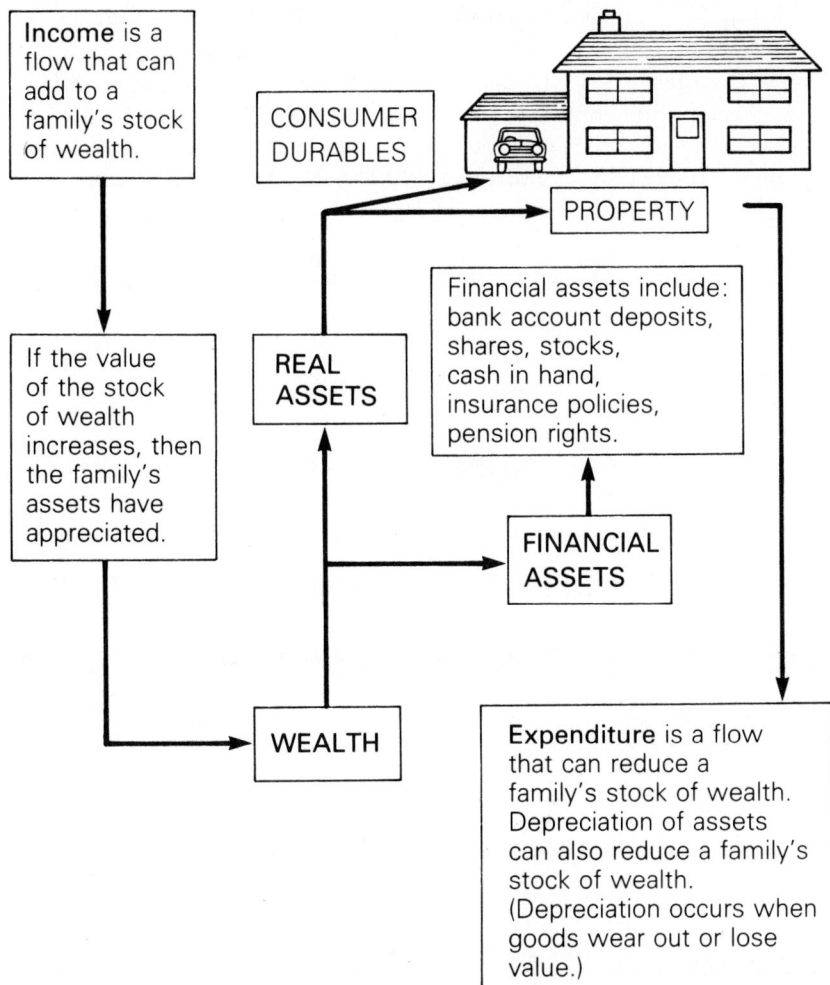

1 a What two forms of wealth exist?
  b Give one example of a real asset.
  c Give one example of a financial asset.
2 Don Osborne has invested in a number of companies this year and the value of the shares has risen. What has happened, all other things being equal, to the value of his total wealth?
3 Don is burgled during the night and loses these consumer durables: his TV, video, antique clock, and £1,000 in cash. Why is Don in a position to replace these items and thus replace his stock of wealth?
4 Don lives in a quiet suburb. Recently an exclusive golf course has been built nearby. The local comprehensive is nearby too, and has an excellent reputation. Parents are anxious to move into the area.
  a What will happen to the value of his house?
  b Will his stock of wealth appreciate or depreciate in value?
5 Don's car has recently broken down and the garage tells him it is beyond repair. At the same time his collection of paintings has been revalued for insurance purposes from £1 million to £2 million. Using the terms appreciation and depreciation explain what has happened to the total value of Don's assets.

Extension 2

The paradox of poverty

Read each account carefully.

THE MYERS FAMILY: Simon and Toni Myers have three children. They live on a council estate two miles from the nearest large shopping centre. There is a small corner store nearby but the goods are very expensive. Simon is a trained fitter but has been unemployed for the last 18 months. The estate is heated by electricity. The family can only afford to keep one room warm. Two of the bedrooms are damp because of a design fault in the construction. The family used to have an old second-hand car but it frequently broke down and, last year when they couldn't afford the tax and insurance, they had to sell it. They have a small kitchen and an old fridge that has broken down twice this year. They walk to the shops each week and because of the difficulties of carrying shopping by bus they would prefer to return by taxi but cannot afford to do so.

THE FOSTER FAMILY: Chris and Liz Foster have two children and live in a smart privately owned detached house on the edge of a thriving country town. Chris is a computer programmer and works from home. Liz teaches in a local primary school. Their home is heated by gas central heating, and solar panels provide an additional source of cheap energy in the summer months. Every two years they buy a new car and sell their old one. They've found that this helps keep maintenance and servicing costs down to an acceptable level. They shop once a fortnight at a large cash-and-carry store three miles from where they live, and buy in bulk. They keep their deep freezer well-stocked and this helps keep its running costs very low.

1 You are the local bank manager. Both families come to you for a loan. Which family would you be more willing to lend the money to? Give reasons for your answer.

2 If you decided to loan money to both families, what rate of interest would you charge each and why?

3 How does their ownership of wealth help the Foster family make savings?

4 Explain how the Fosters benefit from economies of scale in their purchase of household goods.

5 The paradox of poverty (a paradox is a statement that appears to be absurd but is nevertheless true) is that life for the poor is relatively more expensive than life for the wealthy.

   How does each of the above families illustrate an aspect of the 'paradox of poverty'?

Coursework

Aim: To investigate attitudes to benefits.

1 Undertake a survey of people (over retirement age) in your area.
2 Find ways of establishing what they see as their most important needs.
3 Examine the extent to which the current benefits available meet their needs.
4 What other factors would need to be taken into account in deciding the level of need?

5 Use the information you collect to write a letter to the Prime Minister from the perspective of:
   a someone you have interviewed who argues that pensioners need more benefits;
   b someone you have interviewed who argues that benefits for pensioners should be reduced.

47 Managing the Economy

In this final chapter we look at how the different parts of the economy fit together.

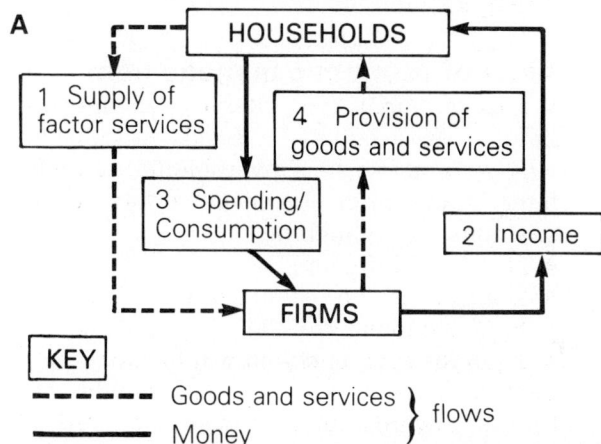

A

```
                    ┌──────────────────┐
            ┌ ─ ─ ─ ┤   HOUSEHOLDS     │◄────────┐
            │       └──────────────────┘         │
     ┌──────┴──────┐      ┌──────────────────┐   │
     │ 1 Supply of │      │ 4  Provision of  │   │
     │ factor      │      │ goods and        │   │
     │ services    │      │ services         │   │
     └──────┬──────┘      └──────────────────┘   │
            │   ┌──────────────┐       ┌───────────┐
            │   │ 3  Spending/ │       │ 2 Income  │
            │   │ Consumption  │       └───────────┘
            │   └──────────────┘
            │       ┌──────────────────┐
            └ ─ ─ ─►│      FIRMS       │
                    └──────────────────┘
```

┌─────────┐
│ KEY   │
└─────────┘

– – – – – Goods and services } flows
───────── Money

B

Diagram A shows how income circulates around the economy. The diagram simplifies the economy as there is only one household and one firm, and there is no international trade or government (public) sector, but it helps us to understand how an economy works:

- members of households supply factor services to firms (that is land, labour and capital);
- these factor services are used by entrepreneurs to make goods and provide services;
- in return for supplying the services, rewards such as wages, rent and interest are given to the households;
- with these rewards the households can purchase the goods and services made by the firms.

The value of goods and services produced (National Output) must be equal to the variety of incomes people receive (National Income), which in turn must equal the amount of spending people engage in (National Expenditure). So:

National Output = National Income = National Expenditure

In a more complex economy we have to remember that there are other sectors involved. There are the government or public sector, a banking sector, and foreign trade (see **B**).

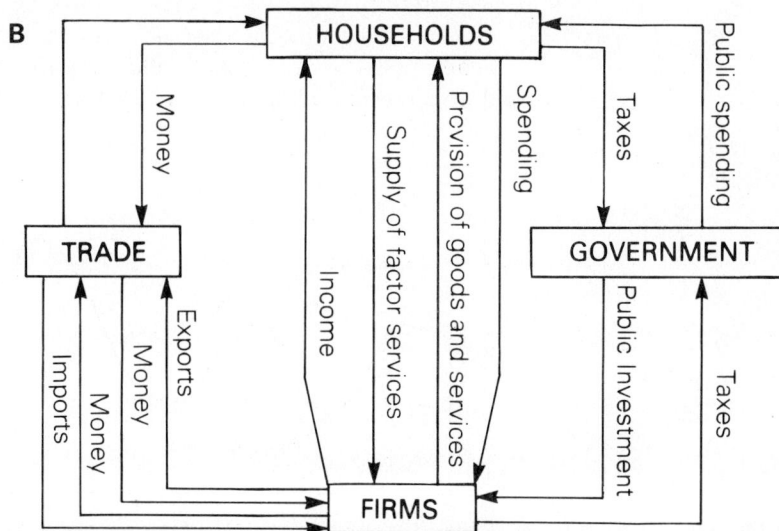

The flow of income

In the simple model of the economy it is easy to see that what households receive from firms as incomes must be spent by them to purchase goods and services, if in turn the household is to receive the same level of income.

In the complex model of the economy, leakages from the circular flow (money which is taken out of circulation) lead to a reduction in the amount of money in the economy. These leakages include:

- savings;
- money spent on imports;
- money invested abroad in foreign industry;
- money paid to the government in taxes.

Equilibrium is restored if there are adequate injections (or additions) to the circular flow of income. These injections include:

- public expenditure;
- money received from countries that purchase our exports;
- money invested by firms and individuals in British industry.

If people decide not to purchase goods then there will be mounting stockpiles. Entrepreneurs unable to sell their products might lay off workers; in turn workers will be unable to purchase goods. The cycle can go on and on, producing deflation in the economy.

If, on the other hand, people demand goods, stockpiles will be reduced, and entrepreneurs will take on more workers to meet the demand for more goods. These workers will demand more goods and entrepreneurs will take on more workers to meet this demand. The economy will reflate under these circumstances.

If the private sector takes more money out of the economy than it puts in, some economists have argued (following Keynes) that government can make up for this and stimulate demand (consumption) in the economy and the production of goods through developing a programme of public spending such as building.

Other economists do not support the case for governments intervening in this way. They argue that in the long run increased public spending would price people out of work and create not only inflation but unemployment too.

Aims of economic management

If a government does intervene in the running of an economy, it needs to consider why it is doing so. Governments normally intervene in order to achieve certain economic aims. These include:
- zero level inflation;
- a surplus in the balance of payments;
- high economic growth;
- a job for everyone who wants one.

Each of these aims, if achieved, would contribute towards an improved standard of living.

The trade cycle

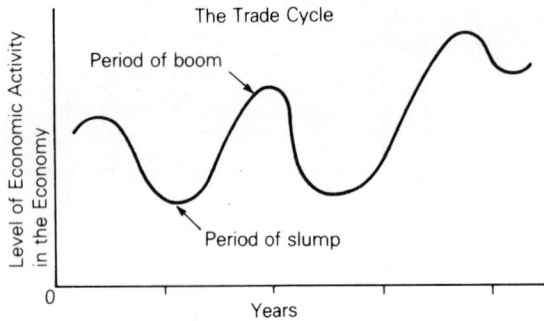

The Trade Cycle

Activity

Imagine an economy with only one firm and one household. The household we are going to look at is the Davis household which has six members: Jean, who owns the firm; Peter who works for her; their two children, Jill and Tim; Jean's uncle, Mick, who helped her set up in business; and then there's Gran . . .

1 a What rewards do Peter, Jean and Mick receive?
  b Why do they receive them?
2 Explain what the family can do with the rewards they receive.
3 The Government has decided to tax the firm and the household. Can you think why?
4 Peter usually gives Jill and Tim pocket money. They use it to purchase the goods the firm produces. Peter forgets to give them any money for a few weeks. What does Jean notice about the amount of finished goods in her warehouse?
5 Jean employs Peter for 40 hours a week and he does 10 hours overtime. What might she now say to Peter about his future hours of work?
6 If Jean reduces Peter's hours of work and earns less profits from her business, explain how others in the family might suffer.

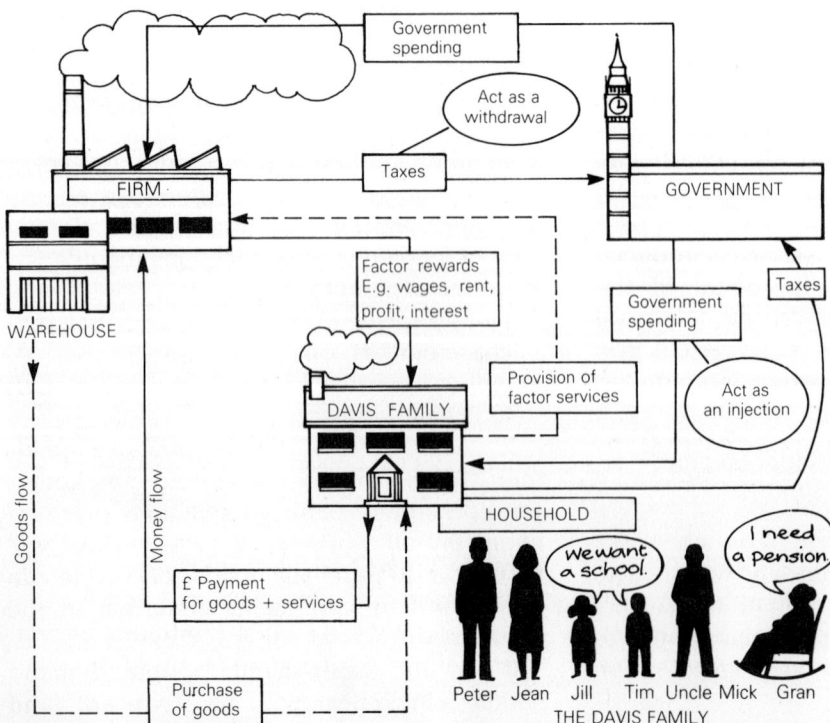

THE DAVIS FAMILY

Economic policies

Governments can realise these aims if they find the right economic policy. An economic policy is simply a way a government can try to achieve its aims. The major types of economic policy include:

- **Fiscal policy**: this uses the tax system to influence economic behaviour. Budget surpluses can remove money if the economy "overheats". Budget deficits or cuts in the taxation levels can stimulate consumption because both methods result in people having more money to spend.
- **Monetary policy**: This method tries to make money more expensive by raising interest rates, or more scarce by restricting bank lending. The government can instruct the Bank of England to call for *special deposits* from commercial banks, i.e. the Big Four; this reduces their liquid assets (or cash available to individuals). Alternatively the government reduces the amount of liquid assets by making the commercial banks use some of their cash to buy government securities – this is known as *open market operations*.
- **Incomes policy**: this method involves government using voluntary or statutory (state) controls to influence people's bargaining power. It has been used from time to time by different governments to try and control inflation.

Keynesians

Keynesian economists argue that government can help stimulate demand by injecting money into the economy. When consumption slumps, people purchase fewer goods which results in fewer jobs being created, and thus demand for goods and services falls further. The government should compensate for this fall in consumer demand, it is argued, and thus create jobs. Once one job is created other jobs arise. This is called the multiplier effect. For example, if Will has an extra £1 of income and spends it buying Bob's chocolates, Bob in turn can buy a magazine and so the effect goes on.

Keynesians believe unemployment in the economy is caused by a lack of demand for goods, so the government has to step in and stimulate spending. If inflation is the major enemy that the government is worried about, then Keynesian economists would argue that a higher level of unemployment might have to be accepted in order to reduce the amount of spending in an economy and thus the pressure spending has on prices.

Monetarists

For monetarists, inflation is the major economic problem. They link its appearance to excessive increases in the money supply.

Government overspending and its effect on the PSBR (Public Spending Borrowing Requirement) needs to be curbed as this leads to inflationary pressures. Public spending bids up the price of factors of production and "crowds out" private spending. With inflation controlled, people can be priced back into jobs. If people are out of work, monetarists argue, they should consider taking a cut in wages to become competitive. Keynesians would argue that this would reduce demand further and put more people out of work.

Monetarists favour a number of other policies:

- **Tax cuts**: this gives incentives to people to work harder and produce more.
- **Curbs on union power**: this, it is suggested, stops wages rising too fast.
- **Privatisation**: this encourages, they argue, greater efficiency and more competition.

Conflict of objectives

Is it possible to achieve all economic objectives? Keynesians would suggest that there is a trade-off between unemployment and inflation:

- a low level of unemployment can be achieved but, with everyone working, prices rise and inflation overheats the economy. This boom can lead to a decline in business confidence and a slump in economic activity appears;
- a low level of inflation can be achieved but unemployment rises if spending is restricted. With people out of work, spending falls further and there is a slump in economic activity that has to be corrected.

Monetarists argue that tight control of the money supply in the short run might increase unemployment, but in the long run falling prices make us competitive in the world economy and price workers back into work.

Who is right? Monetarists or Keynesians?

In the early 1980s falling inflation (given tight control of spending by the Conservative government) saw higher growth but unemployment rose to levels that suggested a lack of demand in the economy was the problem.

In the late 1980s unemployment fell but inflation rose (could Keynesians be right?); at the same time tax cuts appeared to have led to a surge in imports (are monetarists right in arguing that Britain is still not producing enough goods at the right price?). Is there a trade off that is possible?

ECONOMIC TERM

The Bank of England: this is the state bank. It acts as a bank for the government and regulates the activities of commercial banks. It issues bank notes and manages the accounts of the government as well as the PSBR and the National Debt (money owed by the government to past creditors). It keeps accounts for the commercial banks who can use these accounts to settle debts at the end of each clearing session. The Bank of England acts as lender of the last resort, providing a source of funds if commercial banks are in difficulty. It can influence the amount of money in circulation by freezing some of the money the commercial banks deposit with it. The Bank also signals to the financial world changes it would like to see take place in interest rates.

DATA RESPONSE

Pouring cold water on 'overheating'

Sarah Hogg

FEARS that the British economy is "overheating" are exaggerated, according to the National Institute of Economic and Social Research.

Although it has inched up its forecasts for growth in its latest *Review*, published yesterday, the National Institute remains sanguine about the risks. It points out that until May, imports were remarkably low; that the suggestion of a rise in inflation comes from world prices, rather than domestic; and that the fall in unemployment comes at least partly from changing benefit rules rather than purely from a tightening of the labour market.

The National Institute, indeed, takes an unusually optimistic view of economic prospects. It does not believe that the world economy is headed for recession, and while it is forecasting a slow-down in Britain's growth rate, from 3.3 per cent this year to 2.2 per cent next, it believes unemployment is "falling fast".

After next summer, the picture looks a little less rosy: the National Institute believes the fall in unemployment may not continue, while its forecast for inflation creeps up to just under 5 per cent. The balance-of-payments deficit on current account widens to nearly £3½bn for 1988 as a whole, even if public borrowing in the next financial year drops to £1.3bn – lower than envisaged in the Chancellor's present medium-term plans.

This low level of public borrowing is forecast despite the pressures on public spending detailed by the National Institute, which calculates that pay in the public services is rising by an average of 9 per cent this year. That is two percentage points ahead of pay rises in the private sector, and more than twice as fast as inflation. With wage settlements for teachers, nurses and local authority manuals all adding more than 10 per cent to pay bills this year, the National Institute estimates that there has been a considerable escalation since last year, when public service pay increases averaged 7.7 per cent.

However, its forecast suggests the Government will have little difficulty in staying within the limit set for public borrowing this year, aided by a falling bill for unemployment benefit and strong revenues, following from this year's economic growth.

The main problem identified by the National Institute, therefore, is the likelihood of a stustained current account deficit. Its forecasts suggest it will be roughly equal to 1 per cent of national income (against a US deficit equal to 3 per cent of national income this year).

Source: *The Independent*, 20 August 1987

---

1 What has happened to unemployment in the three years covered by the survey? (See the table.)

2 What link could be drawn between unemployment, inflation and the balance of payments?

3 How might increases in public spending affect inflation figures?

4 Why in the long term is the picture portrayed of Britain's economy a bleak one? – Or a little less rosy?

NATIONAL INSTITUTE FORECASTS

Inflation 4th quarter

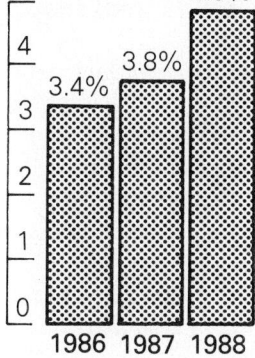

Year	%
1986	3.4%
1987	3.8%
1988	4.9%

GDP growth

Year	%
1986	2.9%
1987	3.3%
1988	2.2%

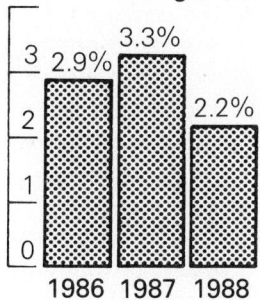

Unemployment 4th quarter (million)

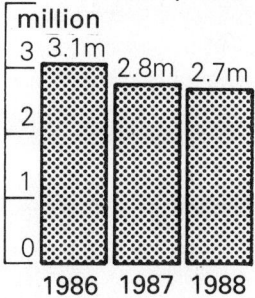

Year	million
1986	3.1m
1987	2.8m
1988	2.7m

Current account £ billion

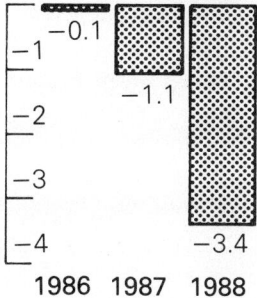

Year	£ billion
1986	−0.1
1987	−1.1
1988	−3.4

Public service pay

Group	1986–87 Rise (%)	1987–88 Rise (%)
Teachers	9.3	12.3
Nurses	10.2	12.5
Local authority manuals	9.0	10.2
Police	7.5	7.6
Civil servants	6.7	7.5
Town Hall staff	6.0	6.4
Armed forces	4.1	5.9
Central gov't manuals	5.4	4.8
NHS ancilliaries	7.7	4.7
Total*	7.7	9.0
Private sector earnings	7.4	7.0
Inflation	3.3	4.2

*Weighted average.

Extension 1

BMA prescribes cigarette tax increases to save more lives

THE GOVERNMENT could raise an extra £1,600m in tax revenue, cut cigarette consumption by 19 per cent and save 15,000 premature deaths a year by increasing the cost of a packet of cigarettes by about 50 per cent over five years, the British Medical Association said yesterday.

The association believes the Government should start by imposing a 21 per cent increase in prices in the next Budget, taking the cost of a packet to about £1.80 and follow that by a 6 per cent increase above inflation each year.

Source: *The Independent*, 7 August 1987

> What about Employment prospects?

> Imports would decline but so too would exports.

> Banning cigarettes could make a lot of difference to labour productivity.

> Taxing cigarettes further could help finance increased government spending.

Divide the class into two groups.

One group is instructed to consider, on behalf of the government, the request by the BMA to increase taxation on cigarettes.

The second group is instructed to consider a letter received from the British tobacco industry asking the government to reject any suggestion of further taxing cigarette smoking.

Each group should consider the arguments that they would present to the government.

The teacher will act as chairperson and will ask a spokesperson for each group to present their case.

The topic for debate is "Taxing cigarette smoking should be a major aim of government policy."

Extension 2

```
        ┌─────────────────────────┐
        │ A  Using monetary policy│
        │    to reflate           │
        │    the economy          │
        └─────────────────────────┘
                    ▲
┌──────────────┐    │    ┌──────────────┐
│ D  Using     │ ◄──┤──► │ B  Using     │
│  fiscal policy│ ┌──────────┐│  fiscal policy│
│  to deflate  │ │The economy││  measures to │
│  the economy │ │  and      ││  reflate     │
│              │ │economic   ││  the economy │
│              │ │policies   ││              │
└──────────────┘ └──────────┘└──────────────┘
                    │
                    ▼
        ┌─────────────────────────┐
        │ C  Using monetary policy│
        │    to deflate           │
        │    the economy          │
        └─────────────────────────┘
```

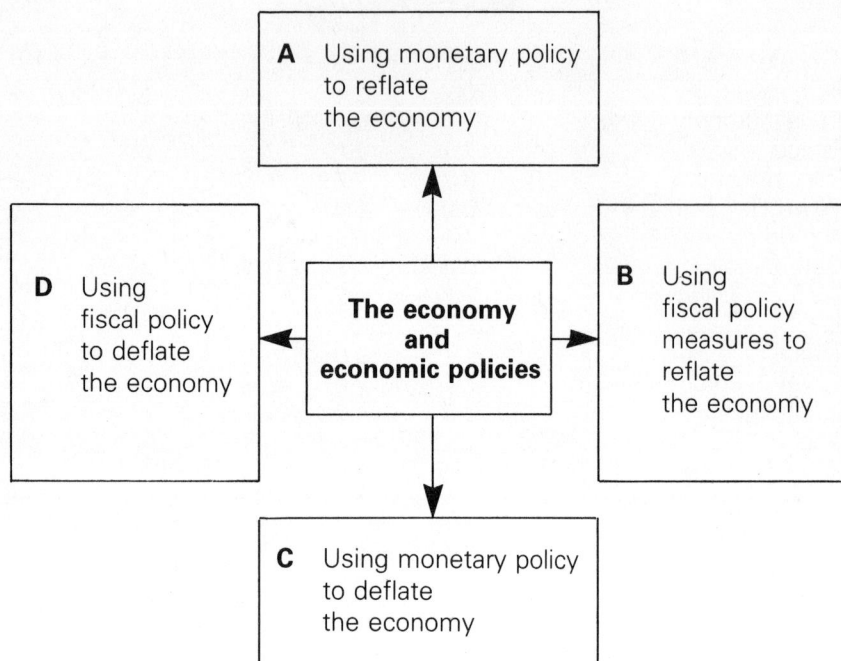

Look at each of the policy options **A–D** and then answer the questions.

1 The government decides to lower interest rates to stimulate the economy. Which of the above routes would it follow?
2 Imports are rising rapidly. The government orders banks to restrict their lending to customers. Which of the above routes does it select?
3 Unemployment has risen to unacceptable levels, consumer demand is sluggish and goods are being stockpiled outside factories for want of customers. The government decides to pump £400m into the economy. Which route has it chosen?
4 The government wishes to increase income tax in order to curb overheating in the economy. Which route should the government choose?
5 Explain how policy objectives can sometimes come into conflict.

Coursework

Aim: To investigate and describe the current state of the British economy.

Use information from newspapers to describe the current state of the British economy. You should refer briefly to information you have collected on:
a inflation (rising prices);
b unemployment;
c economic growth/increase in national income;
d balance of payments;
e the exchange rate.

Identify the various methods that the government has been using to control the economy.

Imagine that you are the Chancellor of the Exchequer. Using all the evidence available to you, produce a report on the economy explaining what you intend to do to manage the economy over the next year. Your report should include the methods you intend to use and an awareness of both the positive and negative aspects of adopting your proposals.

Index